DAYS OF
INFAMY

DAYS OF INFAMY

MacArthur, Roosevelt, Churchill—
The Shocking Truth Revealed

How Their Secret Deals and Strategic
Blunders Caused Disasters
at Pearl Harbor and the Philippines

JOHN COSTELLO

POCKET BOOKS
New York   London   Toronto   Sydney   Tokyo   Singapore

POCKET BOOKS, a division of Simon & Schuster Inc.
1230 Avenue of the Americas, New York, NY 10020

Costello, John.
   Days of infamy : MacArthur, Roosevelt, Churchill, the shocking
truth revealed : how their secret deals and strategic blunders
caused disasters at Pearl Harbor and the Philippines / John
Costello.
      p.   cm.
   Includes bibliographical references and index.
   ISBN 0-671-76985-5
   1. World War, 1939–1945—Diplomatic history.   2. Strategy.
3. United States—Foreign relations—Great Britain.   4. Great
Britain—Foreign relations—United States.   5. World War, 1939–1945—
Cryptography.   I. Title.
   D753.C657   1994
   940.53′2—dc20   94-32498
                                                            CIP

First Pocket Books hardcover printing December 1994

10   9   8   7   6   5   4   3   2   1

POCKET and colophon are registered trademarks of
Simon & Schuster Inc.

Printed in the U.S.A.

To Captain Roger Pineau, USNR (Ret.)
1916–1993

CONTENTS

12 ══

"Nothing to Fear at All"   260

MacArthur's Dereliction, Payoff, and Rewriting of History to Escape Investigation

13 ══

"We Just Did Not Have It!"   278

The U.S. Navy Conceals for Fifty Years that the Unread Intercepted Japanese Naval Traffic Contained the Clues to Pearl Harbor

14 ══

"REMEMBER THE PHILIPPINES!"

Breaking Out of the Pearl Harbor Syndrome

REMEMBER PEARL HARBOR!" was the American wartime call to arms that united a hitherto divided nation in
a crusade of national vengeance against Japan and her Axis
partners, Germany and Italy. The refrain was made into a
popular song and became a strident theme of wartime propaganda that rallied frontline troops who fought from the jungles
of Guadalcanal to the sands of Iwo Jima, just as it rallied the
"Rosie the Riveters" in their battle of war production from
the Bath shipyard in Maine to Boeing aircraft plants in
Washington.

President Franklin D. Roosevelt coined the ringing phrase
"a date which will live in infamy" when he denounced before
Congress on 8 December 1941 the "unprovoked and dastardly
attack" on the Pacific Fleet and called for a formal declaration
of war against Japan.[1] The vehemence of the language that
gave expression to the national outrage made the very words
"Pearl Harbor" a leitmotif of treachery for Americans still un-
born when history shocked them out of an illusory isolationism and into a brutal confrontation with their global destiny.
The shock waves of national indignation were compounded by
a collective incredulity that Japan—a country smaller than
the state of California—had not only dared to attack the United

1

States, but had succeeded in delivering such a humiliating military defeat.

Remembering Pearl Harbor became a wartime fixation that carved itself so deeply into the national memory that its reverberations continued to haunt the American military psyche long after the war ended. Every succeeding president acknowledged the obligation to keep Roosevelt's solemn pledge to "make very certain that this form of treachery shall never endanger us again."[2] The specter of a nuclear Pearl Harbor stalked the ramparts of the United States defenses throughout the anxious decades of the Cold War. It caused President John F. Kennedy to hesitate to order a preemptive attack on Cuba during the 1963 Missile Crisis with the Soviet Union. Twenty-five years later the ghosts of Pearl Harbor were invoked by President Ronald Reagan as justification for the "Star Wars" Space Defense Shield, with its illusory promise to exorcise the recurrent American nightmare of being caught again by a surprise attack.

The emotional aftershocks of the Pearl Harbor attack were so strong that they made most Americans forget that there had been an even greater strategic disaster that had overtaken their military forces in the Philippines. The air raid on the Pacific Fleet, while the most dramatic of the surprise attacks with which Japan plunged the Pacific into war, was not the first, nor the most devastating, blow for the United States. The opening salvos were actually fired a full hour before the first bombs exploded at Pearl Harbor, as Japanese amphibious forces stormed ashore shortly after midnight local time on 8 December across the sandy beaches of the Kra Isthmus on the northern coast of Malaya.

Roosevelt may not have been aware of this when he propped himself up with his painful iron leg braces at the podium of the House of Representatives to make Pearl Harbor the symbolic infamy of a "surprise offensive extending throughout the Pacific area." The emphasis that the president and the American press gave to the attack on the Pacific Fleet—even though the full extent of the disaster was carefully camouflaged to avoid giving comfort to the enemy—overwhelmed the coverage given to the disaster that had overtaken American forces in the Philippines ten and a half hours later.[3] News of this second day of infamy on the other side of the international date line had reached Washington early that morning, but neither in his speech to Congress nor at any other time did Roosevelt publicly acknowledge the Japanese air raid that made blazing fireballs of the bombers parked at the Clark Field Army Air Force in the Philippines. This was a strategic disaster that made the loss of four battleships seem relatively insignificant. The bombers from Formosa had caught the greatest concentration of American airpower outside the continental United States like sitting ducks. The loss of more than half its strength in a single blow doomed the defense of the Philippines even before it could be begun. It also contributed to the loss of Malaya and the Netherlands East Indies, because the long-range B-17 bomber force had been the linchpin of a secret pact the United States had made to defend British and Dutch territories in the Far East. Within two weeks an invading army had forced General Douglas MacArthur into a headlong retreat with the Filipino and American armies to the Bataan peninsula. Within three months Malaya, Singapore, and then Burma were overwhelmed in a tidal wave of conquest that brought the Japanese control of the Borneo oil fields, for which they had gone to war. A month later, shortly after MacArthur's escape to Australia, the remnants of his armies in the Philippines surrendered: 12,000 GIs and 64,000 Filipino troops laid down their arms on 9 April 1942 at the finale of the greatest military defeat ever inflicted on United States forces in the field.

"Remember the Philippines," however, was never to be invoked as a reminder that 8 December 1941 was a second date in the calendar of infamy. The disaster that had overwhelmed MacArthur never became an American battle cry. It was not to be immortalized by wartime propagandists and drummed into the popular consciousness by the tunesmiths of Tin Pan Alley. Nor was MacArthur ever called to account for the debacle, even though its strategic fallout was from his command failure far more devastating to the United States and her allies than were the strategic consequences of the disaster at Pearl Harbor. The debacle of Clark Field was forgotten as the search for the culprits for the spectacular American military setbacks in the Pacific commenced.

It was not MacArthur, but the Hawaiian commanders Admiral Husband E. Kimmel and Lieutenant General Walter C. Short who were to be summarily relieved and found guilty of dereliction by a special Presidential commission. This was the first manifestation of what may be characterized as the "Pearl Harbor Syndrome," the process by which the Roosevelt administration and the military closed ranks to conceal the true extent of the strategic surprise with which Japan had overwhelmed the United States. The military miscalculation and the diplomatic blunders that had set the Pacific stage for twin disasters in the Philippines and Hawaii were kept concealed, because all the eight secret wartime inquiries were restricted to investigating only the unpreparedness in the command chain to Pearl Harbor. The administration's exercise in damage control avoided opening up the issue of the far more disastrous command failure in the Philippines by MacArthur, which would have raised questions about the overarching responsibility of the president and the chiefs of staff.

The irony was that as the Pearl Harbor Syndrome seduced the attention of the American public by inflating the scale of the disaster, history was to show that the air raid on the Pacific Fleet was only a short-lived triumph of arms that brought Japan no lasting strategic advantage. It was not just the way that the "sneak attack" had been executed, but the three thousand dead and wounded Americans that instantly ignited a burning national crusade of vengeance whose terrible antithesis was to be clouds of nuclear debris that mushroomed over Hiroshima and Nagasaki four and a half years later. The sinking of the four vintage battlewagons brought no immediate naval advantage, and its long-term consequence was to doom Japan, because the manner of the attacks taught the die-hard American admirals that World War II in the Pacific would be won by the fast carrier task force, not by a lumbering line of World War I dreadnoughts.

The negative strategic consequences of the Pearl Harbor attack had been overlooked in calculations made by Admiral Isoroku Yamamoto, the commander in chief of the Imperial Navy's Combined Fleet, who had threatened to resign unless the Imperial High Command made his daring "Hawaiian Operation" part of Japan's war plan. Its principal objective was to seize control of the Philippines, Malaya, and the Dutch East Indies, but Yamamoto had argued that a knockout punch to the Pacific Fleet was essential to keep it from interfering for the six months to a year needed to secure the Pacific defenses of Japan's new empire. For all its tactical brilliance, that air raid on Pearl Harbor proved a strategic disaster. The overcautious striking force commander, Vice-admiral Chuichi Nagumo, had opted for withdrawal rather than risk launching further air strikes to bomb the fuel-oil tanks and destroy dock installations, and there was no plan for a sustained submarine blockade that would have denied the Pacific Fleet its forward base. The errors were compounded by Nagumo when he did not hunt down the two American carriers that were not at their moorings on 7 December 1941.

Yamamoto's bold plan not only failed to deliver the knock-out punch to the Pacific Fleet, but it was just six weeks, not six months, before the American carriers went onto the offensive by raiding the forward Japanese bases in the Marshall Islands. It was these same carriers that ferried sixteen Army B-25 bombers to within striking distance of Tokyo on 11 April 1942 for Lieutenant Colonel James H. Doolittle to use in the raid that mortified the Japanese High Command. This dramatic demonstration of Yamamoto's failure to deliver on his strategic promises resulted in an attempt to remedy the strategic defects of his original plan with the "Midway Operation" to lure the American carriers into a decisive battle. This was to be the first step to an invasion of the Hawaiian Islands to once and for all deny the U.S. Navy its base for operating against the western Pacific.[4] But even as Yamamoto sprang his elaborately over-choreographed trap, it was uncovered by U.S. Navy codebreakers in time for the weaker American carrier force to ambush the combined fleet. In the two-day Battle of Midway that began on 4 June 1942, the American carrier planes won the victory that avenged Pearl Harbor and turned the tide of the naval war in the Pacific War irreversibly against Japan.

The U.S. Navy had recovered from their initial setback to regain control over the central Pacific within six months of the start of the war, but it took more than a year for MacArthur to recover the strategic initiative in the southwest Pacific land campaign on New Guinea—at the cost of many thousands more Allied lives than were lost at Pearl Harbor. Notwithstanding MacArthur's role in a far greater strategic calamity, it was to be Kimmel and Short who would pay for a tactical disaster by having their reputations destroyed for their failure to deduce, from inadequate intelligence and deficient warnings from Washington, that enemy bombers would fly in out of the blue on a peaceful Sunday morning to attack the fleet anchorage that was thousands of miles from the nearest Japanese base. But as the records were eventually to reveal, it was the Philippines command that had been far more derelict for being caught unprepared, a full half a day *after* the war had broken out. MacArthur was not only aware from his intelligence that the Japanese were about to commence hostilities, but that their air forces were massing to attack from Formosan airfields only two hundred miles north of Luzon. But even after receiving news of Pearl Harbor and telephone warnings from the War Department not to get similarly caught with his planes on the ground, MacArthur did just that by failing to heed his air commander's urgent and repeated request to launch the preemptive strikes against Formosa in accordance with the Philippines war plan that specifically called for him to "conduct air raids against Japanese forces and installations within tactical operating radius of available bases."[5]

"We supposed that an official investigation would be made, was how High Commissioner Francis B. Sayre expressed his surprise that the military command in the Philippines had never been called to account.[6] While he reasoned that it was because "the war was on, and minds were immersed in the immediate problems of resistance," this did not excuse MacArthur in the eyes of fellow general Claire L. Chennault. "If I had been caught with my planes on the ground, I could never again have looked my fellow officers squarely in the eye," wrote the former commander of the American volunteer squadrons in China. "The lightness with which this cardinal military sin was excused by the American high command has always seemed to me one of the more shocking defects of the war."[7]

"Our General and leaders committed one of the greatest errors possible to military men—that of letting themselves be taken by surprise. The error can be exceeded only by treason," wrote Lieutenant Edgar D. Whitcomb.[8] As Whitcomb was one of the Army Air Force B-17 navigators who had witnessed the attack on Clark Field, his reaction reflected the amazement of many puzzled survivors of the debacle in the Philippines that a full-scale Congressional investigation into the Pearl Harbor disaster could conclude that the Hawaiian commanders were guilty of dereliction of duty for being taken by surprise, while MacArthur's far greater culpability was never made the subject of *any* official reprimand or inquiry.

Geography was only one of the factors contributing to the workings of the "Pearl Harbor Syndrome." Hawaii, though not a state of the union, was still considered by most Americans to be psychologically, if not physically, contiguous territory. Nor did the attack on the Philippines arouse the same emotions. Not only was it not blazed across newspaper headlines, but the Commonwealth—while under the Stars and Stripes— was an uncomfortable vestige of an American colonial adventure that was in the process of being shuffled off into independence. The Philippines were soon invaded by the enemy, unlike Hawaii, which would have made it difficult to recall its commander in the midst of battle. This was not the case with Kimmel and Short. MacArthur's dramatic flair for self-publicity quickly erased any memory of his initial command failure as he became a magazine-cover icon, the personification of an embattled American hero, even as he went down to defeat in defying the high tide of Japanese military aggression in the Philippines. MacArthur progressed from the conqueror of New Guinea to the savior of the Philippines, to be hailed by his many admirers on Capital Hill as an "American Caesar." His appointment as the Supreme Commander of Allied Powers in the occupation of Japan in 1945 made it politically impossible to call him to account when Congress set up its Joint Investigating Committee to ascertain how it was that the Japanese had succeeded in taking the United States by surprise four and half years earlier.

"Why, with some of the finest intelligence available in our history, with the almost certain knowledge that war was at hand, with plans that contemplate the precise type of attack on the morning of December 7—Why was it possible for Pearl Harbor to occur?"[9] The questions that the Congressional investigators set out to answer in a marathon ten-month-long hearing applied with equal, if not more, pertinence to the debacle in the Philippines. But they were never asked. MacArthur escaped a Congressional investigation, because in 1945, to have attempted to tarnish the reputation of the heroic American general who was ruling Japan as an American proconsul would have had a devastating impact on the spirit of the American public. He was the beneficiary, not a victim—as the Hawaiian commanders were—of the "Pearl Harbor Syndrome," whose public manifestation was the belief that discovering who really was to blame for the disaster could restore national amour propre. This was in part the emotional fallout from the constant "Remember Pearl Harbor" drumbeat that buried the humiliation of the Philippines as it increased the American hunger for an answer that would purge the national conscience. For the president, who had to don his war cloak to rally the nation into battle as its commander in chief, duty and expediency dictated that Roosevelt and his administration had, at all costs, to avoid the blame that could have destroyed public confidence in his leadership in the hour of supreme crisis. So the national interest, as well as geography, made Kimmel and Short convenient scapegoats.

For more than half a century MacArthur's reputation has

survived largely untainted by the Philippine debacle, thanks to the same "Pearl Harbor Syndrome" that had constrained the Congressional investigation and which continued to straightjacket the postwar debate only to its Hawaiian context. Its narrow focus encouraged the historical tunnel vision that inspired the still-continuing search for the "smoking gun"— the single piece of evidence that so-called revisionists believe will finally prove that Roosevelt was at the center of a sinister conspiracy to deny Kimmel and Short any warning of the approaching Japanese task force, because he wanted to get the United States into the war.

Ironically, it appears that the revisionists may have been right all along about where the real responsibility should be placed— but for all the wrong reasons. What they have failed to appreciate is that the best evidence for making the case that the Roosevelt administration was to blame was not to be uncovered in the context of Pearl Harbor, but by excavating and sifting the historical records relating to the reinforcement of the Philippines. The conundrum surrounding the spectacular collapse of United States military and diplomatic strategy toward Japan in 1941 cannot be unraveled simply in terms of the Hawaiian command. The air force in the Philippines and the Pacific fleet at Pearl Harbor were the two most potent American pieces on the chessboard of the Pacific. They were being played by the strategists in the War and Navy Departments in Washington in response to the dictates of the United States policy toward Japan that was determined by the president and his cabinet.

Yet eight wartime investigations, together with the 1945 Congressional investigation—and most of the stream of books that has kept the Pearl Harbor controversy alive for half a century— have fallen victim to the "Pearl Harbor Syndrome" by attempting to explain it only in terms of a Hawaiian command failure. This is comparable to trying to rationalize how a chess game was won and lost from the moves made in one corner of the board. Such myopic methodology can never provide more than a lopsided interpretation of the game that Japan won both strategically and tactically. But by taking into account the moves made across the whole Pacific chessboard, it can be shown that the Pacific Fleet was taken by surprise as the inevitable consequence of a major strategic miscalculation: that MacArthur's air force in the Philippines could deter Japan from further aggression in the Far East.

History, according to a foremost modern practitioner, "is

a continuous process of interaction between the historian and his facts, an unending dialogue between the present and the past."[10] The dialogue with the records that have come to light since the public debate began with the Congressional Investigation Committee's hearing half a century ago shows that the single "smoking gun" theory is as shortsighted a historical quest as is attempting to understand the attack on Pearl Harbor without taking into account the sequence of events that also led to the military disaster in the Philippines. What emerges as the fatal underlying mechanism is that United States foreign policy was allowed to dictate military strategy in a dangerous reversal of the precedence by which the Roosevelt administration might more prudently have weighed the decision to confront Japan with a trade embargo. The policy set the stage, but it was the conviction that the advancing of a relatively small force of strategic bombers to the Philippines could provide a potent enough projection of United States military power that risked declaring what amounted to all-out economic warfare against Japan by cutting off supplies of crude oil, all for a very small percentage of which came from American wells.

The Japanese attacked Pearl Harbor, not because it was their major strategic objective, but to prevent the Pacific Fleet from interfering with their invasion of the Philippines to clear the way to securing by force the alternative oil reserves of the Netherlands East Indies, whose government-in-exile had joined with the Americans and British in the embargo. To the American military planners, the Philippines and Hawaii were interdependent elements in the same strategic equation. Ever since before World War I it had been a fundamental tenet of the United States Pacific strategy that Pearl Harbor, not the Philippines, was the forward bastion for projecting American military power into the western Pacific. The sprawling archipelago five thousand miles to the west of Hawaii had long been held to be indefensible without committing resources to their defense on a scale for which there had been neither the budget nor the political inclination in Congress during the penny-pinching years of the Depression. The Philippines had remained a lightly garrisoned outpost in line with the so-called ORANGE War Plan that required the American force on Luzon, in the event of Japanese invasion, to withdraw to the Bataan Peninsula. There they would dig into prepared positions and try to hold out until the battleships of the Pacific Fleet had smashed their way across the Pacific to cover the landing of an army to relieve the siege. This had remained the basis of the United States' Pacific war plan until the summer 1941, when Japan's military power had increased so substantially that the schedule for the fleet's march across the Pacific had been revised from six months to over two years.[11]

The long-maintained strategic doctrine not to reinforce the Philippines was turned on its head at the end of July 1941. This followed the President's decision to push Japan for her incursions into Indochina with trade sanctions that resulted in an oil embargo and the consequent need to reinforce the Philippines to deter Japan from restoring to forceful seizure of alternative supplies in the Netherlands East Indies. MacArthur was recalled to the colors in Manila to take command of all U.S. Forces in the Far East and the additional troops, artillery, tanks, and aircraft that were to be sent out to the Philippines. The centerpiece and justification for this strategic about-face in the Pacific was a two-hundred-strong heavy-bomber force that was to come from the reallocation of deliveries of B-17s originally earmarked for the defense of Pearl Harbor and from the British, who would give up the Lend/Lease contract that gave them one out of every three of the four-engine Flying Fortresses.

To induce Winston Churchill to release the R.A.F.'s B-17 allocation, it was agreed that the powerful strategic bomber force built up in the Philippines under MacArthur's command would also be committed to defending Malaya and Burma, in addition to covering the Dutch East Indies. This deal was struck with the British during the first Anglo-American floating summit meeting held aboard the warships of the two nations in a remote Newfoundland bay. Winston Churchill and his chiefs of staff—whose previous pleas for American help in defending Malaya had been rejected—eagerly agreed to the strategic horse trade. It was enthusiastically endorsed to U.S. Army Chief of Staff General George C. Marshall, although he had earlier rejected any reinforcement of the Philippines, calling it a "strategic error of the first magnitude."[12] But as the secret minutes of the secret Anglo-American staff discussions reveal, this clandestinely concluded de facto Far East defense pact was a far more important outcome of the first Churchill-Roosevelt summit than the much-ballyhooed rhetoric of the Atlantic Charter Declaration. The secret Anglo-American defense pact against Japan was to lead to an ill-conceived strategy based on American airpower in the Philippines and British battleships in Singapore. But far from acting as the "big stick" essential to the successful conduct of a policy of economic warfare against Japan, the combination of maladroit diplomacy and military bluff invited Japan to make a preemptive strike before her oil reserves were too far depleted and MacArthur's military buildup in the Philippines posed a serious threat.

The Roosevelt administration's decision to embark on economic warfare against Japan was fraught with risk—and not only because of shifting the front line of the United States' Pacific defense perimeter to the Philippines, which required sacrificing the air defenses of Pearl Harbor. The buildup in the Philippines could not be completed until April 1942, but with every B-17 that made the long island-hopping journey across the Pacific, Pearl Harbor ceased to be regarded as a front-line fortress by the fall of 1941—according to the records that reveal that urgent and repeated requests of the Hawaiian commanders for more diplomatic intelligence fell on deaf ears. The preoccupation with reinforcing the Philippines had relegated Pearl Harbor, at least in the minds of military planners in Washington, to a relatively safe position well to the rear of new front line of American military power in the western Pacific. But the reassuringly interlocking circles radiating out from the Philippines that were drawn onto the map of the Pacific were nothing more than paper inspired by too much of the military wishful thinking that suggested it would even be possible for MacArthur to threaten to bomb Tokyo if the Soviet Union would consent to let the B-17s land in Vladivostok. The belief that the strategic picture for the United States in the Far East had been transformed was illusory. The B-17 production schedule was no substitute for having the force in place before embarking on a high-risk policy of confrontation with Japan. The same brand of wishful thinking that had flawed the whole foundation of the American strategy toward Japan in the fall of 1941 was also to play its part in the intelligence breakdown that denied vital information to the Hawaiian commanders on the ground, the thinking being that they did not need MAGIC, because the threat to Pearl Harbor had receded with the reinforcement of the Philippines.

It can now be seen that Kimmel and Short had every reason to blame Washington for contributing to their unpreparedness to meet the Japanese air raid on Pearl Harbor. But MacArthur had no excuse for being caught so terribly by surprise on the second day of infamy.

THE STRATEGIC SITUATION IN THE PACIFIC, 7–8 DECEMBER 1941

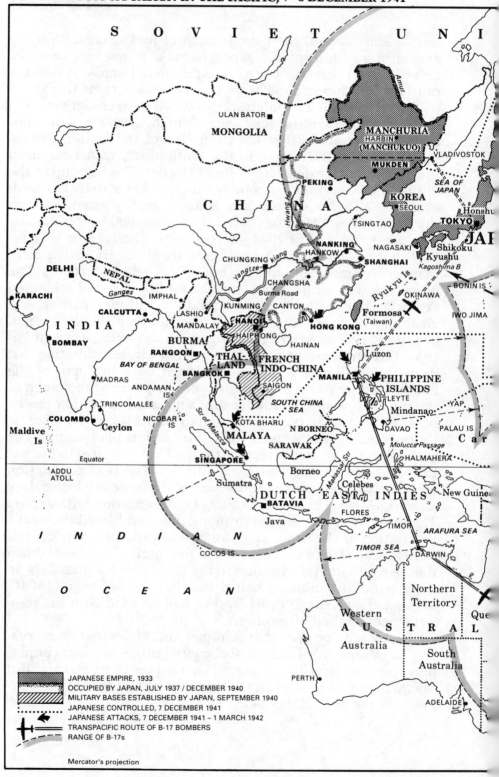

JAPANESE EMPIRE, 1933
OCCUPIED BY JAPAN, JULY 1937 / DECEMBER 1940
MILITARY BASES ESTABLISHED BY JAPAN, SEPTEMBER 1940
JAPANESE CONTROLLED, 7 DECEMBER 1941
JAPANESE ATTACKS, 7 DECEMBER 1941 – 1 MARCH 1942
TRANSPACIFIC ROUTE OF B-17 BOMBERS
RANGE OF B-17s

Mercator's projection

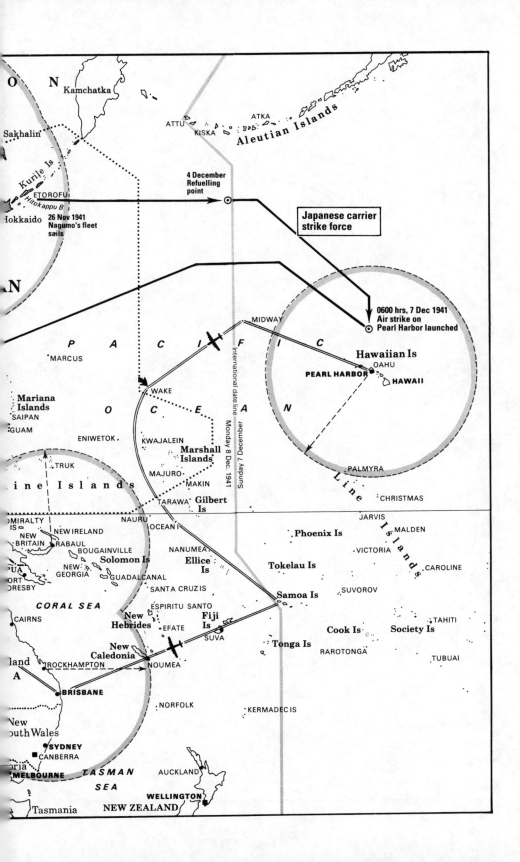

O N Kamchatka

Sakhalin'

ATTU
KISKA
ATKA
Aleutian Islands

Hokkaido

Kurile Is

ETOROFU
Hitokappu B

4 December Refuelling point

26 Nov 1941 Nagumo's fleet sails

Japanese carrier strike force

N

0600 hrs, 7 Dec 1941 Air strike on Pearl Harbor launched

P   A   C   I   F   I   C
MIDWAY

MARCUS

Hawaiian Is
OAHU
PEARL HARBOR
HAWAII

Mariana Islands
SAIPAN
GUAM

O   C   E   A   N

WAKE

ENIWETOK

KWAJALEIN

Marshall Islands

International date line
Monday 8 Dec. 1941
Sunday 7 December 1941

TRUK

ne Islands

MAJURO

MAKIN

TARAWA
Gilbert Is

PALMYRA

CHRISTMAS

Line Islands

ADMIRALTY IS
NEW IRELAND
NEW BRITAIN
RABAUL
BOUGAINVILLE
Solomon Is
NEW GEORGIA
GUADALCANAL
SANTA CRUZ IS

NAURU
OCEAN I

NANUMEA

Ellice Is

JARVIS

Phoenix Is

VICTORIA

MALDEN

CAROLINE

Tokelau Is

SUVOROV

Samoa Is

PUA
PORT MORESBY

CORAL SEA
CAIRNS

ESPIRITU SANTO
New Hebrides
EFATE
Fiji Is
SUVA

Tonga Is
RAROTONGA

Cook Is

Society Is
TAHITI

TUBUAI

New Caledonia
NOUMEA

and
ROCKHAMPTON
A
BRISBANE

NORFOLK

KERMADEC IS

New South Wales

SYDNEY
CANBERRA

oria
MELBOURNE

TASMAN SEA

AUCKLAND

WELLINGTON
NEW ZEALAND

Tasmania

1

"THE BLACKEST DAY IN AMERICAN MILITARY HISTORY"

MacArthur's Air Force in the Philippines Is
Caught in a "Second Pearl Harbor" Ten Hours
After the Attack on the Pacific Fleet

Pearl Harbor! It should be our strongest point!" Lieutenant
General Douglas MacArthur repeated sleepily into the receiver of his bedside telephone.[1] It was 3:40 A.M. in the Philippines when the commander of U.S. Army Forces Far East was woken in his penthouse suite at the Manila Hotel by the call from Major General Richard K. Sutherland. MacArthur's chief of staff had himself been roused by the night duty Signal Corps officer from the Fort Santiago headquarters of the U.S. Army Forces Far East (USAFFE) who had picked up a California radio station's report of an electrifying news flash from the White House.

"The Japanese have just attacked Pearl Harbor, Hawaii, by air" was the electrifying announcement that interrupted broadcasts of Sunday afternoon concerts and football games coast-to-coast, bringing Americans the stunning news just before two o'clock East Coast Time on 7 December 1941 that they had been plunged into war with Japan.[2] Across the International Dateline in Manila, it was in the early hours of Monday morning 8 December when the American commanders in the Philippines rubbed the sleep out of their eyes to learn of the Japanese attack on the base of the U.S. Pacific Fleet.

15

Three floors below MacArthur in the Manila Hotel, Rear Admiral Thomas C. Hart was already dressing in his more modest quarters. The commander in chief of the Asiatic Fleet had a head start on the Army commander in chief because he had been called forty minutes earlier by the Marine duty officer at his headquarters, who had warned him to "put some cold water on your face." Shortly afterward Lieutenant Colonel William T. Clement arrived in person from the Marsman Building, carrying the signal sheet from the Honolulu Naval Air Station on Ford Island: "AIR RAID ON PEARL HARBOR THIS IS NOT [sic] DRILL."[3] Hart immediately sat down on the edge of his bed and drafted for Clement the war dispatch to be sent to the ships and aircraft of the Asiatic Fleet. "PRIORITY. JAPAN STARTED HOSTILITIES. GOVERN YOURSELES [sic] ACCORDINGLY."[4]

Admiral Hart's personal, if misspelled, call to arms contrasted with MacArthur's reaction. He left it to his chief of staff to inform the U.S. Army forces in the Far East that a state of war existed with Japan. His immediate response had been to turn to his bedside Bible for his customary ten-minute contemplation of the scriptures with which he began each day. MacArthur did not record for history what text he selected that morning, but in light of his puzzling inaction it is unlikely that he read St. Paul's injunction on the need for resolute leadership: "If the trumpet give an uncertain sound, who shall prepare himself for battle?[5]

Uncertain trumpets and the surprising lack of a clarion call to action from MacArthur's headquarters that fateful morning left his subordinates puzzled and confused about how to respond to the threat of an impending Japanese attack. The apparent failure of their commander in chief to accept that his forces were already engaged in a life-and-death struggle with Japan was even more inexplicable because he had received immediate orders to execute his war plan from Washington, where an attack on the Philippines had been anticipated.

"My God! This can't be true. This must mean the Philippines," Secretary of the Navy Frank Knox had exclaimed when he was handed the signal that Pearl Harbor was under attack.[6] This was also the reaction of Harry Hopkins when Knox telephoned the White House at 1:47 P.M. Franklin D. Roosevelt's aide also believed "there had been some mistake and that surely Japan would not attack Honolulu." According to Hopkins's detailed account, the president's view was that it was "probably true" because it was "just the kind of thing that the Japanese would do and that at the very time they were discussing peace in the Pacific they were plotting to overthrow it." At 2:28 P.M. the chief of the Office of Naval Operations, Admiral Harold R. Stark, called with confirmation. The president told him to "execute the agreed orders to the Army and Navy in the event of an outbreak of war in the Pacific." At the emergency three o'clock conference of the chiefs of staff and secretaries of state, according to Hopkins's penciled notes, the president instructed "MacArthur ordered execute [sic]."[7]

The War Department radioed the presidential directive order to Army headquarters in Manila at 5:30 A.M. It specifically instructed MacArthur to put his war plan into operation in a radiogram that directed "carry out tasks assigned Rainbow Five." Additionally it directed him "to cooperate with the British and the Dutch to the utmost without jeopardizing the accomplishment of *your primary mission of defense of the Philippines* [emphasis added]."[8] An hour before receiving this formal notification that the United States was officially at war with Japan and while still at his hotel, MacArthur had been given verbal instructions to this effect in a transpacific telephone call from Washington. The chief of U.S. Army war plans, Brigadier General Leonard T. Gerow, personally recalled confirming that Pearl Harbor was still under attack.[9]

"I wouldn't be surprised if you get an attack there in the near future," Gerow warned MacArthur, who responded with the assurance that his forces were on full alert and ready for action.[10] The record, however, shows otherwise. Twenty-three years later MacArthur would write that Gerow had given "the impression the Japanese had suffered a setback at Pearl Harbor."[11] The surviving War Department record, however, indicates that General Gerow had stated that "considerable damage" had been suffered to aircraft and installations on Oahu.[12] Moreover, when he arrived at his headquarters at 4:30 A.M., MacArthur found waiting for him the radiogram from General George C. Marshall, the chief of staff of the Army, warning that the Japanese envoys in Washington had been given a local one o'clock deadline to deliver Tokyo's final diplomatic message. The significance of the timing was not clear, but all Pacific commands were cautioned to "be on the alert accordingly."[13] This alert had been overtaken by the attack on the Pacific Fleet, but it ought to have alerted MacArthur to the fact that the United States was irrevocably at war with Japan.

One of the first missions MacArthur was specifically required by the USAFFE (U.S. Army Forces Far East) War Plan to put into effect was "air raids against Japanese forces and installations within tactical operating radius of available bases."[14] For Major General Lewis H. Brereton, handpicked by MacArthur to be commander in chief of the Far East Air Force, the urgency for launching this preemptive air strike against the Japanese bases in Formosa was his first concern when he was awakened by Sutherland's phone call that morning and told that Japan had attacked Pearl Harbor.

"It came as no surprise to me," Brereton recorded in his diary. That the Japanese would launch into war had been expected, but like all the other American commanders in the Pacific theater he had not anticipated that the opening attack would be made against the Hawaiian base that night.[15] Brereton and many of his officers had only shortly before returned to their quarters after attending a late-night party held in his honor at the Manila Hotel and hosted by the 27th Bombardment Group, whose A-20 light bombers were still aboard freighters en route to Manila. Because there were no patrols to fly the next day, the party did not break up until after two A.M.

While the unsuspecting commander of the U.S. Army Air Force and his officers applauded what their invitations promised would be the "best entertainment this side of Minsky's," the celebrated New York striptease theater, the curtain was about to go up on the Japanese program. It called for a sequence of attacks on American and British installations timed to explode like gargantuan firecrackers exploding westward with the advance of the sun rising over the Pacific. Starting with the massive carrier raid at Pearl Harbor, the first detonation would be followed by landings on the northern coast of Malaya and dawn raids on the Philippines. The U.S. Navy seaplane base at Davao, on the southern island of Mindanao, was to be raided by planes from a Japanese carrier task force that had steamed west from Palau, the westernmost island of the Carolines. The main punch was to be delivered simultaneously against the American airfields south of the sixteenth parallel on Luzon by two hundred fighters and bombers of the Japanese Navy's 11th Air Fleet. Targets on the northern half of the island had been assigned to the 150 shorter-range aircraft of 5th Air Group of the Imperial Army, whose main strength had been concentrated across the South China Sea to support the Malayan invasion force.[16]

MacArthur and his subordinate commanders were well aware that American forces in the Philippines were a potential target for attack, even if they were unaware of the magnitude of the Japanese forces ranged against them. They had been repeatedly warned by their own intelligence reports and alerts from Washington that Japan might break out at any moment by attacking British, Dutch, and possibly even American territory in the Far East. Earlier that night, during the course of the reception at the Manila Hotel, Brereton had been advised by the chief of staff of the Asiatic Fleet that the "situation was hopeless" regarding the diplomatic negotiation with Japan. After receiving confirmation from General Sutherland that it was "only a question of days or perhaps hours until the shooting started," Brereton, convinced that "hostilities might break out at any time," ordered his own chief of staff to put the Far East Air Force on "combat alert" beginning at first light the next morning.

All available bombers and fighters were to be gassed up and ready to take off at short notice. The official history of the U.S. Army Air Force in the Pacific in World War II records, "there can be little doubt that to the airmen of General MacArthur's command the logical defensive use of the long-range heavy bomber in the circumstances existing was to strike at the enemy's concentration of air and naval power in Formosa."[17] Brereton had under his command a force of thirty-five B-17 bombers that had been designed for raiding and interdiction missions without fighter escorts, but Formosa was easily within its three-thousand-mile range. Bristling with guns to defend itself from fighters, the four-engine bombers were regarded by the U.S. Army Air Force as one of the most advanced weapons systems of the day. The B-17s had the capability to carry seventeen thousand pounds of high explosives over a thousand miles and deliver this awesome destructive power with pinpoint accuracy from an altitude of five miles, thanks to a super-secret gyro-stabilized Norden bombsight.

"It is true that the number of planes available was nowhere near that required for a decisive striking force," the official history notes, "but the defensive value of the B-17 lay entirely in its offensive power and the alternative to its use in that manner was to save it for possible destruction on the ground."[18] Brereton was ready to put his heavy bomber force to the test, and at four A.M. he ordered that all units should be made ready for action, because he "knew we could expect an attack from the Japs at any time after daylight."[19] Anticipating that MacArthur would approve a dawn strike against Formosa, he ordered Colonel Eugene L. Eubank, the commander of his bombardment forces, to fly down "without delay" from Clark Field, where the B-17s were based, to Far East Air Force headquarters at Nielsen Field, southeast of Manila.

"Well, boys, here it is. It's what we've been waiting for," declared Eubank, who not only looked like but affected the mannerisms of the comedian Will Rogers.[20] He and his staff relished the prospect of being the first Americans to have the opportunity to avenge Pearl Harbor, by bombing the Japanese airfields and port of Takao on the southern tip of Formosa, where the transports were waiting to ferry Lieutenant General Mashaharu Homma's 14th Army to invade the Philippines. At 5:30 A.M. Eubank's operations officer ordered all B-17 commanders at Clark to report to Group Headquarters as dawn broke over the only airstrip on Luzon whose turf runway was firm enough to operate the fifty-thousand-pound four-engine bombers. The hastily built airfield apron was still undrained, and the B-17s had to be parked out near the runway without the benefit of camouflage. The three that had been rostered for patrol that morning were stood down, so that the two squadrons of the 19th Bombardment Group could carry out the Formosa mission at their full strength of seventeen aircraft.[21]

Five hundred miles north of Manila, a combined five hundred fighters and bombers of the Japanese army and navy were ranged on the airfields of Formosa ready to launch a series of raids on the U.S. air bases in Luzon. Takeoff had originally been set for two hours before dawn, to bring them over the American airfields at sunrise and catch them off-guard. But dense banks of coastal fog had rolled in shortly after midnight to blanket the Takao airfields, threatening a serious hitch in the most crucial element of Japan's Far East war plan. The weather conditions were to delay the clockwork precision of the 11th Air Fleet's attack on Clark Field by nearly six hours, costing—the Japanese expected—all hope of achieving surprise in a strike that was intended to destroy the American heavy bombers. As they waited helplessly by their grounded planes, the Japanese navy aircrews anticipated encountering swarms of American fighters by the time they arrived and finding that the B-17s had been evacuated to the southern Philippines, where they would be beyond their reach.

The Japanese command worried that this could prove to be a fatal setback for their Philippine invasion plan, which required establishing air superiority over the beachheads in the two days before General Homma's invasion force started landing his troops. With every hour that passed concern mounted that the American heavy bombers would arrive to turn the tables on them. Intelligence reports had confirmed there were up to three dozen B-17s based in the Philippines, constituting the largest concentration of strategic air power outside the continental United States. The threat was therefore taken very seriously by the Japanese pilots as they crouched beside their fogbound planes and anxiously scanned the gray overcast. Any break in the weather threatened the screech of bombs plummeting from B-17s flying high above the reach of antiaircraft fire. With no advance warning, even the swift Mitsubishi "Zero" fighters could not be scrambled to climb up to twenty-five thousand feet to counterattack before the American bombers had carpeted the airfields and helpless planes with up to sixty tons of high explosives.

"Our defenses were far from complete," was how Lieutenant Commander Koichi Shimada described the situation when he recalled the apprehension that gripped him and his fellow navy pilots, who were "expecting action at any minute" on the Takao airfields. "The air-raid warning system and antiaircraft defenses were totally inadequate," he conceded. "Moreover, we had little of our [fighter] strength left, since in addition to the attack groups sent against Luzon, we had dispatched planes to provide antisubmarine patrol for the invasion convoys headed for Aparri and Vigan."[22] His fears, however, were to prove groundless. During the entire six hours that the Japanese navy's 11th Air Fleet was grounded by fog, not a single U.S. bomber took off to attack Formosa. That the U.S. Far East Air Force missed its golden chance to avenge Pearl Harbor was the result of the extraordinary failure by MacArthur's command. According to General Brereton, it was not for want of repeated efforts on his part to make a preemptive strike.

"After General Sutherland had given me all available information, I requested permission to carry out offensive action immediately after daylight," Brereton wrote.[23] His diary notes that he had set off from Nielsen's Field to make the drive to Fort Santiago, in the old, walled Intramuros citadel of Manila. Arriving around five A.M., he was told that the commander in chief was in conference with Admiral Hart. MacArthur could not, or would not, see him. Brereton, therefore, had to discuss the Formosan air strike with General Sutherland. He advised the chief of staff of his intention to send "all available B-17s at Clark Field" to attack Formosa and to recall the second half of his Bombardment Force that had been flown to Del Monte Field in Mindanao for another strike.[24]

"General Sutherland agreed with my plans," noted Brereton, but he recorded in his diary how he had received permission only to "go ahead with preparations" and that MacArthur's chief of staff promised he would "obtain authority" for daylight attacks.[25] "When I left General MacArthur's headquarters, I was under orders to prepare our heavy bombers for action, but not to undertake any offensive action until ordered."[26] Then he returned to his headquarters at Nielsen Field to meet with Colonel Eubank, who by then had flown in from Clark. The Bombardment Force commander was ready with plans to "mount an operation against targets in Takao Harbor, Formosa" with the primary objective of hitting the "enemy transports and warships." One of the officers present remembered Eubank's impatience to unleash the B-17s.

"Sure, they're ready," he advised Brereton. "They've been ready since before daylight. What're we goin' to do with 'em? That's what I want to know."[27]

"We can't attack till we're fired on," Eubank was told by Brereton, the Far East air commander, according to Colonel Harold Eade, who was present at the meeting.

"As I recall it, when General Brereton arrived at the meeting, he said we could not carry out the plan we had decided on. The orders were we couldn't attack until we were attacked; that we could go out on photo recce in force, loaded with bombs, but were not to use them unless attacked."[28] It was therefore agreed with Eubank that only three B-17s would be prepared to conduct "a reconnaissance of airfields on Formosa."[29]

Eubank, the Bombardment Force commander, and his staff were visibly upset and disappointed because they had assembled plans for an attack on Formosa. MacArthur and his chief of staff, Sutherland, would later claim that the Bombardment Force lacked adequate target information to carry out the mission. But the war alert MacArthur received on 27 November had specifically authorized the Far East Army Air Force to "undertake such reconnaissance and other measures as you deem necessary," even before Japan commenced hostilities.[30] Brereton and his planes had been restricted by USAFFE headquarters to flying no farther than "two thirds the distance between Luzon and Southern Formosa."[31] Sutherland insisted that MacArthur had approved reconnaissance missions that covered "the east coast of the island a little way."[32] This was disputed by Brereton, who said they had not been permitted to conduct reconnaissance north of the treaty boundary between

Formosa and the Philippines.[33] Surviving members of his command claim they conducted reconnaissance missions that reported on the Japanese aircraft assembled on the bases around Takao. Eubank's staff target folders may have been incomplete, lacking such details as bomb release lines for given speeds and altitudes. "But we had something complete enough to make this bombing mission a very far cry from the blind stab it would have had to be otherwise," recalled Captain Allison Ind, an intelligence officer who attended the morning conference at Nielsen headquarters.[34]

"Everyone was very puzzled over why we couldn't bomb Formosa, because the Japanese had committed the first overt act at Pearl Harbor," was how Brereton recalled the reaction of his morning staff conference.[35] He believed that authority to go ahead with the raid had been withheld because it was "entirely possible that the Pearl Harbor attack might not have been construed as an overt attack on the Philippines" by the commander in chief, MacArthur.[36] This was as far as he felt it prudent to state in his diary, which was published in 1946, when MacArthur was at the height of his prestige as one of the heroic American commanders and the supreme Allied commander charged with the occupation of Japan.

According to the notes of an interview Brereton gave Clare Boothe Luce in April 1942, he *had* conferred with MacArthur about the preemptive air strike *before* daylight that morning. The wife of *Time* magazine's influential proprietor Henry R. Luce was told by Brereton that it was MacArthur himself who had refused to sanction a dawn attack against the Japanese airfields and ports of Formosa. According to his statement, his planes *had made* reconnaissance flights that had indicated an invasion convoy had assembled. The commander in chief had insisted that "there were to be 'no overt acts' on the part of the U.S. forces in the Philippine Islands until the Japs struck the first blow at the Filipino people." When told to "stand by and wait," Brereton later told Mrs. Luce, he had left the headquarters building "closer to weeping with rage than he had ever been in his life before."[37]

This revealing interview of Brereton never appeared in *Time*. MacArthur had emphatically denied—and was to repeatedly deny—having seen his air commander that morning. Mrs. Luce was a great admirer of the general and did not wish to embarrass MacArthur, whom *Time* had featured on its cover as a national hero, by airing Brereton's contradictory testimony. It was by then already impossible to establish precisely what had transpired that morning between the commander in chief, MacArthur, his air commander, Brereton, and his chief of staff, Sutherland. The crucial daily logs of the 24th Pursuit Group and 19th Bombardment Group had all been lost during the hurried evacuation from Luzon.

"All records covering the period December 8, 1941, to Dec 16 inclusive were destroyed," was how General Sutherland's official report explained that the journal of events "had to be re-written from memory."[38] This was suspiciously convenient for MacArthur since the actual facts concerning responsibility for the decisions taken at his headquarters that morning were lost in a haze of contradictory recollection and denials. According to the official army historian, who unsuccessfully tried to reconstruct the sequence of events from the conflicting versions given him by the leading participants after the war, the "official records of the events surrounding the attack are practically non existent."[39] Pinpointing MacArthur's accountability also frustrated his principal biographer. According to D. Clayton James, who spent more than a decade researching his subject, the general had "covered his tracks well, and some of his devoted colleagues have tried to sweep away what little he exposed."[40]

What can be established beyond any doubt is that for a full nine hours after receiving news that Pearl Harbor was under attack, MacArthur and USAFFE headquarters withheld permission for launching a preemptive strike on Formosa. Had the bombing mission been undertaken as called for by his war directive, it might have significantly altered the entire course of the Philippines campaign.

"If we had been allowed to raid Formosa, it might have changed the entire course of the war in the Pacific," was the view of Lieutenant General Joseph H. Moore, who was then a lieutenant piloting a P-40 based at Clark Field.[41] Whether a preemptive strike by the B-17 bombers against the Japanese 11th Air Fleet could have saved the Philippines is historically not as significant as the fact that MacArthur's bombers were caught seven hours later on the ground when the Japanese planes raided Clark Field. The seven-hour delay before the operation was finally authorized proved fatal, not only for the Bombardment Force, but for the Philippines, because it cost the air superiority on which the defense of the islands depended. It was a disastrous command failure that was made all the more inexplicable as a result of MacArthur's flat rejection of any foreknowledge of the plan to launch a preemptive strike on the Japanese bases.

"I did not know it at the time, but later understood that General Brereton had suggested to the Chief of Staff, General Sutherland, that we should initiate operations by an attempted 'strike' against Formosa," was how MacArthur was to deny his responsibility to the official U.S. army historian after the war. "Had such a suggestion been made to me, I would have unequivocally disapproved," he insisted, claiming that "it would have been suicidal as well as in direct defiance of my basic directive."[42] MacArthur had already publicly denied his culpability in a 1946 press statement in which he declared that a preemptive bombing of the Japanese air bases "would have had no chance of success."[43]

Yet MacArthur's postwar statements about being unaware of the plan to send the B-17s against Formosa is contradicted by the Philippine War Plan, which specifically contemplated the undertaking of such a mission. His assertions that even if he had known about the proposed raid, he would have rejected it as "suicidal" is belied by the contemporary War Department record that contains a radiogram to General Marshall from USAFFE headquarters that same afternoon, in which MacArthur announced his intention of bombing the Formosan airfields the following day.[44] The inconsistencies in his explanation makes it impossible to explain why a preemptive raid was not sanctioned. It is possible, though unlikely, that his chief of staff, who cavalierly controlled access to the commander in chief, assumed sole responsibility for such an important decision.

Sutherland considered himself something of an expert in air strategy as a result of his limited flying experience. But his own explanation appears carefully crafted to deflect blame away from him and his commander in chief by assigning the decision to Brereton. It was Sutherland who assured the official army historian that it was the commander of the Far East Air Force who was responsible for not launching the raid and that he himself had simply withheld permission until a reconnaissance flight had been made to confirm the potential targets. Sutherland, in his ex-post-facto allegations, also charged Far East Air Commander Brereton with ultimate responsibility for the destruction of the bomber force because he had not obeyed orders to evacuate all thirty-five B-17s to Mindanao. Brereton, in his turn, countered that his decision to retain half the heavy bomber force at Clark Field was necessitated by the need to prevent overcrowding at the Del Monte airstrip, which had been bulldozed out of a pineapple plantation, because of the expected flight of twelve more B-17s from the West Coast. This flight had indeed taken off on 6 December from Hamilton Field north of San Francisco, only to run into the Japanese raid at Pearl Harbor.[45]

Indignantly Brereton pointed out that if MacArthur's headquarters had given him permission early that morning to make the raid on Formosa, his bombers would not have been caught on the ground. He claimed he had repeatedly been denied authorization to launch the attack. He said that after waiting for that permission at Nielsen Field for two hours, he had returned to MacArthur's headquarters to try to press the decision. Confirmation of Brereton's second trip to Manila that morning is provided by the most complete contemporary record to survive destruction in the evacuation of the Philippines. This is the "Summary of Activities of the Headquarters Far East Air Force." It records how at "0715 General Brereton visited No 1 Victoria and requested permission of General MacArthur to take offensive action. He was informed that for the time being our role was defensive, but to stand by for orders."[46] Brereton maintained that had he been permitted to launch a dawn strike by the Flying Fortresses, they "would have disrupted the incoming attack."

Circumstantial support for Brereton's contention was provided after the war by interrogations of the Japanese commanders whose own strike had been grounded by the morning fog. The 11th Air Fleet had not been able to take off for four hours after sunrise, although to the east of Takao the banks of mist had broken up shortly after dawn, which permitted the Japanese army's force of short-range twin-engine bombers and their fighter escorts to take off to attack American military installations in the northern half of Luzon. Commander Ryouske Nomura, an operations officer with the 11th Air Fleet, stated that a preemptive raid by the American B-17s would have disrupted their entire attack plan. Their apprehension was evident in an alert issued after they had intercepted an American radio dispatch around eight o'clock that had been misinterpreted as an indication heavy bombers had taken off from Clark Field and were already heading north. Two hours and ten minutes later when they would have been approaching the Formosan coast, a jumpy Japanese fighter patrol erroneously reported sighting a four-engine bomber. Alarms were sounded on the airfields as aircrews were ordered to don their gas masks.[47] When the fog lifted shortly afterward, they were relieved to find that the sky was blue and empty. Climbing into their cockpits, the Japanese navy pilots took off without wasting any more time, and 108 twin-engine bombers set course south for the Philippines, escorted by 84 Zeros.[48]

Japan's 11th Air Fleet was heading out over the Formosan coast when their army colleagues who had taken off four hours earlier were winging in over their landfall on northern Luzon to bomb the U.S. Army installation at Aparri. A Japanese amphibious force had already occupied the tiny island of Baton, which lay midway between Luzon and Formosa, but this news had yet to reach USAFFE headquarters. It was over five hours since the attack on Pearl Harbor and nearly three hours after MacArthur had been ordered by Washington to execute his Rainbow 5 War Plan. But the Army's antiaircraft batteries on Luzon remained under orders not to shoot at planes unless "that aircraft had dropped an object and that object had hit the ground and exploded."[49] The uncertainty over whether to open fire caused confusion when the incoming Japanese raid was reported flying in by Iba Field. The contacts had been picked up by the only operational radar station, which was set on a bluff above the airstrip on the Zambalese coast north of Subic Bay, a hundred miles northwest of Manila. When the warning was received at Clark Field, all the B-17s were ordered to take off, without bombs. One Flying Fortress remained temporarily grounded by a faulty generator, but eighteen P-40 pursuit planes were scrambled to mount defensive air cover. At Nichols Field, south of Manila, more P-40s took off and headed north to attempt to intercept the raid.

No contact was made. Twenty-five Japanese army bombers, unhindered, attacked Baguio, the Philippine summer capital, and the towns of Tarlac and Tuguegarao in central Luzon. They also hit Camp John Hay, the U.S. Army rest camp on the north coast. Simultaneously reports were being received at MacArthur's headquarters that the port of Davao had been bombed. This air raid had been carried out by the first strike of thirteen bombers and nine fighters that had taken off from the light carrier *Ryujo* shortly after 5 A.M., as the Japanese task force steamed just fifty miles off the Mindanao coast. In contrast to the U.S. Army batteries, those controlled by the U.S. Navy did not hesitate to hit back with accurate antiaircraft fire that downed a Japanese bomber flying in with the second wave of the attack, when the raiders strafed the seaplane tender *Preston*, setting fire to two of her planes moored nearby.

When the reports of the Japanese bombing raids reached Far East Air Force headquarters at Nielsen Field, Brereton concluded that since the Japanese had now committed "overt acts" of war that MacArthur would finally give permission to launch the raid on Formosa. Sutherland had telephoned him at 8:50 A.M. to insist there would be no U.S. strikes against Formosa "for the present."[50] Brereton called him back ten minutes later seeking authority to have the B-17s bombed up when they landed back at Clark so that they could be ready to launch a strike at short notice. MacArthur's chief of staff, Sutherland, would deny receiving this call. But the 9:00 A.M. entry in the Headquarters Summary records: "In response to query from General Brereton received a message from General Sutherland advising him that planes not authorized to carry bombs at this time."[51]

MacArthur's headquarters were still hesitating to implement their prearranged war plan. But the War Department assumed that the Philippines were already operating at war with Japan. Shortly after nine o'clock Brereton had received a long-distance call on the scrambler phone from the commander in chief of the Army Air Force in Washington. General Henry H. "Hap" Arnold later wrote in his memoirs that he called to alert Brereton to the urgent need for dispersing his heavy bomber force so that he would not get caught, as the Hawaiian air commander had been, with them on the ground and "have his entire air force destroyed."[52]

The War Department was more alive to the danger than their Far East commander in chief. Shortly after he had received the reports of the incoming raid, MacArthur received a telephone call from General Gerow at 7:55 A.M., asking if there had been any "indications of an attack."[53] The chief of Army War Plans was told that "in the last half hour our radio detector service picked up planes about thirty miles off the coast." "Our tails are up in the air," MacArthur confidently told Gerow, assuring him that fighters had been sent up to intercept the Japanese raid. But when Brereton telephoned Sutherland again at 9:25 A.M. to advise that "if Clark Field is attacked, we would not be able to operate offensively with the bombers" and again pressed for the "authority to carry out offensive action," his request was turned down again.[54]

"Chief of Staff informed General Brereton that all aircraft would be left in reserve and that the present attitude is strictly defensive," the Far East Air Force Headquarters Summary records. "Bomber command recommends bombs not be loaded at this time due to danger of extensive damage by enemy air action."[55] Then, ten minutes later and just before Colonel Eubank, the Bombardment Force commander, left to fly back to Clark Field, General Sutherland called back to advise: "General MacArthur had decided that a reconnaissance mission could be sent to Formosa."[56] Brereton's diary entry is confirmed by the 10:10 A.M. entry in his Headquarters Summary, which notes that at 10:14 A.M., "General Brereton received a telephone call from General MacArthur. General MacArthur stated that since the attack was not made on Clark, that bombers will be held in readiness until receipt of reports from reconnaissance missions."[57]

MacArthur had by now waited nearly seven hours after receiving the news of Pearl Harbor to put his war plan into effect. That was after he received the radiogram from General Arnold, the Army Air Force commander in chief: "Reports of Japanese attack all show that numbers of our planes have been destroyed on the ground. Take all possible steps to avoid such losses in your area, including dispersion to maximum possible extent and prompt take off on warning note."[58]

The urgent need to get the bombers away was underscored ten minutes later, at 10:20 A.M., when Air Warning Service reported another flight of Japanese aircraft flying in over Lingayen Gulf. More fighters were scrambled, but too late to prevent Vigan and La Union from suffering a sporadic bombing raid by more Japanese army planes. Colonel Eubank, who had just landed back at Clark, sent a coded radio message recalling the B-17s. Preparations were put in hand to equip three of the Flying Fortresses with cameras for the photoreconnaissance mission. "All bombers were ordered to arm and be on the alert for immediate orders," recorded the Far East Air Force Headquarters Summary at 10:45 A.M. "Lacking report of reconnaissance, Taiwan would be attacked in late afternoon. The decision for offensive action was left to General Brereton."[59] The exchange was omitted from Brereton's published diary, which records only that it was at eleven A.M. when he received another call from Sutherland stating that "bombing missions" could now be executed.[60]

"Two (2) heavy bombardment squadrons to attack known airdromes in Southern Formosa at the latest daylight hour today that visibility will permit."[61] His Headquarters Summary confirms Brereton's own account that he directed Eubank to recall the two bomber squadrons from Del Monte Field by the evening and then "telephoned General Sutherland at 11:56 A.M. to give a complete report on the air situation." The B-17s from Del Monte were to fly north "to take offensive action at daybreak the next day."[62] Headquarters Summary corroborates this, recording that "Field Order No. 1 of the Far East Air Force" was sent to the Clark commander by Teletype at 11:20 A.M., confirming Brereton's order to Eubank to prepare for an attack on Japanese targets in southern Formosa with two squadrons of the 19th Bombardment Group.[63] While the seventeen Fortresses lumbered back to Clark Field to be bombed up and fueled and the photoreconnaissance mission waited for the plane to arrive from Nichols Field with additional cameras, the Japanese 11th Air Fleet completed the last leg of its five-hundred-mile flight south.

"At 11:30 a large formation of bombers was reported over the China Sea approaching Manila," was how the Headquarters Summary records how the Far East Air command had been caught so totally by surprise.[64] That no fighter patrols were flying guard over Clark Field was attributed to the "delay in communication that made time and place factors uncertain" at the time when information was sent out to the two pursuit squadrons that were belatedly scrambled to meet the incoming Japanese attack, which was reported, at fifteen minutes before midday, as "a formation over Lingayen Gulf moving south."[65] At the time it was not appreciated that this was the main attack force heading for Clark Field because "communications breakdown prevented identification of these aircraft." The American fighter squadrons ordered to intercept the raid had "not completed gassing." When they did get airborne from Nichols Field, they were redirected too late to cover B-17 bomber base.[66]

At Clark Field itself all but one of the Flying Fortresses were back on the ground by noon, as the fighter patrols came in to land to refuel. In a tactical blunder of the first order, not one P-40 was aloft to intercept the incoming raid. This was the result of a poor communications network and an inexperienced Philippines Air Defense Warning Service. A thick dust haze prevented the squadron of fighters from taking off from nearby Del Carmen Field, while the squadron of P-40s at Iba had been misdirected to intercept what appeared to be another enemy flight reported coming in over the South China Sea. The confused commands plagued Interception headquarters at Nielsen Field, which was responsible for coordinating the telephoned reports from all over Luzon and the radar contacts from Iba. The perceived situation was then relayed by Teletype to Clark Field, where the main interceptor plot was maintained. There, toy planes, colored to represent enemy and friendly aircraft, were ranged on a sixty-foot-long table cut into a stylized shape of the Philippine Archipelago. But the delays in processing the reports, which ranged from "five to twenty-five minutes," made the information hopelessly dated by the time it reached the Interceptor Center at Clark Field.[67]

Colonel Alexander H. Campbell, the aircraft warning officer at Nielsen, insisted he did telephone an alert direct to Clark Field. He recalled being told that the duty officer who handled incoming warnings had apparently gone to lunch. The unidentified lieutenant who answered said he would pass on the warning "at the earliest opportunity." Then he, too, evidently went off to lunch without making sure that the alert was given the urgency it demanded. Campbell, who continued to plot the Japanese planes as they headed south toward Iba and Clark, urged Colonel Harold George, chief of interceptor command, to direct all available fighters onto the advancing Japanese.

Because of the assumption that Clark would have already scrambled its fighter patrols, the incoming raid was less than fifteen minutes flying time away when four squadrons of P-40s from Nielsen Field were finally given orders to head for Clark. But at the Bombardment Force base the fighters and heavy bombers were now lined up wingtip to wingtip to facilitate the refueling, as the aircrew lunched or lounged, smoking cigarettes on the airstrip, watching the three B-17s taxiing out for takeoff on their reconnaissance mission to Formosa. Forty miles to the west, the defenses were also down at Iba Field. A "communications breakdown" resulted in the failure to direct the coastal airfield's P-40 pursuit planes up to an altitude where they could intercept the high-flying incoming Japanese bombers. So when the fifty-four twin-engine Mitsubishis, escorted by fifty Zeros, flashed in over the coast, sixteen of the P-40s at Iba were caught on the ground refueling or circling at too low an altitude and preparing to land.

"Look at those nice planes," a radar plotter returning from lunch called out, failing to make the connection as he saw soldiers running for cover. "The only trouble is that they're Japs," a sergeant shot back as they both crouched for cover behind a sand-filled oil drum. In an oversight no trenches had been dug at the airfield.[68] The Japanese fighters swooped down, lashes of gunfire flickering from their cannons, and a

line of P-40s erupted like a line of fireworks. Pilots who courageously tried to get their fighters airborne were shot down
before they gained any altitude.[69] One of the first bombs blew
away the radar installation. Troops fired up at planes with
rifles, and officers blasted away with their .45 pistols, the only
weapons they had to hand.

The raid on Iba ended as swiftly as it began as the Japanese
raiders headed on to their main target at Clark Field, ten minutes flying time to the east. In perfect V formations of twenty-
seven apiece, Japanese high-flying Mitsubishi bombers were
spotted around 12:35 P.M. shortly after the local KMZH radio
station had brought laughter in the operations hut with the
announcement of an "unconfirmed report" that Clark was already being bombed.[70]

"We heard the roar of motors, coming from the northwest,"
Colonel E. B. Miller, a tank commander recalled. "The roar
was like the deep growl of powerful beasts—snarling as one."[71]

"Look at the beautiful formation of B-17s. They must be
reinforcements from Mindanao," shouted out one of the pilots
lying on the grass after lunch.[72] "Why are they dropping tinfoil?" asked another, mistaking the sun glinting off the tail fins
of bombs spiraling earthward from the formation flying over
at twenty-five thousand feet. The wail of air raid sirens provided the answer as someone yelled out, "That's not tinfoil,
those are goddamned Japs!"[73] Everyone scattered, pulling on
the regulation gas masks, as demanded by standing orders.
The fighter pilots dashed for their P-40s as gunners raced toward the eight antiaircraft guns set up around the perimeter of
the field. Unmanned during the lunch break, only one battery
managed to get into action, and even then the pressure fuses
on the shells had corroded so that they burst at an altitude far
too low to do any damage.

The textbook accuracy of the attack came as a surprise to
the Americans. Until that opening day of the war it had been
a standing joke in the U.S. armed forces that the Japanese were
shortsighted orientals who could not shoot or bomb straight
and whose weapons were inferior. But it was the Americans
who were caught short as the bombs came crashing down on
the rows of neatly parked P-40s and B-17s. The first to be destroyed were the three Fortresses on the photoreconnaissance
mission as they reached the takeoff point at the fear end of
Clark Field. They went up in bright orange fireballs within
seconds of one another. The bombers that Washington had expressly and repeatedly ordered that morning to be dispersed

were caught—like those on Oahu nine hours earlier—bunched together like sitting ducks conveniently lined up for Japanese target practice. Flying Fortresses they may have been in the air, but with full bomb and fuel loads, the grounded B-17s were fireballs waiting to be ignited. As the Bombardment Force intelligence officer, Captain Ind, recalled, "One after another, these vitally needed, expensive, irreplaceable bombers collapsed in bullet-ridden heaps or sagged to the ravenous flames consuming them."[74]

"When the big guys got through, the fighters started raking us, pulling up right over the top of me," remembered PFC Robert Brown of the 17th Pursuit Squadron. "Scared and amazed? I couldn't believe someone was attacking the United States. Absolutely unreal," he would recall. "All these Zeros were so close, I could see the big red dots on their wings. Hell, who could believe this? Us? And here's our planes sitting on the ground."[75] The attacking Japanese pilots could not believe their luck. They had not expected to achieve surprise, but they did not waste the opportunity.

"Our accuracy was phenomenal—it was in fact, the most accurate bombing I witnessed by our own planes throughout the war," recalled Saburo Sakai, one of the Japanese Zero pilots. Instead of encountering the "swarms of fighters" he had anticipated, Sakai noted only five P-40s flying far below. "The enemy planes, however, refused to attack and maintained their low altitude, flying around at fifteen thousand feet while we circled above them," Sakai recalled, counting "sixty enemy bombers and fighters neatly parked." A direct hit on the communications center had destroyed ground-to-air control of the fighters. Unmolested by the P-40s that continued circling seven thousand feet below them, the Japanese bombers concentrated on executing a devastating attack. "The entire airfield seemed to be rising into the air with the explosions," Sakai observed, recalling how "pieces of airplanes, hangars, and other ground installations scattered wildly. Great fires erupted and smoke boiled upwards."[76]

"I saw a guy throw his shoe at a plane, another his .45," was the vivid memory of the attack retained by PFC Victor Mapes.[77] The Japanese "didn't miss anything," according to a fellow private, Anton Bilek. "We look around and see all this devastation, airplanes burning, hangars burning, gas trucks burning. Men yelling and screaming. Wounded and dead all over the place."[78] The ferocity of the attack set the long cogon grass and bushes around the airfield ablaze, sending a wall of

fire roaring toward the landing strip. "We could see our beautiful Flying Fortresses burning and exploding right before our
eyes as we stood powerless to do anything about it," recalled
Lieutenant Edgar D. Whitcomb, a B-17 navigator.[79] The bombing attack came in two distinct waves. During the ten-minute
lull after the Zeros escorting the second flight had sped away,
three of the surviving P-40s managed to get into the air. Lieutenant Moore was one of those who downed one of the Zeros
that returned, cannoning back over the flaming wreckage to
finish off the raid with a concentrated strafing attack. It was
one of only four Japanese navy planes that failed to make the
long flight back to Formosa.

The raid on Clark Field also inflicted damage and casualties at the nearby Fort Stotensburg, the base of the 26th Cav-
alry of the Philippine Scouts. It was so close to the airfield that
to the Japanese bomber pilots its buildings appeared to be one
and the same. Lieutenant General Jonathan M. Wainwright,
the Philippine Ground Forces commander, had his headquarters in the barracks. He had earlier been directed "to take every
precaution against a possible Jap paratroop landing at Clark
Field."[80] Wainwright recalled the frenzy of the early moments
of the attack, when he had flattened himself on the grass as
the Japanese planes roared in over the Zambales Mountains.
"Mother of God, General, what shall I do?" Wainwright's terri-
fied Filipino orderly had shouted as the bombs thudded into
the nearby airfield. "Go out and get me a bottle of beer," the
general had commanded. The afternoon was barely an hour
old when Wainwright found that there was nothing left of
Clark for his Filipino scouts to protect. "All the machine shops
and hangars were down, and most of the officers' quarters and
barracks."[81] According to Lieutenant Samuel Grashio, a P-40
pilot from Nichols Field who flew over the devastation shortly
after the Japanese attackers had flown off at 1:37 P.M., "It was
astounding. Where the airfield should have been was an area
boiling with smoke, dust and flames."[82]

"The first reaction is one of almost complete disbelief that
we could be caught in such a deplorable and helpless condition," said Colonel Miller, who commanded a light tank parked
on the edge of the airfield. "In the morning we had watched
with pride, our air patrols, searching the skies, eager to find
the Japs who challenged the sovereignty of the United States
of America, hoping he would appear! A few hours later—Clark
Field—the Gibraltar of the Far East—the colossal Giant [as

depicted in the newsreels] writhing in its death struggles—the American Eagle—*struck down*."[83]

"I want to report that you no longer have to worry about your Bomber Command. We don't have one. The Japanese have destroyed Clark Field," was how Colonel Eubank acidly broke the news to USAFFE headquarters, according to a member of his staff who was present when he made the call.[84] Apocryphal or not, the sentiment of the Bombardment Force's commander was blunt and to the point. All but one of his seventeen B-17s had been destroyed in the raid on Clark Field—and the casualties might have been even higher had the single Fortress that arrived from Mindanao in the middle of the strafing attack not beaten a hasty retreat back to Del Monte Field. Fifty-five out of the total Philippine strength of 141 P-40 fighter planes had been wiped out, along with some 30 other aircraft. More than a hundred soldiers had been killed, and half as many again had been hospitalized with injuries.[85]

"It was a tragic timetable, one of the blackest days in U.S. military history," was how the Far East air force commander described the events in his diary. The question of responsibility for the debacle at Iba and Clark that Monday must have been uppermost in General Brereton's mind as he set off two hours after the raids to personally report to USAFFE headquarters in Manila. He arrived at 3:39 P.M. at Calle Victoria and was ushered in to see MacArthur after waiting only eleven minutes. What the two discussed was not recorded by either party, but in the aftermath of the defeat the Japanese had inflicted on them that afternoon, neither can have been in any doubt about the strategic disaster confronting them. As Brereton conceded in his diary, the "ultimate collapse of resistance in the Philippines was due primarily to the loss of airpower."[86]

When Brereton left the Calle Victoria late that afternoon to take a personal assessment of the destruction at Clark Field, he left it to the commander in chief to break the news of their disaster to Washington. MacArthur took advantage of the fog of battle to initially conceal the magnitude of his misfortune. As far as the press was concerned, MacArthur disguised his defeat in the time-honored military tradition of not releasing any information on losses that would give comfort to the enemy. The consequences of the Japanese air assault were therefore buried away in the first of his wartime communiqués that concentrated on informing journalists that the Army had been busily rounding up and arresting potential fifth columnists. Only at its tail end were they told that "Clark Field received a series of attacks today, the heaviest occurred at 1:30 with sanguinary results to both sides."[87]

MacArthur may have been justified in covering up for the press the scale of the disaster Japan had inflicted on American forces in the Philippines, but his secret report that evening to the War Department was a masterpiece of evasion. It listed the numbers of aircraft he had left, rather than those destroyed. "Our air losses heavy and enemy air losses medium," he radioed General George C. Marshall, the U.S. Army chief of staff. "Now have available seventeen heavy bombers, fifty to fifty-five P-40s and fifteen P-35s." He had "no losses of other types" and reinforced the impression that the Air Force was still capable of offensive action by promising that he would be "launching a heavy bombardment counter-attack tomorrow on enemy airdromes in southern Formosa."[88] A simple arithmetical calculation exposed just how disastrous a blow the Japanese had inflicted on MacArthur and the tactical nonsense of his plan to belatedly mount a raid with less than half the heavy bombers and only two thirds the fighter strength available to him that morning, when he could contend that such a raid would have been "suicidal." It therefore came as no surprise in Washington next day that MacArthur tacitly conceded his predicament in a cable that revised his aircraft losses upward. Without explicitly giving this as the reason, he reported that after receiving "further information re. damage at Clark Field" he had "required cancellation of proposed attack on Formosa."[89] That same day he also sent off a report that attempted to explain how half the American Air Force on the Philippines had been destroyed in the opening hours of the war. It did not even mention the failure of his command to launch a preemptive offensive raid on Formosa but contrived to make it appear that the defeat he had suffered was the inevitable result of expecting ill-equipped American aircrews to courageously confront vastly greater Japanese airpower.

"Every possible precaution with the limited means and time available was taken by the Far East Air Force. Their losses were due entirely to the overwhelming superiority of the enemy force," was how MacArthur carefully tailored his report. "They had been hopelessly outnumbered from the start but no unit could have done better. Their gallantry has been conspicuous," he continued. "No item of loss can be properly attributed to neglect or lack of care. They fought from fields not yet developed and under improvised conditions of every sort which placed them under the severest handicap as regards to an enemy fully prepared in every way. You may take pride in their conduct."[90]

In making out that his Far East Air Force had been surprised and overwhelmed by the Japanese, MacArthur, in his appeal for magnanimity, evidently believed that by miscasting Brereton as a latter-day Colonel Custer, he would invoke the sympathy rather than the criticism of the War Department and so could cover up the blunders of his own command. For good measure he larded his report by claiming that the accuracy of the Japanese attack could only be explained if their bombers that attacked Clark Field had been "at least partially manned by white pilots."[91] This was another myth that was invoked by both the military and press to explain the success of the attack on Pearl Harbor by Japanese pilots, whose training, ability, and aircraft had been branded as inferior and who supposedly could have achieved their triumph only with sinister secret help from their Axis partner, Germany. This claim was quickly dropped from American government propaganda when it became painfully clear that this was racist nonsense.

The canard was resurrected after the war by members of MacArthur's staff who contrived to explain the Clark Field debacle by claiming that the "job was so well done that there was reason to suspect that the pilots of these planes were Germans."[92] Farfetched stories were circulated to explain away the accuracy of Japanese bombing, including one that alleged mirrors were tied to trees by spies to guide in the raid. Supposedly a Filipino traitor using radio had also talked the Japanese planes in for the attack on Clark Field. In what purported to be a "combat history" of the war in the Philippines, which appeared in 1946, the claim was even made that the Japanese "employed a clever ruse to arrange that many of the Clark Field's planes would be on the ground."[93] Written by a prewar Philippine army veteran, *Triumph in the Philippines* was one of the first of many hagiographies of MacArthur to ignore the record by portraying the raid on Clark as a "sneak attack" that had caught his "woefully small" air force off guard—despite its having been "well dispersed, tactically disposed and ready for action."[94]

The fantasy of German involvement, Japanese trickery, and overwhelming enemy air superiority did not, however, cut any ice with General Arnold. After reading MacArthur's whitewashing report, he telephoned Brereton, who initially took the heat for the disaster at Clark Field from the Army Air Force commander. Arnold observed in his memoirs that he "could not help thinking that there must have been some mistake made somewhere in the Air Force command" and decided "to tell Brereton so." Arnold did not mince his words, demanding "how in the hell could an experienced airman like you get caught with your planes on the ground?"[95] Brereton did his best to explain, in the middle of another Japanese strafing attack on Nielsen Field, that he had "done everything in his power to get authority to attack Formosa on 8 December but had been relegated to a 'strictly defense attitude' by higher authority."[96]

After the blistering phone call from Arnold, Brereton was well aware that the Army Air Force commander in chief was irate and unsatisfied by his explanation. To get himself off the hook, Brereton drove straight to USAFFE headquarters in Manila to seek MacArthur's help in "setting the facts straight." The general reacted furiously. It was the only time that Brereton could recall ever seeing MacArthur mad with anger. "He told me to go back and fight the war," the Far East air commander recorded, noting that as he had walked out of the office, the general called on his chief of staff to get Marshall on the phone.[97] The details of this exchange were not recorded. But the buck-passing had already started. Sutherland reminded Brereton that the heavy bombers would not have been lost if he had obeyed MacArthur's orders to disperse all the B-17 squadrons to Mindanao. "Holding the bombers at Clark Field that first day was entirely due to Brereton" was how Sutherland divested himself of blame to the official army historian after the war.[98] MacArthur, in his deposition and subsequent press statements, flatly denied any prior knowledge of Brereton's plan for a raid on Formosa, confirming only that he had given orders for the evacuation of all the heavy bombers to the safety of Mindanao.

Confronted with MacArthur's denials and having to duck the issue of the tactical blunders made by his own command that left the Luzon airfields without fighter cover, Brereton shifted the blame onto the War Department for not sending adequate fighter defense to protect his heavy bombers.

"The lessons of the war in Europe were ignored by placing the heavy bomber force in the Philippines without adequate protection," Brereton contended. "Our aim in sending the heavy bombers to the Far East was to create a potential threat to Japanese aggression and cause a hoped for delay in the Japanese advance to the south." Even before he had left the United States, Brereton claimed, he had "protested against the danger of exposing a force of heavy bombers to Japanese air attack prior to sending out an adequate defense of fighter aircraft, air warning services and all other means of local defense against air attack."[99] MacArthur "was in accord with my ideas" he wrote, explaining how they had both asked the War Department for four more P-40 pursuit squadrons. Washington's failure was compounded, Brereton argued, by "the result of proportionate failure to establish properly Japan's preparedness, aggressive spirit and strategic plans for the Pacific." According to him "our best military opinion considered an attack by Japan unlikely before 1 April 1942."[100] Even so, had adequate fighter defenses and dispersal airfields been available to the Far East air commander, he declared, "it would have required an intensive and prolonged air campaign" by the superior Japanese air forces to have destroyed his airpower.[101]

"So long as we held the Philippines and had a heavy bomber force, it would have been extremely hazardous for the Japs to bypass them, leaving an air force remaining on their flank and rear," MacArthur's air commander asserted.[102] This was, in fact, the strategic calculation that had prompted the military and political decision makers in Washington in July 1941 to reverse the twenty-year-old policy and make the Philippines rather than the Hawaiian Islands the frontline bastion of the United States defense line in the Pacific. But while Brereton's overall assessment of the importance of the B-17s to the American military posture against Japan was correct, the explanation he provided in his published diary for why the Flying Fortresses were not effectively deployed on their intended mission begs the question of command failures at MacArthur's headquarters which had totally delayed a preemptive raid on Formosa and resulted in the subsequent destruction of half that strategic airpower.

Sutherland, in an apparent effort to shield MacArthur, would later insist that it was solely on his authority that the afternoon Formosan raid was approved. This disclaimer by the chief of staff and his insistence that the twilight raid had been the idea of the Far East Air Force commander, enabled MacArthur to deny ever having spoken with Brereton about a Formosan operation that morning. The assertion Brereton made that he had been blocked by higher authority from sending the Fortress bombers on that mission prompted General Arnold to complain that he was never able "to get the real story of what happened in the Philippines."[103] He also wrote that he did not find that Brereton had provided "a complete and accurate account" and further commented that the version given by MacArthur's chief of staff, Sutherland, "does not completely clear it up by any means."[104]

The mystery deepened after the war, when interrogations of the Japanese revealed the Far East Air Force in the Philippines had not been desperately outnumbered. The tactical blunder made by MacArthur's headquarters in withholding permission for the heavy bombers to raid Formosa became apparent in postwar interrogations of the Japanese 11th Air Fleet commanders, which revealed that, contrary to the general's claims of overwhelming Japanese air superiority, the odds against him in December 1941 had been only marginally more unfavorable than those that had confronted the RAF in the Battle of Britain. Not only had the Japanese feared that the B-17s would disrupt their fogbound first air strike, but their plan had been based on the estimate that it would take a week to "annihilate all American planes in the Philippines."[105] By gaining air superiority on the first day, the Japanese were able to begin landing troops two days later on the northern coast of Luzon. Within a fortnight Manila had been abandoned and American forces were retreating to the Bataan Peninsula, as MacArthur evacuated his headquarters to the island fortress of Corregidor.

MacArthur and his aides missed no opportunity to portray themselves as victims of a second Japanese surprise attack, although the record shows that MacArthur himself had been specifically alerted ten days earlier to the possibility of an attack on the Philippines in the War Department cable of 27 November warning him "hostile action possible at any moment by Japan."[106] The threat to the bomber force at Clark Field had become obvious the previous week thanks to Japanese reconnaissance flights spotted over central Luzon. One particularly brazen snooper flew in over the coast in broad daylight on 3 December. "They've got all they need now," noted Colonel George, the Far East Air Force's interceptor commander, who stated that he had been expressly forbidden by USAFFE headquarters from firing the first shot. "The next time they won't play," he observed presciently. "They'll come in without knocking."[107]

The myth that Clark Field had fallen victim to another Pearl Harbor-style "sneak" attack nonetheless continued to be promoted after the war by MacArthur and his apologists to shrug off the responsibility for the astonishing omissions of the Philippine command in the opening hours of the war. But in contrast to the unheralded attack on the Pacific Fleet anchorage nine hours before, the air raids on the American bomber base in Luzon did not fly in out of the blue without any advance warning shortly after sunrise on a Sunday morning as they had at Pearl Harbor. Across the International Date Line 7 December was Monday 8 December in Manila. It was not dawn, but midday when the B-17s at Clark Field were caught like sitting ducks by Japanese bombs nine hours after MacArthur had been told to put his War Plan into operation—one element of which required sending the B-17s against enemy air bases in Formosa. An offensive strike to counter a Japanese invasion threat had been the rationale for giving MacArthur overall command of the greatest concentration of strategic airpower outside the continental United States.

"Hopes for the active defense of the Islands rested on those aircraft," the official U.S. Army history of the Philippines campaign concludes unequivocally. "At the end of the first day of war, such hopes were dead,"[108] was how it characterized the "tragedy" of Clark Field. "As at Pearl Harbor the Japanese had removed at one stroke the greatest single obstacle to their advance southward," and the strategic consequences of the disaster at Clark Field were such that "Philippine garrison could expect little help in the near future. It was almost entirely surrounded."[109]

Not only were the Flying Fortresses intended to be the cornerstone of the defense of the American island territory, but, as part of a strategic bargain concluded between Churchill and Roosevelt in August 1941, they had become a crucial element in the secret pact by which the United States had guaranteed the security of the British Empire in the Far East. The premature loss of more than half the heavy bomber force becomes even more incredible because—as the records show—in the months before the Japanese attack both the military planners in Washington and MacArthur assumed that B-17s could be deployed not simply in a defensive posture but also as a deterrent to further Japanese encroachment in the Far East, by threatening a strategic air offensive against Tokyo. This assumption was the culmination of an extraordinary series of military and diplomatic miscalculations that set the stage for the Pacific Fleet being caught by surprise at Pearl Harbor.

In the late fall of 1941, the records reveal, Washington had ceased to consider the Hawaiian Islands as the front line of the United States Pacific defense against Japan. After July it was MacArthur in the Philippines to whom the long-range aer-

ial reconnaissance and interdiction force of heavy bombers—
originally destined to reinforce the Hawaiian command—were
redirected. The Pacific Fleet was denied not only essential air
defenses but also vital intelligence because the decision to reinforce the Philippines had convinced the military and diplomatic policy makers in Washington that by December 1941
the Hawaiian Islands were safe five thousand miles inside the
redrawn Pacific defense perimeter.

After the twin disasters of 7 December, the anticipation of
political fallout obliged the president and his advisers to conceal the administration's ultimate culpability for the disastrous Philippine deterrent strategy. The "Pearl Harbor
Syndrome" began to manifest itself as they restricted the investigations solely to the Pearl Harbor attack and focused the
question of military accountability entirely on the Hawaiian
commanders. This directed attention away from the secret
deal Roosevelt had struck with Churchill—the historical record, as the following chapters will show, had made MacArthur
the point man, commanding a scratch Anglo-American Far
East deterrent force against Japan. By sacrificing Kimmel and
Short to satisfy public indignation, the administration's blunders were overlooked as national outrage erupted over Pearl
Harbor. The destruction of the Pacific Fleet battleships had
been such a spectacular affront to American pride that it overshadowed the far greater strategic disaster of the Philippines,
and the geography that put Kimmel and Short closer to the
flames of American public wrath contributed to their becoming the scapegoats, while MacArthur was transformed into a
national hero as he went down to defeat battling the Japanese
in the Philippines.

General MacArthur's reputation as the American Caesar
also enabled him to avoid being investigated to determine why
he failed to promptly execute his war plan to preempt the
Japanese attack on Clark Field. The lack of surviving records
and the conflicting claims about the B-17 raid on Formosa
made by MacArthur and his air commander, Brereton, and
chief of staff, Sutherland, also shielded MacArthur. The official
account of the *The Fall of the Philippines*, published in 1953,
concluded somewhat tactfully that "the historian can be sure
of only five facts: (1) That an attack on Formosa was proposed;
(2) that such an attack was deferred in favor of a photo reconnaissance mission requested by either Brereton or Sutherland;
(3) that about 1100 on 8 December a strike against Formosa, to
take place that day, was finally authorized; (4) that the heavy

bombers were back on Clark Field after 1130 on the morning of 8 December; and (5) that MacArthur planned an attack against Formosa for the morning of 9 December."[110]

Subsequently three explanations emerged to explain what can only be described in hindsight as an appalling dereliction of duty by MacArthur as commander in chief. His own account would have history believe that the instructions he received from Washington did not make it clear that the U.S. forces in the Philippines were under attack following the raid on Pearl Harbor. In the light of the records, this proved an unsatisfactory and unconvincing explanation for MacArthur's inaction that morning for both of his most recent biographers, D. Clayton James and William Manchester. The latter speculated that his fatal "misunderstanding" was induced by a catatonic psychological reaction to the news of the Pearl Harbor attack, just as Napoleon Bonaparte's alimentary ailment had paralyzed his powers of command during the crucial opening rounds of the Battle of Waterloo.[111]

The recent discovery of bank records showing that the general and his staff received a half-million dollar payoff from the Philippine treasury account three weeks later raises a third and far more intriguing possibility. MacArthur's fatal hesitation to launch a preemptive bomber strike on the air bases in Formosa, it can be argued, may have been the result of his divided loyalty to the Manila government, which was hoping to keep the island commonwealth neutral in the conflict between Japan and the United States. While it may never be possible to establish the real reason for MacArthur's inability to discharge his military responsibilities as commander in chief of the U.S. armed forces in the Far East during the opening hours of the war in the Pacific, his failure to commit the B-17s to their intended mission is a matter of historical significance.

The pivotal role that the Philippines heavy bomber force played in the events leading up to the disasters on 7 December 1941 makes the question of why the B-17s were never deployed an issue of far greater importance than the unresolvable debate over whether a B-17 raid on the Japanese air bases at Takao that morning could have changed the course of the war in the Pacific. It can now be demonstrated how the Flying Fortresses under MacArthur's command in the Philippines had supplanted the Pacific Fleet's battleships in Pearl Harbor, which was a dramatic reversal of what had been, until six months earlier, the United States military and diplomatic strategy against Japan.

2

"A STRATEGIC ERROR OF THE FIRST MAGNITUDE"

Embargoing Japan Required Reinforcing the
Philippines as the U.S. Pacific Front Line, to the
Detriment of Hawaiian Defense

The Hawaiian Islands had become a fully garrisoned naval fortress for the first time only a year earlier. Until the spring of 1940, Oahu's great natural harbor had served only as the forward base of the so-called Hawaiian Detachment. This was the single carrier task force stationed there throughout the year, with the Pacific Fleet steaming out from its West Coast home port of San Pedro to make a springtime base at Pearl Harbor for its annual exercises. What had been a temporary anchorage became the fleet's permanent base after the April 1940 exercises, when Admiral James O. Richardson was ordered to remain in Hawaiian waters by Admiral Harold R. Stark, the chief of naval operations, because of "the deterrent effect which it is thought your presence may have on the Japs going into the East Indies."[1]

Richardson, who was the epitome of a seafaring admiral whose devotion to the Navy was matched by an unshakable temperament, had flown to Washington in July 1940. Forcefully, he argued for the fleet's return to the West Coast, where he believed it would be less exposed to the danger of a surprise Japanese attack. His meetings with the president and officials of the State Department convinced him that it was the bureaucrats rather than the admirals of the Navy Department who were dictating naval strategy. As he testified in 1945, he believed that the fleet had been "retained in the Hawaiian area solely to support diplomatic representations and as a deterrent to Japanese aggressive action."[2] In Washington, Richardson recalled, he had gained "the distinct impression that there was an opinion in Washington that Japan could be bluffed."[3]

Admiral Richardson's concern that the fleet had fallen hostage to American diplomacy was reinforced when he received notification, after the Japanese signed their Tripartite Pact with Germany and Italy in September 1940, that the fleet could not now pull back to the West Coast without it being interpreted as a climb-down in Tokyo. Richardson promptly took off again for Washington. But it was not a propitious time to persuade the president to back down. Running for an unprecedented third term in the White House against vocal isolationist opposition, Roosevelt had to satisfy his Republican critics that there was going to be no sellout of the Chinese Nationalists to the Japanese, whose forces had been fighting a bitter war on the mainland of Asia since 1931.

"I know that the presence of the fleet in the Hawaiian area has had and is now having a restraining influence on the actions of Japan," the president told Richardson,[4] when the admiral restated that keeping the fleet based in Hawaiian waters left it "disadvantageously disposed for preparing for, or initiating war operations."[5] In what he recalled as a "hot and heavy" confrontation, Richardson had then stunned the president by expressing doubts about his administration's competence "for the successful prosecution of a war in the Pacific." Taken aback that a senior member of the armed forces would step out of line with such a bold criticism of foreign policy, Roosevelt terminated the uncomfortable conversation by telling the Pacific Fleet commander, "Joe, you just don't understand."[6] Richardson returned to Pearl Harbor convinced that he had "shocked" Roosevelt into reconsidering naval policy.

It was Richardson, however, who was to be shocked three months later on 5 January 1941, when he received a cable from Washington informing him he was to be replaced as Pacific Fleet commander with effect from 1 February by his subordinate, Admiral Kimmel, Commander, Cruisers of the Battle Force. Richardson passed on to Kimmel—who was no less stunned than his predecessor by his appointment to command—the troubling issues raised in a dispatch to Pacific Fleet headquarters from the chief of naval operations. Stark's letter enclosed the communication that Secretary of the Navy Knox wrote to Henry L. Stimson, the secretary of war, on 24 January 1941, voicing the concern in the Navy Department about the "security of the U.S. Pacific Fleet while in Pearl Harbor, and of the Pearl Harbor naval base itself."[7] Drafted by Rear Admiral Richmond Kelly Turner, this letter reflected the conclusions of the Office of Naval War Plans, of which he was newly appointed head, following the British torpedo-plane attack on the Italian Fleet at Taranto in November of 1940.

"If war eventuates with Japan, it is believed easily possible that hostilities would be initiated by *a surprise attack upon the Fleet or Naval Base at Pearl Harbor* [emphasis added]." The study asserted, listing the dangers "in the order of importance and probability," that the likelihood of an "air bombing attack" and "air torpedo attack" against Pearl Harbor was greater than the possibility of enemy submarine operations. "The possibilities of a major disaster to the fleet or naval base warrant taking every step, as rapidly as can be done, that will increase the readiness of the Army and Navy to withstand a raid of the character mentioned," the memorandum continued, urging that priority be given to the "location and engagement of enemy carriers and supporting vessels before air attack can be launched."[8] Navy Secretary Knox accepted that such protective measures were "largely a function of the fleet, but quite possibly, might not be carried out in case of *an air attack initiated without warning prior to a declaration of war* [emphasis added]."[9]

This prophetic forecast reflected the strategic importance of Pearl Harbor as it was seen in Washington eleven months *before* the Japanese made their attack. By chance a letter sent by the secretary of the navy to the secretary of war coincided with a letter addressed to Kimmel by the chief of naval operations that arrived on 1 February. Stark enclosed a report received from the U.S. ambassador in Tokyo, Joseph C. Grew, that warned that a "surprise mass attack on Pearl Harbor" was being prepared by the Japanese "in the event of trouble with the United States."[10] According to Grew, the information had been obtained from the Peruvian ambassador, who had originally learned it from a cook in his embassy. Grew stated "that although the project seemed fantastic, the fact that he had heard it from many sources prompted him to pass on the information."[11] Whether it was an accurate leak could not later be established, but it is an established fact that Admiral Yamamoto, 2 January 1994, ordered the Japanese Combined Fleet planning staff to begin a feasibility studies for the attack on Pearl Harbor.

The Japanese attack of 7 December 1941 gave Knox's letter and Grew's warning a singular significance. They were to be cited at the various investigations and inquiries as clear evidence that the Pacific Fleet command had been given an early warning of the threat of a Japanese air attack on Pearl Harbor. But Kimmel had every reason for not taking the warning at face value. Since the chief of naval operations was unaware of the secret Japanese deliberations, Stark discounted the warning, which "appeared to be hearsay information which was not substantiated."[12] Kimmel was therefore advised by Naval Intelligence that he should be "placing no credence in these rumors" because "no move against Pearl Harbor appears imminent or planned for in the foreseeable future."[13]

What the record does show is that in the early months of 1941 both Washington and Kimmel were focusing on the need to bolster Pearl Harbor against a possible Japanese carrier attack. The new Pacific Fleet commander was a stickler for seagoing drills who prescribed a strict weekly rota of intensive exercises to work up his ships and men into a state of war readiness. Kimmel also instituted a review of the protection for the fleet anchorage that resulted in a request for extending the antitorpedo net defenses. To guard the Hawaiian Islands against a carrier-borne raid, a total of one hundred eighty B-17 bombers were estimated to be necessary for long-range air patrols and interdiction of an approaching enemy attack force. These measures to reinforce Oahu had been called for in a "Joint Estimate" that had been submitted on 31 March after a major review of the defenses by the Army and Navy air commanders at Hawaii.

The assessment, made by Major General F. L. Martin and Rear Admiral Patrick N. Bellinger, had focused on the vulnerability of Pearl Harbor to air attack, which had been demonstrated by the fleet exercises three years earlier, when a successful mock air strike had been launched from the carrier *Saratoga*. Yet even as the request for a massive increase in Pearl Harbor's air defense was received by the War and Navy departments, the focus of Washington's strategic attention was shifting westward toward the Philippines and away from the Hawaiian Islands in the central Pacific. This was in part because the perception of the Pacific Fleet as the major deterrent to Japan was diminished in April 1941, after Kimmel had been ordered to send a carrier, three battleships, four cruisers, and eighteen destroyers through the Panama Canal to join the Atlantic Fleet in the undeclared war against the U-boats that the U.S. Navy was fighting alongside the embattled Royal Navy. This almost one quarter reduction in the Pacific Fleet's strength was alarming enough for its commander in chief, but in May when Kimmel learned that more of his warships were going to be sent to the Atlantic he flew to Washington to protest directly to Chief of Naval Operations Stark and the president.

"Once the fleet was placed there, for the purpose of exerting a deterrent effect upon Japan, it was not maintaining a consistent policy thereafter to weaken the fleet, visibly and plainly, by diversion of powerful units to the Atlantic," Kimmel bluntly informed Roosevelt on 2 June.[14] His point that the Pacific Fleet was already dangerously weaker than the Japanese Combined Fleet was accepted. But the requests for more antiaircraft batteries and long-range aircraft to defend Pearl Harbor from air attack went unfulfilled, except for twenty-one B-17s that arrived at Hickham Field from California on 13 May. While they constituted the greatest concentration of heavy bombers outside the United States at the time, the force was only a fraction of the one hundred eighty considered essential for Oahu's defense.

Admiral Kimmel was not made aware, during his visit to Washington, that a fundamental shift in United States military strategy in the Pacific was in the offing, as the accelerating pace of Japan's aggressive advances in the Far East brought demands for a "get-tough" policy from the hard-liners in the Roosevelt administration. The War and Navy departments were, in the meantime, wrestling with the dilemma of how to confront the growing and separate menaces to the United States in the Atlantic and Pacific, which threatened the strategic nightmare of having to fight a two-ocean war with a one-ocean navy. Contingency strategies had been jointly developed by the Army and Navy for a series of war scenarios in which the potential foes and possible allies were designated by colors. These were the so-called Rainbow plans, which, by the beginning of 1941, had been narrowed down to Rainbow 5, as the most likely eventuality. Developed from the Navy's "Plan D" of October 1940, it was based on the presumption that the United States would eventually be drawn into the war with Germany in the Atlantic theater.

The need for the United States to become actively involved in Britain's lone struggle against the Axis powers became apparent to the president and his military aids—after Hitler's lightning takeover of Europe, which culminated in the shattering defeat of France in the spring of 1940. The majority of the electorate, however, remained wedded to an illusory isolationism, to which Roosevelt had pandered during the fall presidential election campaign, with repeated promises to American mothers that he was not about to send their sons to fight in any foreign wars. Once he was safely reelected to the White House, however, he encouraged the chief of naval operation to complete a strategic blueprint for involving the United States in the Atlantic war. The underlying premise was that since America was starting out with a "one-ocean navy," instead of trying to fight a "two-ocean war," American forces would be concentrated in the Atlantic, while maintaining a defensive posture against Japan in the Pacific. This was in keeping with Chief of Naval Operations Stark's assumption in Plan D that the Atlantic/European theater would be the strategic crucible of the war and Germany could be defeated only with the active participation of United States forces.

On 16 January 1941 Roosevelt had approved the broad outlines of Rainbow 5, and it was the basis of discussions with the British and Canadians at the so-called ABC-1 staff conference, held in Washington under conditions of great secrecy the following month. The Rainbow 5 strategy dictated the objectives of what became an increasingly closely knit Anglo-American defensive relationship in the Far East. Not only did "Europe First" become the basis of United States diplomatic and military strategy through 1941, but the priority given to the Atlantic over the Pacific theater after 7 December was to dictate the way the war would be fought when the British and the Americans became formal allies. It was acknowledged at the time, however, that the agreements reached at the ABC-1 conference were tentative and constituted no political commitment. This was to avoid the charge that the United States was being unconstitutionally committed to an "entangling foreign alliance" without congressional ratification.

While enthusiastically agreeing with the "Europe First" underpinning of Rainbow 5, the British chiefs of staff had also tried very hard at the ABC-1 discussions in March 1941 to persuade the U.S. Navy to send warships of the Pacific Fleet to Singapore, to deter Japan from attacking Malaya. Their contention that "the loss of Singapore would be a disaster of the first magnitude, second only to the loss of the British Isles," was firmly rejected by Admiral Stark, not least because it ran counter to the twenty-year-old strategic doctrine that U.S. ter-

ritories west of Hawaii—including the Philippines—were indefensible. To abandon such a fundamental policy would have,
in Army Chief of Staff Marshall's words, constituted "a strategic error of the first magnitude."[15]

The Philippines had been a military liability for the United
States ever since they had been annexed by a reluctant Congress in 1898, after their liberation from the Spanish Empire
by armed American intervention. Successive administrations
had been reluctant to commit substantial forces to defend the
sprawling island territory after World War I, when Japan
emerged as the most aggressive Pacific power. They remained
a lightly garrisoned outpost, which if attacked, necessitated
that the American and Filipino defenders retreat to prepared
defensive positions on the Bataan Peninsula and there to dig
in and await the lifting of the Japanese siege by the battleships
of the Pacific Fleet, staging from their advanced base in
Hawaii. The commonwealth would cease being a liability at
the end of the decade, when it was scheduled to achieve full
independence. This prompted a movement in the War Department to propose "that the United States forces in the Philippines and the Far East be withdrawn at the earliest practical
opportunity and outposts be established along the approximate line of the 180th meridian."[16] The consequent plan to
make Midway Island, twelve hundred miles to the west of Pearl
Harbor, the outer perimeter of the United States Pacific defense line, was ultimately rejected. Although until the summer
of 1941 the Philippines was universally acknowledged by the
American military planners to be indefensible, with its token
garrison U.S. Army division and a score of obsolescent
bombers. But the island territory continued to extract a powerful commitment from the most senior officers, who, in common with the U.S. Army chief of staff, General Marshall, had
sentimental attachments from their posting there as young
army lieutenants. They were also loath to abandon the emerging Filipino nation in what, they feared, would be taken as a
concession by the United States to the encroaching ambitions
of Japan.

The United States had committed itself to Philippine independence. Any American withdrawal from the Far East at a
time when Japanese aggression was threatening to accelerate,
Marshall argued, would send the wrong signal to Tokyo. Secretary of War Stimson, who had long argued for taking a stand
against Japan, also strongly opposed those members of the
Army General Staff who had proposed abandoning the Philip-

pines. Although by 1941, the islands were more a symbol of American strategic impotence than a forward bastion of military power in the Far East. That spring, Stimson had begun to call for reinforcing the Philippines as a demonstration of the United States' intent to stand firm against Japan. He garnered the support of other hard-liners in the Roosevelt administration, including Treasury Secretary Henry Morgenthau and Harold Ickes, the interior secretary, whose department was ultimately responsible for the civil administration of the Commonwealth territory. The strongest advocate for confronting Japan was Dr. Stanley K. Hornbeck, the long-serving and influential head of the Far East Section of the Department of State.

A dyed-in-the-wool Japanophobe, who had repeatedly urged military action as the Japanese had escalated their war with the Chinese, Dr. Hornbeck argued that the Tokyo regime "will yield not to persuasion, but to fear."[17] Japan's foreign policy became more aggressive during the spring of 1941, in response to pressure from their own military leaders and their Axis partner Germany, who wanted Tokyo to move against Britain's Far Eastern territories. The War Department's debate over whether to reinforce the Philippines intensified. This widening inconsistency in United States foreign policy greatly worried a staffer at the Army War Plans Division who raised the issue in a memorandum at the beginning of 1941: "The military policy should conform to and be capable of supporting our foreign policy in the region. Conversely, the foreign policy should be such that it can be supported by the military policy. At present the two are inconsistent; one or the other should be changed."[18]

This timely warning of the incompatibility of American military and foreign policy toward Japan was fated to be ignored. Only the president had the authority to reconcile the expanding discontinuity between national objectives and the means of the Army and Navy to back them up. Roosevelt's pragmatic presidential style and his inclination to let the rival camps in his administration fight out a compromise allowed U.S. policy in the Far East to drift until a clear-cut decision was forced on him by the rush of events. MacArthur, too, bears a measure of responsibility for the resolution of the Army's strategic equation in the Far East in favor of reinforcing the Philippines at the expense of the U.S. Army Hawaiian Department. On his retirement as chief of staff of the Army, he had arrived in Manila in 1935 to become a military adviser to the president of the Philippines Commonwealth, where he devoted his prestige and considerable political influence, as one of America's most celebrated military figures, to pressing the War Department to reverse its doctrine, by contending that the Philippines could be defended if the islands received adequate reinforcement.

The plan for American forces to retreat to the Bataan Peninsula to await rescue by the Pacific Fleet in the event of an attack by Orange, as Japan was designated in the war plan of the same name, was doubly offensive to MacArthur. He had established his military hero's reputation by leading his American troops of the so-called Rainbow Division into German machine-gun fire on the Western Front during World War I, armed only with a woolen scarf and a swagger stick. But his campaign to reinforce the Philippines had fallen on deaf ears in Washington as the Depression shrank military budgets and the Roosevelt administration struggled to maintain America's overseas commitments. When MacArthur completed his two-year term as U.S. military adviser, he retired from the Army and accepted a lucrative offer from the Philippine government to stay in Manila as commander of the commonwealth's militia. Promoted to field marshal, he was given an inappropriately lavish salary to lead a Filipino army composed of four thousand regulars and twenty thousand minimally trained part-time troops. Sporting a gold-braid-encrusted uniform of his own design, he settled into a custom-built air-conditioned penthouse atop Manila's luxury hotel. But by 1940, as a result of his failure to persuade the United States government to bolster the defenses of the Philippines, MacArthur's military influence with President Manuel Quezon had become more symbolic than real.

"From 1922 until later 1940 our policy with regard to the Philippines was to maintain existing strength, but to undertake no further permanent improvements except as a measure of economy," reported General Gerow, the head of Army War Plans, in a memorandum outlining the steps initiated to reverse the 1939 recommendation that "U.S. forces in the Philippines be withdrawn at the earliest opportunity."[19] At the start of 1941 the U.S. garrison commander, Major General George Grunert, was advised that he could expect only a limited increase in the strength of the 31st Infantry Division but that his force of Filipino Scouts could be expanded to twelve thousand. The War Department cautioned Grunert, however, that there could be no major reinforcement "which might result in involving us in action in a theater which we are not prepared to sustain."[20] But the southward encroachment by Japanese troops toward Indochina in the spring of 1941 succeeded where MacArthur and Grunert's appeals had failed, by convincing the War Department to abandon its hard-nosed strategy against reinforcing the Philippines. At the end of May, General Grunert received approval for the construction of a series of coastal batteries on Luzon. This was followed by an ambitious scheme for building strategic roads and shelters and for expanding the airfields to take heavy bombers, although at the time Grunert's aerial defenses consisted of forty old fighters and a score of obsolete medium twin-engine bombers.

In the spring of 1941 the sixty-one-year-old MacArthur, by now tiring of all his gold braid and lack of forces to command, began to look for a way to restore himself to a more influential military position. He let it be known that he was considering resigning his empty command and penned ingratiating letters to senior members of the administration soliciting an appointment as U.S. high commissioner in the Philippines. Despite MacArthur's obsequious characterization of Roosevelt as "our greatest military strategist,"[21] he did not get the post he coveted. He then begged the president to recall him to active duty with the U.S. Army. When he received no response, he notified General Marshall, the Army chief of staff, of his intention to return and announced his intention of making reservations for the trip back to the United States.[22] He canceled his passage only at the end of June, after receiving a confidential notification from Marshall informing him that Secretary of War Stimson considered him "the logical selection for the Army Commander in the Far East should the situation approach a crisis."[23]

That crisis with Japan was fast boiling over. Two months of secret discussions between Admiral Kichisabura Nomura, Tokyo's newly appointed ambassador in Washington, and the secretary of state, Cordell Hull, had finally run aground. Disregarding the repeated caution urged by his adviser Dr. Hornbeck, Hull had enthusiastically begun discussions with the genial, pro-American admiral under conditions of great secrecy, predicting that confidentiality offered the best hope for reaching an accommodation with Japan. But any chance of an agreement quickly foundered on fundamental issues: Tokyo had rejected the American insistence that any long-term accommodation must be based on a willingness by Japan to pull out of the Tripartite Pact with Germany and Italy. In addition,

Hull demanded that Japan withdraw all her troops from the mainland of China and accept free trade in Asia. He was no less adamant that until the Japanese made peace with Chiang Kai-shek, the United States would continue supplying economic aid and ammunition to the Chinese Nationalists. The secret talks came to a standstill after it became clear to the secretary of state that Foreign Minister Yosuke Matsuoka was not interested in reaching a compromise, after his trip to Berlin and Moscow, meeting with Hitler and Germany's then ally Stalin.

When the Soviet Union was invaded on 22 June 1941 by German panzer divisions, Matsuoka seized on the news to press the Japanese cabinet to cast their lot with the Nazis and declare war. But the government of Prime Minister Prince Fumimaro Konoye, which was taken by complete surprise by the invasion of Russia, did not want Japan dragged into Hitler's widening conflict. The prime minister could remain sitting on the political fence because the Japanese armed services were locked in their own strategic debate. The Imperial Army had long argued for advancing north into Siberia from Manchukuo, the client state that Japan's Kwantung army had established in Manchuria. But the Imperial Navy staff wanted to seize bases in Indochina to launch a southward campaign to take over the rich material and mineral resources of Malaya and the Dutch East Indies.

Japan's bitterly argued strategic debate was not formally resolved until the Imperial Conference of 2 July 1941. In the conference chamber of the Tokyo palace, the emperor, in full ceremonial robes and regalia, presided over the meeting of the cabinet and its military and naval advisers, who made the momentous decision to expand southward "no matter what obstacles may be encountered." Declaring that "our Empire is determined to follow a program which will result in the establishment of the Greater East Asia Co-Prosperity Sphere," Prime Minister Konoye affirmed his intention to secure for Japan the markets, oil, and mineral wealth of the British, Dutch, and French Far Eastern colonies. He won the agreement of the military leaders for an attempt to bring about Japan's national goal by diplomacy; but in the event that this failed, he promised, "preparations for war with Great Britain and the United States will be made."[24] To facilitate the resumption of negotiations with Washington, the pro-Nazi Matsuoka, who had attracted the fatal tag of being "Hitler's office boy" in Tokyo, was replaced as foreign minister by the more temperate Admiral Teihiro Toyoda.

What was intended to be a placatory gesture to Washington was drowned out by all the saber-rattling in the Japanese diplomatic communications among themselves. Unknown to Tokyo, the Americans had been able to eavesdrop on their most secret cable traffic since November 1940, when the Signals Intelligence Section of the U.S. Army Signal Corps succeeded in breaking into the main diplomatic cipher system known as Purple. Designated *97-shiki O-bun Injiki*—"Alphabetical Typewriter 97"—by the Japanese, this electromechanical enciphering machine had been introduced in September 1939 for secure high-level diplomatic communications between Tokyo and its overseas embassies. Unlike the German Enigma and the American Sigaba code machines, which relied primarily on revolving wired rotors to encipher each letter of text, the Japanese encrypting machine was based on a typewriter keyboard whose input was scrambled through a battery of six-level, twenty-five-point Strolger-type stepper-switches as then used in telephone exchanges, with a daily cipher key set up by means of an electrical plugboard.[25]

The process was duplicated after a brilliant piece of mathematical deduction by the signals intelligence service team led by William S. Friedman and Frank B. Rowlett, who designed and built an analogue deciphering device. The so-called Purple Machine allowed the United States to read the intercepts of Tokyo's most secret exchanges between Tokyo and its diplomats. MAGIC was the code name given by the Army to the information obtained from the Japanese diplomatic messages. According to Rowlett, the name arose because "the chief signal officer liked to refer to us as magicians."[26] In 1942 the U.S. armed forces adopted the British practice of classifying all communications intelligence as "ultrasecret" or ULTRA for short. Throughout 1941 the Purple decrypts were known as MAGIC intelligence. Their raw translations of these Japanese messages, for the most part uninterpreted, were locked in leather pouches for circulation by courier to the operational chiefs of the armed services, the president, and the secretaries of war, navy, and state.

As tension with Japan rapidly mounted in the early summer of 1941, Roosevelt and his closest advisers monitored Tokyo's diplomatic exchanges with mounting concern. On 7 July MAGIC intelligence revealed the timetable of Japan's "determination to get bases" from the Vichy administration of

French Indochina, and anxiety rose in Washington after the interception of Tokyo's instructions to their ambassador in Berlin that "Japan is preparing for all possible eventualities regarding the Soviets in order to join forces with Germany."[27] This heightened Washington concerns about whether the Red Army would cope with another frontal assault. In another intercepted foreign ministry message, the Japanese notified their legation in Saigon that "Japan intends to carry out plans by force if opposed by British or United States intervenes."[28] The advance knowledge that Tokyo was committed to advancing her troops into Indochina as a springboard for a southward advance set the alarm bells ringing wildly in Washington. Their inability to counter Japan's next aggressive move was an irritating reminder to Washington of the weakness of the United States in the Far East.

The relative weakness of the Pacific Fleet compared to the Japanese Combined Fleet rendered its deterrent value increasingly ineffective. But the priority of the Atlantic theater dictated by the Rainbow 5 strategy prevented any return of the transferred warships to Pearl Harbor or any major naval reinforcement of the Philippines. Nonetheless, the hard-liners in the state, interior, and treasury departments increasingly urged the president to counter Japan's aggression with economic warfare, calling for a total trade embargo. This would extend the ban on the export of scrap iron that had been put in place as a warning the previous October to curtail Japan's ability to produce weapons grade steel. Cutting off oil was a far more potent weapon, because Japan relied on the United States for all but two percent of her supplies.

The risk in adopting a policy of economic sanctions was that it would prompt Japan to use her military strength to seize alternative oil resources in the Dutch territory of Borneo. The dangers were outlined by Admiral Turner, the head of Office of Navy War Plans, who warned that an embargo "would probably result in a fairly early attack on Malaya and the Netherlands East Indies, and possibly would involve the United States in early war in the Pacific." As chief of naval operations, Stark endorsed Turner's recommendation that "trade with Japan not be embargoed at this time" and passed it on to the president on 20 July with the covering note, "I concur in general."[29] After MAGIC that day disclosed that Japan had "decided to advance on 24th regardless of whether demands accepted or not,"[30] the majority of Roosevelt's cabinet decided to put policy before prudence and make a firm statement to Tokyo. The president, however, shared the Navy's concern about the inherent risks in introducing a total embargo of Japan's trade with the United States.

"I think it will interest you to know that the Japanese are having a real drag-down and knock-out fight among themselves for the past week trying to decide which way they are going to jump," the president had told Ickes, who in his role as "petroleum coordinator" had been pressing for extending economic sanctions to oil.[31] "I simply have not got the Navy to go around and every little episode in the Pacific means fewer ships in the Atlantic," the president explained, declaring that he had no intention of choking off all oil supplies. Rather he said he wanted to "slip a noose around Japan's neck and give it a jerk now and then."[32]

The president's plan for a controlled embargo was put into effect on 26 July, after the news broke that Japanese troops had crossed the border into Indochina. The State Department announced the freezing of all Axis funds to effectively bring all trade with Germany, Italy, and Japan to a standstill. But mindful of the Navy's warning, which had been reinforced by Churchill's cabled concern that all-out sanctions might cause the Japanese "to run amok," the president took care to personally assure Ambassador Nomura that oil supplies were not being totally shut off. Roosevelt intended that low-grade gasoline supplies would keep on flowing to Japan at 1936 levels. But the system of export licenses by which this was to be achieved was to be frustrated by Interior Secretary Ickes and Assistant Secretary of State Acheson, who saw to it that the Treasury Department bureaucrats snarled the Japanese paperwork in red tape. The embargo was made total. Contrary to Roosevelt's expressly declared intention, the noose around Tokyo's neck became a garrote to choke Japan off from all oil supplies.

In contrast with the fall of 1941, when MAGIC intelligence was withheld from the Pacific Fleet commander in chief for three months, during the Indochina crisis in July, Admiral Kimmel was copied with the relevant Purple diplomatic intercepts from Tokyo, including the one suggesting an imminent attack on the Soviet Union. He was also apprised of the key intercept in which Tokyo let its Saigon embassy know that Japan was prepared "to use force" to obtain control of Indochina air and naval bases, and expressed their hope "to avoid friction with Britain and particularly the United States if possible, but risk is necessary."[33] Two days later the full terms of

Japan's ultimatum were also relayed to Kimmel, informing him that "army planning advance on about twenty July" and that Tokyo had ordered diplomats in Hanoi and Saigon to "burn codes" and evacuate personnel because "Japan intends to carry out plans by force if opposition or if British or United States intervenes."[34] The Pacific Fleet also received MAGIC intelligence direct from the Philippines, where the naval cryptographic unit attached to the 16th Naval District, known as Station CAST, was by then operating its own Purple decrypting machine.

This Japanese diplomatic intelligence provided the Pacific Fleet intelligence officer, Commander Edwin T. Layton, with an accurate framework to delineate Tokyo's policy objectives, which in turn enabled him to predict with precision the dispositions that the Combined Fleet would make to support Japan's advance into Indochina. The intercepts proved a far more accurate and timely source of intelligence for Kimmel than the interpretations he received in the personal letters from Chief of Naval Operations Stark. Their value as intelligence was devalued not only by ten-day-long postal delays, but the chatty indecision in which Stark cloaked his evaluations of MAGIC. They veered between cheerful reassurance, to painful obfuscation and hesitant alarm. Without this separate access to MAGIC, Kimmel, whose tidy mind operated with the well-ordered precision of a watch, would have been hard-pressed to obtain any significant intelligence from Stark's letter, which simply predicted "war in the near future," with allusions to a possible advance against the British and Dutch and "seizure and development of naval, army, and air bases in Indochina."[35]

"Just where it will all end I do not know," Stark wrote Kimmel on 24 July, just two days before he received notice that "at 1400 GCT July twenty-sixth United States will impose economic sanctions on Japan." He explained that he himself had opposed sanctions "just as strongly as I could," because the Office of Naval War Plans feared that a total embargo would encourage the Japanese to move into Borneo.[36] The Hawaiian commands received only a six-hour warning, in a 25 July dispatch, of Washington's decision to launch economic warfare. Kimmel was simply advised that "immediate hostile reaction by Japan through the use of military means was not anticipated." Both Kimmel and Short were nonetheless instructed to "take appropriate precautionary measures against possible eventualities."[37]

With the advance knowledge of the Japanese objectives

provided by the analysis of MAGIC, Layton, in conjunction with his other intelligence sources, was able to accurately estimate the probable disposition of the Imperial naval forces covering the Japanese movement into Indochina. Important elements of the Combined Fleet, including two carrier divisions, had been "lost" when the radio call signs used to address them disappeared from the intercepted radio traffic.[38] From the analysis of the pattern in this traffic, it soon became clear that although the two "missing" carrier divisions were involved with the First and Second Fleet covering operations in the South China Seas, the major units of the Combined Fleet were not involved in this operation.[39]

At the staff conference of the Pacific Fleet held on 26 July, Kimmel was therefore able to make his planned dispositions with confidence. In the first test of the newly promulgated Pacific Fleet War Plan, he proposed to counter the possibility of an attack from the Japanese base at Jaluit with a series of long-range air sweeps southwest of Oahu over the ocean toward the Marshall Islands. The Army commander in chief, General Short, after reports were received of the Japanese consulate's burning documents, responded by putting U.S. Army forces on "half alert against sabotage." In the absence of any reports of other "untoward eventualities" over that weekend, Kimmel and Short both concluded that the immediate crisis had passed and that their forces could be stepped down.[40]

It was not until six weeks after the 26 July crisis had passed without incident that Secretary of State Hull discovered that the president's express intention to keep some fuel flowing had been thwarted by overzealous hard-liners. By then it was too late to rectify the situation without sending the wrong message to Tokyo.[41] The United States was now committed to all-out economic warfare with Japan. The New York Times had observed on 27 July that this policy was the "the most drastic blow short of war."[42] If there was any doubt about this in Tokyo, it was eliminated by the announcement made the same day from Washington that MacArthur was being returned to active duty to replace General Grunert as commander of U.S. Army Forces Far East. His recall to the colors as a three-star general was intended to show that the United States was now committed to reinforcing the Philippines to deter any move by Japan to seize the alternative oil supplies in the Dutch East Indies. MacArthur responded by declaring that he "felt like an old dog in a new uniform." He appeared quite oblivious to the risks inherent in this announcing of an overnight reversal in

U.S. Pacific strategy when there weren't adequate military forces in place in the Philippines to back it up.[43]

To meet the fresh demands on his command, MacArthur proposed a year-end deadline for training and equipping an army of 120,000 Filipino militia. This encouraged Secretary of War Stimson to urge the president that "all practical steps should now be taken to increase the defensive strength of the Philippines."[44] Less than five months after General Marshall, the U.S. Army chief of staff, had declared himself against reinforcing the Philippines, the "strategic error of the first magnitude" was committed, and the United States initiated the fatal chain of events whose denouement came months later at Pearl Harbor and Clark Field. This fatal strategy was enthusiastically cheered along by the new U.S. Far East commander in chief in the Philippines.

"It is quite evident that its determination is indomitable," MacArthur declared from his Manila headquarters. The "action of the American government in establishing this new command can only mean that it intends to maintain, at any cost and effort, its full rights in the Far East."[45] The bluster of his first press release as commander in chief contrasted with the private caution of General Sutherland, the head of his staff, that they had been assigned an "insurmountable task."[46] MacArthur could field only one division of 8,500 regular U.S Army troops and 7,850 other forces, including air and coastal artillery corpsmen. The USAFFE—on paper—included 5,200 Filipino Scouts and the grandiosely titled Army of the Philippines of 4,000 troops. But their former field marshall inflated Washington's expectations of his military forces by promising to raise 100,000 trained militia immediately, with another 200,000 Filipinos by the end of the year.

"Tokyo was dumbfounded and depressed," MacArthur assured the editor of *Army and Navy Journal*, boasting of the strength of his rapidly building forces. With the eleven divisions of troops he anticipated commanding in the Philippines by the end of the year, he predicted, "we can successfully resist any effort that may be made against us."[47] But his army existed only in MacArthur's overoptimistic estimate. At the end of July he had just a tenth of that force available to defend the islands, whose total coastline exceeded that of the entire United States. Nor could MacArthur have been unaware that it would take many months of training and a small mountain of rifles to turn the Filipino militia into anything vaguely resembling a fighting force. His optimism should have been tempered two days after assuming his new command when the War Department advised MacArthur that he could expect that "no additional forces, except approximately 400 reserve officers to assist in training the Philippine Army, or additional equipment over and above that now authorized, will be available for your command in the near future."[48] Inflated by his newfound authority as USAFFE commander in chief, he ignored the dispatch and began firing off daily demands for more tanks and antitank weapons, fighter aircraft, C rations, and 120,000 uniforms for a Filipino militia force that had yet to be recruited.

MacArthur was transported far from reality by what his biographer characterized as "overconfidence and unjustified optimism as to the abilities of himself, his staff, and the untried Filipino soldiers." According to Clayton James, the general had fallen victim to "wishful thinking which unfortunately became a contagion which ultimately affected even the War Department and the Joint Army and Navy Board."[49] MacArthur's enthusiasm for his "paper army," which could not begin to materialize as a credible fighting force until the spring of 1942, encouraged the War Department's wishful thinking that this was enough to act as a deterrent to the Japanese. But in Tokyo plans were already being made with a timetable that called for action in the fall of 1941, before MacArthur's forces would be a credible military threat.

Once they had cut Japan off from oil, the lifeblood that fueled their war machine, it was unrealistic of the military planners in Washington to assume that the military leaders in Tokyo would simply sit on their hands and wait for the United States to complete a major buildup in the Philippines that would threaten the Japanese goal to take over the American and European territories in the Far East. This elementary miscalculation opened the way to the twin disasters on 7 December 1941. It was compounded when the policy makers in Washington set April 1942 as their deadline for completing the reinforcement of MacArthur in the Philippines, as the principal United States deterrent to further Japanese aggression. The blunders of the War Department planners were matched by the hard-liners in the State Department, who failed to appreciate that slapping economic sanctions on Japan without having an adequate military force in place in the Philippines would invite the strategists in Tokyo to make a preemptive strike.

The risks implicit in the War Department's strategic about-face in the Pacific deeply troubled the Navy Department planners. Not only did it break the established Pacific defense strategy not to move reinforcements west of Hawaii, but it also ran counter to the dictate of the newly agreed to Rainbow 5 War Plan to concentrate the United States' limited resources in the Atlantic theater. The Cavite Naval Base on Manila Bay possessed neither the repair facilities nor the fuel reserves to serve as a forward base for the Pacific Fleet, and Chief of Naval Operations Stark used this argument to justify not moving any major warships to bolster the weak Asiatic Fleet.

The Army plan for reinforcing MacArthur, which depended on marshalling yet-unavailable forces which would then have to be ferried across an exposed Pacific Ocean supply route that could not adequately be defended, amounted to an astonishing military gamble. It imposed demands on the Army and Navy that neither was equipped to fulfill during 1941. By acceding to the demand of the hard-liners in his administration for an embargo on all of the Axis powers when the U.S. did not have the resources to impose all-out economic warfare on Japan, the president bore the ultimate responsibility for allowing the demands of diplomacy to overwhelm the military and naval capacity of the United States. As the scale of the reinforcement being called for by MacArthur mounted, the Philippines supplanted Pearl Harbor in the minds of the president and his advisers as the forward bastion of American power in the Pacific. This westward shift was made without regard for the impact that such a military buildup on the doorstep of Japan's sphere of influence would have on Imperial General Headquarters in Tokyo. It was a fatal error whose immediate result was to give MacArthur's claims priority over those already made by the Hawaiian commanders for long-range bombers, fighters, and antiaircraft batteries. Only six months earlier the U.S. service chiefs had considered them essential for the defense of Pearl Harbor.

The psychological contagion that distorted Washington's strategic overview of the Pacific following the decision to reinforce the Philippines was made clear by General Marshall in his testimony before the Congressional Investigating Committee in 1945. "We felt reasonably secure about Hawaiian defenses," in 1941, he recalled. At the time he "felt that it was the only installation we had anywhere that was reasonably well equipped."[50] The belief that the Pacific Fleet was secure and no longer *the* frontline bulwark against Japan in turn led to the decision that sending Purple intercepts to Admiral Kimmel could no longer be justified, on the grounds that it presented a risk to the security of MAGIC intelligence. The most telling indication of just how peripheral Pearl Harbor had become to the strategic planning in Washington was that not a single Japanese diplomatic intercept was to reach Pacific Fleet headquarters during the four months from the end of July 1941 to the beginning of December. The Purple machine originally destined for the cryptographic unit at Pearl Harbor had been sent to the British at the beginning of the year. Admiral Kimmel was, therefore, cut off from direct access to critical intelligence. MacArthur's headquarters, in contrast, had direct access to MAGIC from decrypts of the Japanese diplomatic messages produced by the decoding machine that was operated by the U.S. Navy's local code-breaking unit, which that summer moved from Cavite to the safety of the Malinta tunnel on the fortress island of Corregidor in Manila Bay.

Not only was the intelligence capability of the Pacific Fleet diminished after July 1941, but the defenses of Pearl Harbor were also sacrificed to the new priority of sending all available reinforcements to the Philippines. Spurred on by MacArthur's enthusiastic overestimates of the strength of his own ground forces, the U.S. Army Air Force saw the chance it had been waiting for to promote its B-17 heavy bomber as the answer to both defending the Philippines and deterring Japan. But to get MacArthur 165 of the Flying Fortresses required that the British give up their agreed allotment of one out of every three bombers scheduled to roll off of the Boeing production lines at Seattle.

The first batch of twenty Flying Fortresses had arrived in England the previous month to join the Royal Air Force's air war against the Third Reich. So Churchill's agreement was therefore crucial if MacArthur was to get the centerpiece of the reinforcements he had been promised. Such was the pressure on the United States military planners that the president persuaded his chiefs of staff to reverse themselves in August 1941, when they were to make a far-reaching strategic concession to obtain British agreement to the release of the R.A.F.'s allocation of Flying Fortress bombers that were essential to the reinforcement of the Philippines.

3

"WE SHOULD NOT FIGHT ALONE"

The First Churchill-Roosevelt Summit and the
Secret Anglo-American Alliance to Deter Japan

W e are now trying to build up the defense of the Philippines as a direct defense to the Indian Ocean and Singapore, could the British help out on this?" Admiral Stark, the
chief of naval operations, inquired of the British chief of staff,
at their second session of strategic discussion at the first Anglo-
American summit meeting.[1]

The historic first meeting between the U.S. and British
chiefs of staff took place aboard the *Prince of Wales*, the Royal
Navy's newest battleship, which still bore the scars from its
recent encounter with the German battleship *Bismarck*. After
zigzagging at high speed across the U-boat infested Atlantic,
the *Prince of Wales* had dropped anchor the previous day in
the windswept black waters of Placentia Bay, off the rocky
southern shore of Newfoundland. Aboard were the British
prime minister and a full team of military advisers. Also
aboard was a cargo of freshly shot Scottish grouse to entice
the palate—and cooperation—of his American guests as part
of lavish dinners in the convivial, clublike surroundings of the
admiral's quarters. Churchill had insisted, despite wartime
exigencies, that Britain's newest class of battleships be com-

pleted with oak-paneled admiral's quarters so that the Royal Navy's flag officers "travelled first-class."[2]

The *Prince of Wales* had made a majestic spectacle as she and a single escort steamed through the early morning mists of Saturday, 9 August, to anchor off the Agentia, one of the naval bases that had been leased to the U.S. Navy the previous year, in return for fifty old destroyers. The arrival was watched by the president and his chiefs of staff from the bridge of the USS *Augusta*. Off the coast of Maine, Roosevelt and his party had secretly transferred to the heavy cruiser from the presidential yacht *Potomac*, which had embarked on what was publicized to the press as a deep-sea fishing vacation. But landing a strategic deal on the Far East was the real goal as the secret, first face-to-face meeting of the president and prime minister began.

The British team arrived well-rehearsed in the arguments for America's becoming more deeply involved in the Atlantic war. Two months of strategic reversals gave every reason to argue that Hitler would ultimately be victorious if the United States did not soon become openly committed to the struggle against the Axis. Following an abortive attempt to intervene in the Balkans, British forces had been driven out of Crete by the Germans by June, the month that saw the collapse of the offensive in North Africa to recapture Tobruk. In July, with the number of operational U-boats steadily mounting, the "wolf-packs" pushed their operations into the western Atlantic and sinking of merchant ships had risen again to half-a-million tons. In two months the gigantic scale and furious pace of Germany's assault on the Soviet Union had advanced to the outskirts of Leningrad on the Baltic and to Odessa on the Black Sea. The fall of Smolensk in mid July had brought the panzer divisions to within a hundred miles of Moscow, raising grim fears in both London and Washington about how the war would be carried if the Soviet Union went down to defeat. It was clear that Japan had been emboldened by Germany's tide of military victory to make the move into Indochina, and although the Tokyo government was still resisting repeated calls from Berlin to join the war, there were fears that the Japanese military leaders might soon find it advantageous to invade Siberia.

Harry Hopkins, Roosevelt's confidential aide and Lend-Lease administrator, was aboard the *Prince of Wales*, returning from a fact-finding visit to Moscow, which was now being bombed by the Germans. He was conveying Stalin's staggering demands for war equipment, without which it was seriously feared the Red Army could not hold out. Churchill, therefore, had reason to believe that the catalogue of Allied disaster that was being brought to the conference table would prompt turn-about in the United States' commitment to the war. But he was to be disappointed. The opening sessions of the summit were a setback for the British because both Roosevelt and his chief of naval operations resisted participating in Naval Plan 4, under which the U.S. Navy would take over patrol and con-voy duties in the western half of the Atlantic. This bitter disap-pointment over the Atlantic, however, was compensated by the unexpected offer of American help against Japan in the Pa-cific in return for the British giving up Lend-Lease alloca-tions of bombers and anti-aircraft guns for the defense of the Philippines.

The British chiefs of staff enthusiastically agreed to sacri-fice the Royal Air Force's call on the B-17 bombers after the U.S. Army chief of staff, General Marshall, declared that redi-recting the scheduled shipments to General MacArthur would also bolster Britain's defenses in the Far East.[3] The quid pro quo that the United States would now share the burden of defending Malaya was strategic manna for Churchill after his repeated pleas for the Pacific Fleet to send a squadron to Singa-pore had been so firmly rejected only a few months earlier.

Stark and Marshall now proposed the very goal for which the prime minister had been striving ever since July 1940, when he had received the grim assessment: *"The Situation in the Far East in the Event of Japanese Intervention Against Us."* Drawn up during Britain's darkest hour, following the fall of France a year earlier, the grim chiefs of staff's assessment con-cluded that Italy's entry into the war in the Mediterranean had made it impossible to send a naval squadron to Singapore. Leaving the vaunted "Gibraltar of the Far East" an empty for-tress exposed the British and Dutch territories to Japanese aggression. Unless the United States provided at the very minimum "a measure of economic and material support," the report concluded, Britain would be unable to resist the territorial demands anticipated from Japan's expanding em-pire.[4] The chiefs of staff reluctantly advised the war cabinet that unless the Americans committed to a joint Far East de-fense, there was no alternative to piecemeal appeasement. Hong Kong, Malaya, the Dutch East Indies, and Singapore would all eventually have to be ceded to buy off Japan in a policy directed toward maintaining control over India.

Churchill and his embattled cabinet reluctantly faced the prospect that, without United States involvement, Britain would have to appease Japan and with no certainty of being able to retain the "brightest jewel" in the Empire. Not only would giving up Malaya and Borneo deprive Britain of rubber and tin supplies essential to the war effort but any hint that the British government was contemplating such a policy would send shock waves through the Dominion government of Australia. But in what emerges as one of the most extraordinary intelligence coups of the war, the Japanese obtained a complete copy of this British chiefs of staff Far East assessment, together with the minutes of the war cabinet of 15 August 1940 accepting its bleak recommendations.

The British government has never acknowledged that such a critically important set of cabinet documents ever fell into Axis hands. Captured German naval records, however, have come to light that reveal the British bureaucratic bungle that led to the loss of the report in November 1940 and the contribution it made to accelerating Japan's march to war the following year.

Despite the red "Most Secret" security classification, the 1940 British cabinet report was not shipped to Singapore in the captain's safe in a weighted security pouch for quick disposal overboard. As the result of a clerk's error, it was packed into one of the sixty bags of official mail that were loaded into the hold the *Automendon*, a freighter of the Blue Funnel Line, which put out from Liverpool in October as part of a southbound convoy on the first leg of the long passage around the Cape of Good Hope to the Far East. On 11 November this steamer was making a solitary passage across the Indian Ocean when she was stopped by the German armed merchant cruiser *Atlantis*. Before she was sunk, a boarding party retrieved the bags of official mail, which intelligence officers aboard the raider sorted. They extracted the July chiefs of staff report, which was then transferred to a captured Norwegian vessel named the *Ole Jacob*, which was sailed to Japan by a prize German crew.[5]

The British war cabinet documents reached Kobe on 4 December, when the *Ole Jacob* docked, and five days later they were in the hands of the German naval attaché in Tokyo. When Rear Admiral Paul Wenneker read that Churchill would be "unable to send a fleet to the Far East" and that Britain would "avoid an open clash with Japan" until cooperation had been secured with the United States, the strategic significance of this intelligence was inescapable. For months Germany had been urging their reluctant ally to attack the British in the Far East without any success. Now Wenneker reasoned such direct evidence of Britain's weakness from Churchill's own directives could change Tokyo's attitude. After consulting with Berlin, the admiral passed the haul of captured documents to the Japanese naval staff. Their reaction, according to Wenneker's report, was "one of extraordinary interest."[6] Vice Admiral Nobutake Kondo himself sent for the German naval attaché to express his thanks for this valuable intelligence. Although Japanese espionage had confirmed that Singapore remained an empty fortress, this proof that the British could not spare any warships to garrison their fortress in the Far East was powerful support for the Imperial Navy's case for an advance southward, rather than north into Russia, as called for by the Army.

The Japanese government now appreciated that as long as the United States hesitated to meet Churchill's pleas for help in defending Britain's Far Eastern possessions, Japan had only to set up the diplomatic pressure in order to get London to appease their demands. According to the captured documents, Hong Kong, Singapore, and Malaya would fall into Japan's hands like ripe plums. This knowledge provided Tokyo with an incentive to drive a wedge between Britain and her potential ally the United States and was a factor in prompting Prime Minister Konoye to send the conciliatory Admiral Nomura to Washington, in the spring of 1941, with the mission of negotiating an accord with the Americans. This policy had to be pursued secretly and separately from the blustering of Japan's pro-Nazi foreign minister, Matsuoka, who that spring had set off to see Hitler and his ally Stalin. At the same time the Japanese naval strategists made their plans for a southward advance to Malaya and the Dutch East Indies, secure in the knowledge that the British and Dutch had no military ability to resist them. This would leave them free to concentrate the main carrier forces of the Combined Fleet to deal with the U.S. Pacific Fleet.

Confirmation of Britain's willingness to yield to Japanese diplomatic pressure had already been provided by the closing of the Burma Road into China, in August 1940. Churchill had acquiesced to Tokyo's demands and by doing so sent a powerful reminder to Roosevelt of Britain's desperate need for

American assistance. Since the fall of France, in June, the prime minister had been pleading with the president to release fifty World War I destroyers for Atlantic operations against the German U-boats and for a strong force of American warships to visit Singapore "to keep the Japanese dog quiet."[7] After Roosevelt had finally authorized the transfer of the destroyers to the Royal Navy, in the "warships for bases deal," it was not without significance that Churchill ordered the reopening of the vital supply line to the Chinese Nationalists through Burma, in October 1940.[8] The president, however, did not order the dispatch of so much as a single American destroyer to Singapore, for fear that such an overt commitment would have inflamed isolationists and scuttled his chances of being reelected to an unprecedented third term. Even after his November victory at the polls, there was still a discernible softening of Roosevelt's position about coming to Britain's aid in the Far East, as concern about Japan mounted in London and the Australian capital of Canberra. Following a December report of the Singapore Defence Committee on the growing danger posed to Australian security by leaving the fortress ungarrisoned, Prime Minister John Curtin cabled from Canberra that his government was "gravely concerned at the most serious situation."[9]

"It always being understood that if Australia is seriously threatened by invasion we shall not hesitate to compromise or sacrifice the Mediterranean position for the sake of our kith and kin," Churchill had responded soothingly to Curtin.[10] The Australian prime minister was under no illusion about Britain's overextended military resources. His country would have to look to the United States for assurances of help in the event that Japan advanced southward. To placate the rising alarm in Australia, in March 1941 the British chiefs of staff again pressed the Americans to use Singapore as an advance base for the Pacific Fleet during the American-British-Canadian conference. The offer had been rejected despite Churchill's 15 February 1941 cable warning Roosevelt that "drifting straws" indicated "Japanese intentions to make war on us."[11] Nor was there any inclination shown by the United States to heed the invitation when it was reiterated during the joint staff conference held in April in Singapore with the Dutch. The American delegation did, however, agree that portions of their air forces in the Far East should be concentrated under Britain's Far East commander in chief in the event that a Japanese threat materialized.[12] This was only a small step toward Churchill's

hope of a full-fledged Anglo-American-Dutch alliance to stem
further aggressive moves by Japan.

Therefore the British prime minister reacted with some
apprehension and not a little irritation to reports that the U.S.
secretary of state had been secretly negotiating toward an accord with the Japanese ambassador in Washington. The British Foreign Office, which had not been informed of the talks,
had cabled its ambassador in Washington on 21 May, expressing its "misgivings" on the "general principle of compromising
with the Japanese."[13] Lord Halifax conveyed London's views
to Secretary of State Hull "in a somewhat too categorical
matter." According to the Foreign Office record, "Mr. Hull's
reactions were so violent that Lord Halifax withdrew his
communication."[14]

Roosevelt had then moved rapidly to smooth the prime
minister's ruffled feathers over the secret talks with the Japanese ambassador, but Churchill took greater comfort from the
breakdown of the Nomura initiative in July, after the incursion
of Japan's armed forces into Indochina. Any sense of relief
in London that Tokyo's attempt to reach an accord with the
United States had stalled was, however, tempered with concern that the occupation of naval bases and airfields of Indochina now brought Japanese forces within striking distance
of Malaya.

The Dutch reacted immediately by pressing for a public
declaration of joint military action to counter armed aggression against their territories in the Far East. But the British
war cabinet on 21 July concluded that without the United
States' participation they could not commit themselves to anything more than a private assurance.[15] After the United States
announced its embargo on Axis trade a week later, the prime
minister agreed that although this "rather altered the situation," he "still deprecated" giving an automatic assurance to
the Netherlands government that they would go to war with
Japan "irrespective of the attitude of the United States."[16] But
he did not hesitate to join with the Dutch in publicly committing Britain to the American embargo against Japan, although
a report of the Joint Plans Committee cautioned that "the
Japanese government are unlikely to be deterred by threats of
economic action."[17]

The prime minister decided that the time had come for
"making an approach to the United States Government on the
Far East position," since the restrictions it had imposed on oil
imports to Japan would inevitably increase the pressure

on the Dutch.[18] The need to garrison Singapore now became a pressing issue. Just before departing for his summit with Roosevelt, Churchill had received the Admiralty's admission that they "still could not collect a fleet to proceed to the Far East."[19] As the prime minister reviewed their strategic objectives with his military chief in the admiral's quarters as the battleship *Prince of Wales* crossed the Atlantic, one of their primary objectives was to persuade the president to change his mind about committing American forces to a joint deterrent against Japan.

"The Dominions, especially Australia, are concerned by the fact that though we have acted with the United States in freezing Japanese assets, the United States has not given us any assurances of help should any part of our Empire or the Dutch in consequence become embroiled with Japan," the foreign secretary reminded the prime minister in a 2 August memo that accompanied Churchill to the summit. A memorandum prepared shortly before sailing by the British chiefs of staff confirmed that they had not pressed the issue of a joint Far Eastern defense after the Americans had made clear at the spring staff conversations at Singapore that they had "no intention" of even moving to reinforce the Philippines. It was therefore "a complete surprise" on 11 August when the president announced that it had been "decided to reinforce Manila with a squadron of bombers and a few tanks," Churchill somewhat disparagingly recorded in a confidential note preserved in his private wartime file.[20] The prime minister was delighted by this strategic about-face by the Americans, which required that in return for concessions over the B-17s' Lend-Lease deliveries, the United States was now prepared to resolve Britain's intractable dilemma of how to defend their Far Eastern empire from Japan.

In the strategic horse-trading sessions aboard the *Prince of Wales* the British agreed to accommodate the Americans by giving up the Royal Air Force's four-engined bombers so that they could be sent out across the Pacific. The first sea lord, Sir Dudley Pound, and General Sir John Dill, the chief of the imperial general staff, agreed that "a strong defense of the Philippine Islands directly strengthens the defense of Singapore and the Netherlands East Indies."[21] The Flying Fortress bombers, which the War Department had initially regarded as a quick fix to bolster MacArthur's defense of the Philippines, were to emerge from the Churchill-Roosevelt summit as the "big stick" of an Anglo-American strategy that they mistakenly believed would be a powerful threat to curb Japan from further encroachment.

The trade-off of the RAF's B-17s for a Far Eastern defense pact was a strategic salvation for the British and Churchill and his chiefs of staff were prepared to accept all the attendant risks. They did not question the American assumption that a relatively small force of heavy bombers could stand guard over the Philippines, Malaya, and the Dutch East Indies and at the same time constitute an effective strategic deterrent to Japan. This belief was founded on the overselling of the military potential of the heavy bomber. Lieutenant General Henry Harley Arnold, the newly appointed chief of the U.S. Army Air Force, was an ardent advocate of air power. Taught to fly by the Wright brothers, "Hap" Arnold had been an ardent disciple of Brigadier General William C. Mitchell, a predecessor, who had sacrificed his military career to become the American prophet of the war-winning potential of strategic bombing.

The War Department's dilemma over how to defend the Philippines offered Arnold the chance for a demonstration of the capabilities of the B-17 bomber and dramatic vindication of his late mentor's revolutionary doctrines. He had been both father and midwife to the Army's heavy bomber program after the rollout of the first prototype at the Boeing Aircraft Company's Seattle plant in 1935. Arnold spent five years urging the Army Air Force to support the four-engine bomber program and lobbying a penny-pinching Congress to fund large-scale production. The B-17, as it was now officially designated, had been repeatedly modified to enhance its performance, acquiring in the selling process the mystique of a wonder bomber, whose range and onboard armament supposedly made it independent of fighter protection and led to its Flying Fortress moniker.

Originally designed as a long-range heavy bomber to be flown on offshore missions to defend the United States from invasion by hostile enemy fleets, the B-17 had been promoted by Arnold as the weapon system that was the fulfillment of "Billy" Mitchell's doctrine of airpower. Ever since the July afternoon in 1921 when Mitchell led a force of eight World War I biplane bombers to sink the ex-German dreadnought *Oestfriesland* off the Virginia Capes, the Army Air Force contended that the bomber, not the battleship, was the weapon of the future. Equipped with a gyro Norden bombsight, the most closely guarded U.S. military secret, which enabled targets to be attacked from an altitude of five miles, the B-17 bristled with guns to defend itself from enemy fighters.

The Flying Fortress, however, failed to live up to its reputation on the first operation flown by the RAF, against relatively soft targets in France. General Arnold himself conceded that "the long awaited combat showing of the B-17s was a fiasco."[22] Eight of the twenty B-17s supplied to the RAF under their Lend-Lease agreement in July 1941 had been shot down over France in two weeks. German propaganda was derisively referring to the Flying Fortress as the "Flying Coffin," as the RAF blamed their heavy losses of the "wonder bomber" on design problems. These ranged from inadequate firepower and defective turbocharged engines to defective oxygen systems for the crew and the tendency of the C model Fortress to ice up at altitude. Arnold had immediately dispatched a team of investigators to England to rescue the Fortress's tarnished reputation. The U.S. Army Air Force report attributed the heavy bomber's poor performance in action to inadequately trained aircrews and the RAF's refusal to fly the bombers in the tightly stacked formations that were essential for all-round mutual defense against enemy fighters.[23]

General "Hap" Arnold's faith in the Flying Fortress remained unshaken in the last week of July 1941 as his staff worked up the plans for getting the maximum force out to the Philippines. Its three-thousand-mile range, which enabled it to be flown from the West Coast across the island-hopping transpacific route pioneered in the mid-thirties by Pan American Airways, was a very attractive factor when it came to convincing the War Department. So, too, was the timing of the proposal. The plan for dispatching a strong force of B-17s to Luzon reached Arnold's desk on 27 July, the day after MacArthur's recall underscored the necessity of rapidly reinforcing the islands.[24] The next day Arnold's plan received the approval of Secretary of War Stimson. On 7 August the Air Force chief briefed the president on the B-17's capabilities at a staff meeting aboard the *Augusta* as the heavy cruiser steamed north toward the Placentia Bay rendezvous with the British.[25]

Arnold was a bluff and persuasive advocate of Mitchell's philosophy of airpower. He argued that because it would provide MacArthur with the capability of interdicting an invasion fleet still at sea, a force of B-17s was the answer to mounting a defense of the Philippines. In the absence of any other means of providing MacArthur with a strong defensive force, the heavy bombers appeared to the War Department to be

a heaven-sent solution. Overtaken by the press of events, the
ground-based generals unskeptically accepted that the B-17
would live up to the overblown performance claims of their
enthusiastic colleagues in the Army Air Force. Arnold's plan
called for sending to the Philippines most of the 220 B-17s
scheduled to be completed by the end of 1941. To meet this
rapid buildup target, not only would the British have to give
up their allocations, but the Hawaiian Department would also
have to be denied its request for a minimum force of 108 of
the long-range bombers to defend Pearl Harbor against an attack by Japanese carriers.

The Hawaiian air command faced a fait accompli, because
the British welcomed the decision to send the Fortresses to the
Philippines in return for the United States' commitment to the
overall defense of the Far East. Whatever doubts the RAF's
experience may have raised about the B-17's effectiveness as
a bomber, let alone its capability of mounting a credible deterrent against Japan, the British chiefs of staff prudently kept
them to themselves during the Anglo-American summit. A
rapid reinforcement of MacArthur's air force accorded with
the strategic vision of a mutual Anglo-American defense alliance that Churchill outlined on 10 August, in his after-dinner
speech aboard the *Prince of Wales*. He called on the United
States to join with Britain and Russia in issuing a strong ultimatum to Tokyo: "If Japan moves south into the Malay Peninsula, we will throw her out."[26]

The president and his closest aides warmly applauded the
declaration in the oak-paneled privacy of the wardroom of the
British battleship. Churchill had already directed Sir Alexander Cadogan, the Foreign Office permanent secretary, to
draft "a parallel declaration by the U.S., ourselves and Dutch
designed to restrain [the] Japanese from further devilry and
to provide military aide."[27] According to the report that the
prime minister radioed to London on 11 August, he had agreed
with Roosevelt that he would conclude his communication to
Japan "with a very severe warning which I drafted."[28]

"Any further encroachment by Japan in the southwest-
Pacific would produce a situation in which the United States
Government would be compelled to take countermeasures,
even though these might lead to war between the United States
and Japan" was the wording Churchill had drafted for Roosevelt. "I am confident," the prime minister assured the cabinet
on his return home, "that the President will not tone it
down."[29] But after the president returned to Washington, the

very idea of such a strongly worded message appalled the secretary of state, who protested that it would only inflame Tokyo. In deference to Cordell Hull and the sensitivities of the isolationist opposition on Capitol Hill, the president toned down Churchill's full-blooded language, omitting both the word "war" and any reference to Britain.

"We did not get 100% of what we wanted on the Far East," Sir Alexander Cadogan conceded in his diary, taking some consolation that "we must remember it must be read in conjunction with the Joint Declaration, which will give the Japanese a jar."[30] This was the so-called Atlantic Charter, drafted by Churchill and issued jointly with the president. The eight-point declaration proclaiming the Anglo-American commitment to free trade, self-determination, and seeking no new territories and calling for the abandonment of force enshrined Roosevelt's earlier call for the "freedom from fear and want," which was later to be incorporated as the basis of the United Nations Charter.

This euphonious Atlantic Charter, which was never actually signed by the two leaders, was a declaration of principle, drafted to reinforce the impact of the intended ultimatum to Japan and to publicly demonstrate at the same time the unity of Anglo-American purpose, if not yet a shared military commitment. The joint declaration of euphonious principle resulted in the summit being dubbed the Atlantic Charter Conference. But in light of the military commitments that the United States had given on the use of the B-17 bombers to defend British territory in the Far East, Pacific Charter would have been a more appropriate historical tag.

"Onward Christian Soldiers!" was the rousing hymn chosen by Churchill and Roosevelt to lead off the Sunday service attended by contingents of U.S. Navy and Royal Naval sailors on the quarterdeck of the *Prince of Wales*. It was an evocative and appropriate symbol of the new Anglo-American alliance against Japan. Yet as a close observer of the United States political scene, Churchill knew that Roosevelt's commitment was not constitutionally binding without congressional ratification. If Roosevelt needed any reminder of the strength of the isolationist opposition on Capitol Hill, it came on 12 August, when the extension of the selective service bill, essential to maintain the strength of the army, was passed by a single Senate vote. While the president would not actually have run afoul of the Constitution until he was called upon to honor the agreement, the subsequent record reveals that he came perilously close to exceeding the authority of his office. Just how far the president had committed the United States to what Churchill later described as armed support of British territory in the Far East in his private sessions with the prime minister was never to be made clear to the U.S. chiefs of staff.[31]

"What the President and the Prime Minister had to say when together, I know not," General Arnold noted in his diary.[32] "I can't make up my mind as yet whether most of us are window dressing for the main actors, whether we are playing minor roles in the drama." Since the U.S. Army Air Force chief had played a key role in mapping out the military details of the Philippines air strategy and the deployment of the B-17 bombers in defense of British Far East territories, it is particularly significant that he alluded to the "epoch making" outcome of the conference in diary notes.[33] He knew that Churchill would not have agreed to release more than a hundred heavy bombers that originally were intended to extend the RAF's air war against Germany without a firm commitment from the president that the United States really would take on "a direct defense of the Indian Ocean and Singapore."[34]

"The difficulty of the President's position is that he can give no undertaking to come to the help of any foreign power without the authority of Congress,"[35] Foreign Secretary Anthony Eden had cautioned the prime minister before he set sail for Newfoundland. Accordingly, Eden regarded it as essential "to secure some assurance" from Roosevelt that could only be given privately, or it risked running afoul of the isolationists on Capitol Hill. "It would satisfy us," Eden suggested, "if the President could go as far as to tell you that in the event of ourselves or the Dutch becoming involved in hostilities with Japan, while we are pursuing a policy parallel to that of the United States, he would then be prepared to ask Congress to authorize him to take measures to give us all possible help."[36]

Precisely what words were used to express that commitment is unclear. But Roosevelt certainly gave Churchill a "gentleman's agreement" that implied an alliance in the Far East, even if the Americans had not agreed to convoy British ships across the Atlantic or to support Britain's planned occupation of the French port of Dakar, on the West African coast. While the president may have held back guarantees of American armed support if the Japanese moved to threaten Malaya or the Netherlands East Indies, it is clear that whatever commitment was made satisfied the prime minister. Even the limited form of the "assurance" proposed by Britain's foreign secretary was questionable from a constitutional standpoint, since it amounted to a de facto pact, because it was dependent on an ex post facto application for congressional approval. As Arnold himself put it, after the summit the U.S. chiefs of staff took it as stated that Britain and the United States were now in accord on "the handling of Japan if that nation moved farther southward."[37] That was certainly the assumption of the British chiefs of staff and Churchill himself, who in the following months made a number of references on the record to the agreement that he had received from the president.

"We should therefore press the United States government to declare that they would take up arms against Japan if she committed any further act of aggression," the prime minister told his war cabinet on 3 November. "Such a declaration *would be in line with the policy which President Roosevelt had developed orally at the Atlantic Meeting* [emphasis added]."[38] While Churchill frequently declared his belief that he could count on the armed support of the United States if Japan attacked British or Dutch territory, he was well aware of the constitutional limitations on the assurance he had been given.

"No doubt the President would find it necessary to use such language as that, in such-and-such circumstances, he would find it necessary to seek the support of Congress for the measures required by national security of the United States," was how Churchill rationalized the cabinet concerns that Roosevelt's assurances provided a less-than-watertight guarantee if United States territory was not simultaneously attacked.[39] That he entertained a nagging doubt himself explains why Britain did not give the Dutch guarantees of military support in the event of an attack on only the Netherlands East Indies until two days before the Japanese attacked. Only then would Churchill gamble on Roosevelt's unequivocal and specific assurance of "armed support" even though he knew that if put into effect the president would have to seek congressional approval.[40]

While the agreement reached at the floating August summit left both the prime minister and the president in an uncertain predicament, the record shows that both British and U.S. chiefs of staff proceeded with their military plans on the assumption that a de facto Anglo-American alliance had been concluded. The secret commitment to assist in the defense of Britain's Far Eastern empire had been driven by America's need to reinforce the Philippines. The British seized on the B-17 deal and lengthened runways and provided fuel dumps

at a string of airfields to ensure that the Americans would
have no excuse to renege on their promise to operate the heavy
bombers in defense of Australia, Malaya, Borneo, Burma, and
even India itself.

Roosevelt's strategic reversal had been matched by an
equally dramatic about-face by Churchill. Without consulting
the Admiralty, he had promised Roosevelt that Britain would
send a force of capital ships to Singapore. This policy was
fraught with risk. Without adequate forces already in place in
the Far East, the scale of the military reinforcement in the
Philippines and Singapore was just too great before the Anglo-
American forces could project a credible military threat. It
was a foolhardy strategic gamble that rather than determining, the Anglo-American strategy actually invited a preemptive strike by the Japanese. Anticipating that this buildup
would take at least six months, Churchill agreed to take the
diplomatic cue from the United States by accepting Roosevelt's assurance that the State Department would be able to
"baby them [Japan] along" by spinning out negotiations with
Tokyo until the spring of 1942.[41] The prime minister had to
overrule Foreign Office objections that handing over responsibility to the Americans for negotiating with Tokyo was
pregnant with risk and an unprecedented abrogation of British
diplomatic independence. But after returning to London from
the Atlantic meeting, Churchill issued express instructions
that the lead in all future negotiations with the Japanese was
to be handed over to the U.S. State Department.

Whatever the nagging doubt that the prime minister maintained until the attack on Pearl Harbor, he acted as though
he had received from Roosevelt a watertight assurance of full
American military support in the Far East. An indicator of his
confidence was his increasingly testy rejections of the Foreign
Office's uneasiness over Britain's diplomatic relations with Japan having been abrogated to the United States without any
formal guarantee or safeguard. The prime minister himself
alluded to a presumed de facto Anglo-American Far East pact,
a month after war broke out in the Pacific, when he defended
himself against a censure motion in the House of Commons on
17 January 1942.

To rebut the charge that Britain's Far Eastern colonies had
been inadequately defended against the Japanese, Churchill
assured the honorable members that he had taken good care
that Britain "should not be exposed single-handed to the Japanese assault."[42] Picking his words with care, so as not to let

the cat out of the bag and embarrass the president of the United States, he denied the charge of dereliction, citing "the probability," as he put it, "since the Atlantic conference at which I discussed these matters with Mr. Roosevelt, that the United States, even if not attacked herself, would come into the war in the Far East." His "expectation," as he put it, was "reinforced as time went on," when, he said, he had received from the president "greater assurance that if Japan ran amok in the Pacific, we should not fight alone."[43] As the prime minister reminded his critics, his confidence that the United States would come to Britain's aid had not been "falsified by events."[44]

The speech caused consternation in the White House when it was reported in the American press on 21 January 1942. His confidential aide, Harry Hopkins, warned the president, "some day soon Wheeler and his crowd may pick it up."[45] Senator Burton K. Wheeler was the most strident isolationist on Capitol Hill, and he never missed a chance to excoriate Roosevelt. He was soon charging that Churchill's speech was evidence that the president had made a clandestine military alliance with Britain to provoke Japan. It was an allegation that would be resurrected repeatedly during 1945 Congressional hearings on Pearl Harbor. But only tenuous circumstantial evidence could be produced by Roosevelt's critics to support the isolationist accusation, because he was by then dead and no documentary corroboration existed of the true extent of a secret pact with Churchill. The congressional investigating committee, whose Democratic members loyal to the late president were in the majority, concluded that there had been no unconstitutional commitment given to the British in 1941 that had infringed on the right of Congress to ratify treaties and pacts with foreign powers.

While that was technically correct, because whatever assurances Roosevelt had given Churchill at their Atlantic summit had been oral, the record of the joint Army-Navy board contains many indications that there was some merit to the isolationist charge. The chief of naval operations, Admiral Stark, was ex-officio chairman throughout 1941 of the board that served as a supreme war council of the United States and which included both chiefs of staff and their principal subordinates. Many had been present aboard the *Prince of Wales* on 11 August when the deal over the RAF B-17s was struck in return for their assignment to MacArthur.

The declassified minutes of the subsequent joint board de-

liberations indicated that the de facto alliance came into effect
immediately after the August summit, since strategic plans
were made on the assumption that the United States would
go to war if British Far East territory was attacked by Japan.
At its first meeting following the Atlantic summit, concern was
even voiced that "the President might direct the British be
given a seat on the Joint Board."[46] This was an indication of
an extraordinary degree of Anglo-American military fraternity
envisaged by the president. But Army Chief of Staff Marshall
declared that he would resist Roosevelt's attempt to involve a
British representative so directly in the supreme war council
of the United States. When the board next met, on 14 September, the head of naval war plans, Admiral Turner, submitted
the Navy's plan for dealing with "offensive operations" by the
Japanese. It took into account not only an attack on the Philippines but also joining operations with the British and Dutch
forces to defend Malaya. A month later on 10 October, the joint
board reviewed and approved a strategic review submitted by
the British chiefs of staff that listed the fuel and bomb depots
in Malaya and Borneo, and Australian airfields from which the
B-17s could operate in defense of British and Dutch territory.

Further indications that the de facto Anglo-American alliance guided the Far East military contingency planning of the
joint board in the Far East is contained in the minutes of their
meeting of 3 November. This came when Rear Admiral Royal
E. Ingersoll, the deputy chief of naval operations, listed the
circumstances under which the United States would find itself
at war:

> In the case of a Japanese attack against *either* the Philip-
> pines *or* British *or* Dutch possessions the United States
> *should resist* the attack. In the case of a Japanese attack
> against Siberia, Thailand or China through Yunnan, the
> United States should not declare war [emphasis added].[47]

When Admiral Stark was questioned in 1945 by the Congressional Investigating Committee, he was pressed on the issue of whether "any formal agreement" had been drawn up by
the president to offer armed support or one "which would be
predicated on a forecast that the British or the Netherlands
East Indies were attacked," that the United States would go
to war. "No, sir, I know of no such agreement," the former
chief of naval operations declared. While Stark may have been
truthful as regards the lack of specific document to this effect,

the principle was certainly enshrined in the joint board's records.[48]

The board's minutes and the subsequent course of U.S. military planning in the Far East leaves very little room to doubt that the United States would "resist" with armed intervention in support of the British and Dutch even if Japan did not simultaneously attack American territory. Ingersoll's notes show that he had checked "Yes" for "War" in only two of five possible eventualities of Japanese attacks: "Philippines" and British or Dutch Malay" [sic]. The recommendation that the joint board would prepare for war under these circumstances did not presume approval having been obtained by the president from Congress or a previously ratified treaty with these two foreign powers. How the president would have persuaded Congress to declare war if the Japanese had attacked only European territory in the Far East on 7 December remains a moot point. Yet the underlying strategic principle enunciated by the U.S. chiefs of staff and accepted by the joint board is that they were planning armed support for Britain.

In a curious twist of historical coincidence, even as Churchill and Roosevelt were agreeing on a mutual deterrent policy against Japan at their floating summit in Placentia Bay, the Japanese were agreeing among themselves on their strategic campaign objectives. On 7 August the Imperial Navy staff met in Tokyo to review Admiral Yamamoto's war plan, which was the product of months of work by the Combined Fleet staff.

"If we are told to fight, regardless of the consequences, we can run wild for six months or a year," Yamamoto had earlier warned Prime Minister Konoye, "but after that I have utterly no confidence. I hope you will avoid war."[49] When it became clear that hostilities were inevitable, the Combined Fleet commander in chief drew up his plan to achieve a quick victory against the Americans with a knockout blow against the Pacific Fleet. But the more conservative members of the naval staff postponed a final decision on the carrier raid on Pearl Harbor until the tactical concept had been thoroughly tested on the plotting boards at the fleet's annual war games. These were delayed, at Yamamoto's request, until the first week in September. The Imperial Navy's concern that their warships and planes, as the biggest consumers of Japan's shrinking oil reserves, were facing ultimate immobilization galvanized the war preparations. On 15 August the naval staff joined the army staff at Imperial General Headquarters for a four-day conference. They agreed on a joint operational plan only after the army war games, during which they had rehearsed the military scenario for Japan's conquest of Southeast Asia.

The Japanese timetable for capturing Manila and the subjugation of the Philippines was two months long. Three weeks was the timespan targeted for the campaign to subdue Malaya and Singapore, and five months for the occupation of the British-ruled territory of Burma that was to follow. Simultaneous operations were to bring the rich oil fields of Borneo under Japanese control, and by the fourth month Java and the remainder of the Dutch East Indies were to be integrated in Japan's "Co-Prosperity Sphere." Mid-October 1941 was the date for the completion of Japan's war plan, and this was the deadline given to Prime Minister Konoye for negotiations to bring about that goal by diplomacy, or Japan would resort to war. His chances of success were not auspicious after news of the Atlantic Charter Conference reached Tokyo. Reporting rumors picked up on the Washington grapevine, Ambassador Nomura alerted Tokyo on 16 August that the Churchill-Roosevelt meeting was a clear indication that Britain was maneuvering to get "a Japanese-American war started by the back door."[50]

Tokyo reacted by instructing Nomura to explore the possibility of a face-to-face meeting between the Japanese prime minister and the American president. But Roosevelt had no intention of letting himself be bullied in a "Far Eastern Munich," as British Prime Minister Neville Chamberlain had been, in the dismemberment of Czechoslovakia in 1938. The State Department response to Nomura's discrete inquiry was that before a summit could take place, Japan would have to commit to withdrawing its troops from China and repudiating the Tripartite Pact with Germany and Italy—preconditions that dashed Konoye's hope that a Japanese-American summit might slow the accelerating momentum of the war preparations.

"Although I feel sure we have a chance to win a war right now, I am afraid that the chance will vanish with the passage of time," Konoye was warned by the Navy chief admiral, Osami Nangano, at their liaison conference on 3 September.[51] The next day the Japanese cabinet met to approve the list of "minimum" demands and "maximum" concessions. These were dictated by the military to diminish any room for diplomatic maneuvering with the United States, and the Foreign Ministry was informed that the last ten days in October would be the final deadline for diplomacy, after which Japan had to be "resolved to go to war with the United States, Great Britain and the Netherlands, if necessary."[52] On 6 September this was submitted to an Imperial conference for the rubberstamp of Hirohito's formal approval. The emperor, however, surprised his generals and admirals by breaking his traditional silence to read an antiwar poem written by his grandfather.[53]

"Since all seas of the world are brothers / Why do the winds and waves of strife rage so violently?" the emperor piped in his reedy voice. He explained in halting sentences to his conference of ministers and service chiefs that he was "striving to introduce into the present the Emperor Meiji's ideal of international peace."[54] Startled but unmoved by the unprecedented Imperial intervention, the military leaders insisted on adhering to their 16 October deadline for a diplomatic breakthrough with the United States. The chance of success was made more remote by their refusal to concede even a token troop withdrawal. Nor was Japan's gratuitous offer to "guarantee the neutrality of the Philippine Islands" intended to break the diplomatic ice in Washington.[55]

Five days after the Imperial conference, the Pearl Harbor attack plan was finally put to the test on the plotting tables of the Naval War College, in a closely guarded compound in the suburbs of Tokyo. Using colored markers spread out over large charts of the western Pacific Ocean and the China Sea, the interlocking naval operations that were intended to effect a swift Japanese takeover of Southeast Asia were put to a rigorous test during ten intensive days of war gaming. While the staffs of the 3rd Fleet and the 11th Air Fleet rehearsed and refined their plan for invading the Philippines and the conquest of Borneo, the 2nd Fleet staff practiced the invasion of Malaya and Thailand, and the 4th Fleet ran through the attack on Wake Island and Guam. Only thirty, out of over a hundred, Combined Fleet staff officers participating in the map maneuvers were permitted into the east wing of the red-brick war college, where the charts of the Hawaiian Islands were laid out.

Yamamoto himself supervised the rehearsals for Operation Z, the code name given to the Pearl Harbor attack plan or Hawaiian Operation as it was designated. Several run-throughs only served to underscore the risks that the carrier strike force would run if the element of surprise could not be achieved. The potential for heavy losses worried the naval staff. Like Prime Minister Konoye, Yamamoto was also given a six-week deadline to convince the skeptics that the remaining tactical and technical problems could be solved. A race against time to modify torpedoes to run in shallow water was under way, as the pilots of the bombers trained at flying low in at deck level over lines of anchored capital ships. Dropping their torpedoes at this lower altitude would ensure that the weapons would not plunge into the mud forty feet below the surface of Pearl Harbor.

While the Japanese were preparing for war, the strategic bombing force that the United States and Britain were counting on to deter Tokyo from further aggression in the Far East began to arrive in the Philippines. When General Marshall, the Army chief of staff, returned to Washington from the summit he found a memorandum dated 14 August warning that "the ability of the Philippine Islands to withstand a determined attack with present means is doubtful."[56] After the guarantees given the British, it became imperative for Marshall to ensure that MacArthur's heavy bombing force not only could be built rapidly but would constitute an effective deterrent to Japan as well as be adequate to defend the Philippines and Malaya. To satisfy himself that General Arnold's Flying Fortress bombers could fulfill the mission, Marshall accompanied the chief of the Army Air Force and Secretary of War Stimson to the Boeing plant at Seattle. They were treated to a flying display that put an "improved" B-17D model through its paces, including a demonstration of how the lumbering four-engine bomber could operate as a giant torpedo plane.[57] Impressed, Marshall returned to Washington and on 26 August gave orders for the history-making flight of nine of the Fortresses across the Pacific.

Staging so many Fortress bombers across the ocean to Luzon without arousing the Japanese suspicions required that the B-17s, after refueling at Hawaii and Midway Island, then make the long over-water haul southwest via Ocean Island to Australia to avoid flying within range of Japanese reconnaissance planes from the Marshalls. From Australia the bombers headed north to the Philippines. Anticipating that Tokyo would protest any military buildup, the War Department prepared a press release that would announce the movement of the B-17s to the Philippines as a scheduled replacement of the obsolescent bombers already based in the islands.

Such diplomatic doublespeak proved unnecessary. To the relief of Stimson and Marshall, all nine Flying Fortresses made it safely to Clark Field on 12 September, apparently unnoticed by the Japanese. General Arnold was delighted that his Flying

Fortress had proved itself capable of a navigational feat that was also a grueling endurance test of the heavy bombers. His confidence riding high, he decided to recommend to the War Department that MacArthur get a minimum of 165 B-17s by the end of the year—more than two thirds of the scheduled production. But when General Brereton, whom MacArthur had requested as his Far East Air Force commander in chief, arrived in Washington for a final briefing by Marshall before he set out for Manila, he expressed concern that too rapid a buildup of the heavy bomber force might prompt a preemptive Japanese strike. Marshall and Arnold reassured him that they were taking a calculated risk and expressed confidence that the thousand-mile radius of operation of a token force of heavy B-17s in Luzon could forestall hostile action by the Japanese against the Philippines or the oilfields of the Dutch East Indies.[58]

"Strategic Concept of the Philippine Island" was the title of the War Plans Division memorandum accompanied by a map that the Secretary of War received on 8 October 1941. It was predicated on the assumption that the current B-17 bomber reinforcement program had already made the "cost of an operation" to invade the islands "so great that Japan will hesitate to make the effort except as a last resort." Although only thirty-five heavy bombers had actually reached the Philippines, the report concluded that "the air and ground units now available or scheduled for dispatch to the Philippines islands in the near future have changed the entire picture in the Asiatic area."[59] The memorandum prompted Secretary of War Stimson to declare that four-engine bombers now gave the Army the opportunity "to get back into the islands in a way it hadn't been able to for years." He at once pressed the president to order an immediate increase in production rate of the B-17s, and he gave MacArthur's priority over all other commands— including Hawaii—for deliveries of the Flying Fortress. This was yet another indication of the degree to which the strategic focus had shifted away from Pearl Harbor by the fall of 1941. This was despite a 20 August update to General Arnold from the Hawaiian Department air commander, General Martin, that predicted that as the Japanese "can probably employ a maximum of 6 carriers against Oahu," a minimum of thirty-six B-17s "would be required to disable and destroy the carriers." This prescient forecast, which the Hawaiian Army Air Force commander had underlined for special emphasis, stated that an "*early morning attack is therefore the best plan of action to the enemy* [emphasis added]." He therefore urged Arnold to give "immediate consideration to the allotment of one hundred and twenty-eight [B-17s]."

Even this number was "a small force when compared with the importance of this outpost," Martin contended, adding that this necessary protection could be provided "at less cost to the government than a modern battleship."[60] Within the week, however, General Arnold had received a copy of an Army Air Force recommendation of 26 August for a minimum force of 128 B-17s for the Philippines by February 1942. It was approved, although another memorandum of the same date warned that "under no circumstances could the Hawaiian bombardment force be reduced without gravely endangering the security of the Pacific coast." The two hundred long-range bombers that had originally been earmarked for the "most vital outpost" of Hawaii could not be made available. MacArthur, on the other hand, was slated to get the "four Heavy Bombardment Groups" that were deemed necessary "for the maintenance of a strategic defensive in Asia and for the protection of American interests in the Philippines."[61]

"We turned our endeavor to set up sufficient force in the Philippine islands," was how General Marshall would later explain the switch in strategic emphasis from Hawaii to the Philippines.[62] The War Department had decided that General Martin was not going to get the thirty-six B-17s he had asked for as the minimum forces necessary to defend Pearl Harbor. As the U.S. Army chief testified, they had "given Hawaii all we could afford to give them up to that time."[63] The Hawaiian air commander, therefore, faced the frustration of seeing his airfields turned into mid-Pacific refueling stops for the bombers he so badly needed to defend the fleet. This left Pearl Harbor far more vulnerable because without the B-17s to supplement the Navy's PBY flying boats, there were too few long-range aircraft for the around-the-compass reconnaissance essential for providing an early warning of the approach of a Japanese carrier task force.

The door was, therefore, left wide open for the Japanese to exploit, not because the Hawaiian commanders were sentries who fell asleep on their watch, but because Admiral Kimmel and General Short were denied the aircraft needed to mount an effective guard on the approaches to Pearl Harbor. The extent to which the shift in Washington's strategic focus had been redirected to the Philippines was never communicated or explained to Admiral Kimmel or General Short. All that

Pacific Fleet headquarters knew was that MAGIC intelligence dried up and the Hawaiian Department did not receive the long-range bombers and antiaircraft batteries that had been requested not once but twice by General Martin. The Hawaiian commanders were made to carry the major share of the blame for the inadequacies in their defenses. They were victims—not culprits—of the dramatic reordering of United States military priorities in the Pacific, as the U.S. Army chief of staff implicitly admitted in 1945 when he came under cross-examination before the congressional committee.

"We turned from meeting the demands of Hawaii and fulfilling the Martin-Bellinger request for 190 B-17s," Marshall conceded.[64] Faced with insufficient numbers of heavy bombers to provide for the defense of both Hawaii and the Philippines, the U.S. Army chief of staff had given the Philippines priority on the basis of an Army Air Force assessment that had laid down that "Any threat against the Western Hemisphere would hardly be conducted were a strong American bombardment force present in Asia capable of destroying Japanese shipping within its radius of action."[65] The joint board at its 19 September meeting had "concurred" with Marshall's view that sending B-17s to Luzon rather than Oahu "would have a profound strategic effect and that it might be the decisive element in deterring Japan from undertaking a Pacific war."[66] Before the congressional committee the U.S. Army chief of staff confirmed the central role that the B-17s had played in the high-risk Anglo-American deterrent gamble.

"If we could make the Philippines reasonably defensible, particularly with heavy bombers in which the air corps had at that time great faith," Marshall testified, "we felt that we could block the Japanese and block their entry into the war by their fear of what would happen if they couldn't take the Philippines."[67] The underlying flaw in Washington's strategic calculations was that the fifty or so heavy bombers that could be flown to the Philippines by the end of the year was an inadequate force to defend the Philippines and even the two hundred scheduled to be on Luzon by April 1942 would not have acted as a deterrent to Japan's plans.

The Anglo-American deterrent strategy may have been an ill-conceived military and diplomatic gamble, but it was not a deliberate attempt to get "a Japanese-American war started by the back door" as Ambassador Nomura predicted after the August Atlantic summit. This was to become the favorite charge leveled against Roosevelt by the isolationists and postwar revisionists. The most compelling evidence against the charge is that Roosevelt would not have sought to engineer a confrontation that left Japan no way out but to attack the United States. Such a policy would have been diametrically opposed to the "Europe First" strategy of Rainbow 5, to which both the Americans and British subscribed. There was no doubt that, with the connivance of his chief of naval operations, Admiral Stark, Roosevelt intended to steer the United States into a naval war with Germany sooner rather than later. But this objective gave him every reason *not* to get embroiled in a simultaneous war in the Pacific. He was constantly reminded in 1941 that there were not sufficient ships, aircraft, or material resources to sustain supplies to Britain, the Soviet Union, and Nationalist China. To court certain hostilities with Japan and the consequent global war that would erupt would have made nonsense of the very foundation on which United States strategic planning was based.

As events were to show, the weight of evidence argues that Roosevelt had provided Churchill with a guarantee in the event of an attack by Japan on British territory that could be construed as exceeding his constitutional authority if a simultaneous attack on U.S. territory was not forthcoming. That was a gamble that the president appears to have been willing to take because of the military straitjacket the United States had been forced into by committing itself to economic warfare with Japan. But the Anglo-American deterrent gamble that emerged from the consequent need to reinforce the Philippines was an effort to deter Tokyo from, not goad Tokyo into, attacking British, American, and Dutch territory in the Far East. It was the result, not of a sinister conspiracy between the president and prime minister, but a profound misreading of Japanese diplomatic resolve, military capabilities, and political psychology.

Stereotypical Anglo-Saxon racial attitudes played their part in Roosevelt and Churchill's belief that a scratch force of bombers and battleships would be a sufficient threat to cow the Japanese into halting their southward advance long enough for a truly powerful deterrent force to be built up in the Philippines and Singapore. Their poker game of diplomatic bluster and military bluff was soon to collapse because of Washington's failure to appreciate that the hand they intended to play required them to "baby along" the Japanese for six months, while the oil embargo forced Tokyo to play their hand within three months.

The very idea of babying along the Japanese was yet another indication of the traditional Anglo-American tendency to patronize Asian nations. It led to Washington's fatal misreading of Tokyo's request to resume negotiations. The hardliners in the State Department concluded that Nomura's willingness to hear American demands for the withdrawal of Japanese troops from Indochina was the result of the economic sanctions. This misassumption, coupled with an overconfidence that MAGIC would provide both insight into and a forewarning of the Japanese military agenda, led to the patronizing myopia that characterized the final rounds of diplomatic maneuvering with Japan.

The warning signs in the diplomatic traffic that gave clear indication that the military leaders in Tokyo were running out of patience were ignored in Washington. Only Churchill appears to have grasped the significance of the time factor, shrewdly calculating that if the Americans' bluff was called, Roosevelt would find a way of persuading Congress to live up to the secret commitment he had given to Britain.

4

"An Imperfect Threat"

The Military Miscalculation that Flying Fortress
Bombers in the Philippines Were a Strategic
Deterrent to Japan

When President Theodore Roosevelt sent the Great White Fleet of battleships on its epic round-the-world voyage in 1907 to demonstrate Uncle Sam's determination to cow the emerging Pacific power of Japan, he proclaimed the need for the United States to "speak softly and carry a big stick."[1] Thirty-four years later when his cousin Franklin made his attempt to reprise his predecessor's brazen gunboat diplomacy in the fall of 1941, the United States spoke too loudly and wielded too little a stick. His bid to browbeat Japan was not made with naval power—the U.S. Navy could no longer compete in the Pacific—but with heavy bombers. This aerial-deterrent strategy emerged from a 21 October memorandum on the Flying Fortress bombers, in which the secretary of war had set out a stratospheric flight of military wishful thinking by the U.S. Army Air Force.

"A strategic opportunity of the utmost importance has suddenly arisen in the southwestern Pacific," Henry Stimson assured the president in a breathtakingly overoptimistic assessment of the potential of American airpower in the Philippines. "Our whole strategic possibilities of the past twenty years have been revolutionized," he wrote. "From being impotent to influence events in the area, we suddenly find ourselves vested with the possibility of great effective power. Indeed we hardly realized our opportunities in this respect."[2] According to this three-page single-spaced memorandum, the growing U.S. heavy bomber force in the Philippines, while still an "imperfect threat," according to Stimson, "if not promptly called, bids fair to stop Japan's march to the south and secure the safety of Singapore, with all the revolutionary consequences of such an action."[3] On the assumption that the United States would soon muster enough B-17s to deter Japan from attacking the Philippines, the secretary of war went on to describe the "strategic possibilities" that General Arnold envisaged opening up for MacArthur's aerial bombardment force.

Stimson had been assured by the U.S. Army Air Force chief that with sufficient airpower in the Philippines the Japanese could be deterred from further aggression by threatening them with a strategic bombing offensive. This was made possible by the very long operational range of the B-17 and B-24 bombers, which were graphically presented as red and blue circles encompassing Tokyo on the National Geographic map that accompanied his memorandum. The proximity of the Philippines to Japan, which for so long had made the island a strategic liability for the United States, could now be turned to advantage, since MacArthur's heavy bombers were within striking distance of the Japanese home islands.

The "imperfect" nature of the Flying Fortress as a deterrent force, however, was obvious from the map. To raid Tokyo required the cooperation of Stalin, since the three-thousand-mile range of the B-17 required making shuttle-bombing runs on a dog-leg flight path that took them from the Philippines over Japan to land on Soviet airfields at Vladivostok and the Kamchatka Peninsula. This operation, General Marshall had already been assured by General Arnold, would be "a comparatively simple matter," and Stimson had no hesitation in conveying to the president how the threat of a strategic bombing offensive now gave a "power" to the United States that "can hardly be overestimated."[4]

If a strong enough force of B-17s could be established in the Philippines, Stimson contended, the mere threat of subjecting Tokyo to devastation from the air "might well remove Japan from the Axis powers."[5] The implication that heavy bombers alone could provide the U.S. with the proverbial "big stick" to deter the military leaders of Japan left Roosevelt "a bit bewildered," according to the note he appended when he sent Stimson's memorandum to Harry Hopkins for his evaluation.[6] But General Arnold had already taken care to brief the presidential aide on the B-17 deterrent strategy. So although Roosevelt may have initially been skeptical that MacArthur's heavy bombers really "had changed the whole picture in the Asiatic areas," after meeting with Stimson and Marshall on 30 October, he was persuaded that the United States would soon possess the necessary airpower to raise its strategic hand against Japan.[7]

Unaware that Washington was already planning to escalate the diplomatic poker game, Churchill cabled Roosevelt on 5 November of his concern. "When we talked about this at Placentia you spoke of gaining time, and this policy has been brilliantly successful so far. But our joint embargo is steadily forcing the Japanese to decisions for peace and war."[8] He therefore urged the president to issue a stern warning to Tokyo not to send troops into China's Yunnan Province to cut the Burma Road supply route to Chiang Kai-shek.[9]

"What we need now is a deterrent of the most general and formidable character," the prime minister proposed. "No independent actions by ourselves will deter Japan because we are so much tied-up elsewhere."[10] But Roosevelt turned down Churchill's request because there was "at least an even chance" that it would have the opposite effect. Replying to the prime minister on 7 November that American efforts were being concentrated on continuing "to strengthen our defenses in the Philippine Islands," Roosevelt said this would "tend to increase Japan's hesitation."[11] The effectiveness of the B-17 as a deterrent to Japan was evidently on Roosevelt's mind that day, since he raised the issue indirectly by canvassing his afternoon cabinet meeting on "whether the people would back us up in case we struck at Japan down there."[12]

Just how imperfect the threat to bomb Japan really was should have become obvious when soundings made by the U.S. of Moscow on the possible use of Soviet Far East airfields for what was described as possible "ferry flights" were ignored. Facing the advance of the German panzer divisions on Moscow, Stalin had only just recalled five Red Army divisions from Siberia to join the desperate battle for the capital. He had taken this calculated risk only after he had received assurances from Soviet Military Intelligence. Their spy Richard Sorge, a German journalist with high-level diplomatic connections in Tokyo, had obtained intelligence confirming that the Japanese had decided to move southward and not attack the Soviet

Union. Siberia's frontier with Japan's puppet state of Manchu-kuo was now sparsely guarded, and Stalin was not about to agree to U.S. bombers operating against Japan from Soviet air bases. It would have jeopardized the fragile neutrality that existed between Moscow and Tokyo.

Stimson and Marshall had already been carried so high on the Army Air Force's flight of strategic fantasy by Arnold that they did not wait for Soviet agreement before convincing the president that the presence of a force of heavy bombers in the Philippines was enough to give the Japanese nightmares about bombs raining down over Tokyo. MacArthur's own ambitions also fueled the belief that his Far East Air Force was an instrument of enormous tactical and strategic potential. Ironically, he himself had been a late convert to airpower, serving as one of the judges who at the the 1925 "Billy" Mitchell court-martial found the general guilty of indiscipline. Mitchell continued until his death, in 1936, with his outspoken public criticism of the Army for not recognizing the potential of strategic bombing in general and the inadequacies of the air defenses of Pearl Harbor in particular. Sixteen years later, when MacArthur embraced Mitchell's theories with the unquestioning ardor of a zealous convert, he fell victim to the same wishful contagion that infected the deliberations of the joint Army Navy board, which on 19 September decided to accelerate the military buildup in the Philippines by assigning MacArthur priority for B-17 deliveries.

The confidence of the U.S. Army Far East Command soared with every flight of bombers that rumbled in over MacArthur's Manila headquarters, migrating from the West Coast in stately flocks whose daily progress across the trackless Pacific was anxiously monitored by the secretary of war. Following the arrival by sea in mid-September of a troop convoy carrying fourteen companies of U.S. Army regulars and the news that a contingent of U.S. Marines was at sea en route from Shanghai, MacArthur's confidence knew no bounds. When the War Department promised him fifty thousand more American troops by February 1942, he cabled Marshall that the Philippines mobilization was "proceeding in a most satisfactory manner."[13] He reported that his Philippine defense program was "progressing by leaps and bounds," transforming "a feeling of defeatism to the highest state of readiness I have ever seen."[14] Assured by the Army chief of staff that the USAFFE now had the "highest priority" for men and equipment, MacArthur promised to have two hundred thousand strong Filipino militiamen under arms by the end of 1941.

"Lewis! You are as welcome as the flowers in May," MacArthur declared as he warmly embraced General Brereton when he arrived in Manila on 1 November. He carried with him Marshall's assurances that yet more reinforcements were on their way. "They are going to give us everything we asked for," MacArthur delightedly told his chief of staff after learning that his bombardment force was to be increased to at least 170 B-17s and longer-range B-24s by February 1942. They would be augmented by 86 light bombers and two additional squadrons of P-40 pursuit planes. Brereton had also brought with him the preliminary studies Washington had made for a strategic air offensive against the Japanese islands. Carried away by the prospect of being able to strike Tokyo, MacArthur directed his new Far East air commander to at once urge the Army Air Force planning staff to accelerate the completion and shipment to Manila of five hundred target maps.[15]

The usually levelheaded Marshall was also infected with the Army Air Force's inflated vision of the strategic opportunity for MacArthur's bombing force. On 15 November the Army chief of staff summoned selected senior news correspondents and newspaper bureau chiefs to an off-the-record Sunday morning briefing at the War Department. After swearing them to secrecy, he told the astonished journalists that "we are preparing an offensive war against Japan, whereas the Japs believe we are preparing only to defend the Philippines."[16] Marshall told them, without explaining how, that "we know what they know about us and they don't know that we know it." Expressing his concern that if the secret leaked, the "fanatics" in Tokyo would "demand war immediately" so as not to lose face.[17] But if the message were to filter through to Japan discreetly that the United States was considering bombing Tokyo and possessed "the equipment with which to do it," it would cause the Japanese to think twice before embarking on further aggression. This was no bluff, Marshall assured the startled pressmen. "Flying Fortresses will be dispatched immediately to set the paper cities of Japan on fire, in the event of war," he declared. "There won't be any hesitation about bombing civilians—it will be all-out."[18]

Marshall did not reveal that it was MAGIC eavesdropping on Japanese diplomatic communications that enabled him to be so confident that the Japanese had not yet discovered the ace card that the United States military believed they were holding. But the hints that he dropped that it might soon have to be played indicated the degree to which Washington overestimated its own military capability and underestimated the Japanese military mind. Without Soviet cooperation any strategic bombing offensive against Tokyo was an empty bluff. But Marshall had already approved the shipping of incendiary bombs to the Philippines solely for the purpose of making good on the threat to set the "paper cities" of Japan ablaze."[19] On 15 November, four days after the extraordinary briefing, *The New York Times* carried a story that revealed that the United States heavy bomber force in the Philippines had the ability to "drop bombs on Japan, land in Siberia, refuel and re-bomb and repeat the enterprise on a return trip to Manila."[20] This speculative piece had not been written by any of the journalists present at the secret Sunday briefing, but it alerted Tokyo. At the same time it aroused the concern of more levelheads in the War Department about the wisdom of trying to intimidate the Japanese with empty threats.

"Strategic Air Offensive Against Japan" was the heading of a sober memorandum that cast doubt on MacArthur's scheme to bomb Japan. Drawn up by Brigadier General Lawrence S. Kuter and presented to the U.S. Army chief of staff on 21 November, it cautioned that "a sustained air offensive against the Japanese was never discussed" in detail with Brereton before his departure for Manila. Marshall was advised that "we are going much too far on the offensive side" in light of what Kuter described as the "smallness of the proposed army air force in the Philippines." Even if the Soviets agreed to let their airfields be used for the shuttle-bombing of the Japanese home islands, Marshall had dangerously overestimated the ability of MacArthur's relatively small bomber force. The U.S. Army Air Force had already received requests to prepare target maps for "the location of 600 industrial objectives in Japan proper," but MacArthur would have a force of only two hundred B-17s by April 1942, and Marshall was reminded that the Victory Plan that had been prepared as a strategic blueprint for Rainbow 5 presumed that a force of eight thousand bombers would be required "for the positive assurance of destroying 154 industrial objectives in Germany.[21] Kuter concluded his report by warning that the inflammability of the city of Tokyo had been "considerably overestimated" in the Army Air Force proposal which called for a "general incendiary attack to burn up the wood and paper structure of the densely populated Japanese cities."[22]

Bombing Japan may have been a more imagined than real strategy, even before the Soviet refusal to cooperate killed the plan. But MacArthur's overblown faith in the strategic and tactical capabilities of his force of heavy bombers remained unshaken. After reading the Philippines' section of the Rainbow 5 War Plan, which Brereton had brought with him, MacArthur rejected as "too negativistic" the "citadel defense" strategy that required him to withdraw USAFFE forces to the Bataan Peninsula in the event of a Japanese attack. Citing the dramatic transformation that airpower had made in his command, he pressed the War Department for permission to move the ammunition and supply reserves from Bataan up to the forward areas of Luzon. This was part of his audacious new plan for a beach-defense strategy, which he claimed was now practical because troops and tanks at his disposal would be able to smash any assault force that survived interdiction at sea by the Flying Fortresses.

The Asiatic Fleet commander in chief was not nearly so sanguine. The weakness of Admiral Hart's force of three cruisers, thirteen destroyers, eighteen submarines, and half a dozen PT boats required that it be withdrawn southward if a Japanese attack materialized. MacArthur violently disagreed with Hart over what he saw as the Navy's determination to cut and run, and he argued that he should take over control of all naval air operations over the approaches to the Philippines. Hart, who believed it was the Navy's responsibility to direct overwater air operations, had appealed to Washington, complaining that MacArthur was "going far beyond the war plans" by trying to assume command over the Asiatic Fleet's aircraft in order to direct them "to strike at any enemy force committed to attack." This brought a ripsnorting letter from MacArthur telling Hart that it would be "manifestly illogical" to assign "such a powerful Army air striking force to an element of such combat inferiority as your Command."[23]

Marshall and Stark had to step in to resolve the dispute between their warring commanders. They sided with MacArthur, and on 19 November the joint board approved his revision in the Rainbow 5 War Plan. It provided for sending more air units to the Philippines and gave MacArthur authority for his beach-defense plan to fight a Japanese invasion at the waterline. This extraordinary concession was another indication of how far American military strategy in the Far East had drifted from reality. Even with forces ten times greater than those MacArthur anticipated he could command by April 1942, it would have been impossible for them to cover all the potential beachheads on Luzon. Securing all of the Philippine archipelago against invasion was an insurmountable task. Such was MacArthur's enthusiasm, however, that even Admiral Hart was persuaded of the new strategy's practicality, and he recommended to the chief of naval operations that instead of retreating, the Asiatic Fleet should now be committed to fight in the Philippines.

The magnitude of the strategic and tactical miscalculations made in Manila and Washington was little short of astonishing. To keep up with the military demands placed upon them by the adoption of the policy of economic warfare, the War Department had uncritically embraced the doctrine that airpower alone could deter the Japanese from making an end-run around the Philippines to seize the oil supplies of the Dutch East Indies. The doctrine was not only unproven, but it depended on the Japanese not attempting a military adventure before April 1942, when a two-hundred-strong heavy bomber force would be in place in the Philippines. Four years later the magnitude of this strategic miscalculation was acknowledged by Marshall himself, when in his testimony to the Congressional Investigations Committee, he accepted that in 1941 there had been a dramatic underestimate of the number of bombers needed to constitute a credible deterrent.

"We now think in terms of thousands. At that time one hundred was a very large figure," Marshall conceded under crossexamination.[24] But the 1941 record shows that no proper estimate had been made of what the size would be of a strategic bombing force that would constitute an effective deterrent to Japan. The Army chief's willingness to cut by more than half the original estimate of 200 as the requisite number of B-17s necessary for the defense of the Philippines was another strategic blunder because it was dictated by the rate at which the Boeing Aircraft Company could produce the heavy bombers. When fewer than fifty could be sent to the Philippines by December 1941, Marshall testified, he had been prepared to cut his estimate to accept that even this limited number "would probably deter the Japanese from making an attack."[25] Stimson's "strategic opportunity" fell victim to a gross strategic miscalculation by the War Department planners. Yet from the first touchdown of the Flying Fortresses at Clark Field in September until the Japanese attack three months later, Washington remained transfixed by a deterrent strategy that had no soundly calculated military foundation. The determination to believe that MacArthur's "big stick" grew ever more menacing with every B-17 that reached the Philippines was encouraged by the racially engendered attitude that only a fraction of the bomber force necessary to defeat the Germans would be sufficient to strike terror into the minds of what were presumed to be less stalwart and more panicky Asiatics.

"As you well know, however, the final success of the operation lies on the knees of the gods, and we cannot tell what may momentarily come out from Japan," Stimson had cautioned Roosevelt when he first put forward the idea of the deterrent based on a strategic bombing offensive.[26] Stimson made his prophetic caveat knowing that there was mounting evidence from the MAGIC intercepts that the patience of the Japanese military leaders was rapidly evaporating. Only five days later, on 16 October, the Konoye government collapsed, when his prime minister could not meet the military's deadline for a diplomatic accommodation with the United States.

General Tojo, who only two weeks earlier had cautioned Konoye that "the way of diplomacy is not always a matter of concession, sometimes it is oppression," now became head of a cabinet dominated by hard-line admirals and generals.[27] Tojo, nonetheless, reacted to another admonishment from the emperor by agreeing to make a final effort to reach diplomatic resolution with the United States, before Japan embarked on war.

The fall of the Konoye government had not been foreshadowed in the Japanese diplomatic messages. This should have been a warning to the policy makers in Washington, who had grown increasingly dependent on the Purple intercepts, that Tokyo's diplomatic traffic might not provide insight into or advance warning of every move that Tokyo made. The chief of naval operations had access to intelligence other than that obtained from diplomatic intercepts, but almost none of it was relayed to the Pacific Fleet. Nor had any MAGIC intelligence been received by the Pacific Fleet in three months, so Admiral Kimmel was in the dark about what action should be taken in response to the alert that was received from Washington. Addressed to Admiral Kimmel from the chief of naval operations, Admiral Stark—with instructions it be forwarded to General Short—the dispatch warned of "a grave situation" resulting from the resignation of Konoye's cabinet. Anticipating that the new regime in Tokyo "would probably be strongly nationalistic," Stark warned the Pacific Fleet commander in chief that "hostilities between Japan and Russia are a strong possibility." Since the "U.S. and Britain are held responsible by Japan for her present desperate situation," advised the chief of naval operations, "there is also a possibility that Japan may attack." All U.S. commands in the Pacific were, therefore, ordered to "take due precautions including such preparatory measures as will not constitute provocative actions against Japan."[28]

Without MAGIC, Kimmel and Short were left to ponder just what "preparatory measures" they should take to meet the crisis. The Pacific Fleet headquarters had no insights into Tokyo's diplomatic objectives which were essential for an accurate evaluation of Japan's current military and naval intentions. The only diplomatic background that the commander in chief obtained during the 16 October alarm was from the vague and often contradictory interpretations of Purple intercepts that Admiral Stark included in his personal letters to Kimmel. These ranged from a 22 September reassurance, relayed via the Asiatic Fleet commander, Admiral Hart, that expressed Stark's belief that "the Japanese appear to be making some effort at reaching a satisfactory solution," to a letter he wrote to Kimmel the following day advising that "conversations with Japs have reached an impasse" and there was a "strong warning and a threat of hostile action."[29] While it may have been apparent to Kimmel from newspaper reports that the negotiations with the Japanese envoys were foundering, the only clue to what military action Japan might be contemplating came from Stark's 16 October estimate of a "strong possibility" of an attack on Siberia.[30]

"I do not believe the Japs are going to sail into us," Stark wrote on 18 October, reassuring Kimmel that the president's intention was to "continue to strive to maintain the status quo in the Pacific."[31] Any intelligence that Kimmel might have been able to glean from such communications was further devalued because the letters took up to a week to reach him. Why the chief of naval operations should have chosen to keep his Pacific Fleet commander informed by personal letters—which were subject to delays—instead of relaying through secure naval communications channels the actual MAGIC intercepts, or proper intelligence estimates, was never explained. The evidence suggests that after the relief of Admiral Richard, Stark and all other Navy high commanders had become wary about taking the initiative concerning the Pacific Fleet without first consulting the president. Stark's resort to personal letters was an "off-the-record process" that may have protected him, but it left Kimmel in a difficult predicament when it came to seeking clarifications or responding rapidly with his own thoughts. As a method of communicating intelligence the personal letter was an anachronism more appropriate to the sedate days when the Navy was under sail. In the mid–twentieth century, when time was of the essence, Stark's procedure was a "helluva way to run a railroad" and was worthy of censure.

Kimmel had already reacted to the 16 October dispatch predicting a possible Japanese attack on the Soviet Union and had already made his deployments. This estimate, as it turned out, coincided with those of Commander Layton, the Pacific Fleet intelligence officer. He believed that the most likely area for Japanese military operations was against the maritime provinces of Siberia on the far rim of the Pacific. Accordingly, Kimmel put the U.S. Battleship Force on twelve-hour sailing notice and ordered that six submarines be prepared to depart for Japanese waters. He also held back the battleship *West Virginia* from sailing for the West Coast for a scheduled refit. Twelve more patrol planes were sent to Midway Island and plans were made for dispatching more Marines and fighter aircraft to outlying Wake Island. When Kimmel informed the chief of naval operations of these measures on 22 October, he received a curt "OK" from Stark in a letter that did not reach him until three weeks later.[32] By then the threat of imminent Japanese action had subsided.

The accuracy of Kimmel's overall assessment of the October crisis had also been confirmed by the report that Stark forwarded to him after it was over, from the Navy's liaison officer in the State Department. "Japan may attack Russia or may move southward," was the estimate given by Captain Roscoe E. Schuirmann, who concluded that "in the final analysis this will be determined by the military on the basis of opportunity and what they can get away with, not by what cabinet is in power."[33] General Short had been reassured, too, by a 20 October dispatch he had received from the War Department which stated that "Tension between the United States and Japan remains strained, but no repeat no abrupt change in Japanese foreign policy appears imminent."[34] According to his own G-2 intelligence chief, Colonel George W. Bicknell, an "attack on Russia from the east" was the most probable eventuality. "Japan, if faced with certain British military resistance to her plans, will unhesitatingly attack the British," Bicknell forecast, but this would happen "without a simultaneous attack on American possessions, because of no known binding agreement between the British and the Americans for joint military action against Japs, and . . . the American public is not yet fully prepared to support such action."[35]

Short would later attest that these two estimates of possible Japanese moves against the Soviet Union "weakened as far as I was concerned the probability of an immediate war between the U.S. and Japan."[36] As a result he focused the attention of the Hawaiian Department on alerting "all our guards against sabotage."[37] The intelligence estimates reaching both of the Hawaiian commanders were deeply flawed because what little diplomatic information reached them was skewed by Washington's preoccupation with the Philippines. But Bicknell might have made a very different interpretation had he known the extent to which the joint board was basing its plans on the assumption that the United States was already in a de facto military alliance with Britain in the Far East.

"Arrangements are on foot for our ships to use American bases in the Philippines," Lord Halifax, the British ambassador, confidently noted in his diary a few weeks later.[38] But Admiral Kimmel remained ignorant of this important shift that had taken place in the United States Pacific strategic equation. In Stark's 7 November letter, which reflected the growing pessimism of the chief of naval operations, Kimmel learned only that relations with Tokyo had deteriorated.

"Things seem to be moving steadily towards a crisis in the Pacific. It continually gets worser and worser!" Stark warned. "It doesn't look good," he gloomily observed, predicting that a "month may see, literally, almost anything."[39] Stark's alarms and qualified uncertainties on whether the negotiations could ever succeed in reconciling "two irreconcilable policies" were an inadequate substitute for the "horse's mouth" intelligence that was contained in MAGIC. Had Kimmel received any of the November Purple decrypts available to Washington, he would have seen, from Tokyo's many urgent references to the need to reach a diplomatic agreement by a November deadline, that the crisis would come to a head again by the end of the month.[40]

Precisely when, and by whom, it was decided to deny Kimmel and Short the intelligence from MAGIC could not be established by the congressional investigators. A parade of senior Army and Navy staff officers testified to having no knowledge of any such ban or responsibility for setting it up. There was no doubt in the minds of the investigators that the unwritten ban on sending MAGIC to the Hawaiian commands was the result, in part, of an obsessive concern for its security that had been prompted by a series of alarms. The most heart-stopping incident came at the beginning of May 1941, when a series of Purple intercepts disclosed that Tokyo had alerted the Japanese ambassador in Washington to the German warning that "it appears certain the United States Government is reading your code messages."[41] Since the alert was relayed in the Purple cipher, which continued to be used, it was clear that they did not suspect that this high-level crypto-system had been compromised. The need for tight security was underscored in August, when U.S. ambassador Grew reported from Tokyo that a trusted pro-American source in the Japanese Foreign Ministry insisted that any information he supplied be transmitted to the United States in a secure military cipher because only one State Department code remained unpenetrated by Japan's code breakers.[42]

The War Department had already adopted stricter security measures in May, after a "lost" memorandum on MAGIC together with another document referring to the Purple decrypts were found in the president's office desk drawer.[43] The Army and Navy had until then rotated the White House MAGIC delivery on a monthly basis. After May the Army courier provided Roosevelt with only an oral briefing. When the Navy took over deliveries in June, the president asked to see individual Purple messages. This was arranged through his naval aide, whose deputy, Lieutenant Commander Lester R. Schulz, would later testify that the Army had subsequently "sent nothing to the White House."[44]

If the president, as commander-in-chief, was not permitted full access to MAGIC for a month, it is not surprising that the Hawaiian commanders were arbitrarily denied access to the Japanese diplomatic traffic. The decision to cut off this vital flow of intelligence to the Hawaiian commanders, after the June Indochina crisis, was tantamount to blindfolding two sentries, yet still expecting them to stand guard over the Pacific.

Even as the October crisis passed into history, the Imperial Navy staff in Tokyo approved the strike against Pearl Harbor. This came only after Yamamoto had threatened to resign unless his "Hawaiian Operation" was adopted as an integral element in the war plan. "If the situation is going to force us into action," Yamamoto had written to Vice Admiral Shigetaro Shimada, the new navy minister, knocking out the Pacific Fleet was necessary in order to obtain the six months necessary to complete the southward offensive.[45] During the first week of November, the Combined Fleet completed its final training exercise and rehearsals for the Pearl Harbor attack. Imperial General Headquarters set X-day, when Japan would go to war, for the first week in December. On 5 November, they issued a general directive for war, which stated, "In the interest of self-defense and survival, the Empire is due to open hostilities with the United States, Britain and the Netherlands in the first ten days of December. Preparations are to be completed for the various operations involved."[46]

The same day Yamamoto issued *Combined Fleet Operational Order No. 1*. Seven hundred copies were printed and distributed to the warships involved in the southward offensive. Security was tight. On Yamamoto's orders the hundred-page final section, which detailed the Pearl Harbor plan, was detached and circulated under conditions of even stricter secrecy to only the commanders of Admiral Chuichi Nagumo's carrier striking force. While the Japanese completed war preparations, Tojo's new cabinet was coming under pressure from the navy minister who wanted fast action, not slow diplomacy.

"The situation is urgent: we must have a decision one way or the other," Shimada told the prime minister, reflecting the concern of his fellow admirals that with each passing day Japan's oil reserves were running lower.[47] From Tokyo Ambassador Grew warned the State Department on 3 November that General Tojo soon might not be able to restrain his cabinet's demands for "an all out, do or die attempt to render Japan imperious to foreign embargoes, even risking national harakiri rather than cede to foreign pressure."[48] Uneasiness that time might be running short was also voiced by the joint Army-Navy board, which met the next day in Washington to consider a State Department policy paper that advocated stepping up aid to China and issuing a stern ultimatum to Japan. This diplomatic policy was in direct conflict with the strategic requirement that a confrontation with the Japanese be avoided while the military reinforcement of the Philippines was being completed.

"Mr. Hull is of the opinion that there was no use to issue any additional warnings to Japan if we can't back them up," General Marshall advised at the board's meeting. He observed that the secretary of state's concern was justified because it would be mid-December before they could get MacArthur sufficient numbers of heavy bombers to provide the "impressive strength" that would "have a deterrent effect on Japanese op-

erations."[49] At the time, it was evident that they did not have
the airpower in the Philippines to back up any ultimatum to
Tokyo. The U.S. Army chief of staff went on to remind the
board that the U.S. commitment to an Atlantic strategy made
it essential that they avoid any flare-up in the Far East that
would diminish their ability to keep Britain and the Soviet
Union in the fight against Germany. Admiral Ingersoll, the deputy chief of naval operations, also argued for rejecting the
memorandum, because, in his opinion, the State Department
recommendation was based on the false premise "that Japan
could be defeated in military action in a few weeks."[50]

Admiral Stark concurred. He pointed out that the tankers
needed to support offensive operations by the Pacific Fleet in
support of the Philippines could not be provided without precipitating a major fuel supply crisis in America. "Assuming
the fleet could be moved to the Far East," the chief of naval
operations further cautioned, "no repair facilities are available at either Manila or Singapore."[51] His reference to the
British naval base as an alternate reflected the degree to which
the Anglo-American strategy in the Far East had become
intertwined.

"It would take some very clever diplomacy to save the situation," was how General Marshall summed up the dilemma
now facing the United States. He declared himself in favor of
making "certain minor concessions which the Japanese could
use in saving face."[52] The joint board therefore unanimously
rejected "the issuance of an ultimatum to Japan." They resolved to advise the president to "put off hostilities with Japan
as long as possible" and proposed that the State Department
be directed to make minor agreements "to tide the situation
over for the next several months."[53] Previously the foreign policy makers had dictated to the military; now the joint board
issued a strong warning to the State Department to avoid any
diplomatic missteps that might precipitate Japan into war.

"The only current plans for war against Japan in the Far
East are to conduct a defensive war in cooperation with the
British and Dutch," Marshall and Stark reminded Roosevelt
in the six-point memorandum that went to the White House
on 5 November. MacArthur's strategic bombing force could
not become "a positive threat" until mid-December. The president was told it would be March 1942 before the "potency of
this threat will have reached the point where it might well be
the deciding factor in deterring Japan."[54] This amounted to an
admission that it would take five months before the Anglo-

American deterrent strategy could become effective. Until then it was nothing but a bluff.

Britain's seaborne contribution had also lost credibility. Churchill had assured Roosevelt at their August summit that he would dispatch a "formidable, fast, high class squadron" to activate the naval fortress of Singapore. Then he ran into stiff resistance from the Admiralty, who argued that there was no squadron that was powerful enough to act as a deterrent to the Japanese. They proposed instead sending a couple of the World War I–vintage battleships to the Far East. The prime minister rejected sending these "floating coffins" to deter Japan, and pressured the first sea lord relentlessly until he agreed to send out the *Prince of Wales*. The Admiralty, nevertheless, had succeeded in whittling the promised Singapore fleet down to a single battleship task force.[55] "There is nothing like having something that can catch and kill anything," the prime minister cabled Roosevelt confidently on 2 November, when Admiral Sir Tom Phillips sailed from Britain in the battleship that had hosted the Atlantic Charter summit. It was accompanied by the battle cruiser *Repulse* and escorting destroyers for the long haul round the Cape of Good Hope to the Far East.

"The firmer your attitude and ours the less chance their taking the plunge," Churchill assured the president.[56] The ability of Task Force Z to "catch and kill anything" was called into question when the aircraft carrier *Indomitable*, which had been assigned to the squadron, ran aground on a Bermuda reef. Phillips, a short man whose pugnaciousness had earned him the sobriquet "Napoleon," determined to press on to Singapore regardless of his task force's now having to operate without any air cover in the South China Sea within range of Japanese airfields in Indochina. The prime minister ignored the opportunity to recall the admiral from the disaster into which he was steaming when he received a warning from the South African prime minister, who had visited Force Z docked at Capetown.

"If the Japanese are real nippy, there is an opening here for a first class disaster," Jan Christian Smuts cabled Churchill on 16 November.[57] But the British prime minister did not want to see the folly that was so obvious to the veteran Boer general. Sending a task force unprotected by air cover into Far Eastern waters, where Japan exercised an overwhelming sea and air supremacy, was only courting disaster. Churchill's expectation that a single Royal Naval battleship would be more than a match for the Japanese again reflected the West's esteem for Asians.

Japan was no more likely to be deterred from her strategic plans by a single battleship flying the British naval ensign in Singapore than by thirty-five American heavy bombers on Luzon. MAGIC had already disclosed that Tokyo knew that the "greater effective power" of MacArthur's air force was a charade. The intercepts from the Japanese consulate in Manila had reported how few heavy bombers were operating from Clark Field. Japan's air attaché in Berlin had noted the poor performance of the B-17s flown by the RAF. This was over-looked in Washington, although by November, Imperial General Headquarters in Tokyo was well aware that there would not be enough B-17s in the Philippines to challenge their war operations timetable. By mid November it should also have been as clear to Washington as it was to Tokyo that without Soviet cooperation not a single American bomb would fall on Tokyo. Stalin needed to maintain the goodwill that was permitting freighters to carry American Lend-Lease supplies unmolested through Japanese controlled waters to Vladivostok.

Japan was no longer willing to be babied along by the United States Army. Time and again the phrases in the Purple traffic echoed with urgency and crisis. But no alarm bells rang in Washington. On 4 November Japan's ambassador, Nomura, was informed that the professional diplomat Saburo Kurusu was being sent to Washington because of the "gravity of the negotiations."[58] If the current discussion led nowhere, "relations between our two nations will be on the brink of chaos," he was advised. The next day the terms of the "last possible bargain" were spelled out to Nomura, who was told that "there will be no room for personal interpretation."[59] The 5 November dispatch from Tokyo contained two sets of proposals. The "A" list detailed the conditions Japan would accept for a permanent settlement, which the ambassador was told to present "at the earliest possible moment" because "speed is an absolutely essential factor."[60] The "B" proposal for a modus vivendi, or temporary accommodation, was to be submitted in the event that there was "a remarkable difference between Japanese and American views." Tokyo again warned Nomura that the situation was "critical" and that the two proposals represented his government's "final step" to reach a settlement with the United States. "Absolutely no delays" were to be permitted since it was vital that "all arrangements for the signing of this agreement be completed by 25th of this month."[61]

The indications that should have alerted the War and Navy departments to Japan's march toward belligerency appeared in MAGIC with accelerating frequency throughout the month of November. A deadline of 25 November was set by Tokyo for the completion of negotiations. This was the day that the Striking Force was due to sail to attack Pearl Harbor, although this could not have been foreseen in Washington. No one suspected that the date signaled that Japan's military juggernaut had started rolling. Washington's overconfidence that MAGIC would explicitly forewarn if Japan intended to launch into hostilities had actually drained the intercepts of urgency. Hull knew when he received the "A" proposal from Nomura, on 6 November, that Tokyo had a fallback modus vivendi. In accordance with the joint board's memorandum, he played for time. The secretary of state received Nomura cordially, promised to study Tokyo's proposal for a long-term settlement, but commented that it did not appear to contain "any recessions from the position consistently maintained by the Japanese government."[62] That afternoon at the White House, the secretary of state did concede that "relations were extremely critical" with Japan when he warned Roosevelt and the cabinet that "we should be on the lookout for a military attack anywhere by Japan at any time."[63]

Yet no warning to that effect was sent out to the Pacific Fleet. The presumption must be that Washington did not alert the Hawaiian commanders because now the Philippines were considered the front line in the Pacific. MacArthur was receiving MAGIC and it was assumed that the USAFFE commander in chief was making his own similar intelligence deductions. At the Department of State the babying along process continued, and Hull withheld giving Nomura the official response to Tokyo's "A" proposal until 15 November. By then Ambassador Kurusu had arrived in Washington, bringing a renewed sense of urgency to the negotiations. Four days earlier MAGIC had revealed that Tokyo had complained to their ambassador in Washington "that the United States takes this lazy and easy going attitude." The American response continued to be spun out despite the Purple intercept that disclosed that the Japanese embassy, on Massachusetts Avenue, was making preparations to repatriate nonessential personnel by sea, which was a sure indication that the final round of the crisis was approaching.[64] Still the secretary of state declined to give Tokyo's envoys an answer. Instead, he dropped hints that there might be a prospect of reaching a temporary agreement on trade but maintained that any final settlement would require Japan to withdraw from the Tripartite Pact. MAGIC had already revealed that this was an unacceptable condition for Tokyo and that trade concessions would be too small a carrot with which to lure Tokyo into continuing negotiations when their major objective was to restore oil supplies.

"The fate of our empire hangs by a slender thread of as few days, so please fight harder than you did before," Japan's envoys were urged by Japan's foreign minister, who alerted them on 15 November that the twenty-fifth was the "deadline set for the solution of these negotiations."[65] MAGIC had revealed this and the instruction to the ambassadors that they give up on the "A" proposal for a permanent settlement and be ready to present Tokyo's "B" plan for a modus vivendi. The Japanese were about to make their final effort to save the solution. Once again the forewarning induced complacency in the State Department rather than a sense of urgency. There were plenty of additional clues in the Purple traffic that provided confirmation. They included references to the "laxness" of the U.S. government's "stalling for time" when "the crisis was fast approaching."

After eight years of navigating the increasingly turbulent rapids of American foreign policy, the six months of fruitless discussions with Nomura had left the seventy-year-old secretary of state weary of the diplomatic process in general and fed up with Tokyo's apparent deceitfulness, as it had been revealed in the MAGIC intercepts. Hull had instantly disliked the brusque approach of the self-important Kurusu, who had arrived with Ambassador Nomura for a meeting with the president on 17 November. They found the secretary of state irritable and tense, but Roosevelt—who had postponed his annual Thanksgiving trip to his Georgia retreat at Warm Springs—was at his most affable. For an hour and a half, discussion ranged back and forth over the three key issues that the United States insisted on as the basis of any negotiated settlement with Japan: trade equality in the Far East, Tokyo's willingness to withdraw from the Tripartite Pact, and the return of the invading Japanese army from mainland China and Indochina. Hull's impatience, at one point, led him into a bitter denunciation of Japan's "Hitlerian policy of expansion." He was interrupted by Kurusu, who tried to interject a note of urgency by warning of an "imminent explosion" unless an accord could be reached.[66]

"There is no last word between friends," the president

chipped in, offering to remain in Washington through the holiday weekend if it would help achieve a settlement. The Japanese envoys seized on this indication of American willingness to communicate and they cabled Tokyo for permission to put forward the "B" modus vivendi proposal. "It seems very clear that they are of a mind to bring about a compromise after making sure of our peaceful intentions," Japan's envoys reported, speculating that Roosevelt's apparent receptivity might be because "the United States has turned more and more than ever toward the Atlantic of late."[67]

The ambassador's opinion was well founded. A furious public outcry had arisen in the U.S. when, on 31 October, two weeks after eleven crewmen had been killed when a torpedo damaged the U.S. destroyer *Kearney*, a U-boat sank the *Reuben James*—another destroyer patrolling the North Atlantic shipping lanes—taking the lives of 115 of her crew. Roosevelt used this first destruction of a U.S. combat vessel to justify ratcheting up the American commitment to the war against Hitler and ordered the arming of all U.S. merchant ships. His announcement brought out isolationist demonstrators who paraded outside the White House with placards calling for the president's impeachment and protests that the United States was not so much drifting as being carefully steered by Roosevelt into a shooting war in the Atlantic. Yet what the president was trying to do, as his chief of staff set out in their 5 November memorandum, was avoid any immediate conflict.

The strategic arguments in favor of keeping the war from spreading were clear from the headlines in the press. In Russia, the Germans had stepped up their drive toward Moscow and had rolled through the Ukraine toward the oilfields of the Caucasus. The War Department was already circulating grim estimates by its Plans Division that Hitler was on the verge of defeating the Red Army. Britain's Atlantic lifeline to the United States was again under siege by U-boat "wolf-packs," even as her army in North Africa had been driven back to Egypt by General Erwin Rommel's Afrika Korps offensive. The worsening situation from Churchill's standpoint was confirmed by a 13 November cable from the London representative of Colonel William J. Donovan, Roosevelt's intelligence coordinator. He relayed the order in which Churchill had ranked the four possible permutations for American intervention: "(a) United States without Japan (b) United States and Japan both in War (c) neither at war (d) Japan without America (this possibility unthinkable!)"[68]

Neither Britain nor the United States wanted war to break out with Japan. But the diplomatic poker game that Washington had been playing with Tokyo was now at a critical juncture. Roosevelt and his cabinet were now confronted with the choice of either bowing to the demands of military strategy or raising the diplomatic stakes, with the risk that Tokyo would challenge the Anglo-American deterrent gamble. Concessions would buy three more months, and possible Soviet cooperation, so that MacArthur's Air Force would be approaching its full strength even if, because of Soviet reservations, he could not carry out the threat of a strategic bombing offensive against Japan. An outright rejection of Tokyo's last-ditch modus vivendi initiative risked provoking Japan to call the United States' military bluff by lashing out against the Philippines.

While this may not have been the worst-case scenario for the British, it would pitch the United States into a two-ocean war with naval and military resources inadequate for a single theater of operations. Wartime isolationists and postwar revisionists would argue that it was Roosevelt's policy to force a confrontation with Japan so that the cornered nation had no choice but to climb down or go to war with the United States to save face. All the declassified secret records, however, show that the president *did not* set out to defy the military logic that dictated some diplomatic concessions that would buy three more months of peace in the Pacific. Indeed, it was the president himself who took the initiative in persuading the secretary of state to soften the policy demanded by his hard-line officials. For the first time since Japanese troops launched their war in China in 1931, Dr. Hornbeck and the Far East Section were ordered to prepare a compromise position based on Japan's modus vivendi proposal.

The president and the secretary of state knew of Japan's last-ditch fallback "B" proposal from MAGIC. Kurusu had hinted at it during the 17 November White House discussion when he asked, "if the Japanese were now to withdraw their troops from Indochina, could the United States ease their oil and economic pressure to the point of sending small quantities."[69] That same evening Hull broached the idea to Lord Halifax, the British ambassador to Washington, with the comment that it was "attractive enough to warrant it being tried at least."[70] That same day Henry Morgenthau, the forceful secretary of the treasury, also drafted a memorandum for a "carrot-and-stick" policy intended to restore oil supplies to Japan in step with a phased pullout of troops from Indochina. It fleshed out an idea that Roosevelt himself had proposed the previous month for buying more time to reinforce the Philippines by offering Japan a six-month truce. As he put it, "some oil and rice now—more later," in return for freezing troop movements and a commitment "not to invoke Tripartite Pact even if U.S. gets involved into European War."[71]

The next day Secretary of State Hull carefully presented to Nomura and Kurusu the general outline of a proposal by which "Japan should evacuate southern French Indochina, and in return the United States should rescind the freezing order."[72] Hull also told them that "if the atmosphere remains calm in this manner, there will be no need for sending warships to Singapore or strengthening military facilities in the Philippines." All the records suggest that the secretary of state was not simply preempting Japan's "B" proposal but preparing the way for playing the Anglo-American Far Eastern deterrent as a bargaining chip. Tokyo's modus vivendi, in contrast, did not contemplate a withdrawal from Indochina—or the Tripartite Pact. It simply sought a maintenance of the status quo. Hull was to learn this three days later from the MAGIC intercept that curtly instructed Nomura to "present our B proposal of the Imperial Government and no further concessions can be made." The envoy was told that if the American government did not accept it by the deadline—now only a week away— "the negotiations will have to be broken off."[73]

On the morning of Thanksgiving Day 1941 the two Japanese ambassadors arrived at the State Department to formally initiate a last attempt at an accommodation by presenting Tokyo's proposal for a modus vivendi. Hull objected because it called for the United States to cease supplying aid to Chiang Kai-shek during the three months it was in force. At the same time he was careful not to give an impression of any prior knowledge of the other stumbling blocks it contained. He promised to think it over "fully and sympathetically," telling the Japanese envoys that he would have to defer giving a final answer until he had consulted with the representatives of Britain, China, and the Dutch government-in-exile."[74]

Despite what Nomura reported as Hull's "complete evasion" of detail, the impression he gave to Tokyo of the secretary of state's reaction was sufficiently positive for Japan's envoys to be granted a four-day extension of the original deadline. They were cautioned, however, that there were "reasons beyond your ability to guess why we wanted to settle Japanese-American relations by 25th."[75] Once again no intelligence ana-

lysts in Washington deduced from MAGIC the obvious suggestion that Japan might already be committed to some hostile
operations that were about to be set in motion. In the State
Department, the postponement of the deadline was misinterpreted as indication that Tokyo was still anxious for a negotiated settlement and could continue to be babied along. Yet it
was obvious, from this particular MAGIC, that if a modus vivendi could not be agreed by 29 November (Tokyo time), Japan
might launch into hostilities, because Nomura and Kurusu
were alerted that if the deadline passed: "After that things are
automatically going to happen."[76]

Cordell Hull would later testify before Congress that he
was "clutching at straws" when his officials at the State Department set to work over the weekend in a "desperate effort
to get something worked out that might stay the hand of the
Japanese army and navy for a few days, or weeks."[77] The first
draft reached Hull's desk on Monday morning. It proposed that
the United States would restore commercial relations and "a
required quantity of oil" sufficient for civilian needs only. In
return Japan would pull back from southern Indochina, agree
to limit her forces in the north of the French territory to
twenty-five thousand, and refrain from further "armed ad-
vancement" for three months while negotiations continued to
settle the major points at issue with the United States.[78] Although the American modus vivendi made no offer to meet
Tokyo's call for halting Lend-Lease aid to the Chinese Nationalists, it did propose the Philippines as a possible venue for
Japan to begin direct talks with Chiang Kai-shek. To allay the
Nationalist Chinese fears of a sellout by Washington, a ten-
point list of the demands that had to be met in a permanent
settlement with the United States was to be attached to the
modus vivendi proposal as an appendix.

The State Department's willingness to even consider this
last-minute temporary deal with Japan to avoid war makes
sense only in the context of the U.S. military's need to complete
reinforcement of the Philippines. It was only after Japan's attack that the United States' having been prepared to make a
temporary deal with Japan became an embarrassment, so it
was later dismissed as a straw-clutching exercise. Contrary to
this impression that Hull was to convey in his testimony at
the congressional hearing, a heated exchange of letters on 28
October 1941 with his principle Far East adviser indicates that
he took a much more favorable view of succeeding with the
modus vivendi at the time.

The letter to Dr. Hornbeck, which was removed shortly afterward from the official State Department records, reveals that Secretary Hull thought that the proposal was an "important factor in facilitating the conversations and avoiding a breakdown."[79] The proposal he wrote had been carefully constructed to give "our army and navy what they solemnly and most urgently represented as an urgent need for several weeks more time in which to get ready to defend on two ocean fronts." He assured his hard-line adviser that granting Japan "the privilege for ninety days of purchasing lower grade products in the amount of some two million tons, plus some flour and cotton and other foodstuffs would be entirely in accordance with a policy of moving gradually toward a peaceful basis for ninety days in return for a tremendous movement on the part of Japan." It was essential that they offer concessions, which Hull characterized as "absolutely microscopic," in return for Tokyo's calling a halt to military operations for three months, in order to buy the United States the time needed to complete the scheduled military reinforcement of the Philippines.[80]

"It was at this most critical stage with possible war on both fronts threatening that I formally made this proposal in reply to that of the Japanese," Hull explained in his letter to Dr. Hornbeck. "The truth is that the benefits to this government, if the chance for an agreement had been realized—and of course it was only a chance—would alone more than have justified the concessions offered to Japan for 90 days."[81] The president, however, was less hopeful of success for the modus vivendi than his secretary of state. In the message that he cabled Churchill outlining the terms of the American proposal, he stated, "This seems to me to be a fair proposition, but its acceptance or rejection is really a matter of internal Japanese politics. I am not very hopeful and we must all prepare for trouble very soon."[82]

While the president's telegram confirms the American uncertainty about whether Tokyo really would agree to the terms, at the meeting of his inner cabinet on 25 November, he did not question whether the United States should attempt a temporary accommodation with Japan. Before the meeting that Tuesday afternoon Secretary Hull had taken care to canvass support for his draft proposal from the secretaries of war and navy. The memorandum proposing concessions was signed by the army chief of staff and the chief of naval operations. It endorsed the principle of concessions, which the chiefs had already approved in the modus vivendi, with the proviso that its presentation must not be allowed to halt the B-17 buildup or the troop convoys being sent to the Philippines.

"It adequately safeguarded our interests," Stimson noted, in his diary, of the modus vivendi. When he expressed his own doubts that Tokyo would go along with all the details, the secretary of war told the cabinet meeting that he was in favor of any measure that brought more time to reinforce MacArthur. That was the unanimous opinion of those present, who agreed that the proposal should be given to the Japanese envoy that day. Then they turned to discuss what should be done if Tokyo did not accept the American proposal. Stimson's diary records that Roosevelt feared that if Japan broke off negotiations after the Friday deadline, "we were likely to be attacked perhaps as soon as next Monday because the Japanese are notorious for attacking without warning."[83]

The "difficult proposition," the president also remarked, "was how we should maneuver them into the position of firing the first shot without allowing too much danger to the United States."[84] Roosevelt's statement was to be misinterpreted by revisionist historians as evidence for their contention that the president was intent on maneuvering Japan into war. It is more plausible, however, to interpret this remark as Roosevelt voicing his doubt that Tokyo would actually accept the terms of the U.S. modus vivendi. Any other interpretation does not square with the context in which it was made, namely *after* the decision had already been taken that the secretary of state should at least make the attempt at an accommodation.[85]

After receiving the endorsement from the president and the cabinet, Hull then summoned the Chinese ambassador. The previous day Secretary Hull had outlined to the representatives of Britain, China, the Netherlands, and Australia the possible terms that the United States would agree to for a ninety-day temporary accommodation with Japan. The respective ambassadors had listened politely and agreed to refer the terms of the modus vivendi to their governments for comment. Only the Chinese ambassador, Dr. Hu Shih, had remonstrated with Hull that if Japanese troops were to remain in Indochina, they should be reduced from twenty-five thousand to five thousand. The State Department was then bombarded by "numerous hysterical" cables, as Hull described the clamor stirred up by Chiang Kai-shek's supporters. They typified the selfishness of the Chinese and their "lack of a disposition to cooperate," according to the secretary of state, who brushed them aside as an intrusion "into a delicate situation with no idea of what the facts are."[86] So when the Chinese ambassador arrived for his Tuesday evening briefing, Hull did not conceal his displeasure that Chiang Kai-shek's supporters were already branding the modus vivendi proposal as appeasement.

"Our proposal would relieve the menace of Japan in Indochina to the whole Pacific Area," Secretary Hull declared, warning Hu Shih, "We can cancel this proposal, but it must be with the understanding that we are not charged with the failure to send our fleet into Japanese waters, if by chance Japan makes a military drive southward."[87] The official minutes of this conversation give no indication that the secretary of state offered the Chinese ambassador any reason to expect that Nationalist Chinese displeasure was going to deflect the United States from attempting an accommodation with Tokyo. The only concession Hull made was to tell Hu Shih that he would send a "fuller explanation" to calm Chiang Kai-shek's fears.

The following afternoon the Japanese envoys arrived at the State Department anticipating a sympathetic response to their modus vivendi proposal, in light of the hints they had been given at their meeting the previous Friday. But the secretary of state did not to go ahead with the U.S. offer of a temporary accommodation with Japan. Nomura and Kurusu were brusquely handed the ten-point appendix to the modus vivendi, which, standing alone, read as an uncompromising list of the oft-repeated American terms and conditions that Japan must fulfill for a permanent settlement with the United States.

The secretary of state was keenly aware of the likely reaction of the Japanese because MAGIC had revealed that Tokyo's irreversible deadline was just seventy-two hours away. In a telephone conversation with Stimson that morning Hull stated that he was "ready to kick the whole thing over."[88]

Japan's envoys were "dumbfounded." As Nomura reported to Tokyo, he was shaking with anger when he told Hull "furiously" that the United States' ten-point note could only be interpreted as an "ultimatum."[89] The secretary of state had remained as "solid as a rock." The decision to abandon the modus vivendi may not have amounted to an "ultimatum" in the strict sense of the word, but in the circumstances, it was clear to all concerned that Japan would interpret it as a unilateral abandonment of the negotiating process by the United States. Dropping the proposal can, therefore, be argued to have made war all but inevitable, an outcome that Roosevelt himself must have anticipated when he ordered the sudden overnight reversal in American policy. Considering that it was such a dramatic about-face, it is significant that each of the parties involved offered conflicting explanations. After Japan's attacks ten days later it is understandable that members of the Roosevelt administration—and especially Secretary Hull—should have wanted to distance themselves from the charges that they had been willing to appease an aggressor. New evidence that has come to light, however, suggests that the true reason why the modus vivendi was dropped was that Roosevelt had received intelligence from Churchill that Japan was making preparations to go to war.

5

"A PRETTY SWEEPING INDICTMENT OF U.S. POLICY"

What Was Responsible for the Abrupt Decision
to Drop the Modus Vivendi Negotiations?

Wednesday 26 November 1941 was a critical juncture in the history of the United States. That morning the president awoke to confront a head-on collision between the demands of foreign policy and dictates of military strategy. Only hours after his cabinet had agreed on an attempt to buy the three months needed to complete the reinforcement of MacArthur in the Philippines, the decision to offer Japan a modus vivendi was abandoned, breaking up those negotiations and the underpinning of the whole Anglo-American Far East deterrent strategy.

Since the United States' global strategy was predicated on babying along Tokyo to avoid war breaking out in the Pacific, Roosevelt had to have been aware of the potentially disastrous consequences of such a dramatic policy reversal. What effectively amounted to a unilateral American decision to terminate negotiations with Tokyo's envoys cannot simply be put down to the "second thoughts" of the secretary of state that the modus vivendi was unfair to the Chinese Nationalists. Yet that has been the accepted explanation ever since the ailing Cordell Hull testified at the congressional hearings on 22 November 1945 that he was responsible for the decision to abandon the initiative, because by 26 November 1941 it had become "perfectly evident that the modus vivendi aspect was not feasible."[1]

Pale and trembling, the white-haired former secretary of state was given leave to submit his twenty-two-thousand-word prepared statement in writing. Out of consideration for his manifestly frail health and throat complaint, Hull was spared the rigors of a continuous and full cross-examination. In three separate appearances amounting to little more than an hour of considerate questioning, he repeatedly denied any foreknowledge of the Japanese attack. He insisted he had "never heard of anything, except, as the danger became more imminent, there was conference among the staff people." He testified that "As to that the President had said to them 'I do not know.'" In this way Hull ducked the question of whether Churchill had been given an assurance of armed support from the United States to defend British territory in the Far East. The former secretary of state was equally opaque when it came to pinning down precisely what had prompted the decision to abandon the modus vivendi, other than his recollection that to have proceeded with it would have run "the serious risk of collapse of Chinese morale and resistance."[2]

The minutes of the secretary of state's stormy confrontation with Ambassador Hu Shih the previous evening do not suggest that he would willingly have bowed to the "hysterical" overreaction of Chiang Kai-shek. But in his published memoir, Hull does refer to Churchill's "lukewarm" reaction to the modus vivendi as having triggered his concern for the Chinese, which ultimately prompted him to decide against submitting it.[3]

"What about Chiang Kai-shek? Is he not having a very thin diet?" were the actual words used by Churchill in his overnight cable to the president, which arrived in the White House at five minutes before one on the morning of 26 November.[4] The prime minister's anxiety about supplies to China, however, must have been subordinate to his overriding strategic concern, which was the need to buy more time to reinforce the joint Anglo-American defense in the Far East. This was apparent from the caveat with which he concluded his telegram: "Of course it is for you to handle this business and we certainly do not want an additional war."[5] Confirmation of the prime minister's deference to the secretary of state's proposal for offering concessions in order to gain time can be found in the private diary kept by the British ambassador in Washington.

"Endless talks these last two days with Hull about the question of a temporary and limited agreement with the Japs," Lord Halifax wrote of the modus vivendi proposals. "London is inclined to be stiffer than Hull wants to be, but I think this is very difficult for them, having left the whole business to Hull,"[6] he commented, noting, "we were handing over our diplomacy pretty completely, however unavoidable it may have been to do so."[7] However reluctant the Foreign Office was to see Britain's relations with Japan held hostage to the United States, the records show that Churchill stood by his agreement with Roosevelt that Washington should handle the babying-along diplomatic process. On 25 November he minuted his approval of the American modus vivendi terms to the foreign secretary. "My own feeling is that we might give Hull the latitude he asks," he told Anthony Eden. "Our major interest is no further encroachments and no war, as we have already enough of the latter."[8]

The British prime minister, who was never an ardent supporter of Chiang Kai-shek, gave no indication in this memorandum that his approval of the American proposal would be withheld out of sympathy for the plight of the Chinese Nationalists. He had shown scant concern for the Nationalists a year earlier, when he had peremptorily ordered the closure of the Burma Road supply line to Chunking when Britain was pressed to do so by diplomatic pressure from Tokyo. Churchill was as aware as Roosevelt and his secretary of state that sparing the feelings of their petulant Chinese ally was far less important than bargaining for the time to establish a credible Anglo-American deterrent against Japan. With Admiral Phillips and the Royal Navy task force still two days away from the Ceylon port of Colombo and more than a week from Singapore, the prime minister knew that this was no time for precipitating a diplomatic crisis that might cause the Japanese to lose patience and jump into war.[9]

After minuting his approval of the American policy on 25 November, something evidently happened that caused the prime minister to have reservations about the modus vivendi. According to Halifax's diary entry, it was still Tuesday in Washington when he "got a message in the evening to ask Hull to hold his hand until Winston had sent a message to the President."[10] Halifax was so convinced that no last-minute caveat from Churchill would deter the secretary of state from presenting the proposal the next day that he observed, "I hope it won't be a case of our grumbling and giving way, which does no good at all.[11]

The conviction expressed by the British ambassador makes it all the more puzzling to find that Churchill, in his Nobel Prize-winning account of World War II, very specifically denied that he had any hand in persuading the president to abandon the agreed-on policy. In contradiction to the documentary record, he even wrote that he had not even been asked to approve the modus vivendi or Hull's ten-point appendix. He, nonetheless, was careful to point out that this reiteration of the demand that Japan withdraw from Indochina and mainland China "not only met our wishes and those of associated governments, but indeed went beyond anything for which we had ventured to ask."[12] He flatly rejected Hull's claim that his "lukewarm" response was what finally prompted the decision to abandon the U.S. proposal for a temporary accommodation with Japan.

"I understood the dangers attending the thought 'the British are trying to drag us into war,'" Churchill wrote in the volume he entitled *The Grand Alliance*. "I therefore placed the issue where it belonged, namely in the President's hands."[13] This denial indicates a suspicious degree of oversensitivity, on Churchill's part, to any suggestion that he might have played a role in persuading Roosevelt to terminate negotiations with Japan. Even more significant is that he was later to categorically deny that he had direct access to the intelligence contained in the Japanese diplomatic traffic. In his memoir, published in 1951, he claimed that the Americans only infrequently and belatedly passed the occasional MAGIC intercept to him. The Japanese diplomatic intercepts, he wrote, "were repeated to us, but there was an inevitable delay—sometimes of two or three days—before we got them."[14]

This declaration by Churchill was a complete fabrication, as he well knew when he wrote it. He never anticipated that either the British or the Americans would ever permit researchers access to their most secret code-breaking records. Unfortunately for Churchill's reputation as a reliable source of history, the Americans commenced declassifying their huge World War II intelligence archive in the late seventies, and the British were belatedly to follow suit nearly twenty years later. The U.S. records show that Army Chief of Staff Marshall, after a great deal of soul-searching and despite the reservations about the Navy, had authorized in January 1941 that Britain be supplied with not one but two of the precious Purple decoding machines, as part of the exchange of secret technical information.[15]

One of the decoding machines originally built to be shipped to Pearl Harbor was instead crated up and sent under close escort aboard a British warship across the Atlantic, where, together with its precious twin, it was delivered to the code breakers of the closely guarded Government Code and Cipher School at Bletchley Park, an estate in the rolling hills of Buckinghamshire eighty miles north of London. These two Purple machines began spewing out Japanese diplomatic decrypts in February, after the British cryptanalysts had been trained in their operation by a joint U.S. team consisting of Lieutenant Robert H. Weeks and Ensign Prescott H. Currier of the U.S. Navy and Major Abraham Sinkov and Captain Leon Rosen from the U.S. Army.[16]

Churchill, despite his claim to the contrary, had been eavesdropping on Tokyo's most secret diplomatic communications since early April. This was the source, as it now turns out, from which he had been considerably concerned to learn that the Japanese ambassador in Washington was holding talks with the secretary of state about reaching an accommodation in the Pacific.

Roosevelt had not told Churchill about the Nomura-Hull conversations, nor had the State Department informed the British ambassador in Washington. But as the contents of the MOST SECRET intelligence file now shows, the prime minister was able to eavesdrop on the Japanese communications to an even greater degree than was the president. Released in the fall of 1993 to the Public Records Office, the first-ever declassification of the Purple decrypts produced at Bletchley Park reveals that the prime minister not only had more detailed access to the Purple messages than the president but was also receiving a wider variety of Japanese communications. The larger number of Japanese linguists at Bletchley Park enabled the British to apply their decoding machines to tapping a greater number of Tokyo's worldwide secret transmissions than was practical for the smaller teams of the U.S. Army and Navy. But in his memoir, Churchill lied to make it appear that he had less advance knowledge of Japan's intentions than Roosevelt.

"We did not know at any given moment all that the President or Mr. Hull knew," Churchill stated in his memoir, reinforcing the falsehood with what can now be seen as a tongue-in-cheek aside: "I make no complaint about this."[17] This was the accepted version of Britain's eavesdropping on Japanese communications until research for Admiral Layton's memoir turned up the U.S. Navy cryptanalysts who had accompanied the Purple machines to Bletchley Park. Their accounts were confirmed because of the Japanese decrypts obtained from Bletchley Park by Colonel Henry C. Clausen in 1944 for his Pearl Harbor investigation are part of the *Congressional Record*.[18]

The degree to which Churchill's version was based on a deliberate misrepresentation was finally exposed in 1993 as a result of a commitment to more open government on the part of Prime Minister John Major. Consequently the Foreign Office abandoned its long-standing policy of denying that they had ever eavesdropped on the secret communications of a power with whom they were technically at peace.[19] The declassification of Bletchley Park's Purple translations exposed a major falsehood that had been maintained for fifty years in the official histories and the authorized accounts of Britain's wartime code breaking in order to protect Churchill's reputation.[20]

The prime minister, we now know, received several deliveries each day, depending on the number of intercepts and the success of Bletchley Park's prolific code-breaking effort. The translations arrived at Downing Street by special courier. The covering notes on blue paper from Sir Stewart Menzies stamped MOST SECRET were simply signed "C," the traditional title adopted by the head of Britain's Secret Intelligence Service, who channeled the communications intelligence to Churchill and other selected service chiefs and ministers. Each pouch contained ULTRA from German Enigma intercepts as well as a selection of the most interesting decrypts of intercepted communications of foreign powers, which were then returned from Downing Street after the prime minister had read them. These decrypts were referred to as "BJs" or "Black Jumbos," although the cognomen derived from the blue color of the cardboard jackets reserved for the most secret Foreign Office documents.

Churchill's disclaimer of having had direct access to Purple is especially significant since the recent declassification has revealed that not only did the Japanese intercepts he was reading differ in their translations from the American versions, but Bletchley Park was intercepting Japanese diplomatic communications that were not picked up by the United States. In addition to intercepting the critical exchanges between Tokyo and the Japanese ambassadors in London and Berlin,

Bletchley Park had by the fall of 1941 extended its eaves-dropping to cover Japan's consulates and legations all over the world. This is clear from intercepts sent to the British prime minister that came from Japanese consulates in Mombasa and other far-flung outposts, in addition to their embassies in Rome, Madrid, Angora (now Ankara), Moscow, and Vichy. The intelligence in the "BJs," which were the British equivalent of MAGIC, was not restricted to Japan. It included reports from French, Italian, Spanish, and Turkish diplomats. Even the occasional American diplomatic exchange has not escaped the official weeders, proving that when it came to eavesdropping, Churchill was as keen to know what Washington was telling its diplomats as he was to keep abreast of Tokyo.

Since many of the Bletchley Park Purple messages do not appear in the declassified American MAGICs, it is self-evident that Britain was not exchanging all its Japanese intelligence with the United States. Nor did Washington pass on all their recoveries to the British, apparently on the assumption that this had been made unnecessary by the gift of the decoding machines. When it came to the issue of protecting the Purple secret, the U.S. Army and Navy, for whom MAGIC security had become a fixation, would have been shocked by the unnecessarily wide distribution that the British gave their Japanese decrypts. These show that neither the prime minister, nor even relatively junior ministers had any reason to complain that they were not receiving the reports on Tokyo's most secret diplomatic communications. The Bletchley Park "BJ" distribution lists disclose that it was not unusual for as many as twenty copies to be made for circulation to intelligence sections of the armed services and ten or more Whitehall departments, right on down to the Colonial Office level!

The gaps in the serial numbers of "C's" wartime Black Jumbo bulletins that have been made available indicate that only a carefully selected portion of the total decrypts received by Churchill have been declassified by the Government Communications Headquarters (Britain's supersecret electronic espionage and code-breaking establishment known as GCHQ), which inherited the wartime Bletchley Park archives. Even the release of what is obviously only a carefully weeded selection of the diplomatic communications that were sent to the prime minister from 1940 through 1942 shows just how far Churchill manipulated the historical truth when he denied direct knowledge of Japan's intentions.

"History will bear me out, particularly as I intend to write that history myself," the prime minister was accustomed to declare when settling contentious War Cabinet discussions in his favor. Preoccupied with how he would be judged by history, he had declared his intention to "yield to the temptation of adapting facts to my phrases."[21] The extent to which Churchill had filtered history through the roseate lens of his compelling prose and his inclination to suppress inconvenient facts and unflattering details is nowhere more evident than in connection with relations with Japan during the critical fall months of 1941. This was to be the case with the report Sir Robert Craigie, His Majesty's ambassador in Tokyo, wrote for the Foreign Office following his repatriation to Britain in 1943. Craigie had been effectively sidelined by Churchill's decision to leave it to the United States to "baby along" Japan. In his report he reminded the Foreign Office that when on 20 November he had learned from reliable sources in Tokyo of the secretary of state's initiative, he had sent a "most immediate" cable to London "strongly urging that this proposal be accepted as the basis of further discussion, and indicating the direction in which I believed the Japanese proposal to be susceptible of improvement."[22] His assessment was highly critical of American diplomacy, particularly regarding the decision to drop the modus vivendi.

"I consider that had it been possible to reach a compromise with Japan in December 1941 involving the withdrawal of Japanese troops from Indochina, war with Japan would not have been inevitable," Craigie wrote, contending that the U.S. president and secretary of state were "fully conscious of what they were doing" when they rejected the modus vivendi and knew that it would precipitate hostilities with Japan.[23] The report, which one senior member of the Foreign Office noted was a "pretty sweeping indictment of U.S. policy," sent Churchill into a fury.

"It is a very strange document and one which should be kept most scrupulously secret," Churchill scrawled on Craigie's report in prime ministerial red. "A more one-sided pro-Japanese account of what occurred I have hardly ever read." That a former British ambassador "writes of the breach with Japan as if it were an unmitigated disaster" angered Churchill, who wrote on his copy, "It was a blessing that Japan attacked the United States and thus brought America wholeheartedly into the war."[24] Until 7 December, that was by no means a foregone conclusion, and the prime minister was aware that in addition to the concern expressed by British ambassadors in Tokyo, the Foreign Office was rumbling with discontent that Britain had effectively abrogated her dealings with Tokyo to the United States. "I cannot help wondering whether the Americans have in fact any very real conception of what is passing in Japanese minds," one senior member of the British embassy in Washington had minuted his ambassador on 10 October. Complaining that the Americans were "keeping us in the dark," he noted he had a "real concern" that "if negotiations are to prove to be abortive and there is to be war, we cannot be certain of immediate U.S. participation and it is we (with the Chinese and the Dutch) who will have to bear the heat and burden of the day."[25]

"Nobody but Congress could *declare* war," the prime minister had emphatically reminded the 12 November cabinet, which considered the urgently expressed concerns from the Australian government and the Admiralty that a "complete understanding had not yet been reached" with the United States in the event of Japanese attack on British territory. Conceding that the president faced difficulties "as a result of the slow development of American opinion and the peculiarities of the American constitution," Churchill declared his confidence that Roosevelt was a "great leader" and that it was "in the President's power to make war without declaring it."[26]

"Should the United States become involved in war with Japan, the British declaration will follow within the hour," the prime minister had announced the previous evening, in a speech at the lord mayor of London's banquet at the Mansion House.[27] His ostentatiously public declaration was part of his ongoing effort to remind the Americans of Britain's unflinching support in their diplomatic stand-off with Japan. But he did not expect a similar reciprocation. "The American President had no such power," he told his colleagues the next day and conceded that "it remained possible, though unlikely that the United States would disinterest themselves if we were to declare war on Japan."[28]

Churchill's pronouncements appeared to be little more than whistling in the dark to the Australians, whose high commissioner in London was told after the cabinet meeting that it was "not possible to maintain a 'tidy diplomatic front' in the Far East or move without regard to the United States." The prime minister knew that he had to rely on Roosevelt's assurances, and on the Anglo-American agreements on a coordinated defense and diplomatic strategy against Japan that had been secretly agreed to four months earlier. The uncertainty about what guarantee of American armed support the president could provide if negotiations for a Pacific accord broke down was not resolved, but the babying of Japan was left to Washington. In the increasingly likely event the "baby" lashed out as a result of an American diplomatic blunder, Churchill could only pray that Roosevelt and his secretary of state would have a moral, if not constitutional, obligation not to leave Britain in the lurch.

This was why the prime minister subsequently took such offense at the harsh critique of U.S. diplomacy written by Britain's dispossessed ambassador in Tokyo and why he should go to extreme lengths to deny any suggestion that he himself had played any part in influencing Roosevelt's decision to abandon the modus vivendi. Nor could he reveal that he had been monitoring the Japanese diplomatic communications without admitting that he had been fully aware of the degree to which Washington had mishandled the crisis by ignoring the repeated indications of urgency in the Purple traffic. If Secretary Hull's pointing a finger at the prime minister was correct, then it can be argued that the influence Churchill had on the president's decision must have resulted from a much more important and urgent concern than his "lukewarm" support for the temporary accommodation with Tokyo.

Just what it was that prompted Roosevelt to call off the attempt to reach a temporary accommodation with Japan on 26 November is a question of far more historical importance than the debate over whether war could, or could not, have been averted if the secretary of state had proceeded as agreed. All the parties concerned were fully aware of the potential repercussions of dropping the agreed-on temporary accommodation, which were intimidating for both the United States and Britain, and the final decision could only have been sanctioned by the president himself. In light of the new documentation, it must be asked whether Roosevelt himself would have judged it in the interests of the United States to put the whole Philippine defense strategy at risk simply for the sake of Nationalist Chinese morale. Given the degree to which it is now apparent that the whole of American foreign policy in the Pacific had become hostage to reinforcing MacArthur as the principal deterrent to Japan's southward advance, it is impossible to believe—as historians have hitherto—that the secretary of state awoke on 26 November to pangs of consciousness about Chiang Kai-shek and recommended that MacArthur be sacrificed to satisfy the "hysterical" protests of the Nationalist Chinese.

"Hull wanted peace above everything because he had set his heart on making an adjustment with the Japanese and had worked day and night on it for weeks," noted Roosevelt's aide Hopkins, providing contemporary evidence of the secretary of state's determination.[29] Hull's commitment to the modus vivendi is supported by the recollections of one of his aides, who happened to be present when the secretary of state returned from a discussion on the issue with the president. Hull was "very agitated," according to Landreth Harrison, and he expressed his exasperation with those at the White House who "do not believe me when I tell them that the Japanese will attack us. You cannot give an ultimatum to a powerful and proud people and not expect them to react violently."[30] Harrison's account conflicts with the version given by Secretary Hull at the congressional hearings and repeated in his memoir that it was the result of Churchill's "lukewarm" reaction and his concern for Chiang Kai-shek. According to Harrison, the contemporary account given in Hull's angry exchange with Hornbeck makes it clear that it was the president who took the decision to abandon the modus vivendi that Wednesday morning, over the secretary of state's strongly voiced objections.

This is plain from Hull's angry words in response to Dr. Hornbeck's oleaginous assurance that "in days to come you will look upon the decision *which was made* and the action you took yesterday with great satisfaction [emphasis added]."[31] Hornbeck, the State Department's Far East adviser who had put the odds at five-to-one against Japan's going to war, wrote to the secretary of state on 27 November to justify the restoration of the hard-line policy toward Japan. He smugly consoled Hull that his modus vivendi proposal would have had only a "small chance" of success because the Japanese would have eventually rejected a "not . . . completely honest document" whose main intent had been "to give us more time to prepare our weapons of defense."[32] Hornbeck may have been correct that the temporary accommodation, from the American side, had been formulated so as to complete the reinforcement of the Philippines, but his contention stung the secretary of state into writing an angry response.

"We differ so entirely, however, that I must in writing offer my dissent," Hull told Hornbeck. "It is no answer to the question of whether this proposal is sound and desirable at this most critical period to say that it probably would not have been accepted by Japan in any event. If that sort of demagoguery stuff would be rung into this sort of undertaking, then there could never be any settlement between countries except at the point of a sword."[33]

According to the diary kept by the British ambassador, "the Chinks having made a proper row about the United States plan for a temporary agreement with Japan, Hull has apparently abandoned this, anyhow for the time being, and has given the Japs a general essay on high principles instead."[34] Two days later Halifax recorded how Secretary Hull had "opened up on the way in which his careful efforts to postpone the row had been blown out of the water by the intervention of many people who didn't understand how delicate the balance was."[35] The version that Hull gave to Lord Halifax, "hardly veiling his language," confirms that given in his exchange with Hornbeck. He "let go about Stimson and other members of the Cabinet," singling out Laughlin Currie, the president's Chinese Lend-Lease administrator, who, he complained, "had been swept off his feet by the violent telegrams from Chiang Kai-shek."[36] Hull made it clear that he was "pretty tried [sic] with the President's methods of being receptive to advice other than that which he received from the State Department."[37]

Lord Halifax, who as Britain's foreign secretary had earned the hostile sobriquet "Holy Fox" for his high-minded scheming behind Churchill's back to send peace-feelers to Hitler the previous year, sympathized with the frustration Hull had endured "when great men got loose from their advisors."[38] The fastidious British ambassador was careful, however, to reassure the secretary of state that he would have no "complaint against the matter of Winston's messages to the President, because he always knew what they were."[39] In the "postmortem" that he cabled to London on 29 November, Halifax reported that Hull had spoken with "considerable bitterness of the part by T. V. Soong, both in the unbalanced advice given to Chiang Kai-shek and also for the breach of confidence to the press."[40]

A Harvard-educated financier and a former Nationalist Chinese premier and foreign minister, Soong was Chunking's principal string-puller and extremely effective lobbyist in Washington. Hull made no effort to conceal from Halifax his bitterness that Soong had succeeded in "swinging Stimson, who had been forward in pressing to gain time, onto the other tack of supporting the Chinese view."[41] Despite the ambassador's assurances that Churchill had been "fully prepared to support the interim agreement," Halifax noted, and although the secretary of state had not reproached the British government, Hull had given the "impression" that the prime minister's message of sympathy with Chiang Kai-shek had played some part in convincing him of "the impossibility of proceeding with the interim agreement." Halifax was told that it was the Chinese leader's intention "to get us embroiled with Japan and that he looked like being successful."[42]

Cordell Hull, when he came to explain the dramatic U-turn in American policy on 26 November in his postwar memoir, made no bones about the role played by Britain's lack of support as expressed by the prime minister's "thin diet" cable. Not only was this to be vigorously denied by Churchill in his memoir, but the Foreign Office records show concern in Whitehall that Japan might have construed the American proposal as appeasement. But British diplomats in Washington moved swiftly to counter charges that they had sheltered behind the Nationalist Chinese protests while conspiring to get the United States into a war with Japan. When Dr. Hornbeck suggested at his meeting on 28 November with Sir Ronald Campbell of the British embassy that the "decision not to present the modus vivendi proposal was a joint responsibility to which all had contributed," he was told of Lord Halifax's displeasure. The ambassador begged to differ after he had learned from Assistant Secretary of State Sumner Welles that "Mr. Hull felt that it has been useless to go on with the idea of the modus vivendi because of our attitude."[43]

Britain's paramount concern was to avoid any damaging leaks from the State Department suggesting that Britain was in any way involved in influencing United States policy, particularly on a decision that might well lead to the outbreak of hostilities with Japan. Dr. Hornbeck was therefore told very firmly that "attempts to cast blame were to be avoided." It was decided that unless they detected "attempts to fix the blame on us in the U.S. press," the best policy for the British ambassador was to "duck" any questions as to the responsibility for the abandonment of the modus vivendi.[44]

The Foreign Office was reminded that the Americans had, in fact, kept the British embassy so much in the dark about the conduct of their negotiations with Tokyo's envoys that the actual text of Hull's ten-point message delivered to the Japanese ambassadors on 26 November was not given to them until 1 December.[45] Nonetheless, so important was it considered in London to distance the British ambassador from the eye of the diplomatic storm that it was agreed "to have another go at

Hornbeck discreetly, in a way that he can minute the record."
As the State Department Far East adviser had himself put it,
"historians looking to the facts in future would look to these
records."[46]

When it comes to establishing the facts, however, the British and American records offer conflicting versions of what
really caused one of the most dramatic U-turns in United
States diplomatic history.

6

"If the British Fought, We Would Have to Fight"

How Churchill Obtained Guarantees of "Armed Support" from Roosevelt

The president's unminuted style of cabinet government left history no official record of what had prompted his decision to abandon the attempt to reach a temporary accommodation with Japan. The U.S. chiefs of staff had repeatedly reminded him of the need to gain the three months required to complete the reinforcement of the Philippines. The potential consequences to the United States of the overnight policy reversal were so awesome that it could only have been taken by Roosevelt. The diary of the secretary of war, which purports to detail the actual process of how the president made the fateful decision, gives a very different explanation from that given by the secretary of state.

Significantly, Stimson did not present concern for Chiang Kai-shek as a major factor in his account of why Roosevelt ordered Hull to drop the modus vivendi on the morning of 26 November. He describes how he made a telephone call to the White House that Wednesday, shortly after learning from Hull that "he had just about made up his mind to give up the whole thing in respect of a truce and simply tell the Japanese that he had no further action to propose."[1]

"A few minutes later I talked to the President over the tele-

131

phone," Stimson wrote. "I asked him whether he had received the paper which I had sent him last night about the Japanese having started a new expedition from Shanghai down toward Indo-china." He described this in his diary as a report of a Japanese convoy of "30, 40 or 50 ships" that had been sighted at sea "south of Formosa." The president was "shocked and at once took it as further evidence of bad faith on the part of the Japanese."[2] In an extended version of the diary entry Stimson wrote that Roosevelt reacted dramatically: "He fairly blew up—jumped up into the air, so to speak, and said he hadn't seen it and that changed the whole situation." Stimson recorded that "I at once got another copy of the paper I had sent last night and sent it over to him by special messenger."[3]

Stimson's account, which so precisely pinpoints the evidence that prompted the president's decision to abandon the modus vivendi, turns out to be as flawed as that left by Hull. On Stimson's own admission the convoy report was sent by him on Wednesday afternoon, after he had found it waiting for him on his return from the cabinet meeting that had approved the terms of the temporary accommodation with Tokyo. But accepting this chronology of events depends on the president's not having received this convoy report until the following morning. The mystery of how such an allegedly explosive piece of urgent intelligence could have failed to reach the White House is made more puzzling because it was accompanied by a MAGIC intercept. In this case it was the decrypt of an intercepted British secret communication, not a Japanese one. Stimson's letter enclosed a War Office estimate from London on Japan's intentions that had apparently been decoded by the U.S. Army four days earlier. This is the presumption to be drawn from the injunction on it: "In order that the source may be protected do not reveal to the British that you have received the following information."[4]

It is curious that neither the intercepted British intelligence nor the convoy report was alarming enough to anger the short-tempered secretary of state when Stimson telephoned him and "told him about it and sent copies to him and the President of the message from G-2."[5] The intelligence in the report certainly did not amount to sufficient evidence of Japanese bad faith to have caused the president to blow up and order a reversal of a foreign policy decision that he knew might risk war with Japan—which he had committed the United States to avoiding. It was a four-day-old report of "ten to thirty troopships"—not the thirty, forty, or fifty ships Stimson recorded in his diary—that were not even at sea! The original 25 November letter, in fact, noted that this convoy was "a more or less normal movement" of Japanese transports "in the Yangtse River below Shanghai."[6]

As it turns out, this report was not dramatic or particularly news. Not only had the convoy's arrival at Shanghai been foreshadowed in a month-old MAGIC intercept, but the accompanying British intelligence estimate had predicted that "Japan will make a last effort at an agreement with the U.S." before the worst-case scenario materialized, which forecast an invasion of Thailand if negotiations broke down.[7]

The reason for doubting that this could have been an alarming enough piece of intelligence to seriously upset Roosevelt when he allegedly first learned of it is that Stimson's 25 November report, which supposedly failed to reach the White House the previous afternoon, came to light in the Philippine section of the secretary of war's most secret papers, which were kept in his office safe. That it *did* reach Roosevelt is evident because it was returned to Stimson on 27 November from the White House by Major General Edwin "Pa" Watson, the president's military aide, who enclosed a note that "he found inside the pocket of a very distinguished gentleman."[8] Since Roosevelt's aide would hardly have been rifling the pockets of anyone but the president, it is logical to assume that the "very distinguished gentleman" can have been none other than the president himself. General Watson returned the original convoy report to Stimson, together with the British estimate, both of which still bear the creases indicating it was quarter-folded to slip into a coat pocket.

The inference may therefore be drawn that Roosevelt sent the 25 November report back to the War Department because had it been filed with the president's correspondence, it could not be claimed that Roosevelt had not received the "evidence of bad faith on the part of the Japanese" until the following morning. When T. V. Soong and the Chinese ambassador had their meeting with Roosevelt on the *afternoon* of 26 November, they were given the impression that the modus vivendi had already been dropped. According to the report Lord Halifax sent to London, the president had told the Chinese diplomats "he had received the news *last night* that 30 Japanese troop transports carrying 30 to 40,000 men had just left Shantung for the South" and that "if this movement was correct, the Japanese were breaking faith while negotiations were under discussion, and if so war might break out at any time [emphasis added]."[9]

The amended wording of Stimson's follow-up letter is further evidence for believing that Roosevelt had received the convoy report on the 25 November, and it was only the next day that he inflated its significance to justify dropping the modus vivendi negotiations because of Japanese bad faith. In the 26 November version we find that Stimson has embroidered the report on the convoy in an obvious attempt to make it appear a more alarming piece of intelligence than it actually was.

"Later reports indicate that this movement is already under way and ships have been sent south of Formosa," Stimson had added, although the actual G-2 intelligence on the convoy at the time shows that it was still in the Yangtse. A penciled note by the secretary of war also records "no new direct reports of captains at sea since the five ship's capt[ains] last reported from Shanghai."[10] Moreover, he took care to advise the president that his report was "highly abbreviated from the original verbal information," a qualification that would not have been necessary unless the second report was intended to serve as camouflage for some much more alarming intelligence that had arrived at the White House *after* the president had received Stimson's "missing" letter the previous afternoon.[11]

Neither the timing nor the unalarming contents of Stimson's convoy report suggest that it could have been the alarming "evidence of bad faith on the part of the Japanese." The charade over the convoy suggests that Roosevelt must have received some more startling warning of Japan's commitment to war by the morning of 26 November that prompted the withdrawal of the proposal. Circumstantial corroboration is provided by the diary of Treasury Secretary Morgenthau, who arrived that morning in the presidential bedroom to find that Roosevelt had been taken back by some important news that he did not want to discuss. "He had not touched his coffee," Morgenthau noted. "He had some kippered herring which he had just begun to eat when Cordell Hull called up. The president was trying to talk to Hull and eat his food at the same time, but by the time he finished his conversation his food was cold and he didn't touch it."[12]

If the already outdated Shanghai intelligence was not the evidence of Japanese treachery, what was the information that reached the White House that morning that prompted the president to so abruptly reverse United States policy? The information must have provided more evidence of Tokyo's "bad faith" than the convoy report to have warranted Roosevelt's decision to abandon any further negotiations. In the records of the secret wartime investigations into Pearl Harbor evidence emerges that also points to credible intelligence of imminent hostile actions by Japan.

"On November 26 there was received *specific* evidence of the Japanese intention to wage offensive war against Great Britain and the United States [emphasis added]" was the unequivocal conclusion of the 1944 Army Pearl Harbor board.[13] It proved impossible to establish precisely what the intelligence was, but indications were that it was a report on "the concentration of units of the Japanese fleet at an unknown port ready for *offensive action* [emphasis added]."[14]

Yet when Admiral Kimmel attempted to question Admiral Stark at the naval board of inquiry about what this intelligence was that "gave specific evidence of Japan's intention to wage offensive war," he could not get his question answered.[15] Although the tribunal was sitting in secret session, the former chief of naval operations declined to answer on the grounds that to do so would "involve the disclosure of information that was detrimental to the public interest."[16] Stark was rescued by the court's ruling that he did not have to disclose "state secrets."[17] The Shanghai convoy report was hardly that, and so the presumption must be that a far more important piece of intelligence had been received that the president evidently shared only with the Army and Navy chiefs of staff. Stark and Marshall must have known precisely what it was because of the consistency with which both evaded the question at the congressional hearings. Marshall testified that he had "no specific recollection" of what he talked about in his telephone call to the president that Wednesday morning.[18]

"We were playing for time" was all that Stark would concede because he, too, was "unable to separate and clarify just what happened on the dates around the 25th."[19] The two chiefs of staff's cloudy memories about the "state secret" that prompted the president to drop concessions they had repeatedly urged as essential to buying time to reinforce MacArthur strongly supports the contention that there was a "missing" warning received at the White House on 26 November. The chiefs of staff and the president were so very keenly aware that the reinforcement of the Philippines had not yet been completed that they had every reason that Wednesday morning to continue "playing for time," and not to withdraw the modus vivendi and not to submit only the ten-point restatement of the hard-line memorandum, which could only be interpreted in Tokyo as an ultimatum.

Last-minute reservations by the British prime minister about Chiang Kai-shek's "thin diet" and the protests of China-hands in the Roosevelt administration would not have been enough to have triggered such a dramatic policy reversal in the face of such strong pleas by the chiefs of staff for more time to reinforce MacArthur. They were as aware as the secretary of state that abandoning the negotiations risked precipitating war in the Far East, so whatever information reached the White House that Wednesday morning must have amounted to "specific evidence of the Japanese intention to wage an offensive war," as the Army Pearl Harbor board concluded.[20]

The reaction of the president and his chiefs of staff that Wednesday morning was immediate and irreversible. It indicates that they had received an incontrovertible warning that war was imminent, no matter what action the United States' diplomats or military commanders initiated. Like a chess player caught in an inescapable "checkmate in five moves," the president of the United States was confronted with a "no win" situation.

There was no way out of the dilemma. To have continued negotiations with Tokyo after having received what was a credible warning that Japan's military forces were irrevocably committed to attack could have been politically disastrous for the president. Roosevelt would have risked being branded an appeaser and his ability as a war leader would have been discredited, as Britain's former prime minister, Neville Chamberlain, had been after Munich. To argue, as Secretary of War Stimson did, that the United States should strike first, risked both military and political disaster. With the reinforcement of the Philippines still uncompleted, the disparity between the American and Japanese forces in the Far East would have risked certain defeat and opened the president to the isolationists' charge that he had engineered an attack on Japan simply to get into war with Hitler. Japan's pact with the Axis powers was defensive, in that it required Germany and Italy to go to war only in the event of an attack on the Japanese, not if they themselves initiated war.

The American leadership had no option on the morning of 26 November other than that of "letting the Japanese fire the first shot," as the president himself put it.[21] Roosevelt and his chiefs of staff had been trapped in a military and diplomatic impasse of their own making. MacArthur's heavy bomber force, on which their whole Pacific strategy had become dependent, was still too puny a military "stick" to deter Japan and was still not powerful enough to guarantee the defense of the Philippines. The realization that the Anglo-American strategic gamble in the Far East had collapsed caught Roosevelt like a poker player with a weak hand who had caught sight of his opponent's aces.

Foreknowledge that the United States' strategic bluff was about to be called by Japan rather than concern about Chiang Kai-shek is a more logical explanation of what prompted the president to effectively discard his cards rather than reveal he had gambled everything on the illusory strategic bombing card. To prevent the enormity of their military miscalculation in the Philippines from being exposed, the Roosevelt administration disguised the real reason for their abrupt withdrawal from these negotiations. Citing concerns for the Nationalist Chinese and invoking the secretary of war's "missing" convoy report as evidence that Japan was negotiating in bad faith, the United States portrayed itself as standing on high moral principle. In the face of potential political fallout from the attack on Pearl Harbor, the need to protect the president from being blamed for what political opponents on Capitol Hill would characterize as a monumental strategic blunder became even greater. The decision to throw over all attempts at obtaining a temporary accommodation with Japan was the president's only politically defensible recourse.

"Whether this was the right course to take only history can judge," noted the British Foreign Office assessment delivered a month after war broke out with Japan. This document conceded, significantly, that the Nationalist Chinese protests, together with "the short message from the Prime Minister," were the determining factors in the American decision to withdraw the proposals for a temporary accommodation and to submit a restatement of the principles of a Far Eastern settlement. "At the time and in the light of the subsequent actions of the Japanese it would seem that no serious agreement could have been reached with Japan." The British postmortem concluded smugly that "it was better that the negotiations should end on the comprehensive statement of principle made by the United States government rather than tail off into a wrangle to avoid some inglorious and unworkable compromise."[22]

Once the decision had been taken by the president, no time

was wasted by the U.S. chiefs of staff, who battened down the military hatches and tried to get as many B-17 bombers out to MacArthur as possible before the Japanese attacked. The records of the War and Navy departments confirm that the strategic equation in the Far East—as it was read that Wednesday by the military leadership in Washington—was that war with Japan was now unavoidable and imminent. But so completely had the strategic calculations become hostage to the notion that the Philippines was the front line that little attention was given to the Hawaiian commands. In the flurry of decisions taken to bolster MacArthur before the attack came, the defenses of Pearl Harbor were further stripped to reinforce the Philippines. This was where both logic and intelligence indicated that the Japanese would launch their strike on the United States.

When General Marshall returned to Washington on 27 November from attending army maneuvers, he summoned an emergency conference in his office at 10:30 A.M. The minutes of this Thursday morning meeting show that he specifically warned his staff that the president and secretary of state believed that with the anticipated breakdown of negotiations, Japan "will soon cut loose and attack the Philippines."[23] Without explaining how he knew, the Army chief of staff declared, *"We are familiar with their plans to a certain extent* [emphasis added]." The Army chief of staff chose not to explain what the Japanese plans were or how he knew about them, either then or at the congressional hearings four years later. He directed that MacArthur be sent an "unequivocal" war warning authorizing him to attack threatening convoys and make reconnaissance flights over Formosa—even at the risk of provoking the Japanese. The emergency conference also decided to request that the Navy use its two carriers at Pearl Harbor to ferry two Marine pursuit squadrons to Wake and Midway from Hawaii to protect the upcoming flights of B-17s to the Philippines. It is therefore no small irony that the U.S. Army has to be credited with fortuitously saving the Pacific Fleet's carriers from destruction because they had not returned to Pearl Harbor by 7 December.

Marshall was willing to further reduce the Army's air defense of the Pacific Fleet anchorage even though, he acknowledged, it would run the risk that "there will be nothing left at Hawaii until replacements arrive." His decision is the clearest-cut confirmation that Washington, in the ten days before war broke out, did not consider that a Japanese plan to attack Pearl

Harbor was a serious possibility.[24] That Washington's focus was exclusively—and fatally—focused on an anticipated attack on the Philippines is evident from Roosevelt's cable that same day to High Commissioner Sayre in Manila, which Admiral Hart took as a war warning "straight from the horse's mouth."[25]

The Asiatic Fleet commander had also received orders from Washington to begin unrestricted submarine operations as "soon as formal war eventuates."[26] No such specific warning indicating the imminence of conflict was sent to Admiral Kimmel. But Hart was instructed to coordinate joint operating plans with the British and Dutch because "the situation will be far more complex if hostilities ensue without a formal declaration of war."[27]

The chiefs of the Army and Navy sent a joint advisory to the president advising that "considerable Army and Navy reinforcements have been rushed to the Philippines, but the desirable strength has not yet been reached."[28] MacArthur must have offered up his own prayer for more time on 27 November when he received the dispatch putting him on full war alert. In Washington's estimate it was no longer a question of whether, but when the Philippines would be attacked. This became a matter of urgent and vexing concern in Washington, and the president had to repeatedly remind his cabinet that Japan had to fire the first shot. But with the U.S. commanders in the Philippines ordered to prepare for joint operations with their opposite numbers in Singapore, there was a real possibility of a trigger-happy British fighter pilot preempting the prerogative of Congress to decide when the United States went to war.

"If the British fought we would have to fight," Roosevelt had told his cabinet the previous day. To reconcile this with the constraints of the Constitution, he announced that he intended, in the event that Japan attacked the Malay Peninsula before the Philippines, to appeal to a joint session of Congress to approve armed support of Britain.[29] But the Foreign Office records show that within a week he was to give the British ambassador those guarantees of armed support in advance of the Japanese attack and any appeal to Congress. Indeed, had he been called upon to make good on his commitment to Britain before Japan had attacked Pearl Harbor, it would have been a supreme test of the president's political skill. Getting that vital guarantee of armed support from Roosevelt was what principally preoccupied Churchill, his chiefs of staff, the

Foreign Office, and the British ambassador in Washington for the next ten days.

"How important it is to ensure ourselves of American support in the event of hostilities," Churchill reminded Lord Halifax in a 28 November message that he was instructed convey to the president.[30] To prevent "a melancholy extension of the war" the British ambassador was to ask Roosevelt to consider making a public declaration that "any further Japanese aggression would compel you to place the gravest issues before Congress."[31] The president had already left Washington for his belated Thanksgiving weekend at his retreat of Warm Springs, Georgia, so Halifax had to content himself with meeting the secretary of state the next day to alert him to the latest British intelligence reports that Japanese troop and shipping movements indicated preparations for an invasion of Thailand as a precursor to attacking northern Malaya.

"I am a little bit afraid that the President may hesitate to answer our plain question of whether we can count on the United States support," Halifax noted in his diary that night.[32] While he "felt pretty certain" that they could count on United States armed support, "precisely how quickly I would not pronounce."[33] In his official cable to London he was more optimistic. "Even if the President does not give immediate affirmative answer to our questions and although prophesy is dangerous, I would find it very difficult to believe the United States Government would not very soon support us in the event of hostilities. I know Hull, Stimson and Knox would wish to do so," Halifax assured the prime minister, informing him that Roosevelt was not expected back at the White House until Monday. "The real question to my mind is how quickly the United States would join up."[34] That was the question Churchill had to confront at the war cabinet meeting next day. The Australian government was pressing for "warlike measures" to forestall a Japanese invasion of Thailand, which entailed advancing to the Kra Isthmus, across the border from Malaya. For this United States support was essential, but the Canadian prime minister, William Lyon Mackenzie King, had cabled London warning "in strong terms of the dangers of becoming involved with Japan with no assurance from the United States."[35]

The British prime minister himself was also having second thoughts. He cautioned the War Cabinet that they "must not assume that the outbreak of war between England and Japan would necessarily precipitate the entry of the United States into the war," because "there was a strong party in the United

States who would work up prejudice against being drawn into Britain's war." It was therefore agreed that Britain "would not resist or attempt to forestall a Japanese attack on the Kra Isthmus unless we had a satisfactory assurance from the United States that they would join us should our action cause us to become involved with Japan."[36]

The prime minister decided to tell the Australian government that "United States armed cooperation is so desirable that she should be advised of our intentions." Prime Minister Curtin in Canberra was cabled, "We realize the constitutional difficulties of securing prior undertakings but the United States should at least be asked whether any objections are raised to our proposals."[37] At the same time Churchill directed the British ambassador in Washington to go to the White House to seek answers for an "extremely fluid" situation, which the foreign secretary announced could be resolved only by "an answer from the United States Government which would justify a more forward policy."[38]

The responses obtained by Lord Halifax during an hour-and-a-half lunch meeting with the president and his aide Harry Hopkins that Monday afternoon, while generally positive, were not entirely what Churchill wanted. Roosevelt declined to go along with a request for a parallel declaration with Britain warning Japan about the serious consequences for any incursion into Thailand. But he did agree to question Tokyo about the reason for its latest southward troop movement into Indochina, since, he told Halifax, it was "plain that they were not going there for their health."[39] Rather than giving the assurances Churchill had requested, the president asked what the British government intended to do if an unsatisfactory reply was received and the Japanese sent those troops into Thailand.

The British ambassador reported to Churchill his personal conviction that Roosevelt "would be inclined to support" whatever action was taken by Britain to defend her interest. He cited how the president "spoke all the time of the United States airpower in the Philippines and long distance naval blockade" as the key to dealing with Japan, although he acknowledged that any such action "of course means shooting."[40] The whole tenor of the conversation, according to the ambassador, indicated Roosevelt's recognition that "any of these hypothetical actions [could] be a prelude to some further action and threat to our common interests against which we ought to react together at once."

Halifax reported how Roosevelt had at one point remarked in an aside "that in the case of any direct attack on ourselves or the Dutch, we should obviously all be in it together." He had also assured the ambassador that "we could certainly count on their support, though it might take a short time, he spoke of a few days, to get things into political shape here."[41] The president had given this assurance to the British ambassador in response to Churchill's request, but Roosevelt knew that he could not put the United States on the line with Britain in the Far East without congressional support.

Roosevelt therefore appears to have committed a technical breach of the constitution by giving such clear, although unwritten, indications to the British, which he knew Churchill wanted to interpret as a guarantee of American armed support, in advance of having the approval of the U.S. legislature. The groundwork for this had still to be carefully prepared, because nine months earlier Congress had passed the Lend-Lease bill by a narrow margin. Moreover, it was only after his meeting with Lord Halifax that the president issued instructions to his three closest advisers, the secretaries of state, war, and the navy, to draft a speech for him to deliver on Capitol Hill within three days. He intended this to be couched as a bipartisan appeal to the United States Congress to issue a declaration of support for Britain against a Nazi-like Japanese war of aggression in the Far East.[42]

"I feel pretty clear that if we get into war with Japan we can count on the United States," the British ambassador confided in his diary that night.[43] But Churchill recognized that he still had to move cautiously because a presidential aside across the White House lunch table was a long-way short of a cast-iron written guarantee of United States support endorsed by Congress.

"Our settled policy is not to take forward action in advance of the United States," the prime minister instructed the foreign secretary, after reading Halifax's 2 December telegram from Washington. "If they move, we will move immediately in support. If they do not move we must consider our position," he wrote in a memo to the foreign secretary, noting that in the event of a Japanese attack on Thailand's Kra Isthmus "we should not take forestalling actions without a definite guarantee of United States's support."[44] To make absolutely certain of Roosevelt's agreement, Halifax was cabled with instructions to obtain confirmation that "the President's assurance of armed support" in the event of a Japanese attack on Malaya would also cover "armed support" if Britain proceeded with an operation to intervene in the event of Japanese incursion into Thailand. The president was to be told the British would go ahead only if a similar assurance was received that "we have the armed support of the United States if our action resulted in hostilities with Japan."[45]

Even before the president's confirmation was received, the prime minister, after reviewing Halifax's report at the 4 December war cabinet meeting, announced that Roosevelt's promise of armed support that was implicit in his statement that "we should all be in it together" in the event of an attack on British or Dutch territory was "very satisfactory." Britain now at last had adequate assurances of American support to be able to assure the Dutch that if Japan attacked them first, "we should at once come to their aid and that we had every confidence that the United States would do so also."[46] Instructions were issued to the British commander in chief Far East to prepare to put in motion Operation Matador, the plan to forestall a Japanese attack on the Kra Isthmus, in anticipation that Roosevelt would agree to Britain's request that the United States join Britain in jointly assuring the government of Thailand of their support.

Halifax was also instructed to obtain the president's clarification of the United States' guarantees of support if the British sent troops into Thailand's Kra Isthmus. Roosevelt unhesitatingly confirmed that his assurance of "armed support" for Britain if Japan attacked Malaya meant just that, advising the ambassador to tell the prime minister that the "character of this armed support must be decided by the Staffs." But he was still reluctant to support Churchill's call for simultaneous warnings to Tokyo not to use Indochina "as a base for further aggression," or to support a British intervention in the Kra Isthmus, or to join in a guarantee to the Thai government.[47]

"We are particularly grateful for his confirmation of our interpretation of his assurance of support," the prime minister responded to the president via the British ambassador next day.[48] The critical nature of such official guarantees made it essential for Churchill to employ the formal channel through the British ambassador rather than communicate with the president directly by the private, "Former Navy Person" channel that he had been using to exchange views with Roosevelt. In his cable of 5 December the prime minister instructed Lord Halifax to return to the White House to press Roosevelt to extend the guarantee of support for the proposed Matador plan. Since Britain "cannot technically give the Thais a guarantee of non-aggression," the ambassador was to explain, "we should like therefore to assure them that in the event of attack by Japan we will both help them to the best of our ability."[49] The president was also to be informed that "there was no longer room for hesitation": Britain had to join with the Dutch in a public commitment "to cooperate *immediately* to the fullest extent of its available resources in the event of the other party being forced to take military action to repel an attack on any of its territories in the Far East."[50]

On the morning of 5 December the ambassadorial Rolls-Royce once again made its stately progress down Massachusetts Avenue carrying the poker-faced Lord Halifax to yet another session at the White House, this time to pin down Roosevelt on the issue of Thailand. He succeeded in persuading the president to agree to issue a warning to Japan about any incursion into Thai territory, but only on condition that separate communications be sent to Tokyo by the British and the Dutch within twenty-four hours of the American diplomatic note. "He would prefer the United States to get in on the act first," the British ambassador explained in his report to London. "On account of political considerations here, it was important that their action should be based on independent necessities of United States defense and not appear to follow on ourselves." Roosevelt also told Halifax that he was contemplating sending a direct appeal to the emperor and that the State Department would issue some form of assurance of United States support to the Thai government.[51]

Later that afternoon Halifax had to cable back to London that it was "most annoying," but he had received a telephone call from Assistant Secretary of State Sumner Welles advising him that the president had "changed his mind and wishes to suspend decision about conveying assurance to Thailand." The news that Roosevelt might be having second thoughts may have vexed Churchill, but he nevertheless proceeded on the assumption that it was too late for the president to withdraw the assurance of United States armed support for Britain that had already been secured.

"We have authorized forestalling action at Kra Isthmus if necessary, and are about to assure Dutch that we will help them if attacked," Churchill had already cabled the Australian prime minister, requesting of him, "Please treat President's attitude with utmost secrecy."[52] The British prime minister wasted no time in instructing Lord Halifax to ask the president for clarification of what action Britain should now take regarding Thailand. The ambassador set off for the White House again carrying the RAF report of a Japanese invasion convoy sighted off the Cambodian capes that was apparently heading directly for the Gulf of Thailand.

When shown the sighting reports, Roosevelt told the British ambassador that if the Japanese transports were seen "steering west or south-west across the Gulf of Thailand (Siam), we should obviously attack them, since they must either be going for Thailand or Malaya." Halifax was delighted with this statement and mightily reassured to learn that the president had after all decided to send a message to Bangkok "to the effect that the United States will regard it as a hostile act if the Japanese invade Thailand, Malaya, Burma or the East Indies." But when he was asked directly about whether the United States would support a forestalling British move into the Kra Isthmus, the president became equivocal, declaring that "he would not cross that bridge before we came to it, and that you could not tell exactly how the thing would start."[53] Halifax offered his apologies in his report that he had not been able to obtain from the president clear agreement on the outstanding issues, but his cable was warmly welcomed by the prime minister.

"This removes all political difficulty from initiating Naval or Air action and I agree with the President that 'we should obviously attack Japanese transports in conditions prescribed,'" Churchill memoed to the foreign secretary and the British chiefs of staff at noon in London on 7 December. He asked that the precise wording that Roosevelt had suggested be used in the message of support Britain had to send to Bangkok. Then he drafted yet another cable for Lord Halifax that reiterated "from your recent telegrams we understand we can rely on armed support of the United States if we become involved in hostilities with Japan." So that there should be no mistake, he listed the three circumstances under which the president had already agreed to armed support: "(a) Japanese invasion of Malaya or Netherlands East Indies (b) Action on our part in Kra Isthmus to forestall or repel Japanese landing in that Isthmus (c) Action on our part in Kra Isthmus in event of Japanese encroachment on Thailand by force or threat of force." The British ambassador was then told to approach Roosevelt again for clarification of precise "conditions" for a preemptive British attack on the Japanese invasion convoy before it reached its target.

The reassurance proved unnecessary. As a handwritten note on the cable draft records, it received the prime minister's approval at 8:30 P.M., but "in view of Japanese commencement of hostilities instructions were given to cancel it."[54] This unsent cable together with the exchanges from the British ambassador to the U.S. in the prime minister's confidential file can leave no doubt that Roosevelt by the eve of Japan's attack on Pearl Harbor had given a number of clear, carefully worded assurances of United States "armed support" of Britain in advance of delivering his intended appeal to Congress.[55] What the American records reveal is that Roosevelt gave such unprecedented—and arguably unconstitutional—assurances only after taking steps to render an appeal to the legislature unnecessary. It turns out that he had resorted to a highly questionable ruse to ensure that Japan would simultaneously attack the United States as well. He had given orders for a live fleet of expendable U.S. Navy "warships" to be stationed across the South China Sea to serve as "fishbait" for the Japanese invasion force.

Getting things into "political shape," as the record reveals, had involved Roosevelt in a far more dubious tactic than having an appeal drafted for Congress comparing Japan's aggression to that of Nazi Germany's. After returning from a belated Thanksgiving break at his Warm Springs retreat in Georgia, the president even resorted to subterfuge in order to give the Japanese an irresistible opportunity to fire upon the Stars and Stripes. He instructed Admiral Stark to order the Asiatic Fleet to send out a line of vessels to act as a tripwire across the South China Sea in what was clearly intended as a sacrificial "fishbait" mission.

"The President directs that the following be done," was how the chief of naval operations prefaced his 2 December signal. The phrasing was an indication of Stark's discomfort at having to order Admiral Hart to "charter three small vessels."[56] Roosevelt wanted it made clear that Hart need take only the "minimum requirements to establish identity as U.S. men of war." Filipino crews were to don U.S. Navy uniforms and in expendable craft head out to specific locations that were calculated to put them in harm's way of a Japanese invasion force steaming toward Malaya.

Admiral Hart, who was already sending out air reconnaissance patrols, was not fooled about the true nature of this dubious mission by its characterization as a "defensive information patrol." He could not, however, disobey a presidential directive, and on 3 December, he reluctantly sent the Asiatic Fleet's steam yacht into the danger zone. Two days later Japanese patrol planes buzzed the *Isabel*. But they did not take the bait to precipitate another incident like the one involving the *Panay*, when the bombing of the U.S. Navy gunboat on the Yangtse River in December 1937 had almost brought the two nations to war. To Hart's surprise the *Isabel* returned safely to Cavite on 7 December. Meanwhile the schooners *Molly Moore* and *Lanikai*, under the command of Lieutenant (later Rear Admiral) Kemp Tolley, sailed out on another "fish bait" mission into the Gulf of Thailand.

The news of the attack on Pearl Harbor, which led to the *Lanikai* being recalled, had overtaken Roosevelt's subterfuge. The president could have been badly discredited had his orders for the "fish bait" mission leaked out before the Japanese attack. As it happened, the commitments he had given to the British had almost triggered the secret alliance two days earlier, when the Netherlands High Command in Bandoeng, alarmed at the incursions of Japanese planes over Java and Borneo, prematurely ordered the implementation of the A-2 section of the Rainbow 5 War Plan. This called for joint retaliatory operations by the Royal Australian Air Force and MacArthur's air force in the Philippines. The alarm brought the Australian war council into emergency session after the British chiefs of staff prematurely issued an alert from London that war was imminent.

Lord Halifax had to make a late-night visit to the White House on 5 December to inform the president that "the time has come for immediate cooperation in the Dutch East Indies."[57] When Roosevelt balked at this, the British ambassador had to relay a warning to London that the jittery Dutch must be prevailed upon to rescind their order. This was eventually done, but not until after assurances that the United States was about to enter the war had already been flashed to Singapore. From there they had been relayed to the Asiatic Fleet by Admiral Phillips, who had flown in on 29 November from Colombo in advance of the arrival of his flagship the *Prince of Wales* to assume command of Britain's Far East Fleet. The existence of this secret undertaking to go to the aid of the British and Dutch even if the Japanese did not attack United States territory came as a complete surprise to Admiral Hart, the commander in chief of the Asiatic Fleet.

"Learn from Singapore we have assured Britain of armed support under three or four eventualities," Hart radioed the chief of naval operations in Washington. "Have received no corresponding instructions from you."[58] The Asiatic Fleet commander's communication was taken as evidence of a secretly agreed and unconstitutional Anglo-American defense pact in the Far East when it surfaced at the time of the Pearl Harbor congressional hearings in 1945. The British records show that what had been agreed to at the joint American-British-Dutch staff talks was PLENAP B, which required the cooperation of their respective naval forces in the event of a Japanese attack on all three countries.[59]

It would have been more damaging if the congressional investigating committee had been permitted to examine the conduct of MacArthur's command in the Philippines, because it would have exposed the whole of the Anglo-American deterrent gamble. The verbatim transcripts of the secret conference MacArthur held in Manila after Admiral Phillips had flown down from Singapore on 4 December reveal just how closely Britain and United States plans were enmeshed before war broke out—and how much these plans were based on wishful thinking and high-blown rhetoric rather than reality.

"I have three great defensive lines, the first is on the shore, the second is on the shore, the third is on the shore," MacArthur declared. Wrapping himself in the same rhetoric that Churchill had used in 1940, he vowed to "fight to destruction on the shoreline." Declaring that he had "nothing to fear at all," the general paced the conference room as he confidently predicted that his "ace units" of B-17 bombers would smash the Japanese invasion fleets before they landed. Any enemy forces that managed to get ashore would be mopped up by his dozen light tanks and 125,000-strong army.[60]

Admiral Phillips was so impressed with the picture MacArthur painted of his airpower that the British admiral decided to abandon Singapore for Manila Bay, which was to become "the Scapa Flow of the Far East"—a reference to Britain's North Sea naval bases in the Orkney Islands north of Scotland. This amounted to a reversal of what had already been agreed to in the spring staff talks. Under PLENAP B the Asiatic Fleet was required to head north and operate with the British naval forces from Singapore in the event of an attack on the Philippines. Now the British Far East fleet commander proposed that in the event of war it would be strategically advantageous for the Anglo-American and Dutch naval forces to operate from Cavite, where they could be protected by MacArthur's vaunted airpower.

"Clearly, until you have a fleet you can't do much except act on the defensive," Phillips said, noting that he would wait for more warships before going on the offensive. "It is quite clear that to stick your head out where the enemy is with a very inferior force would be foolish."[61] The surreal nature of the Anglo-American staff conference at Manila abruptly ended on the afternoon of 6 December when RAF reconnaissance reported that a large Japanese task force was headed for Malaya. This sent Phillips flying back to Singapore "to be there when the war starts."[62] Within four days the British Far East Fleet commander was to succumb as a consequence of his pugnacious nature, by ignoring his own warning. Admiral Phillips's disastrous decision to do battle with the Japanese invasion force without the air protection he had told the Americans was so essential was to cost him his life and the lives of over a thousand British sailors when the enemy torpedo bombers found the *Prince of Wales* and the battle cruiser *Repulse* steaming off the Malayan coast.[63]

The assurances that MacArthur gave the British admiral make it difficult to comprehend why the American general failed to deploy his "Ace units" of B-17 bombers after he learned of the attack on Pearl Harbor. Not only was airpower the linchpin on Anglo-American strategy in the Far East, but in contrast to the Hawaiian commanders, MacArthur had received very specific advance warnings that the U.S. forces under his command would be a target for a Japanese attack if war broke out in the Pacific.

7

"SURPRISE AGGRESSIVE
MOVEMENTS IN ANY
DIRECTION"

Imperfect War Warnings from Washington

"This dispatch is to be considered a war warning" was the header on the priority cable sent by the Navy Department to all Pacific commanders on 27 November alerting them that:

> Negotiations with Japan looking toward stabilization of conditions in the Pacific have ceased and an aggressive move by Japan is expected within the next few days. The number and equipment of Japanese troops and the organization of naval task forces indicate an amphibious expedition against either the Philippines, Thai or Kra peninsula or possibly Borneo.[1]

The Pacific Fleet commander, Admiral Kimmel, was directed to "execute an appropriate defensive deployment preparatory to carrying out tasks assigned" in his war plan and to inform the Hawaiian Department's General Short and Admiral Bloch, the commander of the 14th Naval District. Guam and Samoa were also to be advised and directed "to take appropriate measure against sabotage."[2]

Admiral Stark would later claim that as far as the Navy warning was concerned, "we used language which we thought was strong enough to indicate to them that Japan was going to strike."[3] The chief of naval operations, who had agreed on the wording of the war warning with Admiral Turner, his chief of war plans, failed to appreciate the limited intelligence picture available to the Hawaiian commands, which was the context in which the dispatch would be read by Admiral Kimmel. For the third time in two months, the Pacific Fleet commander was confronting a major crisis without any access to the MAGIC diplomatic intercepts, which were indicating just how serious a crisis was brewing this time. Lacking the Purple decrypt of Tokyo's instructions to their Washington embassy, neither Kimmel nor Short were aware of the extent to which the intercepts stressed there would be a serious consequence to Japanese-American relations if a resolution could not be reached by the end of November. Negotiations with the United States had to succeed "otherwise things are automatically going to happen."[4]

While General MacArthur and Admiral Hart, with access to MAGIC, had been able to track the collapse of the negotiations, the Hawaiian commanders had only the information they gleaned from press and radio reports by which to measure the seriousness of the crisis. The only direct indication they received of just how strained relations were came from Ambassador Kunisu who arrived by Pan Am Clipper in Honolulu on 12 November en route to Washington. Before boarding the giant four-engine flying boat in Manila, he had told the press he had "no great hopes for a successful conclusion to negotiations."[5] This pessimistic forecast was corroborated in the letter Stark wrote two days later, which did not reach Kimmel until 24 November. The anxious but equivocal assessment of the chief of naval operations concluded, "what we will do in the Far East remains to be seen."[6] Still more unsettling for Kimmel was the enclosed copy of a memorandum that Stark and Marshall had jointly sent to the president on 5 November urging that "no ultimatum" be sent to Tokyo for at least two months because "war should be avoided while building up defensive forces in the Far East."[7]

This was the first indication Kimmel had received of a strategic tug-of-war going on in Washington between the military and foreign policy makers. Only ten days earlier he had himself written to Stark, bluntly expressing his concern that the diplomatic confrontation with Japan would inevitably lead to a military showdown in the Pacific and urging that "more consideration be given to the needs of the Pacific Fleet."[8] Kimmel was therefore reassured to read that Marshall and Stark had

informed the president that the Pacific Fleet's inferiority relative to the Combined Fleet now prevented "an unlimited strategic offensive."[9] But any hope he may have entertained that
Washington appreciated his view of the strategic equation in
the Pacific was dashed when he learned from hints dropped in
Stark's letters that the military buildup in the Philippines was
part of a deterrent strategy.[10]

The continuing determination of the policy makers in
Washington to postpone a showdown with Japan while at the
same time increasing the strength of MacArthur's armed forces
on Tokyo's doorstep, displayed a dangerous contradiction in
American strategy. According to Kimmel's intelligence officer
Commander Layton, it became a "hot topic" of corridor gossip
at Pacific Fleet headquarters the day after the receipt of a dispatch declaring, "Chances of favorable outcome of negotiations
with Japan very doubtful."[11]

Kimmel was alerted on 24 November to the Navy Department's concern that "*surprise aggressive movements in any direction including attack on the Philippines or Guam is a
possibility* [emphasis added]."[12]

This dispatch went to all Pacific commands. In the absence
of the background to the crisis that could have been supplied
by MAGIC intelligence, however, Kimmel was left in the dark
over what action was appropriate to counter "surprise aggressive movements in any direction." Its value as a warning of
imminent hostilities by Japan was also negated by the requirement that the "utmost secrecy" be observed so as not to "com-
plicate an already tense situation."[13] Not surprisingly, Kimmel
did not find the message sufficiently alarming to take it up
immediately with General Short. That same day Stark expressed his concern about the "gravity of the situation" in another letter to the Pacific Fleet commander, in which he stated
that he would "not be surprised over a Japanese surprise attack." But he did not imply that it would be against Pearl
Harbor, either then or in his 3 December letter, which attempted to distill MAGIC intelligence, but only resulted in pre-
dictions. "I won't go into the pros and cons of what the United
States may do. I will be damned if I know. I wish I did," the
chief of naval operations wrote Kimmel. "From many angles
an attack on the Philippines would be the most embarrassing
thing that could happen to us," he wrote, adding that while he
believed "it was not time for the Japanese to proceed against
Russia," he was anticipating "an advance into Thailand, Indochina, Burma Road area as most likely."[14]

"I was trying to acquaint him with the picture as I saw it and there was a 'possibility' of a surprise attack," was how Stark attempted to explain to the 1944 naval court of inquiry his conflicting and confusing estimates. "I didn't feel at the time that he needed to start using everything he had on a war basis and the word 'possibility' was used advisedly, though I knew the situation was certainly no better, and if anything, deteriorating."[15] Yet he persisted in maintaining that his 24 November dispatch warning of the possibility of "surprise aggressive movements in any direction" ought to have alerted the Pacific Fleet commander to the possibility of an attack on Pearl Harbor.[16] It was indicative of the mindset in Washington that there was a failure to make the distinction between intelligence for strategic, as opposed to tactical, purposes. It is self-evident that the warnings to the theater commanders omitted to take into account that they would be read in the context of the intelligence picture as it was seen locally. Why Stark believed that Kimmel should have drawn that conclusion from his dispatch is not clear, since it listed only potential Japanese targets five thousand miles from Hawaii, on the other side of the Pacific. Kimmel, in both his testimony and his memoirs, argued that it was unreasonable for the chief of naval operations to have expected him to have deduced this from such a vague caution, which was *not* repeated in the 27 November war warning.[17] Washington's alerts served therefore only to reinforce, not recast, the intelligence picture that Kimmel was already receiving from his intelligence officer: the Japanese forces were assembling for strikes in the Far East, but not the mid-Pacific.

"An intelligence officer always has to establish a framework for defining the scope of the strategic picture," Admiral Layton wrote. "Within it he can assemble scattered elements to piece together the overall pattern, rather like a jig-saw puzzle."[18] He fully supported Kimmel's claim that if they had been receiving MAGIC in November, the diplomatic intelligence would have enabled them to make the accurate evaluation of Japanese intentions that had been possible during the July crisis. Not only did the deadlines in the Purple intercepts reveal that Japan was accelerating toward belligerency, but some of the messages did contain intelligence reports from areas of special military interest, including Thailand, Malaya, Singapore, Borneo, the Philippines, and even Hawaii. But the intercepts that contained pointers to Pearl Harbor as a Japanese target had all been overlooked by the analysts in Washington because they had turned their backs on Hawaii that summer to focus on the Philippines.

General Short and Admiral Kimmel were to repeatedly testify that their response to the war warnings would have been very different had they been privy to MAGIC. Whether their intelligence staffs would have been able to pick up the clues that Washington missed is a matter for speculation, but in all probability the Hawaiian commanders would have been at least energized to the general danger by all the alarms that were reverberating in the Purple traffic at the end of November. Like a distant fire alarm sounding from buildings on the other side of town, the threat indicators the Hawaiian command received from Washington directed all attention to the Philippines, Malaya, Borneo, and other possible targets on the far side of the Pacific. Had Stark used the phrase "in any direction" in the war warning, his later claim that Kimmel should have inferred on 27 November that this included Hawaii would have been more persuasive. But the two separate alarms, as they were sent, indicated only that the chief of naval operations anticipated that the conflagration about to be started by the Japanese would erupt thousands of miles to the west of the Hawaiian Islands.

"The phrase 'war warning' cannot be made the catch-all for all the contingencies hindsight may suggest," was how Kimmel answered Stark's wooly claim to have warned of an attack on Pearl Harbor, during his examination before the 1944 naval court of inquiry. The majority agreed with Kimmel that it was unreasonable to expect him to have inferred that the fleet anchorage was a potential target. The war warning of 27 November, with its references to possible Japanese amphibious operations far removed from the Hawaiian Islands, only served to confirm the estimates of the Pacific Fleet intelligence staff that the only possible threat was a raid from the Japanese bases in the Marshall Islands. Kimmel had already proposed to deploy the Pacific Fleet to counter an attack from the southwest, as required by his war plan. With the intelligence available to him, he concluded that "an air attack on Pearl Harbor, or anything else other than a surprise submarine attack was most improbable."[19] There was nothing in the 27 November war warning that caused him or his intelligence staff to think otherwise.

"When I read the dispatch, it gave me a jolt," was the first reaction of the Pacific Fleet intelligence officer to the Navy Department's 27 November war warning.[20] Layton had never seen such a message before, and his first reaction on reading the dispatch was that the targets for attack agreed precisely with his own estimate, which was "the Japanese would continue their push southward and I was apprehensive that they would not risk leaving our Philippine forces on their flank." This was the gist he gave to Admiral Kimmel. "Our initial discussion was brief, because he wanted this message paraphrased and delivered to General Short,"[21] Layton recalled, testifying that he entrusted it to Captain John Bayliss Earle. He had just arrived from 14th Naval District headquarters bearing the War Department warning that had been received some ninety minutes earlier at Fort Shafter.

"This is the same dispatch in substance that we have just received," was how Layton remembered Kimmel's reaction to the War Department warning.[22] It was not so strongly worded as the Navy's, making no mention of war, stating only that "negotiations with Japanese appear to be terminated" and "Japanese future action unpredictable but hostile action possible at any moment." No likely targets for attack were listed, but General Short was advised that prior to hostilities he should "undertake such reconnaissance and other measures as you deem necessary." The dispatch arrived with a "first priority" designation, but any sense of urgency and immediate danger was diluted by its injunction that "United States desires that Japan commit the first overt act." This "should not be construed as restricting a course of action that might jeopardize your defense," the general was told, but whatever measures he did take "should be carried out so as not, repeat not, to alarm the civilian population or disclose intent."[23]

Short responded immediately by putting the troops of the Hawaiian command on the first level of war alert. In contrast to the Navy procedure, which started high and tapered off to Number 3, the Army command had recently revised its order, so that its Number 1 alert called for "defense against acts of sabotage and uprising within the islands, with no threat from without."[24] So in response to his instruction to "report measures taken," General Short informed Washington, thirty minutes after receiving his war warning, that he was "in liaison" with the Navy and that the Hawaiian Department was "alerted to prevent sabotage."[25] Short reasoned that Washington would advise him if they disapproved of the level of his alert, and they did not. Moreover his action was endorsed by a War Department dispatch received by his intelligence officer, warning, "Acts of sabotage and espionage probable,"[26] and the adjutant general the next day also advised, "Critical situation demands all precautions be taken immediately against subversive activities."[27]

"The danger of sabotage was paramount in my mind, and seemed to me the chief danger which the War Department feared," was how General Short justified his decision not to go to a higher level alert that would meet a possible external air raid.[28] During the next ten days, therefore, every effort was made to adhere to the order "not to alarm civil population." Antisabotage measures were confined to the Army bases and airfields, where planes were grouped to make them easier to guard. Antiaircraft batteries were not manned round the clock and ammunition for the guns was kept locked in the bunkers.[29] The warning Short had received from Washington indicated no external threat, and even the Army chief of staff, General Marshall, later conceded that the measures Short had taken against sabotage were based on a "reasonable" assumption. It was only with the advantage of hindsight, testified the Army chief of staff, that he reproached himself. "That was my chance to intervene and I did not do it,"[30] Marshall allowed, in an implicit acceptance that he, too, carried a measure of responsibility for the low level of the alert. This, however, was not accepted by the secretary of war.

"The fact is that it presented *with the utmost precision* the situation with which we were all confronted," Secretary Stimson told Congress in 1945, with a certainty that contradicted the testimony of the chief of staff. The Army war alert, the former secretary of war declared, had been worded to reflect a situation that was "delicate and critical" because "we did not want to precipitate war." In contrast to Marshall, he contended that Short had not exercised the "judgment and skill" commensurate with an officer who "had been placed in these high posts of command."[31] Yet even with the benefit of MAGIC intelligence, which the secretary of war testified he had mistakenly believed was reaching the Hawaiian command, his assertion was demonstrably wrong. Stimson's stand on the sufficiency of the war warning appears to have been influenced by the report he received from Henry C. Clausen, a wartime major in the Judge Advocate General's Department who had been assistant recorder to the three-month-long Army Pearl Harbor board in 1944. This former trial lawyer had been appointed by the secretary of war to conduct a one-man investigation of "potential errors" in the Army Pearl Harbor board, which had censured General Marshall for not forwarding critical MAGIC intelligence to the Hawaiian departments.

"With a modicum of intelligence and enough business acumen to run a small cigar store, the disaster at Pearl Harbor could have been avoided," Clausen peremptorily asserted in his coauthored memoir, *Pearl Harbor: Final Judgement*, which was published shortly before his death, in December 1992.[32] "Most definitely there was no reason why the Japanese attack should have been a surprise," Clausen stated at the conclusion of a colorful and often self-congratulatory personal account of his mission, which had been to clear Marshall of the charges made by the U.S. Army board.

That Clausen may have relied too heavily on his legalistic talents as a courtroom advocate, rather than make a careful and impartial weighing of the historical facts, is evident in the fact that he made no secret, as an army officer, of his partisan distaste for naval officers in general and intelligence officers, such as Layton, in particular.[33] In an account that indicates that he distrusted the testimony of anyone who was not a fellow Freemason, Clausen concluded that "the most important factor in the disaster of Pearl Harbor" was Kimmel's "criminal neglect of duty." The "neglect" was Kimmel's failure to inform the Hawaiian Department that the main force of Japanese carriers could not be located during the first week of December.[34]

Admiral Kimmel maintained that this was intelligence of purely naval concern and that it would not have conveyed anything of importance to the Army command. Clausen, however, provides no justification for his assumption that General Short's G-2 intelligence section might somehow have been able to divine from the fact that some of the Japanese carriers could not be located that they were bearing down to attack Pearl Harbor. How this deduction could have been drawn by the G-2 staff at Fort Shafter when the best analysts at Pearl Harbor failed to make that deduction is not explained. Clausen, nonetheless, holds this as another instance that supports his contention that the second-most important factor in bringing about the disaster was that General Short "allowed Kimmel to lead him around by the nose."[35] This assertion has as little historical foundation as Clausen's contention that the two Hawaiian commanders never liaised. The record showed that the two met on 28 November, and there were also subsequent Army-Navy staff meetings.[36]

"We arrived at the conclusion at this and succeeding conferences that the possible Japanese actions would be confined to the Far East and Thailand most probably, and Malaya, the Netherlands East Indies and the Philippines the next most probable objectives in the order named," was how Kimmel recalled his meeting with Short to the Naval court of inquiry. "In general, we arrived at the conclusion that no immediate activity beyond possible sabotage was to be expected in Hawaii."[37] His estimate that the threat to Pearl Harbor was minimal was reinforced by the order he had received from Washington to use his carriers to ship fighter reinforcements to Wake and Midway. Since the ferrying mission would take the carriers away from the Pacific Fleet base for more than a week, in addition to drastically reducing the number of fighters available to defend Oahu, he, not unreasonably, assumed that "no attack on Pearl Harbor could be expected in the immediate future." Admiral Kimmel did, however, take advantage of the two missions by having the carrier planes conduct extensive air patrols of the southwestern approaches to the Hawaiian Islands, the one sector where a Japanese strike might uncoil, from their base at Jaluit in the Marshall Islands.

The *Enterprise*, under Rear Admiral William F. Halsey's Task Force 8, sailed from Pearl Harbor on Friday, 28 November, for Wake, where a squadron of Marine Corps fighters were flown in to beef up the defenses of the island. Its landing strips had become a critically important way station for the B-17 bombers being flown on their air route across the Pacific to reinforce the Philippines. As soon as he left Hawaiian waters, Halsey dispensed with the slow battleship force, so that his carrier task force could make their best speed to Wake. Because he was heading into waters in which hostilities might erupt at any moment, he ordered his captain to have their ships "operating at war conditions," with torpedoes and bombs armed. They were "to regard any submarine seen as hostile and sink them . . . [and] shoot down any plane seen in the air . . . not known to be one of our own."[38]

Halsey's belligerent order anticipated that Japanese submarines were the immediate danger to the Pacific Fleet. That morning he had issued a fleet directive calling for all captains to exercise extreme vigilance and to "depth bomb all contacts expected to be hostile in the fleet operating areas."[39] The following week when the *Lexington*, the Pacific Fleet's remaining carrier, sailed with Task Force 12 to ferry fighter planes, Rear Admiral John H. Newton also dispensed with the escorting battle force. It returned to Pearl Harbor, where it was considered safer from submarines and well protected from air attack by the army fighters and antiaircraft batteries ringing the naval base.

The order that stripped Pearl Harbor of part of its air defenses and dispatched the Pacific Fleet carriers on a ferrying mission was a significant factor in persuading both the 1944 Army and Navy Pearl Harbor boards that Admiral Stark and General Marshall bore a full measure of responsibility for the disaster. Their culpability was not entirely concealed by the smoke screen puffed up in Washington in 1945 by the wartime chiefs of staff, in an attempt to absolve themselves and their subordinates from any blame. The recent attempt by Clausen to exhume Stimson's invocation of a doctrine of absolute military responsibility, with the claim that Short and Kimmel were sentries on guard duty, begs the question of the inadequate orders given them by Washington.

It was the War and Navy departments who were responsible for depriving the Hawaiian commands of adequate air defense and long-range air reconnaissance. The "sentries" were not only ill-equipped, but also denied the intelligence from MAGIC that was essential for the effective discharge of their duty. It must be remembered that the United States was *not* at war on 7 December and the warnings the Hawaiian commanders received from Washington alerted them only to the possibility of Japanese attacks thousands of miles away from Pearl Harbor. Stimson, however, was not the only Washington principal who resorted to the sentry argument to duck his responsibility for the blunders that opened the door for the Japanese to attack Hawaii. Senior officers in the Navy Department also found it convenient to make the comparison when their turn came to testify before the congressional inquiry committee.

"We expected all military services and outlying detachments to act in every way as if we were actually at war except for making attacks on the enemy, if encountered or initiating movements against enemy forces," declared Admiral Turner.[40] As director of war plans and the Navy Department's chief strategist, the overbearing Turner carried more blame than any other Navy Department officer for the imperious attempt to control the interpretation and dissemination of intelligence. His campaign had resulted in bitter internecine turf-fighting in the Navy Department, but he disclaimed any responsibility for the ambiguities of the Navy's war warning, even though he had drafted it for Stark and specifically predicted Japanese attacks would be confined to the western Pacific. Turner, therefore, shared with Stark and Marshall the major burden of responsibility for neglecting one of the cardinal rules of intelligence: Warnings to field commanders are always read and acted upon within the local context.

A telling example of how the different viewpoints of Washington and Pearl Harbor determined their different interpretations of intelligence came when the first piece of MAGIC in four months reached the Pacific Fleet on 28 November. It was the so-called "Winds" execute code setup by which the Japanese embassies and consulates were to be posted of developments in the event of a breakdown in communications. The instructions for the word code had been intercepted by the Americans on 19 November in a cable that established a series of messages to be inserted into the daily weather forecast. Tokyo Radio would broadcast that there was a "danger of cutting off our diplomatic relations," according to a prearranged sequence.

1. Japan-U.S. relations in danger: *HIGASHI NO KAZE AME* (EAST WIND RAIN)
2. Japan-U.S.S.R. relations in danger: *KITA NO KAZE KUMORI* (NORTH WIND CLOUDY)
3. Japan-British relations in danger: *NISHI NO KAZE HARE* (WEST WIND CLEAR)

The British had also intercepted the "Winds" code setup and passed on to the Americans the same country-pair designators, which had been transmitted by the Tokyo Foreign Ministry in a more abbreviated form in a 28 November cable addressed to their legations in South America. Since translations of both sets of instructions became available in Washington on the day that Tokyo's 29 November negotiating deadline expired, the assumption was made that an "East Wind Rain" broadcast would amount to Japan's declaration of war on the United States. Prompt cards with the three sentences of the alert in Japanese and English were produced. They were circulated to all Navy and Army radio operators at the intercept stations, who were directed to pay special attention to the daily news bulletins broadcast by Tokyo on the short wavelength. Teletype traffic from the listening posts to the War and Navy department signals intelligence units soared as false alarms flooded in during the first week of December, none of which was found to coincide with the precise "East Wind Rain" wording. On 4 December the U.S. consul in Batavia and the

U.S. Army liaison officer in Bandoeng reported separately to Washington that the Dutch East Indies headquarters had intercepted a genuine "winds execute" message.[41]

Postwar analysis of surviving records failed to produce any confirmation that a genuine execute was ever transmitted or picked up. But a major controversy was to erupt during the congressional hearings following claims that an "East Wind Rain" alert had been received in Washington and had later been destroyed. The hunt for the "missing" *Higashi No Kaze Ame* intercept sparked a furious wild-goose chase that conveniently, for the Navy Department, lured congressional investigators away from examining the more important issue of what intelligence was contained in the intercepts the U.S. Navy made of signals transmitted in the cypher systems that remained for the most part unread before the attack on Pearl Harbor. "East Wind Rain" continued to distract some postwar revisionist historians who were fixated in their belief that the "missing" report of the broadcast would be the proverbial smoking gun that proved that Roosevelt knew of the Japanese attack and deliberately withheld the war warning from the Hawaiian commanders. (See Appendix II.)

The MAGIC containing the "Winds" code instructions, while not a war warning per se, was sent to Pearl Harbor, where it provided the Pacific Fleet intelligence staff with their first direct intelligence of just how close to the brink of hostilities the United States' relations with Japan were. Admiral Kimmel was later criticized for not sharing the setup with General Short, who testified that he could not remember having seen a specific "East Wind Rain" alert. But Colonel Kendall J. Fielder, the Army G-2 (intelligence) chief at Fort Shafter, stated in his testimony that he had learned of it on 5 December from a War Department dispatch instructing him to "contact commander Rochefort immediately thru commandant fourteen naval district regarding broadcasts from Tokyo reference weather."[42] Without access to the current MAGIC intercepts, which illuminated the precarious state of American-Japanese relations, the "Winds" code intercept just did not have the same significance as a warning that war was imminent for the Hawaiian commanders as had been assumed in Washington.

Putting the clock back and rerunning historical scenarios can never provide conclusive proof that events would have taken a different turn had more accurate information been available to the decision makers. But the contents of the original intercepts of the Purple traffic does lend credence to

Kimmel's contention that "knowledge of these intercepted Japanese dispatches would have radically changed the estimate of the situation made by me and my staff."[43] If Kimmel had known how close Japanese-American relations were to the breaking point, he said, he "would have rejected the Navy Department's suggestion to send carriers to Wake and Midway." MAGIC would have provided him the intelligence that he said would have prompted him to immediately order the recall of the Pacific Fleet's third carrier, *Saratoga*, from the West Coast, where she had been sent for an overhaul.[44]

Lack of access to diplomatic intelligence, as Kimmel and Layton argued persuasively, left them less prepared than they would have been had they received MAGIC to anticipate or counter the Japanese attack on Pearl Harbor. Not one of the thousands of intercepted and translated Purple messages contained any direct reference to Japan's intentions to attack Pearl Harbor, but Kimmel would later testify that if he had had the intelligence available in Washington that he was denied, he might have been able to spring an "ambush on the Japanese force as it approached Hawaii."[45] He did not explain how he would have been able to achieve this with the Pacific Fleet at a three-to-one disadvantage in carrier airpower. The odds were that he would have suffered an even greater disaster than that which overtook him on 7 December 1941. But Kimmel believed he would not have suffered the ignominy of being taken by surprise.

It is more likely that access to MAGIC intelligence might have raised the level of the alert at the Hawaiian commands, because it would have made them more aware of Japan's rapid march toward hostilities. Therefore, it would have been less likely that the Pacific Fleet could have been caught so totally by surprise with all air and antiaircraft defenses down. Just how close war was approaching only started to become evident at Pacific Fleet headquarters on 1 December when Kimmel received an alert relayed from British headquarters in Singapore that "Japan will commence military operations on 1 December against the Kra Isthmus."[46]

On the same day, in addition to the "Winds" code, a third piece of MAGIC intelligence was received at Pearl Harbor from CAST, the U.S. Navy code-breaking station in the Philippines. It was a report of an intercept from Japan's embassy in the Thai capital, which stated, "Absolutely reliable agent in Bangkok reports that on 29th conferences were in progress considering plans to force the British to attack Thai at Padang base near Singora as counter move to landing at Kota Bharu."[47] This was yet another indicator that Japan intended to provoke a preemptive occupation of the neck of the Malayan peninsula. The report from CAST also confirmed the disappearance from the Japanese naval radio traffic of the call signs of their main force of carriers. This latter intelligence was a greater cause for concern at Pacific Fleet headquarters than the possible attack on Malaya.

"What! You don't know where the carriers are?" Admiral Kimmel demanded at his 2 December morning briefing by his fleet intelligence officer on the disposition of the Japanese. Layton presented his chart displaying the estimated positions of the combat fleet units. He routinely updated it daily, on the basis of information he received from the naval code-breaking unit at Pearl Harbor, which was code-named HYPO. Commander Rochefort was in charge of what was known as the Combat Intelligence Unit to disguise true function, which included some of the best code breakers and communications analysts in the Navy. It was their task to analyze the intercepted radio traffic direction-finding data, and the intelligence reports received from the military and naval attachés at U.S. embassies and consulates. But when HYPO's analysts for ten days failed to detect any of the radio call signs identified with the main force of Japanese carriers, Layton had noted against three of the five Combined Fleet carrier divisions: "Unknown—Home Waters."[48]

The commander in chief asked his intelligence officer to explain why he was so uncertain about the whereabouts of the most important units of the Japanese fleet. Layton said that while Rochefort believed that analysis of the radio traffic indicated that at least part of Carrier Division 3 was heading for the Marshalls, there was no reliable indication of their precise location. He explained that HYPO's best estimate was that they were in "home waters, probably in the vicinity of the Kure Naval Base." Kimmel's reaction to this uncertainty was part of the memorable—and frequently misinterpreted—exchange that Layton would later recall for the congressional hearings.

"Then you don't really know where Carrier Division 1 and Carrier Division 2 are?"

"No, sir, I do not. I think they are in home waters, but I do not know for sure where they are. But I feel pretty confident of the location of the rest of the units."

"Do you mean to say they could be rounding Diamond Head and you wouldn't know it?"

"I hope they would have been spotted before now."[49]

The exchange was to become one of the most quoted epitaphs on the Pearl Harbor disaster. Critics of the Pacific Fleet commander read an element of levity and even sarcasm into his words. But Layton explained in his memoir that Kimmel was in deadly earnest and that he often employed irony when he wished to drive home an important point.[50] It shows that Kimmel was weighing the options available to him in the context of the time required for their implementation. Layton acknowledged that his own response seemed lame, but that it highlighted the one major piece that could not be located when he assembled the intelligence jigsaw puzzle for the Pacific Fleet in the week before war broke out. He emphasized, however, that apart from the "missing carriers," the estimate of Japanese naval dispositions that he and Rochefort had pieced together proved to be a remarkably accurate *strategic* picture of Japan's intentions and naval dispositions. It was their *tactical* estimate that was fatally flawed, because they had not been able to pinpoint with any certainty the location of the two carrier divisions, which would have indicated the part of the Pacific into which the Combined Fleet was concentrating its major striking power.

The difficulty of locating the carriers had been compounded when new Combined Fleet call signs came into effect on 1 December. HYPO's analysis of the radio traffic identified only two of the five Japanese carrier divisions—but only in a negative sense. This was possible because of the rigid pattern in which the Japanese organized their naval communication networks. Each fleet communicated on a distinct radio circuit, which Layton compared to "a mother hen" that kept its "chickens" under its radio "wing."[51] The assumption was that even if the "mother hen" did not turn up in the intercepted radio traffic, then the call signs of her "chickens" would indicate her presence. This led to the mistaken estimate that at least one and probably two Japanese carrier divisions were in the 2nd Fleet, which intelligence reports, including radio direction-finding analysis, indicated was concentrating for a southward operation.

The dramatic increase in radio traffic on the 2nd Fleet circuits was, however, commensurate with a concentration for a southward movement. This had been corroborated by sighting reports from the captains of merchant ships who reported

Japanese troopships heading south from Shanghai in the first part of November. This movement and "heavy concentrations" of naval units in the radio traffic lead Rochefort to report to Layton on 23 November that "CARDIV 3 definitely associated with 2nd Fleet operations."[52] During the latter part of November, so many signals were being exchanged between 2nd Fleet and bases in Formosa, Hainan, and Indochina that HYPO's analysts believed that the fleet "will comprise a good portion of the [Japanese] navy."[53] Confirmation had also been received from CAST at Cavite that one of these forces, spearheaded by a substantial submarine force, was heading for the Marshalls and the Carolines. The island chains in the western Pacific, which had been mandated to Japan after World War I, were the obvious jumping-off point for an offensive against American bases in the Pacific. A carrier task force in the more westerly Carolines could also cover the flank of an invasion fleet that was concentrating in the ports of Indochina and Hainan for an advance toward Malaya, the Philippines, or the Dutch East Indies.

Contrary to the myth of a large-scale deception operation mounted by the Japanese, Layton explained that the erroneous conclusions he reached with Rochefort about the whereabouts of the Combined Fleet carrier divisions were genuine mistakes resulting from the lack of firm information. He discounts the effort made by some senior officers in Washington to discredit Rochefort by giving credence to the deception claim in a secret report titled *Black Magic in Communications* that was circulated in the Navy Department in the spring of 1942.[54]

"Did the Japanese Paint Us a Picture?" was the title of the section that claimed that HYPO had been taken in by fake radio call signs intended to disguise the whereabouts of the Combined Fleet carriers. "The Japs did not even attempt deception," was how Rochefort angrily responded to the charge. "There was plenty of deception out here, but it was all self-deception."[55] In his testimony and later memoir, Layton detailed how the errors made on the dispositions of the carrier divisions were not the result of deliberate Japanese deception but were the result of the U.S. Navy not being able to read the JN-25 fleet code and therefore having to rely too greatly on analysis of radio traffic.

The process of traffic analysis, as Layton stated, by its very nature was "inconclusive, sometimes contradictory and very often incomplete."[56] He detailed how in the final weeks before war broke out in the Pacific the estimates of Japanese naval dispositions that he and Rochefort were making were strongly influenced by their growing conviction that the Combined Fleet's strength was being concentrated solely on the southward movement. The reports of invasion forces assembling to attack Malaya and the Dutch East Indies convinced Layton that Japan was also preparing to strike against the Philippines. He knew Admiral Yamamoto was a careful strategist, and Layton had often played cards with him when Layton served as U.S. naval attaché in Tokyo in 1938. He therefore believed that the Combined Fleet command in chief would be reluctant to leave his flank exposed to U.S. counterattack. That is why Layton calculated that Yamamoto would send a strong carrier force to the Marshalls, where it could stand guard and also launch a strike against the Pacific Fleet.[57]

Given the information available at the time, the conclusions reached by Layton and the HYPO analysts were entirely logical. They also assumed that at least some of the Japanese carrier divisions would be allocated to the defense of the home islands. "Had these carriers or carrier divisions or the carrier commanders-in-chief been addressed in any messages of the thousands and thousands that came out from the Naval General Staff, regardless of the silence of the carriers, then the thought of radio silence would have been paramount," Layton told the congressional investigating committee.[58] Since two of the three unplaced Japanese carrier forces were not addressed as such—even once—by Combined Fleet headquarters in radio traffic, this persuaded Rochefort that they must be in touch by landline at their home anchorage, guarding against a possible attack from the Pacific Fleet.

"The fact that service calls lasted for only one month indicates an additional progressive step for active operations on a large scale," Rochefort noted on the change in Japanese warship call signs, in his summary report on radio intelligence, on 1 December.[59] According to Layton, Kimmel had underlined that sentence at the Monday morning staff conference when he discussed his own concern that a powerful carrier striking force might be assembling at Jaluit in the Marshall Islands, just over two thousand miles to the southwest of Pearl Harbor. This possibility of an enemy carrier raid from the Mandated Islands had been foreseen in his War Plan 46, which in the event of war required the Pacific Fleet to "prepare to capture and establish control over Caroline and Marshall islands area, and to establish an advance base at Truk."[60] For months Layton had been gathering information on the Japanese bases in the

Marshalls, which Kimmel incorporated into the running estimate of his action memorandum, "Steps to Be Taken in Case
of American-Japanese War Within the Next 24 Hours."[61]

So essential was it for Kimmel to know precisely what
Japanese forces were heading for Jaluit that the previous week
the Navy Department had arranged with the Army for a
high-level reconnaissance mission by specially modified B-24
bombers. They would fly over the Marshalls from Wake taking
photographs, which Layton arranged would also cover the islands of Ponape and Truk.[62] The long-range bombers assigned
to carry out the mission were not scheduled to arrive in
Hawaii until 5 December. In the interim Kimmel had to make
his plans based on the radio intelligence estimate of a major
concentration of Japanese forces taking place at their base in
Jaluit atoll—and that this was the principal threat to Pearl
Harbor in the event of war breaking out.

The Pacific Fleet command was therefore focusing its attention on a potential enemy threat developing to the southwest
of the Hawaiian chain. So when Kimmel began to receive selected MAGIC information again at the end of November, nothing in it indicated that there was any direct threat to the
Pacific Fleet. The information he received from the Purple diplomatic intercepts only served to confirm Layton's estimates
that the main focus of the Japanese operations would be in the
South China Sea with a lesser buildup in the Marshalls. He
remained in the dark about the actual origin and true significance of Purple until a reference to the code popped up in
a dispatch received on 3 December summarizing two more
MAGICs, which revealed Tokyo had ordered a number of its
embassies to destroy their codes and secret papers. The first
identified the legations as "Hong Kong, Singapore, Batavia,
Manila, Washington and London."[63] Confirmation was provided by a second decrypt supplied by the British that actually
referred to the destruction of the Purple machines at these
embassies.[64]

"What is Purple?" Kimmel asked his fleet intelligence officer after reading the dispatches. To answer him, Layton
consulted Lieutenant Herbert M. Coleman, the fleet security
officer who had recently returned from Washington. His description of Purple as "electrical coding machines" confirmed
Layton's assessment that the Japanese must be destroying
their encrypting devices because they were preparing for "any
and all eventualities."[65] It was standard security practice for
a nation on the brink of belligerency to destroy all its codes

and ciphers in the countries whose territory was to be attacked. These "codes-destruct" MAGICs, as they came to be called, superseded the "Winds" code setup as the clearest indication yet that Japan was about to go to war. Yet when they were evaluated by Layton in the context of the intelligence picture of the major concentration of Japanese forces five thousand miles away, there was no reason for him or Kimmel to revise their estimate that the possible immediate threats to Pearl Harbor were a raid from the Marshalls, a submarine attack, or sabotage.[66]

Admiral Kimmel testified that he did not see any reason to pass on to General Short this important piece of intelligence concerning Japanese code destruction. The Pacific Fleet commander was to be severely criticized by the congressional investigating committee for not immediately advising the Hawaiian Department commander that the Japanese were destroying their codes. This was the result of Short's having testified that he would have immediately raised the level of the Army's alert had he been told of "the fact that they had ordered their code machines destroyed . . . because to us that means just one thing—that they are going into an entirely new phase and that they want to be perfectly sure that the code will not be broken for a minimum time, say of three or four days."[67]

This omission by the Pacific Fleet commander was to be magnified by hindsight into such a glaring failure that Congress considered it "inexcusable." But despite General Short's assertions after the event, it is by no means certain that he would have reacted any differently than Kimmel to the codes-destruct MAGICs. The Pacific Fleet had not gone to a higher alert because this additional evidence that Japan was on the brink of war had not increased the threat of an immediate attack on the Hawaiian Islands. Japan's military and naval buildup was clearly focused on British, American, and Dutch territories five thousand miles away and long-range air reconnaissance would give early warning of any enemy task force from the Marshalls. The precautions against submarine attacks were the Navy's concern, and guarding against sabotage was an Army responsibility.

The estimates of probable Japanese action in the event of hostilities breaking out in the Pacific were reinforced in Kimmel's mind by Rochefort's 4 December estimate. Based on analysis of Combined Fleet radio traffic, he reported that "the large number of high-precedence messages and general distribution might indicate that the entire [Japanese] navy is being prepared for action."[68] Layton therefore advised Kimmel that the main Japanese invasion forces had evidently sailed from the ports of Formosa and Indochina and were observing radio silence as they steamed toward Thailand, Malaya, and Borneo. Radio intelligence and long-range air patrols to the southwest revealed no indications of any immediate threat developing toward Hawaiian waters from the Marshalls. So Kimmel permitted the *Lexington* task force to sail the next morning, to ferry fighter reinforcements to Midway, which he testified he would not have agreed to if he had suspected an imminent attack on Pearl Harbor. The cruisers of Task Force 5 also put out that Friday for a patrol sweep out to Johnston Island, to cover the sector threatened by any Japanese carriers in the Marshalls.

The tactical overview of probable Japanese naval operations was not altered when Pacific Fleet Headquarters was copied with a dispatch from the chief of naval operations on Thursday evening instructing Guam and Samoa to "destroy all secret and confidential publications and other classified matter which is necessary for current purposes and special intelligence."[69] These isolated naval outposts were on islands thousands of miles away and were technically under the operational command of the Asiatic Fleet. But Kimmel might well have attached more significance to the orders and realized that the outbreak of war was closer at hand if he had been copied with the instructions that the Navy Department had simultaneously sent out to U.S. naval attachés in Tokyo, Peiping, Shanghai, and Tientsin. They were ordered to report the destruction of their codes and confidential documents by radioing confirmation in plain language using the words "JABBERWOK" and "BOOMERANG."[70] But by copying only the Asiatic Fleet commander with these messages, Washington again deprived the Pacific Fleet command of the larger context for the Guam/Samoa signal and the 6 December order to these outlying island bases to destroy "secret and confidential documents now or later under conditions of greater emergency."[71]

Kimmel was to be faulted for not appreciating the significance of the Navy Department's codes-destruct orders. He had already put his command on the first-level war alert, and the new information did not imply any need to raise it by indicating a direct threat to Hawaii. It has to be remembered that he interpreted them in the context of the repeated warnings he had received from Washington that led him to expect the war would break out with Japanese attacks in the Far East,

not the central Pacific. None of the MAGICs that he received
indicated that the Japanese consulate in Honolulu had been
ordered to destroy its codes too.

The only indication that the Pacific Fleet commander received that Tokyo's diplomatic outpost on Oahu was also destroying its codes did not reach him until 6 December from
Captain Irving Mayfield. The 14th Naval District intelligence
officer had received the information from Robert Shivers, the
head of the Honolulu FBI, which had tapped the telephone line
of the cook at the Japanese consulate. Mayfield immediately
reported to Rochefort that "the Consul General was burning
and destroying all his important papers."[72] Rochefort in turn
informed Layton at the same time that Saturday afternoon as
the 14th Naval District commander, Admiral Bloch, reported
it to Washington.[73] Layton did not regard the news as particularly significant, however, because, as Kimmel was to explain,"such reports had been made three or four times in the
course of the year."[74] Despite his later testimony that the destruction of codes meant war, General Short also did not react
with alarm when he learned of the burning of documents at
the Japanese consulate.[75]

The significance of the Honolulu code burning was lost on
the Hawaiian commands because they had not been supplied
with the full diplomatic intelligence picture that had been provided by MAGIC. Had the Pacific Fleet intelligence staff been
provided with the MAGIC intercepts revealing that the Japanese consulate was keeping Tokyo informed of very detailed
shipping movements in the fleet anchorage—which had been
available for a month in Washington—the importance of the
FBI reports might not have been dismissed. This was also what
happened to the report of a suspicious telephone call received
on Friday by Mrs. Mori, the wife of a dentist in Honolulu. She
was a stringer for a Japanese press agency and already under
FBI surveillance. The tap on her telephone revealed a transpacific telephone discussion with a newspaper reporter in Tokyo that was ostensibly about what flowers were in bloom
and the weather. But in addition to mentions of hibiscus and
poinsettias, the caller wanted to know such unhorticultural
information as what warships were in the harbor, whether airplanes made daily flights over Oahu, and if the naval base
was equipped with searchlights.[76] The very high cost of the
extended telephone call convinced the FBI that Mrs. Mori was
an undercover agent using floral code words to report on the
activities at Pearl Harbor.

Captain Mayfield, however, found "there was nothing in the message in line with previous information indicating Japanese movement." He concluded that the FBI was probably being unduly jumpy when he telephoned Layton. They concluded that the FBI report was not urgent enough to justify a meeting on Saturday evening, and they agreed to discuss the transcript the next day.[77] Colonel George W. Bicknell, Short's assistant G-2 intelligence officer, who also received a call from Shivers that same afternoon, decided that the phone call was sufficiently suspicious to rate immediate attention. Bicknell himself drove down to FBI headquarters in Honolulu and persuaded his chief, Colonel Kendall J. Fielder, to delay Short's departure for a dinner engagement so that he could read the report. After a brief discussion on the porch of the general's quarters, Short decided he was unable to "make heads nor tails of it." He was later to testify that although the Mori telephone exchanges appeared "very fishy," he concluded at the time that it was "nothing very much to get excited about."[78]

Once again the local intelligence did not fit the picture the Hawaiian Department had been given of war erupting on the other side of the Pacific. Short's conviction that it was British or Dutch territory in the Far East that would be attacked had been reinforced the previous day by the War Department's relay of the gist of the false alarm of 5 December, when the Netherlands Far East command had prematurely invoked the secretly agreed-on Allied plan that would have the Australians and Americans commencing reconnaissance flights over Japanese-held territory.[79] This message, like codes-destruct MAGICs, did nothing to alter the expectation at the Hawaiian commands that the islands were safely distant from impending Japanese attack.

All the intelligence received at Pacific Fleet headquarters by 6 December indicated that the South China Sea was about to explode as the cockpit of war. The overall correctness of this intelligence estimate appeared vindicated when confirmation was received from the commander of the Asiatic Fleet that a "25-ship convoy with an escort of 6 cruisers and 10 destroyers" had been sighted steaming south from the southernmost tip of Indochina.[80] Not far behind was another convoy of "10 ships with 2 cruisers and 10 destroyers" also on a southwesterly course making twelve knots. Thirty more Japanese transports and a large cruiser had been reported in Camranh Bay. Admiral Hart, from Asiatic Fleet headquarters in Manila, predicted that "all forces will make for Khotron" on the Isthmus of Kra, which marked the frontier between Siam and British Malaya.[81] A quick calculation by Layton confirmed that if the Japanese convoys maintained their present course and speed, the invasion forces would hit the landing beaches early the following day, which was when he concluded that war would erupt in the Far East.

Layton advised Kimmel that since Japan's objective was to get the oil in the Dutch East Indies, it was his conviction that they would also attack the Philippines, because they would be reluctant to leave their flank of seaborne communications vulnerable to an American counterattack. Following the briefing, Kimmel called an emergency meeting of the Pacific Fleet staff to review the situation. He sent his intelligence officer to present his analysis to Admiral Pye, the Battle Force commander.

"Oh, no. The Japanese won't attack us, we're too strong and powerful"[82] was the reception that Layton received from the admiral and his staff aboard the *California,* moored in majestic isolation at the head of "Battleship Row" off Ford Island. When Layton returned to report this response to Kimmel, he snorted. After reviewing the advisability of ordering the Battle Force to sea, he decided against it. Not, according to Layton, because he worried about a possible surprise air raid, but because he wanted the fleet to be ready for launching the immediate attack on Japanese bases in the Marshalls ordered in his war plan.

According to Layton, it was Pye's refusal to accept that hostilities were imminent that tipped the decision against sending the battleships to sea until the carriers returned to provide air cover. Sending the fleet to sea over a weekend would also have raised an alarm, which the Hawaiian commanders had been specifically cautioned against by Washington. So the battleships, moored against their line of white-painted dolphins offshore from Ford Island in the center of the vast sweep of Pearl Harbor, remained at only the lowest level of alert against sabotage. Ports and watertight doors were open to the cooling trade winds, and boiler rooms maintained only sufficient steam pressure to run auxiliary machinery. Crew members not scheduled to be on watch spent Saturday evening ashore, and the annual "Battle of the Bands" music-fest took place at the newly completed fleet entertainment center.

The eleventh-hour FBI phone-taps, which afterward appeared so obvious as threat indicators, were missed at the time by the Hawaiian commands because they simply did not fit with the other pieces in the intelligence jigsaw. All the warnings Kimmel and Short had received from Washington and the estimates of their intelligence staffs pointed to Japanese attacks thousands of miles away. The burning of secret documents at the Japanese consulate and Mrs. Mori's "fishy" telephone conversation were too indistinct and imprecise to break through the perception that Hawaii was thousands of miles away from the danger of Japanese attack. Had they been evaluated in the context of MAGIC—and specifically the intercepts of the Honolulu consulate's espionage reports, which Washington had not relayed to the Pacific Fleet—their true significance might well have been appreciated by the Hawaiian commanders.

8

"AFFIRMATIVE MISREPRESENTATION"

The Bureaucratic Battle to Control MAGIC
Intelligence Keeps Vital Information from the
Hawaiian Commands

I magine that in all probability there is considerable opportunity left to take advantage for a surprise attack," was the
afterthought of the Japanese consul general in Honolulu, who
added in his cable to Tokyo on 6 December that "there are no
signs of balloon equipment" protecting the fleet anchorage
from low-flying aircraft.[1] Nagao Kita did not know that a carrier striking force was heading toward Hawaii that Saturday
afternoon when he sent his daily log of the warships in Pearl
Harbor, noting that "cruisers and airplane carriers have all
left."

"It appears that no air reconnaissance is being conducted
by the fleet air arm,"[2] Kita reported in response to Tokyo's
instructions to report on the aerial defenses of Oahu. It was
this particular focus and the consul's comment that the fleet
anchorage was wide open to a surprise air raid that would
certainly have aroused the suspicion of Rochefort and Layton
had they seen this intercept. But HYPO did not have the ability
to read the Japanese diplomatic traffic, and the intercepts of
the consulate traffic were sent to Washington for decrypting.
They then became part of the MAGIC, which were denied to
the Pacific Fleet. Had HYPO been able to monitor the radio

messages beamed out from the aerials atop the two-story Japanese consulate on Nuuanu Avenue, the stream of ships-in-harbor reports would have raised a suspicion of an espionage operation that was more than routine surveillance.

On 2 December, Kita had been instructed by Tokyo that "in view of the present situation, the presence in port of warships, airplane carriers and cruisers is of the utmost importance."[3] He was asked to report on antiaircraft balloons and antitorpedo net defenses in the anchorage, details that could only have been needed if the Japanese were considering an air attack on Pearl Harbor. An intelligence officer such as Layton or Rochefort could just not have missed the mounting evidence that the Japanese might be contemplating a Taranto-style carrier raid on the Pacific Fleet.

This particular intercept from the Honolulu consulate, with its revealing clues, did not reach Washington for a week, where it was fated not to be translated until 23 December because of the low priority given to decoding the non-Purple consular traffic. After it was picked up on 2 December from the radio transmission, this intercept had been sent to the Army communications center at Fort Shafter, where it was forwarded, along with all non-Purple traffic, to the War Department by surface mail, as an economy measure. It had been copied to Rochefort at HYPO as a matter of routine, but the Office of Naval Communications had not supplied Rochefort's unit the recoveries for the J-19 cipher used by Kita because the Pacific Fleet Combat Intelligence Unit had not been tasked with working on Japanese diplomatic cyphers. But HYPO did get a last-minute opportunity to access the cables the consulate sent after 2 December, because that day Rochefort received a handwritten, top-secret note from Lieutenant Yale Maxon of the 14th Naval District intelligence office.

"There are available to us, through a very confidential source, rechecks on cables [i.e. copies] received in the code from time to time by the principal Orange establishment here [the Japanese consulate in Honolulu]," Rochefort was informed. "If you are interested will you please communicate with, or see Lt. Carr or myself and we can get the information to you."[4] Access to the Japanese cable traffic had been arranged by Maxon's chief, Captain Mayfield, who had recently met with David Sarnoff, the president of RCA Corporation, whose subsidiary operated the transpacific cable link. Sarnoff had authorized his Honolulu office to secretly provide naval intelligence with copies of the cable messages sent and received by the Japanese consulate. Before the beginning of December, the consul general had used only RCA's transpacific cable when atmospheric conditions interfered with his radio transmissions. Shortly after Maxon's arrangement began, Kita complied with Tokyo's instructions to destroy his most secure J-19 digit books. He then resorted to cabling by RCA all his ships-in-harbor reports in lower-grade codes that had been designated LA and PA-K2 by the Americans.

Rochefort wasted no time in taking up the 14th Naval District's offer. He assigned the consulate cables to Warrant Officer Farnsley C. Woodward, the only HYPO cryptanalyst with recent experience with the Japanese diplomatic cipher systems. He began that Wednesday afternoon with the cables in LA code, which was the easiest to crack. When they turned out to be mostly routine administrative cables, Woodward began work on the more secure PA-K2 cables.[5] If the current keys had been made available to HYPO by Washington, it would have taken him only six hours or so to work through a day's worth of signals. But Woodward had to recover the daily key to the cipher from scratch. As fate would have it, he handicapped himself by assembling the messages in the wrong order, an error that took him four days to discover, so Japanese bombers had come and gone before a single one of Kita's ships-in-harbor reports was broken out of the consular traffic by HYPO.

Even if the consul general reports had been broken out by Rochefort's team before 7 December, there can be no certainty that any one of the messages relating to the Pacific Fleet anchorage would have changed the course of history. The evidence that the Japanese were paying suspiciously close attention to Pearl Harbor's air defenses might well have prompted Kimmel and Short to order a full alert against an air attack. But there was one message in particular that Layton singled out as having had the potential—had it been broken out in time—for sounding a more significant alarm. This was the lengthy RCA cable the consulate had relayed to Tokyo on 3 December. It was a report from a German émigré agent in the pay of the Japanese named Bernard Julius Otto Kuehn that involved a complex system of signals for reporting Pacific Fleet movements to a submarine patrolling offshore.[6] It listed prearranged light combinations to be shown from the windows of Kuehn's Lanikai beach house for night communication and a sequence of roman numerals on a yacht's mainsail to be used by day. This was to be backed up by a series of coded "want ads" to be broadcast by a local radio station.[7]

The Lanikai-lights cable was the first PA-K2 cable Woodward had picked to work on, owing to its length, but because of his chapter of errors, it was not broken out by him until 10 December. Although the German spy's report to Tokyo was made with no idea of when or even if Pearl Harbor was a potential target for attack, the complex system Kuehn laid out for communicating information on a daily basis happened to list the "6th" as the last date for making a report. But as Layton pointed out, if this signal had been available to him, the coincidence of the date would have assumed a special significance on Saturday, 6 December, when he became convinced that Japan was going to go to war the next day.

The so-called lights message would have had even greater importance for the intelligence officers of Pearl Harbor had HYPO's cryptanalysts managed to break out any of the other enemy ships-in-harbor reports made that week. One Kita report that would have attracted attention was the Tokyo request for information on balloon and torpedo-net defenses that the consulate had received that Saturday: "Please wire immediately . . . movements of the fleet subsequent to the fourth."[8] But these indications of an impending Japanese air attack on the Pacific Fleet were destined never to become intelligence, since none were broken out in time. The J-19 and PA-K2 consular cipher systems were fully accessible to the cryptanalysts in Washington and Cavite, but at those stations they were given a low priority because the Purple traffic was considered a far more important source of potential intelligence. A number of revealing Honolulu consulate reports had been translated in Washington, but not one of them was thought significant enough to be relayed to Pacific Fleet Headquarters.

The most revealing intelligence was in the intercept of the strictly secret instructions to the Japanese consul general on 24 September, relaying the Imperial Navy Ministry's request for regular "ships-in-harbor" reports on the Pacific Fleet anchorage. The manner in which these reports were to be made was so distinctive that it would have aroused immediate suspicion:

    1. The waters [of Pearl Harbor] are to be divided roughly into five sub areas. (We have no objection to your abbreviating as much as you like.)
        Area A: Waters between Ford Island and the Arsenal.
        Area B: Waters adjacent to the Island south and west

of Ford Island. (This is on the opposite side of the Island from A.)

> Area C: East Loch
> Area D: Middle Loch
> Area E: West Loch and the communicating water routes.
> 2. With regard to the warships and aircraft carriers, we would like to have you report on those at anchor (these are not so important), tied up at wharfs, buoys and docks. Designate types and classes briefly). If possible we would like to have you mention the fact when there are two or more vessels alongside at the same wharf.[9]

The first "bomb-plot" message was not decrypted and translated until 10 October, by coincidence the same day the second signal was broken out. The two-week lapse between its interception and translation was the result of both bad weather, which had delayed the Pan Am Clipper flight from Honolulu to San Francisco, and the low priority Washington accorded to J-19 traffic. The Japanese Foreign Ministry's decision not to equip the Honolulu consulate with the machine cipher the Americans had dubbed "Purple" unwittingly helped conceal their Hawaiian operations. Between September and December five times as many shipping reports were broken from the Purple used by the Japanese consulate in Manila as from the low-grade cipher messages from the Consul General in Honolulu.[10]

The American naval analysts who reexamined all the intercepts, with the advantage of hindsight six-months after the raid on Pearl Harbor, rated the 24 September intercept as one of the vital missed clues to the attack. This secret 1942 reevaluation of the "Diplomatic Background to Pearl Harbor" concluded that the message revealed that the Japanese had a special interest in "trying to discover the pattern of anchorage procedure" of the Pacific Fleet. After the attack it was obvious that the consul general had been told to superimpose an invisible grid over the Pearl Harbor anchorage of the kind used for planning a bombing attack—hence its designation as the "bomb plot message." The significant clue was missed by the analysts in Washington, who before the attack did not appreciate that the Honolulu reports were radically different from the reports of American shipping movements that Japan's consulates in Manila and the West Coast ports of the United States were making. Nor was it realized that there must have been a special reason why the Pearl Harbor reports included not only the comings and goings of individual warships, but how they were lined up when in the anchorage. This distinction was underlined in another intercept of 29 September, which added four more mooring and dockside locations, which were designated by two-letter codes.[11]

None of the "bomb-plot" intercepts were rated by the naval analysts in Washington as important enough to be sent to the Hawaiian commanders. Layton drew an analogy with an old cowboy maxim that "the nearest rattlesnake is always bigger" to argue that this particular MAGIC, whose significance had escaped Washington, would have been apparent to the analysts at Pearl Harbor. Lieutenant Commander Alwin D. Kramer had his attention sufficiently caught by Tokyo's instructions to the Honolulu consulate to have asterisked the first intercept as "an interesting message" on the gist sheet that he included, on 10 October, when it was circulated with the daily MAGICs. (Kramer's designation OP-20-GZ indicates that he headed the translation unit of the 20G section of the Office of Naval Communications, the unit that handled codebreaking as well as codes for the U.S. Navy.)

Even the asterisk that was appended to the intercept, however, failed to evoke any particular interest among his superior officers, whose job it was to review the "bomb-plot" signal for its relevance to the Pacific Fleet. No one who saw it considered relaying it to Admiral Kimmel for comment. At the congressional hearings Admiral Stark testified he could not remember seeing any of the Japanese messages. Even if he had, he claimed, Tokyo's "bomb-plot" message would not have struck him as anything more important than "just another example of their great attention to detail."[12] The head of naval war plans testified that he had "no recollection of ever having seen that dispatch of 24 September." Had he done so, Rear Admiral Turner testified, he would have referred it to the director of naval intelligence rather than "initiated a dispatch on that subject myself."[13]

Army intelligence did not pass on to General Short the information in the "bomb-plot" messages because the G-2 organization functioned in a much more compartmentalized way within the chain of command. Only General Sherman Miles, the head of the Military Intelligence Division (MID), who was also assistant chief of staff G-2, and the head of his Far East Section, Colonel Rufus S. Bratton, received the MAGIC pouches.[14] The Military Intelligence Division had a staff of over four hundred who gathered and sifted information from a wide variety of sources, including military attachés and overseas observers. It also included what Miles described as "a nucleus of what might be called a secret service under Colonel Clear in Singapore" that dealt with the British Secret Service in the Far East.[15]

Yet when it came to producing strategic estimates of Japanese intentions, MID was not required to send out to commanders in the field specific determinations of when, where, or in what force the enemy would strike. This was the responsibility of the operations divisions, not intelligence, which only relayed the material. It was also customary to leave field commanders to make their own estimates. Miles testified that it was the standing policy of G-2 Division not to risk the security of MAGIC by sending intercepts to theater commands. He was, though, under the impression that the Navy was sending out information derived from Purple to the Pacific Fleet.[16] He claimed that the "long-standing agreement or policy of complete interchange of information between the Army and the Navy" persuaded him to believe that the "bomb-plot" message would then have been passed to General Short.[17]

The liaison between Kimmel and Short was not on the same level as that between MID and the Office of Naval Intelligence. General Miles had tried to formalize this cooperation at all levels with a memorandum proposing a British-style joint intelligence committee. But at its first meeting on 11 October 1941, Admiral Turner insisted that interservice cooperation should be limited to the "presentation of such factual evidence as might be available, but to make no estimate or other form of prediction."[18] As a result the MID estimates of Japanese intentions continued to be made independently of the Navy. They tended to be more detailed: the estimate of 29 November listed Japan's options for moving into Siberia by advancing deeper into China to cut off the Burma Road, an objective that might also be achieved by invading into Thailand and Malaya. The possibility of an attack on Hong Kong and Singapore as well as the Philippines and the Netherlands East Indies was not ruled out by General Miles in this estimate, even though, he concluded, the "most probable line of action for Japan is the occupation of Thailand."[19]

Despite the Army's natural concern for "anti-subversive precautions and operations," it is surprising that General Miles failed to pay attention to the "bomb-plot" intercept, which he did not pass on to the Hawaiian commandant. He testified that the Honolulu consul general's report was only "one of a great number of messages being sent by the Japanese to various parts of the world in their attempt to follow the movements of our naval vessels." Yet when he was asked whether any of the other intercepts were so specific, he had to admit: "I have not found any, sir, similar to this in the sense of dividing any particular waters."[20] Colonel Rufus S. Bratton, who was Miles's chief of the Far East Section of G-2, conceded that the two "bomb-plot" messages impressed him with the idea that the Japanese were showing "an unusual interest in the port of Honolulu." When he "discussed this with my opposite numbers in the navy on several occasions," they concluded that the grid subdividing the Pacific Fleet anchorage could indicate a plan for either "sabotage," "a submarine attack," or "an air attack"—or it might simply have been a "device to reduce the number of radio traffic."[21]

Even if the full significance of the "bomb-plot" messages was not clear before the attack, if they had been properly evaluated as intelligence, it would have been clear that Pearl Harbor was the object of a peculiarly detailed Japanese espionage operation. In a Purple intercept of 2 September, decrypted two days later, Tokyo had instructed their ambassador in Washington that "the naval authorities insist this time upon a member of your staff going to Hawaii in the capacity of a courier."[22] This message was rated as "highly significant" in the 1942 report. "If the Japanese Navy demanded a special courier to and from Hawaii, and insisted it be a diplomatic agent rather than a naval officer for better security, there could only be one objective in mind—Pearl Harbor."[23] Another instruction for relay to the Honolulu consulate whose "vital importance" was overlooked at the time, according to the 1942 report, was the instruction to the Washington embassy for the consul general in Honolulu to direct all information to a Captain Kanji Ogawa of the Third Bureau—the section that directed Japan's naval intelligence.[24] These two intercepts that should have alerted the Navy that the Japanese consulate in Honolulu was the center of an intensifying espionage operation were not passed to the 14th Naval District's intelligence officer or the FBI, which was responsible for internal counterintelligence operations.

The importance of this intelligence was missed at the time and was later to be concealed from the congressional investigating committee by ranking naval officers who tried to cover up the Navy Department's glaring failure in 1941 to have properly evaluated and disseminated the intelligence product of the MAGIC intercepts. This is why the Navy's 1942 report on the "Diplomatic Background to Pearl Harbor" was not produced in evidence. Had its conclusions ever become public, Congress might have judged that the unpreparedness of the Hawaiian commanders was due to blunders in the Navy and War departments that deprived Kimmel and Short of critical intelligence contained in the Honolulu consulate messages. The naval intelligence analysis of this traffic remained a classified secret for thirty-five years although it makes a convincing case that there were sufficient indicators of the developing threat to have, if properly evaluated and disseminated, alerted the Pacific Fleet command that the Japanese were paying particular attention to the surveillance of Pearl Harbor in a manner that indicated a possible air attack.

Consul General Kita's reports following the "bomb-plot" messages revealed a marked acceleration in both the frequency and detail of his espionage. On 15 November, Tokyo requested that Honolulu report "twice a week" and "take extra care to maintain secrecy."[25] On 18 November there was a report detailing the speed, procedures, and the time it took for five destroyers to enter through the channel and reach their mooring.[26] That same day the consulate received instructions to "investigate comprehensively the fleet [air] bases in the neighborhood of the Hawaiian military reservation."[27] A day later Tokyo urged that "great secrecy" be observed when investigating vessels anchored in "Area 'N' Pearl Harbor"—Mamala Bay adjacent to the port of Honolulu.[28] On 19 November, a five-day-old intercept was decrypted in Washington that instructed the Honolulu consulate, "We have been receiving reports from you on ship movements, but in future will you also report *when there are no movements* [emphasis added]."[29]

Why the Japanese should have wanted to know such details if they were not contemplating a carrier attack on Pearl Harbor was not a question that was asked by any of the analysts in Washington. Similar instructions had not been sent to any other consulate, but it did not occur to any of the recipients of MAGIC to question why Japanese naval intelligence wanted to know where warships of the Pacific Fleet were anchored according to a very precise reference chart. Captain Theodore S. Wilkinson, the head of the Office of Naval Intelligence, testified that he theorized that the grid was used by the Honolulu consulate to save on cable costs, although reporting when there were no movements was hardly an economy measure.

To Wilkinson it was "evidence of the nicety of their intelligence" and "just another example of their great attention to detail."[30] His misinterpretation reflected the prevailing belief that the Japanese were obsessed with unnecessary detail. This assumption also skewed the reaction of General Miles, who testified that he did not think the Honolulu consulate reports merited "special treatment." But he did admit that he was "more interested in the fact that the Japanese were following our ships in our own waters, Panama, Hawaii and the Philippines," more than in other places in the Far East.[31]

Just how mistaken General Miles and Captain Wilkinson were is apparent from the conclusion of a 1942 analysis by the Office of Naval Intelligence, "Diplomatic Background to Pearl Harbor," that it was precisely the volume and specificity that set the Honolulu consulate messages apart from all the others. A statistical comparison yielded the "interesting point" that the Japanese consulates in Seattle accounted for six and in Panama eighteen of the shipping reports intercepted between August and December 1941. The consul general in Manila sent fifty-five reports, but a total of *sixty-eight* originated with the Honolulu consul. "The significant point is that the Japanese government did not treat the Honolulu and Manila reports as routine matters, but continually kept trying to elicit more information from its representatives." As the 1942 analysis concluded, "The acceleration of messages from Honolulu and Manila in November was *another identification of war preparations* [emphasis added]."[32]

The declassification in the late 1970s of the report "Diplomatic Background to Pearl Harbor" to the National Archives was one of the factors that prompted Admiral Layton to write his memoir. He had always been highly critical of Washington for its failure to send the Pacific Fleet *any* of the Honolulu consulate intercepts. "It does not require any remarkable foresight to discern the significance of this information," he wrote in his memoir. "Repeated transmissions of such detailed ships-in-harbor locations could have had no usefulness unless the Japanese were planning to execute an attack on our fleet while in port. Why? Such detailed reports lost all value once the ships sailed from their carefully designated berths."[33] Layton's words echoed those of Admiral Kimmel, who testified that "knowledge of these intercepted Japanese dispatches would have radically changed the estimate of the situation made by me and my staff."[34] He regarded the lapse as a major dereliction by the Navy Department, characterizing it as "affirmative representation," because he had repeatedly asked whether the Pacific Fleet was receiving all relevant intelligence from Washington and had been assured by the chief of naval operations that it was.[35]

"We believed that we were receiving it. Our estimates and actions were made on this basis," Layton wrote. "But the failure to relay these vital pieces of intelligence deprived us of essential facts and misled us when it came to our assessing the possibility of a Japanese attack on Pearl Harbor."[36] The full extent to which the Navy Department failed to extract the full intelligence from MAGIC did not become evident at the congressional hearings on Pearl Harbor. It was to take nearly half a century for the saga of bureaucratic rivalry, administrative incompetence, and myopic misinterpretation to emerge with the declassification of the files of the original Japanese diplomatic intercepts and the secret Navy assessments that were concealed from the investigators in 1945. What is now obvious is that the underlying failure was that there was no effective procedure in either the War or Navy departments in 1941 for systematically evaluating and disseminating the intelligence contained in the huge volume of decrypts spewed out by the Purple machine.

Each batch of MAGIC decrypts was studied and weighed in isolation because of the security surrounding Purple, which meant that none of the recipients of the couriered pouches could compare or rate the significance of current intercepts against those previously circulated. This might not have been a major handicap had the intelligence sections of the Navy and Army developed an effective process of analysis, instead of relying on the ad hoc assessment of officers with divided responsibilities. The sheer volume of intercepts, which by November 1941 had reached several hundred a day, contributed to the breakdown of the evaluation process that is essential to extracting intelligence from raw data. A struggle for control over MAGIC afflicted both service departments, but it was on the second floor, or "second deck" as it was known, of the Navy Department that the rivalry between three separate departments became so ferocious that conditions of near mutiny proved disastrous to the intelligence process.

Collection of intelligence in the Navy was a divided responsibility shared by the Office of Naval Communications (ONC), which was responsible for intercepting and breaking coded radio traffic, and the Office of Naval Intelligence (ONI), which acted as both a collector and clearinghouse for intelligence.

Their respective areas of responsibility had been set down in a Navy Department manual drawn up for the chief of naval operations on 23 October 1940. This directed the foreign intelligence branch of ONI (known as OP-16) to "evaluate the information collected and disseminate as advisable."[37] Since this information included the product of Naval Communications (OP-20), there was interdepartmental sensitivity that ONI had been assigned the responsibility for the analysis and distribution of the intelligence product of MAGIC. The delicate equation was, however, to be disrupted at the beginning of 1941, when the director of the Office of Naval War Plans set out to ensure that his department had overall control of the flow of all intelligence estimates.

A running feud developed between ONI and Admiral Turner shortly after his appointment to War Plans in the fall of 1940. Turner was brilliant but confrontational, and his sense of self-importance had been inflated by his appointment, which he believed had anointed him as the next chief of naval operations, a post to which he had aspired ever since he entered the U.S. Naval Academy in 1908.[38] Six feet tall, with beetling black brows and a lantern jaw that gave him a Mephistophelian appearance, he intimidated subordinates. Turner was recalled by one member of his staff "as abrasive as a file." The fifty-five-year-old captain was given a spot promotion to rear admiral by President Roosevelt in January 1941 in order to lend weight to Turner's opinions at the secret American-British-Canadian staff conference.[39] A relentless taskmaster, he was referred to as "Terrible Turner" behind his back, but to Admiral Stark he was "invaluable" because the energetic new war plans chief relieved him of burdensome memorandum writing and staff work.[40]

The chief of naval operations had been impressed by Turner's grasp of strategic principle when he reworked Stark's original "Plan D" memorandum into the comprehensive United States strategic war plan known as Rainbow 5.

Turner had earned the confidence of Stark, whose nickname of "Betty," acquired shortly after he entered the U.S. Naval Academy at Annapolis in 1899, was so incongruous for an admiral whose rosy cheeks and mop of white hair gave him a rather fussy, schoolboyish manner.[41] He owed his own appointment to Roosevelt, whom he had known since 1914, when as a junior captain Stark had tactfully refused the then assistant navy secretary's request to captain a destroyer in treacherous waters off the Maine coast. It was Stark's administrative ability and powers of persuasion that during the latter years of the Depression had managed to win support on Capitol Hill for President Roosevelt's soaring naval budgets. Although an astute performer in staff conferences, Stark did not impress Secretary of War Stimson. Stimson confided in his diary that he found the chief of naval operations "a timid and ineffective man to be in the post he holds."[42]

"Betty" Stark may have lacked the iron will and conviction of a fighting admiral, but Turner possessed these fiery qualities in full measure, and they were put to the test when he became the Pacific Fleet's wartime amphibious force commander. Though he exhibited courage and brilliance as a strategist, Turner's opinionated manner made him the kind of admiral "who could not come ashore in a launch without giving detailed orders to the coxswain."[43] He wanted to be—and be seen to be—in command of all he surveyed. This determination to dominate and expand the authority of his office led to bitter clashes as he attempted to establish War Plans as the final arbiter and disseminator of intelligence. It was in keeping with his character that Turner decided to ignore the demarcation lines set down by the chief of naval operations in 1940, by asserting that War Plans should have "the major strategic overall picture for the use of my superiors."[44] Turner may have had little knowledge of the intelligence process, but he rated himself an expert on Japan, though he had only visited Tokyo once, as captain of the cruiser *Astoria*, which had carried the ashes of the deceased Ambassador Hiroshi Saito home in 1939.

Despite his lack of experience in intelligence work, Turner considered his judgment inherently superior to ONI's when it came to analyzing and interpreting strategic information. He maintained that the War Plans staff was "more experienced than the officers in naval intelligence who generally were more junior and were trained rather for the collection and dissemination of information, rather than its application to a strategic situation."[45] Within a month of his arrival in the Navy Department, Turner had persuaded Stark to issue a directive that "ONI makes no estimate of prospective enemy intentions to CNO, but furnishes information to War Plans who would make the required estimate."[46] By February 1941 Turner began issuing intelligence dispatches without any reference to the director of naval intelligence. The War Plans forecast that Japan would go north to invade Siberia contradicted the bulletin sent out the same month by ONI, which predicted the impending Japanese move south into Indochina.

The head of ONI's Far East Section, Captain Arthur H. McCollum, was immediately summoned by Turner to be instructed "that hereafter War Plans would do all the evaluating of probable enemy intentions and that we had to be particularly careful that the director of War Plans got all the pertinent information."[47] Admiral Stark backed War Plans in the dispute by letting it be known that "in the interest of coordination, Turner was the man to do the coordinating."[48] With the tacit approval of the chief of naval operations, War Plans established its own three-man intelligence section. But according to McCollum, the officers appointed were so inexperienced in evaluating information that they had to beat a path down the corridor to pick his brains. They then carried the word back to the director of War Plans, who issued the directives and intelligence summaries that went to the Pacific Fleet. The naval intelligence staff deeply objected to Turner's assumption of the "coordinating role," according to McCollum, who said that it enabled Turner "to keep his hand on our gullets" by maintaining a stranglehold on the whole intelligence process.[49]

No one resented Turner's usurpation more than Captain Alan C. Kirk, who arrived to take charge of ONI in March 1941, after monitoring the real war as U.S. naval attaché in London. Impressed by the way the British Combined Operations Intelligence Center meshed the Admiralty's war plans directorate and its intelligence function, Kirk proposed that the U.S. Navy adopt a similar system. Turner agreed with the idea of a clearinghouse for intelligence, but only if he could run the whole show. He had powerful allies in Admiral Stark and his pliant deputy, Admiral Ingersoll. But "Kirk wasn't any weak sister," according to McCollum. "He immediately went in to bat, and he and Turner were on the mat all the time."[50] Kirk's struggle to prevent the predations of War Plans continued for the eight months that he headed ONI, although he lost a critical first round in the struggle in April 1941, when Turner insisted that "War Plans Division should prepare such sections of the estimate [of enemy intentions] and should interpret and *evaluate all information concerning possible hostile nations from whatever source received* [emphasis added]."[51] Stark sided with Turner by letting it be known that he "approved the position" taken by the chief of War Plans. Turner promptly took advantage of Stark's acquiescence by unilaterally asserting that Kirk's office was "solely a collecting agency and a distributing agency and was not charged with sending out any information which would initiate any operations on the part of the fleet, or fleets anywhere."[52]

Admiral Turner's bid to reduce the function of the Office of Naval Intelligence to little more than a "drop box" in order to expand the authority and prestige of War Plans brought so much confusion and resentment that it upset the process of the evaluation and dissemination of intelligence. Turner's confidence in his exclusive ability to predict Japan's true intention to move north to attack the Soviet Union caused Turner to ride roughshod over the conflicting estimates of McCollum's Far East Section of ONI, which continued to predict a southward advance by Japan. Since Stark's 1940 memorandum outlining areas of responsibility remained unamended, Turner was able to duck and weave before the congressional committee when they tried to determine who had been responsible both for denying MAGIC intelligence in general to the Pacific Fleet and for the failure to recognize the significance of the "bomb-plot" consulate messages.

The smoke from the internecine warfare raging between the departments in adjoining offices on the second deck of the Navy Department was obscuring and interfering with the intelligence process before Kirk's replacement, in October 1941, by Captain Theodore S. Wilkinson. An affable and brainy naval officer who had headed the Class of 1909 at the Naval Academy, "Ping" Wilkinson was an experienced staff officer who had also won a Medal of Honor for bravery in Vera Cruz in 1914. He brought all the right qualifications to the post, except one: Wilkinson lacked any training or first-hand expertise as an intelligence officer. As a former aide to the commander of the Pacific Fleet's cruiser scouting force, Wilkinson had been Rochefort's superior aboard the *Indianapolis* until January 1941, and the two had become friends. Rochefort had sent a letter of congratulations to the new director of naval intelligence, only to learn that his appointment to Washington was not the "grand job" Wilkinson had anticipated.[53]

If Rochefort hoped that having a friend as director of Naval Intelligence would ensure that HYPO would speed information to HYPO, it proved an empty expectation. Wilkinson had arrived to find that much of his authority over intelligence had been assumed by the chief of War Plans. Since he felt his first mission was to oil the stormy waters on the second deck of the Navy Department, Wilkinson was reluctant to challenge Turner's domination. Shortly after he assumed command of

ONI, he missed a critical opportunity to assert his authority on the issue of the "bomb-plot" intercepts.

Captain Howard D. Bode, the head of ONI's Foreign Intelligence Section, concluded that the "bomb-plot" decrypts were sufficiently suspicious to warrant communicating the contents of these intercepts to Rochefort at Pearl Harbor. His interest in them was supported by Commander Laurance S. Safford, the head of the OP-20-G cryptanalysis and security section of the Office of Naval Communications. Safford recalled that he had drafted a message instructing HYPO to begin decrypting the traffic of Japan's Honolulu consulate. But he testified he was prevented doing so by his chief, Admiral Leigh Noyes, the head of ONC, who feared invoking the wrath of Turner, who was by then "coordinating" the distribution of intelligence.[54] With McCollum temporarily away in London, the newly installed Wilkinson lacked the necessary specialist knowledge to tackle Turner himself and persuade him to send this critical piece of MAGIC intelligence to Admiral Kimmel. When McCollum returned a week later, Wilkinson had already decided to let the issue drop rather than get into a fight with the director of naval war plans over a decrypt that he himself considered only "part of the general information system established by the Japanese."[55]

"Our office was an incoming receiving office of information from abroad and from domestic areas," was how Wilkinson accepted the subordinate role of the Office of Naval Intelligence. He testified that by November 1941, ONI was "not concerned with the ongoing directives to the Fleet nor in fact told of the movements and operations of our own forces."[56] But Turner had not yet been able to control the distribution of MAGIC, which the director of naval communications jealously protected, reducing the War Plans chief to frequent rantings against Noyes "and his God-damn secrets."[57] Turner had, however, effectively taken over control of the dissemination of MAGIC intelligence to the Pacific Fleet, and he took particular care to prevent any challenge to the omniscience of his own operational directives. According to McCollum, Turner could—and apparently did—reject any material that did not fit into his own interpretation that it was Japan's intention to attack Siberia, which remained a feature of the directives issued by War Plans right up until 26 November 1941.

The first time that Turner was persuaded to rate a southward advance by Japan as a higher probability than an attack against the Soviet Maritime Territory was the 27 November war warning, which finally endorsed McCollum's prediction of "an amphibious expedition" heading either for "the Philippines, Thai or Kra Peninsula or possibly Borneo."[58] In his testimony Admiral Wilkinson said that he had rated the possibility of a strike on the Philippines unlikely and an attack on Hawaii even more improbable because he had not believed that the Japanese "would expose themselves to great danger, whatever force they brought there and, furthermore they would be precipitating a war with the United States, which theretofore they had given every intention of attempting to avoid."[59]

This overly optimistic view of the awe with which Tokyo regarded MacArthur's command reflected the prevalent skepticism in Washington: Japan, a nation the size of California, would not dare risk a "David and Goliath" conflict with the United States. But the director of war plans later insisted that when he reviewed the 27 November war warnings on 5 December with Admiral Ingersoll in the context of the latest intelligence estimates they had both concluded that there was a "50-50" chance of a "heavy raid" on Pearl Harbor.[60] His assertion was so incredible, given his previous assertion that Japan would attack the Soviet Union, that it appears to have been another element in the smoke screen of dissimilation that Turner produced for the congressional hearing to conceal his having denied vital MAGIC intelligence to Pacific Fleet. He brazenly testified under oath that after discussing the situation with Admiral Stark, their concern not to cry "Wolf!" too often led to their "unanimous" decision that the earlier alerts had been comprehensive even to the point of embracing the possibility of an air attack on Pearl Harbor![61]

On Friday, 5 December, at least two senior members of the military and naval staff did not believe that the Hawaiian command had been sufficiently warned of the danger. One was Colonel Otis K. Sadtler, a thirty-one-year veteran of the Signal Corps who was in charge of the code-breaking operations of the Army's Signal Intelligence Service. In response to what he assumed was a genuine "winds alert," which had been brought to his attention in a telephone call from the head of naval communications, Admiral Noyes, "about 9 or shortly thereafter on Friday, December 5," Sadtler hurried to tell General Sherman Miles, the Army G-2, that the "word is in."[62] Noyes was later to testify that the information turned out to be a false alert. (See Appendix I on "Winds" controversy.) But Sadtler did not wait for verification before drafting a fresh warning for General Short: "RELIABLE INFORMATION INDICATES WAR

WITH JAPAN IN THE VERY NEAR FUTURE. TAKE EVERY PRECAUTION TO PREVENT A REPETITION OF PORT AR- THUR. NOTIFY NAVY."[63] Its terse language was intended to convey a sense of urgency, as was the reference to Japan's sur- prise assault on Port Arthur, which precipitated war with Rus- sia in 1904. Whether such a warning would have prompted Short to a state of maximum readiness was never put to the test, because Brigadier Leonard T. Gerow, the head of army war plans, believed, like his opposite number Turner at the Navy Department, that "the various departments had been adequately warned."[64]

Captain McCollum, however, did not share this conviction. War Plans had so monopolized control of all operational direc- tives that although he was head of the Far East Section of Naval Intelligence, even McCollum did not yet know the de- tails of the war warning that had already been sent to the Pacific commands. On 1 December McCollum thought that the rapidly deteriorating situation warranted their drawing up a lengthy memorandum setting out the latest estimates of dispo- sitions and southward movement of Japanese forces. It was based on reports of convoys he had just received from Shang- hai, Bangkok, and the British, and in keeping with Turner's fiat that circumscribed the ability of ONI to evaluate operational intelligence, McCollum noted how he had carefully avoided "drawing conclusions in each instance."[65] He brought his memorandum to the attention of Stark and other senior officers, including Ingersoll, Turner, Noyes, and Wilkinson, pointing out to them that "war or a rupture of diplomatic com- munications was imminent." When he requested to know "whether or not the fleets in the Pacific had been adequately alerted,"[66] he said he received a "categorical assurance" from Stark and Turner that "dispatches fully alerting the fleets and placing them on a war basis had been sent."[67]

When McCollum learned from MAGIC that the Japanese were burning their code machines, he condensed his earlier memorandum to a punchy war warning that stated "that we felt everything pointed to an imminent outbreak of hostilities between Japan and the United States."[68] He took this memo- randum to the chief of the ONI Foreign Section, Captain W. A. Hearn, and together they bearded Wilkinson. But the director of naval intelligence, anticipating that McCollum's warning would stick in Turner's throat, sent them along the corridor to show it to the director of war plans. Turner took a predict- ably sour view of the draft, "striking out all except the informational parts of it," according to McCollum. He recalled that he might not have pressed his case if he had been aware of the wording of the 27 November war warning. "Finally I raised so much sand in Turner's office that he showed me the dispatch," McCollum recalled, only to find to his surprise that the words "war warning" had actually been included in the message.[69]

"Well, good gosh," McCollum responded in surprise. "I do not know what could be plainer than that, but nevertheless I would like to see mine go too."[70]

"Well, if you want to send it, you either send it the way I corrected it or take it back to Wilkinson and we will argue about it," Turner snapped back.[71]

Four years later the former director of war plans told the congressional hearing that McCollum appeared satisfied and "tore up his proposed dispatch," commenting that the 27 November war warning was "covering the entire situation."[72] But McCollum gave a different version. He said that he was not satisfied that a proper warning had been sent to the Pacific Fleet that reflected all the intelligence available in the Navy Department that Friday. He had therefore returned to Wilkinson later that day with a penciled draft for the director of naval intelligence to show to Turner. "Leave it with me for a while," McCollum was told. But his warning was never sent, and no copies of his draft survive to suggest how it might have been interpreted by Admiral Kimmel. Like the "bomb-plot" message it, too, fell victim to Turner's stranglehold on the intelligence process.

Turner was a national hero and a decorated four-star admiral for his achievements as the wartime commander of the United States amphibious invasion forces from Guadalcanal to Iwo Jima. As soon as the war was over he commenced a campaign to absolve himself from the taint of the intelligence failure of War Plans in 1941 by rounding on Admiral Kimmel. He wasted no opportunity to excoriate his fellow admiral, who was now in forced retirement, battling to clear his name after the disaster at Pearl Harbor. As Layton recorded in his memoir, he had frequent meetings with Turner during the planning conferences for the naval landings in the Pacific campaign. "But, few who worked closely with him in these operations could forget—or forgive—his stormy temper, overbearing ego, and celebrated bouts with the bottle."[73] And Layton never forgot one particularly nasty confrontation that took place in the wardroom of the battleship *South Dakota*, on the eve of the Japanese surrender ceremony in Tokyo Bay, when Turner staggered in, obviously "stoked up" on whiskey, to regale the company with the reason for his celebration.

"Did you see the Navy Department's release about the findings of the Pearl Harbor Court of Inquiry?" Turner demanded in a booming voice that halted all conversation. "They said that goddamned Kimmel had all the information and didn't do anything about it. They should hang him higher than a kite!"[74] Boiling with indignation, Layton interrupted Turner in mid-rant and told him that he was wrong, Kimmel did not have the information, and that Layton knew it because he had been the Pacific Fleet intelligence officer at the time. "Are you calling me a liar?" Turner bellowed across the wardroom before rushing over and grabbing Layton by the throat. Only the prompt intervention of *South Dakota*'s skipper, Captain Emmet P. Forrestel, prevented a "four striper" captain from exchanging blows with a four-star admiral.[75]

Admiral Turner would persist in maintaining to the congressional committee that the Pacific Fleet commander had "everything we had" and denying his own responsibility for choking the Pacific Fleet off from MAGIC intelligence. It was his "impression at the time," he went so far as to testify, that Kimmel was receiving them. He put Admiral Noyes on the spot by contending that in "March or April" 1941 he had been assured by the director of naval communications that not only was the Pacific Fleet commander "getting as much as we were," but "he was getting it sooner than we were."[76] Noyes, who was evasive when it came to specifics, had to cover himself without branding the former chief of war plans a liar. He testified that Turner had "continually discussed" the status of the Purple decrypts at their "almost daily" meetings and therefore "should have understood."[77] When pressed under cross-examination on whether he had ever given the director of naval war plans "any impression that Kimmel was getting information of the type contained in the Purple code intercepts," Noyes refused to budge from his equivocal "not intentionally."[78]

The unwillingness of the former director of naval communications to blame the former chief of war plans for the failure to keep the Pacific Fleet commander properly informed of intelligence, let Turner off the hook. But he was obliged to admit, when confronted with the evidence uncovered by the congressional investigation team, that he was "entirely in error as regards the diplomatic codes."[79] Turner repeatedly asserted that as far as MAGIC was concerned, he "did not know the details at all of the decryption methods and codes."[80] Admiral

Noyes, he claimed, must have "misunderstood what I was trying to get at" because Turner could not recall whether "diplomatic intercepts" had ever been specified in their conversations. Such confusion might have been credible for an outsider, but not for the director of naval war plans who wanted to keep his finger on every aspect of intelligence.

The underlying inconsistencies of Turner's denial did not escape William D. Mitchell, the senior counsel to the congressional investigating committee, who did not believe that Turner could *not* have been aware the Pacific Fleet was denied MAGIC. "You could not do that," Mitchell demanded caustically, "unless you knew precisely just what they had and what they needed from you. Isn't that so?" "No, sir; that is not correct. It was not my duty to inform commanders in chief as to intelligence," Turner shot back. "Sending intercepts or summaries of intercepts, or evaluating them as to authenticity or probability, was not War Plans province and we never under any circumstances sent such information out."[81]

Lying with bombastic self-righteousness, Turner managed to bluff his way through the cross-examination by repeatedly denying he had any responsibility for the failure to send the MAGIC intercepts of the Honolulu consulate traffic to the Pacific Fleet. Since none of Turner's former subordinates had the courage to call the former War Plans chief a liar to his face, he escaped with his reputation, if not his honor, intact by claiming under oath that he had been misled by his colleagues. McCollum, who went on to achieve flag-rank only after his retirement, finally set the record straight in 1961. In a three-volume interview for the U.S. Naval Institute's oral history program, he recounted the full story of the conflict that had led to near-mutinous conditions on the second deck of the Navy Department as a result of Turner's attempt to usurp the intelligence process. He revealed how the domineering head of War Plans had repeatedly sent out his opinionated and erroneous forecasts of Japanese intentions and incorrect warnings and had also suppressed the ONI estimates without any reference to the director of naval intelligence or to the trained officer whose responsibility was to evaluate the data. But because Stark had never updated his 1940 manual to reflect that War Plans was effectively controlling the interpretation and flow of intelligence, Turner was able to deny his culpability for the breakdown in the intelligence process or that he had been in any way responsible for blocking the dispatch of last-minute warnings to the Pacific Fleet. Like Secretary Stimson, Turner found it convenient to maintain that the Hawaiian commanders were sentries who had been properly and fully briefed, yet still failed to be sufficiently alert on watch.[82]

If Turner, as he claimed under oath, had believed that there was a "fifty-fifty" chance of a Japanese attack on Pearl Harbor, his failure to pass that warning on only adds to his dereliction. But the reality is that the strategic focus on the Philippines had reinforced Washington's belief that there was "not the slightest" indication of any threat to Hawaii.[83]

The conviction in Washington that the Japanese attack was being directed thousands of miles to the west of the Pacific Fleet's mid-ocean base was evident from the 5 December Naval Intelligence estimate sent to the president, after being approved by the director of war plans. It indicated Japanese troop concentrations in Indochina and naval vessels at Camranh Bay, off the coast at Saigon, and at Hainan Island, south of Hong Kong, with another concentration in the southern ports of Formosa.[84] The next day when the U.S. ambassador in London relayed an Admiralty signal of an RAF aircraft-sighting report of two large convoys "off Cambodia Point, sailing slowly westward towards Kra 14 hours distant in time," the report was taken as affirmation of the strategic picture as it appeared to Washington.[85] Further confirmation of the Japanese juggernaut moving southward was provided the same day from Admiral Hart's Asiatic Fleet headquarters in Manila. The same convoys, heading either for Thailand or possibly the neck of Malaya, had been spotted by reconnaissance patrols conducted by the Asiatic Fleet.[86]

Turner's "stranglehold" on naval intelligence had diminished both the ability and inclination of its trained staff to discern nuances that might otherwise have been seen as significant. With naval intelligence reduced to a collecting box and sifting information rather than drawing conclusions from its contents, it was inevitable that the last-minute indicators of a possible threat to Pearl Harbor were missed even when they were broken out of MAGIC. These clues may have been relatively insignificant pieces in a complex overall puzzle, but they were fated to be overlooked because they did not fit into the conception of the Japanese war plan as it had appeared to Washington. The extent of this breakdown is only too clear from the sequence of events that occurred in the Navy Department on Saturday, 6 December, when the decrypt of the Lanikai-lights message came to the attention of Mrs. Dorothy Edgers, who had arrived to work in Washington as a translator only a few weeks earlier.

9

"THIS MEANS WAR!"

Intelligence Denial and Miscalculation
by Washington

A t first glance, this seemed to be more interesting than some of the other messages I had in my basket," was how Mrs. Edgers described the Lanikai-lights intercept to the 1944 Navy court of inquiry. "I selected it and asked one of the other men, who were translators working on other messages, whether or not it shouldn't be done immediately."[1] She was told to go ahead by her brother, Fred Woodrough, a Japanese linguist with four-years service as a translator for the Office of Naval Communications. He had recommended his sister for her job because the thirty years she had spent in Japan, where their parents had been Christian missionaries, had enabled his sister to become "much more fluent" than he was.[2] Her boss, Commander Kramer, would portray Mrs. Edgers as a timid personality who was not a very experienced translator, but according to her brother, Dorothy was quite an extrovert, a "born salesman" who had successfully argued that her knowledge of Japanese rated her to equal pay with the other longer-serving male translators.

It is therefore significant that Dorothy Edgers *was not called upon* by the Navy to testify before the congressional committee, because she would have made a convincing witness and was not someone to be brushed aside. That is why that Saturday morning when she began translating the long message from the Honolulu consulate about coded light signals, it struck her potentially important. When she found that it contained garbles, she took it to a "crippie" to get them corrected and was waiting for the corrected decrypt at half-past-twelve, when the civilian translators stopped work for the weekend.

Dorothy Edgers did not want to leave unread until Monday an intercept that she had a hunch might be very significant because it involved signals for the movements of the Pacific Fleet up until the "6th"—which happened to be that very day. So she went to find Kramer and tried to interest him in the suspicious message. But after the most cursory glance he said he did not think it of "sufficient importance" to warrant her staying behind that afternoon to complete the translation. When Dorothy consulted her brother, he agreed with her suspicions and told her she should remain until the translation was completed, although he admitted that he "wasn't about to stay to do it myself."[3]

So Mrs. Edgers went back to her desk, finishing the first rough translation around two o'clock. The contents of the Japanese consul general's report made such an impression on her that three years later when she testified before the Naval court of inquiry, she could still recall the details of "how they were going to communicate from Honolulu to the parties interested in the information on our fleet movements" with "lights in the window of a certain house and there was also something about newspaper advertising."[4] Kramer was not available when she finished the translation and handed it to his chief clerk, Harold L. Bryant, "whose job was to edit the messages and write them up."[5]

That was as close as the celebrated "lights-intercept" espionage message—which the HYPO cryptanalyst was still struggling to break out—came to becoming a vital piece of intelligence that might have put Pearl Harbor on the alert. On Monday morning it was still on Kramer's desk. "He had not looked at it," according to Fred Woodrough, who said it was "quite possible that the English would have had to be smoothed out, but the essential translation work was done."[6] Kramer, whose responsibility at OP-20-GZ was to review all intercepts as well as supervise their translations, was to deny, under oath, any recollection of seeing Mrs. Edger's version of the intercept when cross-examined by the congressional committee in 1945. Asked if he would have considered the "lights message" an important piece of intelligence, Kramer stated, "If I had seen it that Saturday afternoon I certainly would have."[7] He admitted he had failed to give it proper attention in the "ten to fifteen seconds" he said he spent reviewing the raw intercept before he had concluded that it did not appear "materially different from the information we had already."[8] As for Mrs. Edger's claim of having shown a fully translated message to him, he testified that she "was still unfamiliar with the practices and procedures of my office."[9] He disavowed that she had "invited" his attention to a complete version on 6 December and cast further doubts on her claim by asserting that he subsequently had to spend three days "clearing and working with this message" before it was readable.[10]

Kramer's testimony could not be challenged because the original worksheet had disappeared and Dorothy Edgers was not called upon to contest it. Fred Woodrough believed that it was because the Honolulu consul general's intercepts were not in Purple, but in the low-grade PA-K cipher, that his sister could not get Kramer to focus on the consulate's cable. "Al was not the ideal man for the job at that time," Woodrough observed, recalling that like many perfectionists, Kramer was obsessed with detail and often had difficulty making decisions on important issues.[11] He observed how pedantic his boss had become under the heavy pressure he was subjected to during the final weeks of November 1941.

The limited resources of the OP-20-GZ translation unit had been severely taxed by all the false messages from the "winds-code" alert. But the problems were as often imaginary as real, according to Woodrough, who recalled how Kramer "would take even the most trivial piece of traffic and devote the same amount of time changing a comma here and a period there as he would on an important message."[12] Kramer often "got stuck on things," Woodrough remembered, speculating that the mental strain of having to cover up his failures was the real reason for his boss's hospitalization for nervous exhaustion in 1946, shortly before Kramer was due to appear before the congressional committee.[13] Others have claimed that his crack-up was the result of pressure brought to bear on Kramer by his superiors in the Navy Department, who disputed his claim to have seen a genuine "East Wind Rain" report that was deliberately withheld from being sent to the Pacific Fleet commander. [Appendix II] Woodrough recalled that by the first week of December 1941, Kramer's nervous exhaustion was manifest in the disorganization of the partially translated intercepts that piled up on his desk, awaiting the critical analysis and approval that he insisted upon.

"When the volume of intercepts was very high, the stuff just piled up in a basket," according to Woodrough. "Whoever was ready would take the top one and translate it. We picked whichever one had the highest priority, and Purple got top priority."[14] He was therefore not surprised that his sister's translation of the lights message did not attract Kramer's attention that Saturday afternoon, when the Navy had the additional burden of circulating the MAGIC pouches that day. Washington was anxiously awaiting Tokyo's response to the ten-point memorandum that the secretary of state had given the Japanese envoys on 26 November, when he called off the modus vivendi. A Purple intercept to the envoys had already alerted them that "negotiations will be de facto ruptured,"[15] and MAGIC's revelation that Japanese embassies had been ordered to destroy their code systems further indicated the lurch toward hostility.

At 7:20 A.M. on 6 December the naval listening station at Bainbridge Island in Washington State picked up Tokyo's notification to their Washington, D.C., embassy to stand by for an important message. As an even-numbered date, it was the Army's duty day for decrypting Purple traffic, and OP-20-G Washington routed copies of the intercept to the Special Intelligence Section of the Signal Corps. By midday the Army's Purple machine had produced the decrypt of the pilot message preparing Nomura and Kurusu for a long memorandum that they were advised was Tokyo's "deeply" deliberated response to the United States. It was to be transmitted in fourteen parts, and since the "situation was extremely delicate," they were instructed that it was to be "kept secret for the time being." They were told that "the time of presenting this memorandum to the United States" would be advised in a separate message.[16] In the interim they were directed to put the Japanese government's response "in nicely drafted form and make every preparation to present it to the Americans just as soon as you receive instructions."[17] If there was any doubt as to the importance of the forthcoming fourteen-part message, it was underscored— for both the MAGIC eavesdroppers in Washington and Japan's envoys—by the instruction transmitted immediately after the pilot message, reminding the Japanese envoys of the need for strict security in typing up the fourteen parts: "In the preparation of an aide memoir be absolutely sure not to use a typist or any other person. Be most extremely cautious in preserving secrecy."[18]

When the translation of the pilot message reached the desk of Colonel Bratton early that Saturday afternoon, the head of Military Intelligence's Far East Section realized he faced a logistical problem. Unlike the Navy, the SIS code-breaking unit was not yet on full, round-the-clock duty. Its civilian cryptanalysts had already left for the weekend. Bratton therefore had to obtain General Miles's permission to call in the staff and request the Navy's help with the decoding of the fourteen-part message, so that it could be circulated to the White House and the other MAGIC recipients as soon as possible. The arrangements were agreed to by Commander Safford, the head of the OP-20-G, who only that morning had attempted himself to send another war alert to the Pacific Fleet. He had drafted an order for Admiral Kimmel to relay instructions to the garrison at Wake Island to make sure that all its codes and secret documents were destroyed. But because he had added the phrase "in view of the imminence of war," Safford had been unable to get this dispatch approved by Captain Joseph R. Redman, Admiral Leigh Noyes's deputy.[19] When the director of naval communications returned from the secretary of the Navy's daily briefing, there was a strong exchange with Safford because Noyes took exception to the cable he had drafted.

"What do you mean using such language as that," Noyes had shouted, pointing angrily at Safford's proposed dispatch, which clearly impinged on Admiral Turner's authority because it warned that war was imminent.

"Admiral, the war is just a matter of days, if not hours," Safford replied, holding his ground.

"You may think there is going to be a war, but I think they are bluffing," Noyes snapped back.

"Well, Admiral, if all these publications on Wake are captured we will never be able to explain it."[20]

The director of naval communications, anticipating the cable would ignite Turner's Irish temper, insisted on toning down the signal and removing all references to the "imminent outbreak of hostilities." The message was then finally sent to the Pacific commands as "deferred priority," so that when it arrived at Pearl Harbor shortly after midnight, it had lost all sense of urgency and read like another routine administrative dispatch: "In view of the international situation and the exposed position of our outlying Pacific islands you may authorize destruction by them of secret and confidential documents now or under later conditions of greater emergency."[21] So another opportunity was lost to alert the Pacific Fleet to the immediacy of war because it was blocked by a bureaucratic fight on the second deck of the Navy Department. Admiral Noyes's decision to block Safford's relatively mild war warning had been influenced by an exchange which had taken place that morning at his meeting with the secretary of the navy.

"Are they going to hit us?" Knox had asked. To which Admiral Turner replied, "No, Mr. Secretary, they are going to attack the British. They are not ready for us yet."[22]

There was nothing to shake that complacent assumption in the first thirteen parts of Tokyo's long memorandum, which began chattering in from Bainbridge Island on OP-20-G's secure teleprinter line around midday. When the message was broken out by the Navy and Army cryptanalysts, they found that no translation was necessary because Tokyo was sending their memorandum in plain English so that there was no possibility for misinterpreting the Japanese government's intention. Army typists helped OP-20-G prepare the final copies of the text. All that Kramer was required to do was supervise the procedure to ensure that the messages were clear of garbles as they were assembled in chronological order. Since he was not overworked, this makes even more puzzling his failure to pay attention to Mrs. Edgers' translation of the lights message. But the focus that Saturday was all on Purple. This was the result of the high anticipation that had been raised in the War and Navy departments by the pilot message that Tokyo's diplomatic response would contain indications of the timing and nature of Japan's next move—which was expected would be military rather than diplomatic. It turned out to be a false expectation. The first thirteen parts contained no significant intelligence.

"The Government of Japan, prompted by a genuine desire to come to an amicable understanding with the Government of the United States," was the opening of what was nothing more than an extended statement asserting Japan's "utmost sincerity" in the effort made since April "in order that the two countries by their joint efforts may secure the peace of the Pacific area."[23] The self-justificatory memorandum meandered through a summary of eight months of negotiations, which Tokyo claimed had been motivated by "the immutable policy of the Japanese government to insure stability of East Asia and to promote world peace." The United States and Britain were repeatedly accused of conspiring with the Chinese Nationalist government to block Japan's "constructive endeavors" to stabilize the Far East and "realize the ideal of common prosperity in cooperation with these regions."[24]

For all its accusatory language there were no indications of what Japan's next move was going to be. The presumption that the fourteenth part, which was not picked up until after midnight, would provide the final tip-off of when the war would break out, like the "East Wind Rain" alert, was another misconception that was to obsess congressional investigators and postwar conspiracy theorists. But Tokyo's negative response had been anticipated ever since the secretary of state had presented the Japanese ambassadors with the ten-point summary on 26 November and had even been foreshadowed by Nomura's initial reaction that Hull's ten-point note would be taken as an ultimatum in Tokyo. Anything other than a flat rejection would have come as a surprise, so there was nothing startling about the statement that "the Japanese government regrets that it cannot accept the proposals as a basis for negotiation."[25]

"This means war," Roosevelt declared when he finished reading the document, according to his junior naval aide, Lieutenant Lester R. Schulz.[26] The president's practiced eye had no difficulty filleting the bones from thirteen pages of Japan's diplomatic carping, which concluded by accusing the United States of "aiding Great Britain and preparing to attack, in the name of self-defense, Germany and Italy, two powers striving to establish a new order in Europe."[27] Roosevelt's off-the-cuff reaction did not indicate that he expected Japan to immediately attack the United States the next day, which was how his statement was to be misconstrued by those who claim that he had engineered an impasse from which Japan had no way out but to go to war.[28] Roosevelt did not need to wait for the fourteenth part of the response to know that a major rupture with Japan was inevitable. The president had already anticipated that a breakdown in diplomatic negotiations was inevitable. Earlier that evening he had made an unprecedented telegraphic appeal "for the sake of humanity" to the emperor of Japan. Declaring that the United States bore no hostile intentions toward the Japanese, he urged the emperor to "give thought in this definite emergency to the ways of dispelling the dark clouds . . . to restore traditional amity and prevent further death and destruction in the world."[29]

If it was obvious to the president from the first thirteen parts of Tokyo's memorandum that war was about to break out in the Far East, it was by no means so obvious to the senior naval and military officers who read it that Saturday evening. The signed receipts recording the MAGIC deliveries did not survive, and no record was kept of individual reactions to the contents of the pouches. But the recollections given as testimony revealed a surprising forgetfulness. What can be established beyond doubt is that the president received his MAGIC pouch, which was dropped off at the White House by Commander Kramer, shortly before 9:30 P.M.

Neither the chief of naval operations nor the director of war plans could be reached by telephone to alert them to the new MAGIC. Stark was at the National Theater, and Turner was out exercising the brood of Lhasa apso terriers that he and his wife raised as a hobby. According to Kramer's testimony, he therefore crossed them off his courier round, which he began with his wife driving the family car north up Connecticut Avenue to the Wardman Park Hotel, where the secretary of the navy resided. It was around ten o'clock when Knox read the memorandum. After studying the pages for twenty minutes in his suite, the secretary made "a number of phone calls including Mr. Hull."[30] Security prevented a discussion of MAGIC information on open telephone lines, so they arranged to meet at Hull's State Department office with the secretary of war next morning at ten o'clock to discuss Japan's reply. Kramer records that he was asked to be present to answer any questions about the intercepts.[31]

It was 11:20 P.M. before Mrs. Kramer drove up to the Arlington home of the director of naval intelligence on North Uhle Street. Wilkinson was hosting a dinner for Vichy French naval officers, so he discreetly withdrew with General Miles and another guest, Admiral Beardall, the president's senior naval aide, into an adjoining room with Kramer before unlocking the leather pouch containing the thirteen-part message. After some discussion they concluded that "it certainly looked as though the Japanese were terminating negotiations," but neither the director of naval intelligence nor his Army counterpart thought it warranted any immediate action.[32]

According to Kramer's account, which he committed to paper in 1944, Wilkinson did then telephone the chief of naval operations, who by that time had returned home from the theater.[33] Stark was vague in his congressional testimony about whether he had actually discussed the first thirteen parts of Tokyo's response with Wilkinson, and he did not know if he had been called about it before or after he had received a phone call from the president about the latest MAGIC. But he, too, declared that he would not have regarded it as "anything that required action."[34]

More surprising was that Stark's deputy, Admiral Ingersoll, and Admiral Turner both testified that they had read the memorandum on Saturday evening. They concurred that they, too, had considered but rejected sending out another war warning. Such certainty has to be suspicious since Kramer had not taken them the MAGIC pouch containing Tokyo's response. It would have exceeded the top speed of his car to have driven from Arlington out to Chevy Chase, Maryland, where Turner lived, and to have recrossed to the other side of the Potomac again to reach Ingersoll's residence and to then have returned to the Navy Department shortly after midnight, when Kramer put the MAGIC pouch back in the safe. After the duty watch officer at OP-20-G had assured him that the fourteenth part had still not been transmitted by Tokyo, with relief Mrs. Kramer was able to drive her dog-tired spouse home, where they retired around one.[35]

While Kramer had been making the rounds on the Navy's list of MAGIC recipients that Saturday evening, Colonel Bratton was handling the army deliveries. A West Pointer of professorial intellect that belied his bearlike stature and the nickname "Togo," Bratton was well qualified to head the G-2 Far East Section. He had spent four years in Japan, first as a language student and then attending a course at the Imperial General Staff College, later returning to duty in Japan as the U.S. military attaché in Tokyo. Like Kramer, Bratton had been putting in long and exhausting hours managing the Army's decoding and translation of the Purple traffic as the crisis deepened. He was therefore intimately familiar with all the nuances at play in the Japanese diplomatic position. At the 1944 Army board of inquiry, Bratton was to testify under oath "without equivocation and without qualification" that between nine and ten that Saturday evening he organized the delivery of MAGIC pouches to generals Marshall, Miles, and Gerow.[36]

"It was my practice to deliver them their copies before I went to the State Department," Bratton recalled of how he began his second MAGIC courier round that Saturday. He testified that he had first dropped off Marshall's locked pouch with Colonel Walter Bedell Smith, the secretary of the general staff, who was not cleared for MAGIC, with instructions about its urgency. Bratton stated that he then handed a copy of the thirteen parts of the Japanese response to the director of military intelligence, and had a brief discussion about it with General Miles. Bratton then left the pouch for General Gerow with Colonel Charles K. Gailey, Jr., because the head of Army War Plans was not available. He then headed from the War Department to State, to drop off the MAGIC pouch containing Cordell Hull's copy with the duty watch officer around 10:30 P.M.

Bratton's testimony that he had personally delivered to the senior members of the General Staff or their aides the thirteen parts that Saturday evening led the 1944 Army court of inquiry to conclude that General Marshall and his principal officers must therefore have been aware of the implications of Tokyo's response ten hours before the Japanese attacked Pearl Harbor. On the presumption that this MAGIC was tantamount to a war warning, they concluded that the chief of staff of the army "failed . . . to get General Short on the evening of December 6th and the early morning of December 7th, the critical information indicating an almost immediate break with Japan, though there was ample time to have accomplished this."[37]

A year later, when Bratton appeared before the congressional investigating committee, he dramatically revised his testimony. Claiming that his memory had been at fault, he now swore that he had *not* made the rounds with the MAGIC pouch that Saturday evening as he had previously testified. His "recantation" had been obtained by Clausen, who had been directed by Stimson to "discover whether or not he [Bratton] misled the Army Board" into censuring Marshall and the senior members of the Army General Staff for failing to pass the "critical information" to Short.[38] In colorful anecdotal detail, Clausen described in his memoir how he got Bratton to recant his previously sworn statements by confronting him with affidavits sworn by Marshall, Bedell Smith, Miles, Gerow, and six other former War Department officers. Their affidavits all attested that *no* deliveries of the first thirteen parts of Tokyo's memorandum message had been made to them that Saturday evening by the head of the Far East Section. Corroboration for their claim had been provided by the sworn statement of Lieutenant Colonel Carlisle C. Dusenbury, the G-2 Japan desk officer who had been on duty watch that Saturday evening. He stated that Bratton had gone home at nine o'clock, leaving him with instructions to distribute the MAGIC pouches after the fourteenth part was received. Dusenbury said that when it arrived shortly after midnight, he decided that it was not sufficiently alarming to warrant disturbing the recipients in the small hours of the morning. He attested that he therefore went home without making the distribution round because he "did not wish to disturb the usual recipients who were probably asleep, as I did not see the implications of immediate hostilities."[39]

Confronted by Clausen in the "delightful" splendor of the George Cinq hotel in Paris with no fewer than ten affidavits, three sworn by generals, each one flatly contradicting the testimony Bratton had given to the Army court of inquiry, the colonel recanted. Assuring his readers that the colonel had the look of "an impaled fish," Clausen claimed it was the "sad and droopy" look that was familiar to him as a prosecuting attorney when he "had a criminal dead to rights on the witness stand."[40] With the satisfaction of a Grand Inquisitor who had wrung a confession from a recusant, Clausen described how Bratton's memory "had been refreshed" by reading the sworn statements of his brother officers "to the effect that they did not receive these pouches from G-2 on the night of the 6th."[41]

Clausen's glee in "proving," as he put it, that Bratton had lied was a hollow triumph because General Miles had to testify that he had read the thirteen parts of Tokyo's message that evening at Wilkinson's home. The former director of military intelligence told the congressional hearing that he had concluded that it was "of little military significance," since Japan's rejection had been anticipated for some time."[42] In testimony that undermined the object of Clausen's inquisitorial effort, Miles himself had admitted that he had knowledge of Tokyo's thirteen-part response on Saturday when he declared that he had "contented himself that night by calling Colonel Bratton at his home about 11:30 P.M., and assuring myself that a full reply would be disseminated next morning on Sunday and that he would be in our offices then."[43] While he "could not remember exactly what was decided between Colonel Bratton and myself that night," he admitted that he had decided that evening that there was "no reason for alerting or waking up the chief of staff." Miles also said that the head of his Far East Section, during the course of the conversation, "satisfied me that the messages *were being delivered* or would be delivered early next morning when the complete message was in [emphasis added]."[44]

General Miles's testimony may explain the resigned tone of Bratton's affidavit in which he had admitted that "in the light of the evidence before me it did seem advisable to modify some of my statements."[45] It suggests that when faced by the affidavits of a phalanx of brother officers contradicting his earlier testimony, Bratton, as a West Point graduate steeped in the military academy's code of loyalty, may well have decided to put the honor of the "long gray line" before the truth. "I know all of these officers; they are men of honor and integrity," Bratton tersely told the congressional hearing, "and if they say that they didn't receive the pouches from me or Colonel Dusenbury, or one of my assistants then my recollection must have been at fault and I so admit."[46]

Only a matter of weeks after reversing his testimony before the congressional committee Bratton reverted to his original version when he confided in Colonel Raymond Orr, a fellow officer on General MacArthur's staff in Tokyo. He assured Orr that the U.S. Army chief of staff must have been well aware of the implications of the thirteen-part memorandum on the eve of the Japanese attack on Pearl Harbor because he had already been advised that it was coming in earlier that Saturday afternoon. Bratton said that he had vainly tried to persuade Marshall to issue another war alert, but that he had refused and left for his quarters at Fort Meyer after announcing that he "did not want to be disturbed."[47]

Whether Marshall was "disturbed" that Saturday evening remains one of the enduring of enigmas of the Pearl Harbor mystery. The army chief of staff demonstrated a remarkable inability to recollect precisely where he was, what he was doing, or what he knew during all the hours that elapsed after he left the War Department on Saturday and his return to the office mid-morning on Sunday.[48] In addition to having been alerted that Saturday afternoon by the pilot message of Tokyo's incoming memorandum, Marshall had also received news that two Japanese invasion convoys had been spotted steaming for the Malay Peninsula. As the highest ranking military officer in the U.S. Army, Marshall, it might be presumed, would have kept in touch with the onrush of events. His apparent detachment in the hour of supreme national crisis is as peculiar as it was out of character for someone as conscientious as Marshall.

When cross-examined, Marshall admitted that his standing orders required that "if anything came up at night on which I could act that night, on which it was necessary I should act that night, it should be brought to my attention immediately."[49] But the army chief of staff insisted that he had gone to bed that night "without any knowledge that the Japanese were sending any reply at all."[50] Yet when questioned about

his whereabouts on Saturday evening, he could only say, "I
think I was at home," although he admitted that he "could not
be certain about that." Nor could he recall what he was doing
at his quarters, or who his duty orderlies were. He was, however, remarkably "certain" that neither Colonel Bratton nor
anyone else had made a MAGIC delivery at Fort Meyer that
evening. Such equivocal testimony from Marshall, who had a
reputation for precision, must raise many doubts about his
version.[51] It stretches credibility to accept that while the president had telephoned the chief of naval operations, he would
not also have consulted with the U.S. Army chief about Tokyo's
message, which had promoted his remark, "This means war!"

   "I did not receive, or see, any parts of the message mentioned until the morning of 7 December when a conference
was held with the Chief of Staff," General Gerow declared. "If
I had received parts of the message on the night of 6 December,
I would have immediately warned the overseas commanders
and informed the Chief of Staff. Access to the Chief of Staff for
such purposes was always open to me."[52] The testimony of the
chief of army war plans about the intelligence value of Tokyo's
memorandum is in direct conflict with his fellow staff officers,
who, without exception, did not think it required sending out
another war warning. Given the uniformity of their reaction,
it is most unlikely, despite Gerow's testimony to the contrary,
that Marshall would have disagreed with the majority opinion.
After 7 December he may well have concluded that his prestige
would be irretrievably damaged if he, too, had to admit he
had failed to see any special significance in the Japanese response.[53] So either Colonel Bratton lied to tarnish the reputation of the army chief of staff—as Colonel Clausen set out to
"prove"—or Bratton's original testimony was the truth and
General Marshall's reputation had to be protected by perjuri-
ous conspiracy.[54]

   While it may now be too late to resolve the questions raised
by Clausen's affidavits, the conflicting accounts of who saw the
MAGIC that night, far from exonerating Marshall, only serve
to highlight the army chief of staff's failure to be able to recall
his own movements. The most persuasive evidence that he *did
not spend* the evening at his quarters up on Arlington Hill, or
retire early to bed, appears in a newspaper headline in the
following day's *Washington Times Herald:* MARSHALL GOES
TO VETS REUNION. If the report was correct, then Marshall
was at the University Club that Saturday evening, where he
was given a cheering "vote of confidence."[55] There was no rea-

son for the newspaper to have manufactured the report BE-FORE the Japanese attack made the whereabouts of the Army chief that evening a matter of supreme importance. But it does raise a large question about why Marshall went to elaborate lengths to conceal his whereabouts on the eve of Japan's attack on Pearl Harbor.

If Marshall had been the toast of a reunion of Army veterans, why should he choose not to remember what must have been a memorable occasion? Possibly it was because the University Club on 16th Street was several blocks away from the White House. This convenient proximity would have made it easy for Marshall to have slipped in to see the president after the reunion broke up. Given Roosevelt's declared conviction that Japan was on the brink of war, a late-night crisis conference with his army chief of staff and the secretaries of war and the navy would make sense. But there is no record that the president's inner cabinet, which he liked to call his "War Council," ever met that Saturday, nor was any testimony ever given to any of the Pearl Harbor inquiries and investigations that even alluded to such a meeting.

An account that the secretary of the navy confided to James G. Stahlman, a trusted longtime associate of Knox from the newspaper business he had run before being called to Washington, asserts that Roosevelt did indeed call a meeting of his "War Council" at the White House late on the night of 6 December. According to Stahlman, who was at the time a reserve naval intelligence officer in Washington, Knox unburdened the secret to him after returning from his fact-finding mission to Pearl Harbor after the Japanese attack. Angered as he was by the scenes of death and destruction he had witnessed on Battleship Row, the secretary of the navy informed Stahlman that he was shocked to find, after questioning Admiral Kimmel and his staff, that the Pacific Fleet had never received the war warning he had agreed would be sent out at the nighttime session of the War Council. "He told me," Stahlman wrote, "that the following had sat for a considerable portion of the night of December 6, anticipating a Japanese strike somewhere: FDR, Stimson, Marshall, Knox and John McCrea [Stark's aide] and Frank Beatty [Knox's aide].[56] If a War Council session had been convened by the president, then the precision of Stahlman's list of attendees, which did not include Secretary Hull, lends credence to his account. It would explain why there was so much inconsistency over who had seen the Saturday evening

MAGIC pouch and the mystery of the army chief's where-abouts that night.[57]

The "Visitors Log" does not record that Marshall, or any members of Roosevelt's "War Council" were admitted to the White House at any time that Saturday evening, and according to the usher's record, the president retired at a quarter to midnight.[58] This does not mean that a vigil did not take place, only that if it did, it was not recorded. After the events of the next day it might well have been considered politically expedient to conceal that there had been a late-night vigil on the eve of war breaking out, especially since it did not result in a warning to the Hawaiian command. The question of whether Roosevelt and his key advisers "deliberately sat through the night of 6 December 1941 waiting for the Japs to strike somewhere," as Stahlman said Knox had told him, or the president conversed with them on the telephone cannot be resolved without first-hand documentary proof. But these two possibilities make more sense than the "official" version that the president retired to bed without consulting Marshall, who also insisted he, too, slept soundly because he had not seen the memorandum that had moved his commander in chief to declare, "This means war!"

There is something decidedly suspicious about the echoing testimony that would have history believe that a complete air of calm enveloped the United States leadership on the night before the storm broke in the Pacific. It has too much the appearance of being contrived to be convincing. What is more, it is contradicted by the diary kept by one member of the administration, which provides an account that is more in keeping with what might be expected as the tension and uncertainty of the crisis with Japan came to a head. Assistant Secretary of State Adolph Berle recorded that Saturday 6 December should go down in history as "the day, when in practice, the war really started."[59] After taking his daughter that afternoon to the National Theater to see the matinée performance of *The Student Prince* operetta, Berle returned to the State Department, where he spent the entire evening working on the text of the message that Roosevelt was to give Congress in the event of a Japanese attack on British and Dutch territory in the Far East.

At around seven o'clock Berle notes that "Army Intelligence reported that they had intercepted the text of the reply which Japan was to make." His diary therefore provides independent confirmation that Bratton did make at least one stop on his second MAGIC delivery that evening because Berle records, "It was not only a flat turn down, but a coarse and gratuitous and insulting message as well. Bad as this was, the accompanying message, likewise intercepted, was worse. The Japanese envoys were to keep this message locked up in their safe and present it only on receipt of a signal: *and during this time the final dispositions were to be completed* [emphasis added].[60]

What is most noteworthy about Berle's account is that he provides independent corroboration that by Saturday night the Roosevelt administration was bracing itself for war. The assistant secretary of state "turned into bed about one A.M. feeling very uneasy." Like the president, Berle had grasped the ominous significance of Tokyo's response *without* the final part. This makes it more curious that military and naval officers who read the same MAGIC decrypts had concluded that they were "not of great military significance" without the fourteenth part. That night only two significant pieces of the intelligence picture were still missing in Washington: when Japan would attack and whether the blow would fall simultaneously on United States territory in the Pacific. And those questions were not answered when the final part of the Japanese diplomatic response was intercepted by the Navy's Bainbridge Island listening post shortly after midnight.

"Obviously it is the intention of the American government to conspire with Great Britain," the fourteenth part of Tokyo's memorandum began in accusatory language that continued for a full page before concluding: "The Japanese government regrets to have to notify hereby the American Government that in view of the attitude of the American Government it cannot but consider that it is impossible to reach an agreement through further negotiations."[61]

The assumption has often erroneously been made that this was *the* declaration of war and that it had been relayed to Admiral Kimmel that night, it could have saved the Pacific battle fleet from destruction the next morning.[62] But the memorandum was precisely constructed so as *not to be taken* as indicating that the Japanese were going to war. Although the inference was self-evident from its tone, the language used did not specifically indicate there would be a rupturing of diplomatic relations with the United States, and there was certainly not the slightest hint of any intention to attack the United States at Pearl Harbor or in the Philippines. Insulting and gratuitous though Tokyo's diplomatic posturing may have appeared to the assistant secretary of state, the rejection of the American ten-point note amounted to nothing more sinister than formal notice that Japan could not continue with the current round of negotiations.[63]

It is for this reason that the diplomatic memorandum provoked so little excitement among the intelligence staff officers of the War and Navy departments, at least not among those who would admit to having seen it that Saturday. Because it contained no new information about Japanese intentions other than the anticipated breaking off from the current round of negotiations it approved "relatively unimportant" and "of little significance" and "not anything that required action." But because it was the Hawaiian commands that had been denied any notification of its receipt that Saturday, Tokyo's diplomatic response was later to be regarded by congressional investigators as *the final warning* from MAGIC that war was about to erupt.[64]

Whether General Marshall was notified that night or not, what is significant is that it was not anything in the fourteen-part message that finally prompted his decision to issue a final war alert to *all* the Pacific commands next morning. It was the specific instruction from Tokyo concerning the time that the memorandum was to be delivered to the State Department. This message was not transmitted until early on Sunday morning. When it was translated, the one o'clock deadline that jumped out from the translation of the decrypt was the information that finally set the war alarms ringing in Washington.

10

"AIR RAID PEARL HARBOR, THIS IS NOT DRILL"

Kept in the Dark by Washington, the Hawaiian Command Ignored the Last-Minute Warnings

W ill the Ambassador please submit to the United States Government (if possible to the Secretary of State) our reply to the United States at 1:00 P.M. on 7th, your time," was the delivery instruction that Tokyo gave its Washington Envoys.[1] They were also told that after decrypting the next two Purple messages, which thanked the diplomats and the military attaché in Washington for all their efforts, the ambassadors were to "destroy at once the remaining cipher machine and all machine codes. Dispose in like manner also secret documents."[2]

The Purple diplomatic communication to the Japanese Washington embassy that ordered the severing of their most secret communications umbilical cord was a more direct indication of the imminence of war than the Japanese government's formal diplomatic message. Transmitted at 4:40 A.M. U.S. East Coast time on Sunday morning, they were picked up at what was twenty minutes before midnight on Saturday in the Hawaiian time zone.

As the Japanese ambassadors in Washington received their final directions, the forces of the Combined Fleet were steaming from the South China Sea to the mid-Pacific toward their dawn attacks. Ploughing the waters of the Gulf of Siam, an invasion fleet of troop transports and escorting warships was heading for the narrow Kra Peninsula at the frontier of Malaya and Thailand. In the western Pacific two small forces were on course for Guam and Wake Island, while the largest Japanese naval task force was far out in the mid-Pacific under patchy clouds and the waning moon. The twenty-four knots being made by the Hawaiian Striking Force rapidly devoured the distance separating it from its launching point two hundred miles due north of Oahu, where a massive air strike was to fly off at sunrise the next morning to attack the Pacific Fleet.

In Honolulu, to the east of Pearl Harbor, which for most Americans conjured up pictures of tropical playground for the rich rather than a naval base, the lights from the flamingo-pink Royal Hawaiian sparkled off the waters of Waikiki as couples danced on the hotel terrace in the breeze of another balmy tropical night. For listeners at home Honolulu radio station KGMB announced that it would remain on the air playing dance music all night. It was not announced that the arrangement had been made by the Hawaiian Department's air commander. The U.S. Army was paying the tab for the broadcasts, which acted as a homing beacon for the twelve B-17 bombers winging their way in from the mainland and due to arrive at eight the next morning.

On that last night of tropical peace on Oahu there were few indications ashore that the Army and Navy were on a war alert. This was in keeping with Washington's instructions not to alarm local residents. Only the most observant would have noted that at the large Army airfields at Hickam and Wheeler, on either side of the enclosed waters of Pearl Harbor, armed sentries patrolled the rows of bombers and pursuit planes, which had been parked wing tip to wing tip to facilitate guarding them against sabotage.

Only one officer and a single switchboard operator were on night duty at the Naval Control Center on Ford Island, in the middle of Pearl Harbor. Seven PBY amphibian flying boats were drawn up on the concrete slipway, in readiness for a dawn patrol mission over the waters south and west of Oahu. Behind the line of hangars loomed the six massive dreadnoughts moored along Battleship Row, a couple of hundred yards off the eastern shore of Ford Island. Their jutting gun barrels and high fighting tops cut menacing silhouettes against the distant purple backdrop of Diamond Head.

At sea off Barber Point, on the western side where the narrow channel entered the lochs of Pearl Harbor, the duty guard destroyer USS *Ward* steamed back and forth along the approaches. Two Navy minesweepers, the *Crossbill* and the *Condor*, patrolled off the floating boom that carried the heavy steel nets locking off entrance to the deep-water channel to enemy submarines.

On the coastal peaks around the island, the operators of the Army's mobile radar sets were still asleep. They were to be roused in a few hours, when they would get the generators in the equipment trucks powered up for the scheduled turn-on time of two hours before dawn. But even if the electronic beams from their "mattress spring" arrays had been probing the dark offshore waters before four A.M., the 132-mile maximum range of their primitive radars would not have reached far enough to have detected the approaching Japanese task force bearing down on Oahu from the north.[3]

An arrowhead formation of a light cruiser and four destroyers scouted three miles of the two battleships which steamed in line ahead, each flanked by a heavy cruiser. Following behind was the main force of six carriers with the 335 aircraft aboard that were to be flown off to deliver a knockout blow to the Pacific Fleet. During the final hours of darkness, as the Japanese aircrews dozed fitfully, mechanics made final checks on the *Nakajima* "Kate" torpedo planes and the *Aichi* "Val" dive bombers and the Mitsubishi "Zero" fighters. Fate had been smiling on Admiral Nagumo, whose striking force had in ten days traversed undetected more than four thousand miles of the Pacific to the go-no-go point while the Japanese envoys in Washington unwittingly played diplomatic stooge for Tokyo. The previous afternoon, when still some six hundred miles from their target, the Striking Force had received the order to follow through with the planned attack. All hands had cheered Admiral Yamamoto's Nelsonian signal of encouragement: "THE RISE AND FALL OF THE JAPANESE EMPIRE DEPENDS UPON THIS BATTLE EVERYONE WILL DO HIS DUTY WITH UTMOST EFFORTS."[4]

In the early hours of 7 December, shortly after Nagumo had ordered his Striking Force south for their battle charge toward Oahu, he had received a reassuring report from the Japanese consulate at Honolulu, relayed by Tokyo. It confirmed that apart from the two American carriers and the heavy cruiser squadron, the rest of the Pacific Fleet was unsuspecting and at anchor in Pearl Harbor.

It was 2:00 A.M. Sunday in Hawaii and 7:30 A.M. in Washington (in 1941 the time-zone difference was five and a half hours) when Commander Kramer arrived at his office on the second deck of the Navy Department building. According to his testimony, he found the fourteenth part of Tokyo's diplomatic response already on his desk. He was still digesting its language when he was summoned into Admiral Stark's office by Admiral Wilkinson. Following the delivery by McCollum of the latest MAGIC, they all convened again with the chief of naval operations. For Far East Section Chief McCollum the "virulence and tenor of the language" of Tokyo's answer to the ten points was a clear indication "that we could expect war."[5] Wilkinson agreed and supported the proposal made by McCollum and Kramer that it warranted an additional alert to all fleet commanders.

"No, I don't think any further warning is necessary," Admiral Stark declared, rejecting their suggestion.[6] The chief of naval operations then released Kramer, who set off on foot to Pennsylvania Avenue to hand deliver the latest MAGIC pouches to the White House and State Department. The president, who had decided only the evening before that Tokyo was set on course for war, observed almost casually, according to his naval aide, Admiral Beardall, "that it looked as though the Japanese are going to sever negotiations."[7] Kramer then made his way through the echoing marble corridors of the Old Executive Office Building to the State Department, where Knox was meeting Hull. He personally handed a full copy of Tokyo's fourteen-part response to the secretary of the navy at five minutes to ten and, he testified, was back at his own office at the Navy Department on Constitution Avenue by 10:20 A.M.[8]

The Army courier had already delivered the morning MAGICs to the secretary of state by the time Colonel Bratton reached his office in the Munitions Building, adjoining the Navy Department. In his testimony before the Army Pearl Harbor board, Bratton put the time of his arrival as before eight o'clock. But his assistant, Dusenbury, testified that his superior did not arrive until after nine.[9] The hour difference in their claims was significant because Dusenbury claimed that Bratton was reading the final section of Tokyo's message when the translation of the Purple intercept instructing the Japanese envoys to go at one o'clock to the State Department was brought in.

The significance of the delivery deadline, which became so obvious a few hours later, was not immediately apparent to any of those who saw it in Washington that Sunday morning.

In another one in the chain of failures of the intelligence process, the warning that might have saved the Hawaiian commanders from being caught totally by surprise did not go out at once. The delay was then compounded by poor judgment and bad luck.

Colonel Bratton, who was the first to appreciate that the deadline might be timed to a surprise attack, testified that he was "immediately stunned" and launched "into frenzied activity" because the intercept "was peculiarly worded and the implication was inescapable and that was of vital importance."[10] That urgency was paramount was quickly appreciated because it was unprecedented for the Japanese to request a formal meeting with the secretary of state on a Sunday. Bratton later said he had been certain that it indicated "the Japanese were going to attack some American installation in the Pacific area."[11] His testimony confirmed that at the time it did not occur to him that Pearl Harbor and the Pacific Fleet might be the installation in danger.

"Nobody in ONI, nobody in G-2, knew that any major element of the fleet was in Pearl Harbor on Sunday morning the 7th of December," Bratton insisted. Nor was he the only staff officer in Washington to assume that the fleet had put to sea "because that was part of the war plan, and they had been given a war warning."[12] This common misapprehension in Washington was evident among the War and Navy department staff officers who gave testimony to the various wartime investigations and the postwar congressional hearings. The possibility that the Pacific Fleet might be a target had not occurred to anyone in Washington since July, after the westward shift to the Philippines of the United States' Pacific defense front line.

It was only the potential danger to MacArthur's command and the garrison on Guam—not Hawaii—that Bratton said had sprung to his mind and fired his determination to get an immediate alert sent to all Pacific commands. But he could not do this without authority. General Marshall was not in his office at nine o'clock, nor was the chief of Army war plans or his superior, General Miles.

According to Bratton's testimony, he at once tried to telephone the U.S. Army chief at his quarters. The orderly who answered the phone at Fort Myer informed him that the general was horseback riding. Bratton left instructions that it was "vitally important" that he communicate with the U.S. Army chief "at the earliest possible moment."[13] According to Bratton, the U.S. Army chief returned his call just before 10:30 A.M. He told Marshall there was "a most important message," which he offered to bring out to Fort Myer. He testified that Marshall told him curtly: "I am coming down to my office. You can give it to me then."[14]

"Hull is very certain that Japanese are planning some deviltry and we are all wondering when the blow will strike," was how Stimson recorded the apprehension at the Sunday morning conference he had with the secretary of state and Secretary Knox in his office in the Old Executive Office Building. After delivering to them Tokyo's memorandum, Kramer had returned to his office at 10:30 A.M. to find the one o'clock Purple intercept. He testified that he made a quick calculation "to get a picture of how this 1 o'clock Washington message tied up with the movement of the big Japanese convoy moving down the coast of French Indochina."[15] Adjustment for the time-zone conversion revealed that the deadline would occur in the predawn hours off the coast of Malaya, which Kramer, as an experienced naval officer, noted was "the normal times to institute amphibious operations."[16]

Commander Kramer had just concluded that the deadline for the delivery of Tokyo's response would probably coincide with the Japanese invasion force's putting troops ashore on the beaches of Kota Bharu in Malaya, when his yeoman brought in an intercepted message in plain language Japanese. From the English "STOP" at the end, he realized that it was a "hidden word" alert for Japan's embassies of a rupture of diplomatic relations, conveyed in a simple code whose instructions had been sent out in a Purple circular of 27 November.

In his haste to make sense of the message, the normally fastidious Kramer failed to notice that it contained the code word *Minami*, for the United States. His translation indicated therefore only that "Relations with *Japan and England* are not in accordance with expectations [*emphasis added*]."[17] The correct reading, that relations with *"the United States"* were *"on the brink of catastrophe,"* might well have sparked a more intense reaction when he took his translation into Stark's office a few minutes later. It was Captain McCollum, according to Kramer, who ventured that the one o'clock deadline coincided with 7:30 A.M. in Hawaii. The general consensus, however, was that the timing related to a Japanese attack somewhere in the Far East.

"Pearl Harbor, as such, was never mentioned," Kramer testified. This was in part explained because they all assumed that after being warned that Japan might launch into war,

Admiral Kimmel would have sent the fleet to sea. With less than two-and-a-half hours before the deadline, it was decided that Kramer should take the one o'clock intercept to the State Department, after first dropping off the MAGIC pouch for the White House.

After Kramer left the Navy Department, the discussion about the deadline intercept continued in the office of the chief of naval operations, according to McCollum's account. "Why don't you pick up the telephone and call Kimmel?" he recalled Wilkinson's asking Stark.[18] Considering the obsession for security that surrounded MAGIC, McCollum was surprised to see Stark actually lift the receiver of his desk telephone. "No, I think I will call the President," he said, changing his mind and asking for the White House.[19] But he could not be put through because Roosevelt was on another call. This meeting then broke up shortly before Admiral Turner arrived at his office at 11:15. The chief of war plans would testify that he had been informed of the deadline message and that Stark had only discussed what the Asiatic Fleet would do in the event of war. Turner's account is just not credible given the extent to which he was controlling intelligence and the importance the chief of naval operations attached to the message he was trying to discuss with the president.

Kramer by this time had made the MAGIC delivery to the White House and arrived at the State Department, where he delivered the message deadline to Hull, with the comment that according to his calculations, it appeared that "the Japanese intended to carry out their plans against Khota Baru [sic]."[20]

It was around 11:30 A.M. when General Marshall finally arrived at the War Department, a full hour after Bratton's phone call, according to Bratton's original testimony to the Army Pearl Harbor board. The U.S. Army chief of staff denied under oath that there had been any prior telephone conversation with Bratton, who, by the congressional hearings in 1945, had been persuaded by Clausen to agree with the sworn statements of Marshall and his other staff officers that their chief of staff had arrived in his office almost an hour earlier. Precisely when Marshall did arrive or why he had dallied on his Sunday morning ride at a time of national emergency remained unexplained and unresolved.

What is clear is the chief of staff of the U.S. Army, Marshall, was considerably discomforted that Bratton's original testimony made it appear that he was not on the spot that Sunday morning to handle the crisis precipitated by the deadline message. Whether it was 10:30 A.M. as Miles and Gerow attested, or 11:25, as Bratton first testified, the three agreed that they had all assembled in the chief of staff's office. Whether Marshall had or had not seen the first thirteen parts the previous evening, even Bratton noted that the chief of staff that morning had insisted on reviewing not only the final part, but the whole of the Tokyo memorandum. Bratton recalled they had to wait, with rising impatience, to discuss the issue of the delivery deadline. Only after Marshall had finished his deliberations did they agree that it almost certainly indicated Japanese hostile action against some American installations in the Pacific at or shortly after one o'clock that afternoon.[21]

After a brief discussion this conference concluded. The Washington mind-set was so firmly fixed on the Philippines that the deadline was not perceived to relate to a dawn air raid on Pearl Harbor, but to the possibility that an invasion force was heading under cover of darkness toward the coast of Luzon in the Philippines. It appeared to Marshall and his aides that it was MacArthur's forces who were the obvious target and that an invasion of the Philippines would be preceded by air raids on the airfields where the strategic bombing forces were based from the Japanese airfields on Formosa. As a precautionary measure, Miles urged that in addition to sending one to MacArthur an immediate warning be sent to the army commands in Panama, the West Coast, and Hawaii.[22] Marshall concurred with the view that "outlying possessions [should] be given an additional alert by the fastest possible means"[23] and drafted the warning in longhand on a piece of scratch paper.

> Japanese are presenting at one P.M. eastern standard time today what amounts to an ultimatum also they are under orders to destroy their code machines immediately. Just what significance the hour set may have we do not know, but be on the alert accordingly.[24]

Marshall then called the chief of naval operations on the secure White House telephone system. He later testified that he informed Stark in "a guarded way" of his decision to send out a fresh alert.[25] According to Marshall, the admiral believed "we had sent them so much already" that he "hesitated to send more."[26]

A few minutes later, Stark called back to say he had changed his mind and would "go along" with the chief of staff.

Stark proposed that a joint dispatch go out on the naval communications system, which was "quite rapid when the occasion demanded it."[27] Assured by Marshall that the Army could also "get it through very quickly," Stark agreed to use the Army's system and suggested all the Pacific commands be instructed to "inform their naval opposites."[28] Marshall therefore added the rider, "Inform naval authorities of this communication," and asked Bratton to take the draft to the message center for dispatch "at once by the fastest safe means."[29]

"If there is any question of priority, give the Philippines priority," General Gerow told Bratton as he walked out of the door with the war warning. Marshall testified that if he had telephoned the warning, he would have given priority to MacArthur, then Panama, before calling the Hawaiian commandant.[30] He acknowledged that he had considered using the scrambler telephone because the deadline was fast approaching but had rejected the idea because it posed too great a risk to the security of MAGIC.[31]

It was a decision that he was evidently still chewing over in his mind when Bratton returned. Concerned about the delay in getting a cable to reach MacArthur, he sent Bratton back to find out how long it would take to get the dispatch to the Pacific commands. Lieutenant Colonel Edward P. French, the officer in charge of the War Department Signal Center—who testified that he had "never seen him more excited"—assured Bratton that it would take "about 30 or 40 minutes."[32] In the atmosphere of crisis none of the parties, including the U.S. Army chief of staff, appears to have appreciated that time would have to be added to this estimate for ciphering, deciphering, and actual delivery of the warning.

Marshall might also have changed his mind about using the scramble telephone to warn General Short if he had been told that static had closed down the Army radio link to Hawaii. This problem was brought to French's attention *only after* the dispatch had gone out to the Caribbean Defense command and the Philippines at midday. Since Hawaii had not been given priority, French decided to send Marshall's warning in a service cipher via the commercial cable networks, whose transmitters had four times the power of the Army station. He believed, wrongly as it turned out, that the teleprinter at the Hawaiian Department's Fort Shafter headquarters was already directly connected with the RCA office in Honolulu. It was not yet up and running. French's miscalculation was further to be compounded because the cable was sent out at 12:17

without a priority designation. When it reached RCA in Honolulu three minutes after the deadline expired, it was pigeon-
holed for the next delivery to Fort Shafter.[33]

In a script that was more French farce than Greek tragedy,
Marshall's warning was fated not to reach the hands of General
Short until just before three, six hours after the last attacking
aircraft had flown off that afternoon following the disruptions
caused by the Japanese air raid. History can never know
whether the final war warning might have alleviated the magnitude of the disaster. But what is certain is that a mere hour's
warning could not have prevented the Pacific Fleet's being
caught unprepared, even if Kimmel and Short had interpreted
the cable to have required an immediate alert against an air
attack.

At the very least the Army might have broken out the ammunition for their antiaircraft guns, and the watertight doors
and ports of the battleships in the harbor could have been
closed, making them less vulnerable to turning turtle when
flooding occurred as a result of torpedo hits. But there would
not have been any time for the Battle Force to have raised
steam and put out to sea. At best their fighter and antiaircraft
defenses would have been alert and ready to meet the incoming raid. The Japanese, though, it must be remembered, had
planned their attack in the expectation that they might not
succeed in achieving total surprise. So while the casualty rate
among the Japanese planes carrying out the attack would have
been much higher, the raid was so massive that it could not
have been stopped from reaching its target. With fighters aloft
and antiaircraft batteries at the ready, it is probable that fewer
battleships would have sunk, saving hundreds of lives.

What is certain is that Kimmel and Short could not then
have been accused of being "asleep at the switch," even though
the scale of the disaster might have been just as great.[34] The
popular myth that all military and naval personnel on Oahu
were sound asleep until roused that Sunday morning by the
screech of diving Japanese planes and the sound of exploding
bombs is not supported by the record. Throughout the night
at least three naval vessels were on duty patrol off the entrance
to Pearl Harbor.

Every officer in the Pacific Fleet was aware, from scuttle-
butt rumors, if not from the newspapers and radio reports,
that diplomatic tensions between the United States and Japan
were approaching the breaking point. The current war alert,
the third in three months, may have been thin after ten days

without any action. The local sense of urgency among the U.S. service personnel ashore and afloat was also tempered by the perception of a danger limited to sabotage or submarine attack and conditioned by a peacetime attitude of caution and complacency. But neither of the Hawaiian commanders can be charged with complacency.

Admiral Kimmel had taken very seriously the responsibility of guarding the fleet against a surprise attack. Mindful of the historical precedents indicating Japan's penchant for striking without warning, in February he had promulgated a confidential letter to all his commanders envisaging that "a declaration of war might be preceded by (1) a surprise attack on the ships in Pearl Harbor (2) a surprise submarine attack on ships in operating area (3) a combination of these two."[35] The precautions he had instituted against a surprise attack included plans for long-range air and sea patrols, which were updated when the confidential letter was revised shortly before the October alert. So while Kimmel might have had no inkling from the intelligence he had received that Japan might make an air attack on Pearl Harbor, he had, however, taken steps to counter the probable threat that their submarines posed—either alone or as the outriders of a carrier raid from the Marshall Islands.

"It must be remembered that a single attack may or may not indicate the presence of more submarines waiting to attack," Kimmel's confidential letter advised the Pacific Fleet commanders. "It must be remembered, too, that a single submarine attack may indicate the presence of a considerable surface force probably composed of fast ships accompanied by a carrier." To counter the underwater menace, Kimmel's directive required that his task force commanders "be prepared to pursue or meet enemy ships that may be located by air search or other means."[36]

Long-range air reconnaissance was acknowledged by the Army and Navy to be the best defense against surprise air attack from an enemy carrier. Hawaiian air commanders had forecast in their March report that a strike "would most likely be launched from one or more carriers which would probably approach inside of three hundred miles." It would "come at sunrise" since "in a dawn air attack there is a high probability that it could be delivered as a complete surprise."[37] The around-the-compass, deep-ocean reconnaissance patrols out to 800 miles were called for by General Martin and Admiral Bellinger, in their joint report that also called for a force of 180

B-17 bombers as the minimum that would be required to effectively interdict an advancing enemy fleet. But after priority had been given to building up MacArthur's heavy bomber strength in the Philippines, even the inadequate force of twenty-four Fortresses based at Wheeler Field west of Pearl Harbor had been depleted. By December only six flyable B-17s remained in Hawaii.

The Navy's air commander, therefore, had to assume the responsibility for carrying out deep-ocean reconnaissance. The PBY amphibians might have had extremely "long legs," but they were not capable of the interdiction role against approaching warships at sea for which the B-17s had specifically been designed. Admiral Bellinger was further handicapped by possessing only eighty-one Catalinas. Affectionately known as "Cats" by their aircrews, these black-painted flying boats were less feline in appearance than dragonflylike, with wide parasol section wings and bulbous observation blisters protruding from their fuselages.

Ungraceful though these PBYs were, their twin engines could sustain them aloft for sixteen hours. Such long missions, however, took a punishing toll on equipment and the aircrews, cutting back the effective flyable strength of each patrol wing by one third. Since each plane was capable of searching an 8-degree patrol out to a radius of seven hundred miles from Oahu, covering the full 360 degrees around the island on a daily basis would have required at least two hundred and fifty PBYs. The number of PBYs available for long-range air patrols was restricted by Kimmel's war plans which dictated that he keep a sufficient force in readiness for reconnaissance to the southwest to prepare for operations against the Marshalls. Training missions and rotating PBYs went to Wake and Midway. He simply did not have enough operational aircraft to have guaranteed that any approaching Japanese task force could have been spotted a full day before the carrier planes could get within striking distance of Pearl Harbor. With an effective force of only thirty PBYs serviceable for daily patrolling, only a third of the compass rose could be adequately covered in any twenty-four-hour period. The lack of aircraft meant that Kimmel had no choice but to leave nearly sixty percent of the seaborne approaches to the Hawaiian Islands unguarded.

The tactical decision confronting Admiral Kimmel and his air commander was on which sector to concentrate his limited air reconnaissance force. His war plan also called for launching

raids against the Japanese base in the Marshalls, to the southwest of the Hawaiian chain. The PBYs were essential to
carrying out this mission, and Kimmel could not afford to
fritter away his limited force with unnecessary patrols. "Had
I directed their use for intensive distance searches from Oahu,"
Kimmel was to testify, "I faced the peril of having these planes
grounded when the war plan was executed."[38]

Too few aircraft to patrol too much ocean dictated that
Kimmel cut his coat according to the available cloth. He decided to concentrate his main air reconnaissance effort on the
area of the southwestern approaches to Hawaii, which both
intelligence reports and strategic logic indicated was the most
likely sector from which a Japanese carrier force might attack.
His decision to leave the northern sector only intermittently
patrolled during the ten days between the receipt of the 27
November War warning and 7 December was not the result of
Kimmel's falling asleep at the switch, but a calculated decision, that he took in close consultation with his staff. It was
based on the best intelligence available of the direction in
which the enemy would most probably strike. Unfortunately
for the Pacific Fleet commander in chief, the Japanese, through
intelligence reports from Honolulu on the number of patrol
planes on Oahu, were able to exploit Kimmel's tactical dilemma to make their attack from due north, from which an
attack would be least expected and therefore have the best
chance of achieving total surprise.

"I took account of my probable future needs and of my
orders from the Navy Department," Kimmel testified, in justification of his deployment of air patrols. "I decided that I could
not risk having no patrol plane force worthy of the name for
the fleet's expected movement into the Marshalls."[39] After receiving the war warning, Kimmel had authorized the deployment of additional PBY patrol wings to Midway, Wake, and
Johnston islands. Nor were the forty-nine PBYs remaining on
Oahu sitting on the ground at the naval air bases at Barbers
Point, Ford Island, and Kaneohe. In addition to training flights,
they carried out scouting missions, flying to the north and
northwest of Oahu on a rotating schedule, in addition to executing a daily dawn reconnaissance over the fleet's exercise
areas and making deep-ocean reconnaissance toward the
Marshalls.

Taking into consideration the intelligence picture available
to the Pacific Fleet, the dictates of his war plan, the shortage
of aircraft, and the geographic constraints, Kimmel could not

have made any other decision. That was the conclusion his fellow admirals at the Navy board of inquiry came to concerning the charge that the Pacific Fleet commander had failed to mount a proper aerial guard on the northern approaches to Oahu. "The omission of this reconnaissance was not due to oversight or neglect," the board concluded. "It was the result of a military decision, reached after much deliberation and consultation with experienced officers and after weighing the information at hand and all the factors involved."[40]

On the morning of 7 December three PBYs were scheduled to be in the air on dawn patrol off the southern approaches to Pearl Harbor. They carried live depth charges and were under orders to sink any submerged submarine. Four more PBYs were exercising with U.S. submarines off Kaneohe on the eastern tip of Oahu and searching the Lahaina Road off the island of Maui.

At dawn five more PBYs took off from Midway to search the southwestern approaches to the atoll, as two more headed out to rendezvous with the carrier *Lexington*, which was then some 215 miles west of Pearl Harbor heading back from Wake. At sunrise this task force's commander, Admiral Halsey, also launched a squadron of eighteen planes with orders to fly ahead of *Lexington*, out to a radius of 150 miles before proceeding to Oahu to land at the Marine airfield at Ewa, which lay to the west of Pearl Harbor.

Contrary to the popular impression that the U.S. Navy was inactive and asleep that Sunday morning, over thirty Navy planes were aloft shortly after sunrise on 7 December, patrolling the approaches to the Hawaiian Islands from the northwest to the southwest of Pearl Harbor. The pilots of these planes were very much on the alert, but on the wrong side of Oahu to provide a warning when the Japanese attack planes flew in from the unguarded northern sector.

The popular myth that the defenders of Hawaii were asleep at dawn that Sunday owes more to the "Pearl Harbor Syndrome" than to the record, which confirms that the Navy was on guard and did disrupt the attack on Pearl Harbor by midget submarines. Oahu was surrounded by a force of twenty Japanese submarines, poised to attack the Pacific Fleet if it put to sea. The mission to penetrate the anchorage itself was assigned to the two-man midget submarines, each carrying two torpedoes.

This was the only element of Japan's Hawaii operation that failed to achieve surprise or hit any targets. The attack started to run into trouble in the hour after midnight, when the mother submarines, which had piggybacked the seventy-eight-foot-long midgets across the Pacific, released their charges off the entrance to the channel into Pearl Harbor. One of the midgets immediately began experiencing problems with its gyro compass and ran in erratic circles as its skipper tried valiantly to navigate his way in by staying close to the surface to use his stubby periscope. Its conning tower was spotted at 3:42 A.M. fifty yards off the port bow of the minesweeper *Condor*, standing guard a mile and three quarters off the entrance buoys.

"Sighted submerged submarine on westerly course 9 knots," *Condor* flashed by signal lamp to the guard destroyer *Ward*.[41] The four-stacker came racing over to investigate, her skipper Lieutenant William W. Outerbridge sounding off general quarters (maximum readiness). When a half-hour sonar search failed to produce any contact, Outerbridge secured his crew from action on the assumption that the sighting was a jumpy watch officer's false contact. The floating booms carrying the steel wire antisubmarine defense nets were then opened to let in the two guard minesweepers *Crossbill* and *Condor*, around 5 A.M., just as the first glimmers of dawn's gray light began fingering the sky over Diamond Head.

Neither the *Ward* nor the *Condor* reported the incident to the Harbor Control Post at the 14th Naval District Operations Center. Since there had been no alarm, the net defenses remained wide open for two hours, letting in at least two of the Japanese midget subs, which slipped through the channel submerged and undetected. The peacetime complacency by the respective skippers cost another chance to put the defense onto a higher level of alert.

The Pacific Fleet ordinance circulated by Admiral Kimmel had explicitly cautioned all commanders that "a single submarine attack may indicate the presence of a considerable surface force of fast ships."[42] But the gatekeepers to the fleet anchorage that morning reacted to events with a peacetime mentality rather than wartime vigilance. Standing orders required the Operations Center to contact the Pacific Fleet chief of staff and the naval district commandant in the event of any suspected attack. If Lieutenant Harold Kaminiski, the duty officer at the Operations Center, had received word of an unconfirmed submarine sighting, he might well have considered it sufficient justification for rousing the aides of Admiral Bloch. But since no word reached him, no report was made at first light.

If the alarm had been raised after the first midget submarine contact and if the chain of command had responded with alacrity and precision, Admiral Kimmel could have received three hours' warning that Pearl Harbor was a target for Japanese attack. A pattern of miscommunication and misjudgment was to hobble any chance of raising an alarm two hours later, when the first actual exchange of fire between United States and Japanese forces occurred, in an engagement in the waters of the Harbor entrance.

At 6:30 A.M. in the outer entrance to the buoyed channel, the skipper of *Antares*, a supply vessel with a lighter in tow, reported sighting the conning tower of a small submarine having trouble submerging.[43] When his report was picked up on the bridge of the *Ward*, the object was soon spotted by the destroyer's helmsman. Roused from his bunk for the second time that night, at 6:40 A.M., Lieutenant Outerbridge once more went to general quarters. As his destroyer charged toward the stumpy black object, he ordered the forward gun crew to fire at it. The first shell missed, but the second round hit below the conning tower. As the midget submarine keeled over and sank, the *Ward* dropped a full pattern of depth charges to seal its fate.

"We have attacked, fired upon, and dropped depth charges upon sub operating in the defensive area," Outerbridge immediately radioed. The Navy's communication station at Bishop Point, which picked up the *Ward*'s signal, logged it in at 6:53 A.M. The U.S. Navy had drawn first blood sixty-two minutes before the Japanese air attack began. No alarm bells were run at the 14th Naval District Headquarters for another half hour. *Ward*'s report was related to Watch Officer Kaminiski at the Naval Control Center, but after wasting precious minutes trying to get through to Bloch's aide, he gave up. Finally he was able to reach the naval district commander's chief of staff, who in turn called the duty officer on the Pacific Fleet staff. But when Commander Vincent Murphy tried to call Kaminiski back for confirmation of the details, the telephone lines to the control center were engaged. When Murphy reached his own office shortly before 7:30 A.M., he was given another enemy action report by the duty officer on Ford Island naval air station. One of the PBYs on dawn patrol, he was informed, had just "sunk a submerged submarine one mile off the entrance to Pearl Harbor."[44]

Admiral Kimmel, who had arisen at seven for his regular early morning round of Sunday golf with General Short, was not yet shaved or dressed when Murphy telephoned him with the reports. Although "not at all certain that this was a real attack," Kimmel said he would be "right down."[45] He was to testify that he decided not to order an emergency alert until he had personally confirmed the reports. He testified that he had received so many "false reports of submarines in the outlying area, I thought, well, I would wait for verification of the reports."[46] Kimmel was not alone in reacting with peacetime prudence rather than with the urgency demanded by a war situation. Admiral Bloch was also inclined to regard the *Ward*'s action signal as "just another of those false reports." He therefore ordered Kaminiski to get detailed confirmation from the skipper of the duty destroyer.

When Bloch learned that the matter had been already referred to the commander in chief, he decided to "await further developments."[47] The only direct action that the commandant of the 14th Naval District, who was directly responsible for guarding the fleet anchorage, ordered was that the ready-duty destroyer in the harbor sortie the channel to investigate. That it took the *Monoghan* three quarters of an hour to raise steam and get under way is confirmation that it would not have been possible to get the Battle Force to sea before the Japanese raid began. But if general quarters had been ordered by Kimmel at 7 A.M. when he received the action reports, crews would have been on the alert, manning their battle stations and antiaircraft guns, and the watertight hatches in their vessels secured for action.

During the vital half hour that was lost in confused communication and debate over whether an attack by Japanese submarines was really in progress, no officer from either of the two naval commands thought it necessary to inform the Army headquarters at Fort Shafter of the submarine engagement reports. If they had, then it might have prompted the Army duty officer to give more credence to a contact report received by the Army Information Center shortly after seven o'clock. It came from the mobile radar unit at Opana on the bluffs at Kahuku Point on the northernmost tip of Oahu.

Privates Joseph L. Lockard and George F. Elliot of the Signal Corps had been monitoring the flat green traces on the small oscilloscope display of their radar set since four A.M. If the chow truck bringing them their breakfast had made its way up the steep track on time, they would have switched off their set promptly at seven. It was two minutes past the hour when the trace suddenly began flipping up as a contact was made at the extreme edge of the radar's range. As Elliot later testified, he observed "something completely out of the ordinary on the radar screen."[48]

The green blips leaped about with such intensity that at first he thought that the set had developed a fault. After checking out the equipment, Elliot concluded that the trace "must be a flight of some sort."[49] The two operators estimated from the size of the trace on their screen that at least fifty aircraft were bearing down on Oahu from 132 miles to the north.

Lockard called the Army Information Center to report "the biggest sighting he had ever seen," but in his excitement he neglected to pass on his estimate of the number of aircraft.[50] As fate had arranged it, the crew manning the air defense plot at Fort Shafter, which was set up to keep track of an enemy attack, had already gone off duty at seven. Lieutenant Kermit Tyler, the duty officer to whom the call was relayed, was new at the job and inexperienced in radar terminology. But he knew that because a local radio station had been broadcasting all night, a flight of B-17s was coming in that morning from the West Coast. They made their landing approach over the north coast of Oahu—the same route taken by the Japanese. With no electronic system then available to identify friend from foe for the radar operators, Tyler was bound by security regulations from revealing the reason for his certainty that the incoming planes were American bombers.

"Well don't worry about it," Tyler told the radar operator Lockard with a confidence that belied the reality of the situation.[51] The irony was that both men were correct in their respective conclusions. A dozen B-17s were at that time less than two hundred miles away, flying in right behind the first wave of the Japanese air attack because both friend and foe were homing in on the music broadcast by the Honolulu radio station. If Lockard had explained that his radar contact indicated a flight of more than fifty aircraft, Tyler might have responded differently and the Hawaiian commands would have received a half-hour warning of the incoming air attack. The last chance was lost for sounding an alert that might have saved thousands of lives by warning the battleships and the fighter patrols to go on the defense against an air raid.

The radar operators at Opana continued to track the advancing blips of the incoming Japanese planes until they were within twenty miles from the coast, when the radar back-wave turned the trace into a green snowstorm of meaningless echoes. The four other Army radars had all closed down, or the one on the eastern tip of Oahu might have detected the approach of a lone float plane from the cruiser *Chikuma*, which made a high-level reconnaissance run over the fleet anchorage shortly after 7:30 A.M.

"ENEMY FORMATION AT ANCHOR. NINE BATTLESHIPS, ONE HEAVY CRUISER, SIX LIGHT CRUISERS ARE IN HARBOR." *Chikuma*'s pilot radioed back to the Striking Force.[52] Simultaneously a floatplane from the cruiser *Tone* flew over the island of Maui and signaled that there were no warships in the fleet's alternative anchorage off the old whaling port of Lahaina.

The reports were promptly relayed from the flagship *Akagi* to Commander Mitsuo Fuchida, who was leading the first wave of the attack in a "Kate" that was then less than twenty miles from Kahuku Point. The aerial striking force of torpedo planes, dive bombers, high-level bombers, and escorting fighters circled at prearranged altitudes awaiting a signal flare to form up to make their attack runs. The only hitch in the clockwork precision of their battle plan came when the wing leader of the dive bombers force mistook Fuchida's firing of two separate flares, the prearranged signal to let his force know that surprise was total, for the double-flare warning that American fighters were being scrambled. This contingency required the dive bombers to make a diversionary raid on Hickam and Wheeler airfields and the naval air station on Ford Island to deal with American fighters.

The "Vals" promptly peeled away, climbed twelve thousand feet to the west, and then came racing in to the attack down the Wainae Valley. The Japanese dive-bomber pilots discovered their mistake, but were relieved that all the American pursuit planes were still on the ground. Meanwhile, the high-level bombers and torpedo planes circled round to the west of the Wainae range to approach Pearl Harbor from the south. They, too, found that complete surprise had been achieved, and there was no hostile reception as they began their separate attack runs.

The "TO, TO, TO" signal—the abbreviation for *totsugeki* ("charge")—was flashed out from Fuchida's bomber by signal lamp as he led the fifty high-level bombers around Barbers Point on the south of Oahu and in over the entrance to Pearl Harbor. His wireless operator shortly afterward radioed the prearranged Morse code signal "TO RA, TO RA, TO RA"— "surprise achieved"—to the flagship *Akagi*.[53]

Explosions and strafing runs by the dive bombers blasted

apart the rows of parked Army pursuit planes at Wheeler Field, five miles from Pearl Harbor, just as another flight of "Vals" plastered Ford Island with bombs that set hangars ablaze and blasted apart the rows of PBY amphibians lined up on the concrete slips. The "Kates," with the snouts of their long steel torpedoes capped by wooden box fins to stop them from plunging into the harbor mud, peeled off to hammer the moorings on either side of Ford Island.

The air raid erupted with such sudden fury that it was minutes before those on board the warships grasped what was happening. Along Battleship Row, on the westward side of Ford Island, the forenoon watch had just been piped to breakfast as the morning color parties lined up on the fantails, waiting to break out the Stars and Stripes. The bugle calls echoing with the chiming bells of the shoreside chapels were abruptly drowned out by the roar of aircraft engines and the rattle of cannon fire.

The green-painted lead torpedo bomber raced so low over the *Nevada* that it shredded the half-hoisted American flag with cannon fire. The battleship's band continued thumping out the "Star Spangled Banner" without missing a beat as the "Kate" loosed its torpedo, which splashed into the water abeam of the *Arizona*, which was moored ahead of the *Nevada*.

A seaman in the superstructure of the *Maryland*, two rows of battleships ahead of the *Nevada*, managed to break out a machine gun belt to fire on the two following torpedo bombers as the sickening sound of underwater explosions burst the armored flanks of the battlewagons. Exploding bombs were rocking Ford Island when the commander of the 2nd PBY Patrol Wing managed to get off an urgent signal from the control tower at 8:02 A.M. that was taken up by the naval radio station,[54] which flashed it out to the mainland.

"AIR RAID PEARL HARBOR. THIS IS NOT DRILL" was an alarm whose awkward indelibility expressed the precipitateness with which the attack had erupted. It was transmitted just as the "Kates" raced in at deck height to send torpedoes slamming into the *Oklahoma* and the *West Virginia*.

High overhead Commander Fuchida was watching with satisfaction as the raid developed. Encouraged by "tiny white flashes of smoke [and] waverings in the water," the attacking planes focused on the moored pairs of battleships, which made large targets.

At eight o'clock Admiral Kimmel was getting dressed at his Makalapa quarters when his yeoman rushed in to tell him that the signal tower was flashing news of an attack not being a drill. Still buttoning his white uniform jacket, Kimmel rushed outside and stood transfixed on a neighbor's front lawn, where he had a clear view of the planes circling over Battleship Row. "I knew right away," he later recalled, "that something terrible was going on, that this was just not a casual raid by just a few stray planes."[55]

"Pearl Harbor is under air attack, sir," was how Commander Layton's yeoman broke the news by telephone to his chief at his home overlooking Manalua Bay, fifteen miles to the east of the naval base. The curtain drop of Diamond Head had shut him off from sight and sound of the raging attack. He jumped into the Cadillac Roadster of his neighbor Lieutenant Paul Crossley, and they hurtled off, taking the road through downtown Honolulu, with Mrs. Crossley at the wheel.

"The nightmare grew larger and louder the closer we came to the naval base which radiated terrible explosions," Layton was to recall. Choking with emotion more than forty years later he said it was "just like a bad dream that could not be true."[56] He could see the tall columns of smoke rising from Battleship Row as they struggled through traffic jams that got thicker as they approached the naval reservation.

Prompt flooding of the magazines had saved the *West Virginia*. Astern, a simultaneous bomb and torpedo strike had caught the *Arizona*. The great battleship erupted in a volcanic explosion as her forward magazine detonated after being hit by a bomb. At the head of the row, the *Oklahoma*'s port flank had been ripped open below the waterline by torpedoes. Within minutes the battleship had capsized, entombing more than four hundred of her crew members. Alongside the *Oklahoma*'s whalelike, weed-encrusted hull, with its giant phosphor bronze propellers, now upturned to the unfamiliar sky, the *Maryland* had been saved from a similar fate by her armored deck. Like the *Tennessee*, the next battleship astern, she had been protected by her inboard mooring from the deadly torpedo hits.

Not so fortunate was the *California*, which had taken two torpedoes at her lone berth at the head of the row. As the blazing Battle Force flagship settled bows down into the harbor mud, the *Nevada*, in the isolated berth at the end of the line, was straining to get under way, after casting off her moorings. Every gun aboard the battleship that could be trained skyward was blazing away at the dive bombers that swarmed down on the *Nevada*. Across on the other side of the harbor, the destroyer *Helms* ran down a midget submarine. Badly damaged, it was later beached and Ensign Kazuo Sakamaki surrendered to become the first Japanese prisoner of war of the United States.

Just after eight o'clock, little more than half an hour after it had begun, the raid's fury began to abate as the planes in the first Japanese wave began flying off. It was then 1:30 in the afternoon in Washington as the electrifying news of the attack began reaching senior members of the administration.

"My God! This can't be true, this must mean the Philippines," the secretary of the navy exclaimed when he was handed the THIS IS NOT DRILL signal. He called in the chief of naval operations for an explanation. "No, sir this is Pearl," confirmed an equally shaken Admiral Stark.[57] Knox immediately put in a telephone call to the White House. Roosevelt was no less shocked. He also thought at first that Knox meant the Philippines was under attack. Presidential aide Harry Hopkins, who was lunching with Roosevelt in his Oval Office study, was no less incredulous: "Surely Japan would not attack in Honolulu."[58]

It was just after two when the president telephoned the secretary of state. Hull was furious and flabbergasted. But he agreed to receive the Japanese ambassadors who had just arrived in the anteroom to his office. Nomura and Kurusu had postponed their one o'clock appointment because of the delay they had in typing up themselves the fair copy of Tokyo's memorandum of response. Roosevelt advised Hull not to tell the two envoys about the raid but "to receive their reply formally and coolly bow them out."[59]

After making a pretense of studying the fourteen-part message handed him by Nomura, Hull's Tennessee temper got the better of his southern courtesy. "In all my fifty years of public service," he told the bemused pair of diplomats, "I have never seen such a document that was more crowded with falsehood and distortions on a scale so huge that I never imagined until today that any Government on this earth was capable of uttering them."[60]

The Japanese ambassadors, who had not yet learned that their fellow countrymen were attacking Pearl Harbor, started to protest. Hull dismissed them with a wave of his hand, and they bowed themselves out in an embarrassed fluster. As the door closed behind them, a department official later recalled, the secretary of state muttered, "Scoundrels and piss ants."[61]

At 2:28 P.M., the chief of naval operations telephoned the

president to give him the first damage and casualty reports from Pearl Harbor. According to the memo kept by Hopkins, Roosevelt ordered the execution of "agreed orders to the Army and Navy in the event of an outbreak of hostilities in the Pacific."[62] Shortly afterward the presidential press secretary summoned newspaper reporters to the White House to give them the stunning news that the Japanese were attacking Pearl Harbor. In the confusion of the moment, White House Press Secretary Steve Early also announced that an air raid was in progress on Manila.

The CBS radio network burst on the air with the stunning announcement at 2:31 P.M. Eastern time. Their news flash was followed by others as stations from coast to coast broke into their programs to put out the White House bulletin.

Shortly before millions of Americans learned that their nation was being bludgeoned so precipitately into the war, Admiral Bloch was telephoning an eyewitness account of the attack to the secretary of the navy as the second wave of the raid came winging its way to Pearl Harbor from the east over Honolulu shortly after 8:30 A.M. local time. "He could look through a window," Knox recorded, "and see smoke and flames from the ships still burning in the harbor."[63]

The second part of the raid descended from the northeast of Oahu, where the fighters and bombers devastated the naval air station at Kaneohe in eight minutes, before moving on to strafe and bomb the Army's nearby fighter base at Bellows Field. The resumption of the air raid's intensity coincided with the arrival of the B-17s, whose flight from the West Coast had unwittingly concealed the first wave of the Japanese attack. Unarmed and down to their last gallons of gasoline, the Fortress pilots managed to land their planes safely by scattering to the outlying airfields. Not so fortunate were the Dauntless dive bombers from the *Enterprise*, which flew in to a fiercely hostile reception. Four were shot out of the sky by the more agile Japanese Zero fighters. One was brought down by friendly antiaircraft fire, which had begun in earnest now that ammunition was available for the batteries. Not a single Navy fighter managed to take off as the Japanese bombers roared overhead. A few Army P-40 pursuit planes did manage to scramble from Bellows Field during the raid, shooting down eleven Japanese aircraft out of a clear sky that was now being filled with the black mushroomlike puffs of exploding antiaircraft shells.

American retaliation came too late to save the battleships.

As Kimmel scanned the carnage going on across the harbor from the window of Pacific Fleet headquarters in the Submarine Base Building by the harbor front, a spent .50 caliber machine gun bullet came crashing through the window. It tore a hole in the commander-in-chief's jacket, raising a welt on his chest. "It would have been merciful had it killed me," the admiral remarked prophetically to his communications officer, who was standing alongside him, watching the waterspouts of bomb explosions bursting up over the blazing wreckage that only an hour earlier had been Battleship Row.[64]

The second wave of the attack was reaching a crescendo when the destroyer *Monoghan* rammed a midget submarine in the East Loch as it surfaced to coolly fire a torpedo at the tender *Curtiss*. On the other side of Ford Island the Japanese dive bombers were concentrating their attacks on the *Nevada*. The damaged battleship clawed past the blazing wrecks of her sister ships. It was a show of defiance that drew game cheers from the oil-drenched sailors who had managed to crawl to safety on the upturned hull of the *Oklahoma*. Some of the survivors from the *Arizona* who had been hauled out of the water as the *Nevada* passed helped man the battleship's antiaircraft guns. Dockyard tugboats fought to prevent the dangerously listing *Oklahoma* from sinking and blocking the main channel. The fire pumps on the tugs doused the flames that had threatened to engulf the *Nevada* as they nudged it ashore in the shallows off Waipo Point.

The wounded battleship *Nevada*'s dash for safety diverted the Japanese bombers from concentrating their attacks on the *Pennsylvania*, high and dry on chocks in Number 1 dry dock. A bomb plummeted through the boat deck of the Pacific Fleet flagship, while another blew the bow off the destroyer *Shaw*, which was sharing the vast concrete basin with the battleship and the destroyer *Cassin*. The vast dry dock could not be flooded rapidly enough to prevent a conflagration that ignited the magazines and torpedo stores of the two thin-hulled destroyers, which erupted with terrific force just after nine. Layton had just arrived in his office when the *Shaw* and the *Cassin* blew up with a roar that shook the headquarters building.

"Well, Layton, if it's any satisfaction to you, we were wrong and you were right," Captain Charles H. MacMorris, the war plans officer of the Pacific Fleet, chided him. Layton, who recalled feeling physically sick at this juncture, responded glumly, "It is no satisfaction to me whatsoever."[65]

The whole of Battleship Row now lay under a billowing

pall of black smoke. A second pyre was reaching into the sky from the dry dock as the Japanese planes turned their attention away from the battleships to secondary targets. During the final phase of the raid, they damaged the three light cruisers moored on the northern side of Ford Island and sank the old disarmed battlewagon, *Utah*, which served as the fleet's target ship.

It was during the final minutes of the attack that Layton received word from the combat intelligence unit HYPO that they had a direction-finder bearing on the radio transmissions made by the Japanese carriers to their planes. The Army, in a panicky reaction to the attack, had pulled the plugs on the telephone lines that connected Rochefort's unit to the Navy's powerful CKK-X direction-finding set on the high ground north of the harbor. The local unit could only produce a "bilateral fix," and so it was impossible to determine if the Japanese carrier task force was due north or due south of Oahu.

"Goddamnit! We're under attack here, everybody knows we're under attack," Admiral Kimmel exploded, in an uncharacteristic display of temper, when Layton gave him the ambiguous fix. "Here you are, the Fleet Intelligence officer and you don't even know whether they're north or south. For Christ's sake!"[66]

The outburst from the normally phlegmatic Pacific Fleet commander was perfectly understandable to Layton. Kimmel's battleships were exploding and his men were dying: he had suffered the fate that every commander dreads—being taken by surprise by the enemy. Throughout the morning's ordeal, Kimmel was powerless to strike back because he had no clear indication of from whence the attack had come.

Confused and conflicting reports about the whereabouts of the enemy force continued to come in on the heels of the departing Japanese planes. Army units reported an invasion force coming ashore on the north of the island as other reports were received that paratroops were landing on Barbers Point. It later turned out that both alarms had been raised when a mechanic in dungarees had parachuted to safety after his small seaplane was shot down by the Zeros.

If Fort Shafter had passed on the earlier contact report received from the Opana radar station, Layton would have been able to resolve the dilemma and put the Japanese carriers north of Oahu. The prevailing opinion of Kimmel's staff that morning, however, was that the attack must have flown in from the south because the nearest Japanese base was in the

Marshalls. This erroneous assumption was reinforced when HYPO reported they had picked up the unmistakable ham-fisted radio operator of the *Akagi*. Lacking the ability to determine that it was actually transmitting from the north end of the bearing axis, Halsey's Task Force 8 was radioed that "D[i-rection] F[inder] bearings indicate enemy carrier bearing 178 from Barber's Point."[67]

Four Army bombers left from Hickham Field to search the waters south of Oahu, only to find the heavy cruiser *Minneapolis* steaming through the fleet exercise area. In the fog of that morning's battle, their coded report "No carriers in sight" became garbled in translation to read "Two carriers in sight."[68] That afternoon a PBY returning from Midway mistakenly bombed a cruiser of Admiral Wilson Brown's task force heading back to Pearl Harbor from the southwest.

The dense pyres of oily black smoke that continued all day snaking thousands of feet up over Pearl Harbor were awesome symbols of the tactical victory that the Japanese had won. The two raids had cut the operational strength of the Pacific Fleet by eighteen warships. Four battleships and the target ship *Utah* had been sunk; four more had suffered severe damage. Three light cruisers, three destroyers, and three auxiliary craft had been put out of action, or wrecked beyond repair. The Navy had lost thirteen fighters, twenty-one scout bombers and forty-six patrol planes—in addition to the *Enterprise*'s four dive bombers. The Army Air Force losses were even more punishing: eighteen bombers—including four B-17s—and fifty-nine fighters. Damage to airfields and ground installations was extensive. The final death toll, including 68 civilians, was to climb to 2,403—nearly half the lives were snuffed out when the *Arizona* blew up. Another 1,178 servicemen were wounded, many of them burn victims.

Commander Fuchida, who had led the first wave and whose bomber had been slightly damaged by antiaircraft fire, was the last to leave, after circling high above Pearl Harbor photographing the devastation. When he landed back aboard the *Akagi* around noon, he triumphantly reported that the first two waves of the raid had achieved total success at the cost of twenty-nine planes. This was far less than the sixty or more that had been anticipated. When Fuchida reported to Admiral Nagumo on the flag bridge that four battleships had been sunk and four badly damaged, he was anticipating that a third air attack would be sent in that afternoon, to finish off the destruction at Pearl Harbor, and air patrols would be ordered out to hunt for the two missing American carriers. As long as the installations and fuel supplies at Pearl Harbor remained intact and the two American carriers were unaccounted for, the Hawaiian Operation had accomplished only eighty percent of its mission to knock out the U.S. Pacific Fleet.

As the planes were being fueled and bombed up, the question of whether to make another strike became a subject of debate on the flag bridge of the *Akagi*. Commander Genda, whose meticulous tactical planning had been responsible for the success of the operation so far, urged Admiral Nagumo to deliver the *coup de grace* to an already stunned enemy. Nagumo hesitated. He wanted to know from Fuchida whether he believed that the main force of the Pacific Fleet had been put out of action for six months. When that was affirmed, Nagumo and Rear Admiral Ryunosuke Kusaka, his chief of staff, concluded they had achieved their main objective. Fuchida offered to lead another strike to destroy Pearl Harbor's fuel tanks and dockyard facilities, but his proposal was not welcomed with enthusiasm by the staff officers clustered on the flag bridge.

Cautious by nature, Chuichi Nagumo was not an admiral who was willing to take unnecessary risks with his command. He had also been one of the strongest opponents of Yamamoto's Hawaiian Operation because he believed it hazarded too much of the carrier strength of the Combined Fleet. Although only nine planes had been lost in the first wave, twenty had failed to return from the second, and Nagumo reasoned that losses from another strike would be even higher. He had convinced himself that the Striking Force had already accomplished the most important part of its mission and that the Pacific Fleet had been so crippled that it could not now interfere with Japan's main Southern Operation to advance through Malaya, the Philippines, and the Dutch East Indies to secure the Greater Southeast Asia Co-Prosperity Sphere. Nagumo, therefore, decided that "to remain within range of enemy land-based planes was distinctly to our disadvantage."[69]

"Preparations for attack canceled" was the message that *Akagi* sent to the Striking Force by signal flags to prevent the Striking Force from being tracked by radio direction finding. Nagumo followed it with the order to retire at full speed to the northwest. When Fuchida learned of the orders, he rushed back up to the bridge to protest. He was silenced by Admiral Kusaka: "The real objective of the Pearl Harbor operation has been achieved. Now we must prepare for other operations ahead."[70]

Admiral Nagumo's failure to pursue the tactical advantage that had opened up for him that afternoon turned out to be Japan's next biggest strategic miscalculation after the decision to go to war against the United States. The exposed oil tanks at the corner of the Southeast Loch would have been easy targets. Their destruction would have brought the Combined Fleet a far greater strategic victory than putting the Pacific Fleet battleships out of action. The lack of alternative fuel supplies and the shortage of tankers to transport oil in the months that followed, as German U-boats ravaged the United States East Coast shipping lanes, would have prevented the American carrier task forces from operating in the western Pacific for at least six months and possibly even a year. Had the Japanese made a third strike that afternoon, Admiral Yamamoto's strategy for winning the war against the United States would have stood a good chance of succeeding.

"It would have forced the withdrawal of the fleet to the [west] coast because there wasn't any oil anywhere else out there to keep the fleet operating," was how Admiral Kimmel bluntly summed up the strategic victory that the Japanese admiral let slip from his grasp.[71] Nagumo also passed up the other tactical option urged by Genda and Fuchida: disposing of the two American carrier task forces that were at sea. With a three-to-one advantage Nagumo's striking force would easily have hunted down and overwhelmed the *Enterprise* and the *Lexington*. It was the mission for which the planes returning from the first strike had been prepared. The fighters had been armed to defend their carriers and the dive bombers and torpedo planes had been fitted with antiship weapons to sink the American task forces, which could have been located by scouting patrols. But Nagumo gave priority to preserving his carriers, and Captain Genda confidently argued that the demoralized Americans, even if they could locate the Striking Force, would not be able to get through. His pilots had been practicing for months the tactics of defense as well as attack. During the debate on the flag bridge of the *Akagi*, he had told Nagumo: "Let the enemy come! If he does we will shoot his planes down."[72]

It was fortunate that Admiral Kimmel did not learn until the end of Sunday afternoon that the Japanese carrier task force was north of Oahu. What the direction finding had failed to reveal was clarified by a bloodstained package recovered from the cockpit of the Japanese Zero that had crashed into the seaplane tender *Curtiss*. The plot board and navigation sheet recovered from the body of the pilot indicated the route the attack had taken in from the carriers. He was also carrying a card with the current list of radio call signs for all the ships in the Striking Force. From it Layton was able to provide the Pacific Fleet commander with the composition and location of the Japanese force when the raid against Pearl Harbor had been launched.

Dusk was fast approaching, and over five hundred miles of ocean separated the victorious Japanese Striking Force from the nearest American carrier, making any counterattack that Sunday impractical. Unknown to Kimmel, the victorious Japanese were fleeing northward at high speed. A trick of fate had worked to the ultimate advantage of the Americans because, Admiral Kimmel testified, although he had only two carriers, he would have attempted to ambush the Japanese if he had known their whereabouts. If the *Enterprise* had been ordered to attack, Halsey's task force would have been located by the Japanese, whose overwhelming superiority would have made short work of a single carrier. With the *Lexington*'s task force still two hundred miles away to the west of Oahu, Nagumo's exuberant and practiced aircrews would have been able to pick off the two American carriers one at a time with little risk to his Striking Force.

"It was God's mercy that Admiral Kimmel didn't have warning that the Japanese were about to attack Pearl Harbor," was the judgment Admiral Chester W. Nimitz gave after the war on the possible outcome of an action in December 1941 with the Pacific Fleet. "If we had been warned, our fleet would have gone out to sea, and . . . all our ships would have been destroyed one by one in deep water. . . . We would have lost the entire Pacific Fleet and eighteen to nineteen thousand men, instead of the ships and 3,300 men we did lose."[73]

11

"A Dereliction of Duty"

The Wartime Political Cover-up that Made the
Hawaiian Commanders Scapegoats for
Washington's Strategic Miscalculations and
MacArthur's Tactical Blunders

"O n the ground, by God, on the ground!" was how Roosevelt
vented his anger late that Sunday night to Edward R.
Murrow, who noted how "several times the President pounded
his fist on the table as he expressed his frustration at all the
planes which had been destroyed in the Pearl Harbor raid."[1]

"The idea seemed to hurt him," observed the CBS radio
correspondent, whose live broadcasts from London during the
Blitz had brought the war into the homes of millions of Americans. His invitation to a family dinner in the White House on
7 December had been disrupted by the day's momentous
events. At the president's insistence he had waited until midnight, when he was finally ushered into the Oval Office for
drinks and sandwiches. He found Roosevelt "gray with fatigue"
and anxious to talk off the pressures and tensions of that terrible day.

"I have seen certain statesmen of the world in times of
crisis," Murrow later reflected, observing that apart from
Roosevelt's outburst over the number of planes destroyed, he
was surprised to find the president was "so calm and steady."[2]
Before Roosevelt specifically raised the issue of how he had
been taken by surprise by the Japanese attack, they had chat-

ted about how things were going in London, and the president related how the British prime minister had telephoned him shortly after four P.M. that afternoon to tell him how he had first heard the news about Pearl Harbor from the BBC's nine o'clock news broadcast.

Churchill had been weekending at Chequers, the official country residence of the prime minister, northwest of London. He was entertaining the U.S. ambassador, John Winant, and Roosevelt's special envoy, Averell Harriman, to dinner when the butler had brought to the table the fifteen-dollar portable radio that had been a gift from Harry Hopkins, the president's close aide. The news that Malaya and Singapore had been under attack by the Japanese for nearly four hours had somehow not reached the BBC in London, and the radio tubes took so long to warm up that is was not until after the final roundup that the prime minister and his dinner guests learned of the raid on Pearl Harbor.

"We will declare war on Japan," Churchill announced, jumping up, according to the later account of the American ambassador.[3] Winant also recalled that he had told the prime minister he could not do that on the strength of a radio broadcast. So Winant immediately put in a telephone call to the White House.

"What's this about Japan?" Churchill had demanded when Winant passed over the receiver. The president assured him it was quite true that Pearl Harbor had been attacked and they "were all in the same boat now," to which the prime minister had responded, "That certainly simplifies things."[4]

"So we had won after all," was how Churchill was to write of his relief in his memoir, which recorded how that evening he retired to "the sleep of the saved and thankful."[5] The attack on Pearl Harbor had finally relieved the prime minister of his concern about how Roosevelt was going to persuade Congress to come to Britain's aid in the event that Japan had attacked only Malaya.

That Tokyo had also made things a lot simpler for Roosevelt was apparent to the emergency eight o'clock meeting of his cabinet, at which Frances Perkins observed a visible sense of relief in the president. Although it was traumatic, she wrote, to be "the leader of a nation that had been attacked by surprise by an enemy we had always thought of as inferior," the secretary of labor sensed that Roosevelt was not alone in being relieved that "we didn't have to think any longer about what we would do in defense of Singapore if there was no apparent attack on ourselves."[6] According to Perkins, who was the only woman in the cabinet, "that very wave of relief might have produced in him the psychological atmosphere—reflected partially in his facial expression of calmness and tenseness."[7] It was also apparent to the doughty Perkins that Roosevelt was "having a dreadful time just accepting the idea that Navy could be caught off guard," but she did not detect any "recrimination or attempt to blame Admiral Kimmel."[8]

Roosevelt's first wartime cabinet meeting was "total confusion," according to Perkins, whose account noted that the secretary of the Navy rushed in and out of the meeting to relay phone reports from Pearl Harbor. The president, nonetheless, projected "an air of calm" despite Knox's state of agitation. He read out the draft of his appeal to Congress that they should declare that "since the unprovoked and dastardly attack by Japan," they should declare that "a state of war has existed between the United States and the Japanese empire."[9]

The president's intention was to unite Congress in a brief speech—"an understatement and nothing too explosive," according to the memo left by his aide Hopkins.[10] An hour and a half later, when ten senior congressmen joined the cabinet meeting in the Blue Room, Roosevelt was evasive about what he was going to say the next day on Capitol Hill. Among them were die-hard isolationists whose cause had been snuffed out that afternoon when the news of Pearl Harbor broke across the United States. The president, nevertheless, had to field some tough questions about how the Pacific Fleet could have been caught so badly off guard.

"They were supposed to be on the alert," declared Senator Tom Conally, the chairman of the Senate Foreign Relations Committee. "I am amazed at the attack by Japan, but I am still more astounded at what happened to our Navy. They were all asleep. Where were our patrols?"[11] Congress would clearly be critical and demand explanations, but it was agreed that the joint session the next morning would deal only with the declaration of war.

"Well, Mr. President, this nation has got a job ahead of it, and what we have got to do is roll up our sleeves and win this war," another senator declared as the meeting ended just before 11:30 P.M. The grim-faced members of Congress filed out with the senior members of the administration, past the reporters crowding the still brightly lit White House portico. They were observed by the waiting CBS reporter, whose practiced eye noted the "amazement and anger written large on most of the faces" of the cabinet. "If they were not surprised by the news from Pearl Harbor," Murrow would recall in a 1945 radio broadcast, "then that group of elderly men were putting on a performance which would have excited the admiration of any experienced actor."[12]

It was just before midnight when Murrow was welcomed warmly by the president to the Oval Room on the second floor of the White House. During his review of the latest news he had received from Pearl Harbor, Roosevelt had rhetorically inquired, "Did this surprise you?" When the CBS correspondent replied in the affirmative, Roosevelt, evidently anticipating the accusations that would be leveled against him by the isolationists, quizzically asked, "Maybe you think it didn't surprise us!"[13] Then Colonel William J. Donovan, the president's intelligence coordinator, entered the room and the focus of discussion shifted to the Philippines.

Half a world away in the Philippines, it was coming up to midday and the Japanese Navy bombers were winging their way in over the coast to deliver a far more devastating blow to the strategic plans of the United States than their comrades-in-arms had inflicted nine hours earlier on Pearl Harbor. It is not without irony that the last of the Japanese bombers was departing from Clark Field after wiping out MacArthur's strategic airpower at the same time that the extraordinary late-night session at the White House was ending at 1:30 A.M. The reporter left knowing he had the inside track on the story of the decade, but was honor-bound not to report it. In light of the president's table-thumping reaction to the aircraft lost at Pearl Harbor, his fury would have erupted volcanically that night if he had learned that MacArthur's airpower, on which the whole Anglo-American strategy in the Far East hinged, had been destroyed on the ground in a reprise of Pearl Harbor.

There is no first-hand record of how Roosevelt reacted to the debacle in the Philippines, but when the news of the attack broke in the American press two days later, the scale of the disaster in the Philippines was played down. MacArthur's calamity was overshadowed by headlines that gave prominence to the death and destruction in Hawaii and the president's condemnation of Japan for attacking the United States on the "date that will live in infamy."[14] From Manila, in keeping with MacArthur's statement to the press conveying a "message of serenity and confidence," no casualty reports or toll of airplanes lost were given. Reporting from the Philippine capital, The *New York Times* correspondent reported that only "one hangar was damaged and one officer's quarters burned." The euphemism was so extreme that it jarred with a separate report filed from Washington which stated that there had been an "onslaught against the United States military airfields" in the Philippines which had "put them out of commission for the time being."[15]

When the Japanese returned in force over Luzon the next day, after they had wiped out Clark and Iba, the surviving American fighters would only put up token opposition as Manila and its airfields were bombed and strafed. The most devastating raid that Wednesday afternoon "practically wiped out" the naval base of the Asiatic Fleet, according to Admiral Hart, who watched the destruction from the roof of the Marsman Building in Manila. A thousand miles to the west across the South China Sea, Japanese navy torpedo bombers were making short work of the *Prince of Wales* and the *Repulse*, the only surviving components of the ill-fated Anglo-American deterrent.

That afternoon, outside USAFFE headquarters in Calle Victoria, MacArthur was calmly observing the swarms of Mitsubishi bombers flying over at fifteen thousand feet to bomb the nearby U.S. Asiatic Fleet base at the port of Cavite. Ignoring warnings to take cover, he craned upward and calmly called for a cigarette, according to one of the writers who helped embellish the MacArthur legend. "His gold-braided cap was tilted jauntily. His shoulders were back. He was smoking a cigarette in a long holder and swinging a cane."[16] When an aide suggested that the Stars and Stripes flying over the Intramuros should be struck to avoid identifying his headquarters to the bombers, the general waved him off with the comment, "Take every normal precaution, but let's keep the flag flying."[17]

This set the tone for the carefully tailored image of MacArthur that was fed to the press. He was portrayed as a commander braving enemy fire as coolly as he had nearly a quarter-century before in the trenches of the Western Front. But out of earshot of reporters, MacArthur conceded to his chief of staff his fears that his beach-defense strategy was untenable now that air superiority over the Philippines had been lost. But when the Japanese began to come ashore on the north of Luzon on 10 December and on the east coast of the island two days later to begin a pincer movement toward Manila, he hesitated to recast his defense strategy. For more than two weeks MacArthur refused to order the withdrawal of troops and supplies from northern Luzon to the Bataan Peninsula, losing the chance to prepare for the citadel defense of the original Philippine war plan, which he had abandoned as "too negativistic." Not until a full day after the Japanese began landing in strength on 22 December, at Lingayen Gulf and at Lamon Bay southeast of Manila, did MacArthur finally respond to the strategic necessity for a retreat.

Yet despite all of MacArthur's later protests that his ground forces were hopelessly outnumbered, on paper he commanded 135,000—twice as many soldiers as the Japanese commander, General Homma. Half of the defending troops were poorly equipped and ill-trained regiments of Filipino militiamen, who evaporated into the hills as the Japanese advanced, but MacArthur still commanded a respectably strong army, and he contributed to their eventual defeat by holding for too long to his unrealistic beach-defense strategy. On the night of 23 December MacArthur acknowledged his blunder by ordering that the old Orange War Plan retreat to Bataan be put into effect. The next day, as MacArthur accepted the inevitable and ordered the evacuation of his headquarters from Manila, word came from the War Department that he had been promoted to a full general.

The incongruity of MacArthur being awarded a fourth star on the very day that he ordered the belated retreat to Bataan was overlooked by the American press. Also ignored was the fact that his promotion was given in the wake of military defeat, barely a week after Admiral Kimmel and General Short were effectively demoted and removed from their Pacific commands.

The precipitate decision to recall the two Hawaiian commanders in chief came after a fact-finding trip to Pearl Harbor by the secretary of the Navy. On 10 December, the day the Japanese captured Guam, Knox himself set off with a team of aides "to find out why the Japanese had caught the U.S. force unprepared." One of his objectives, as he put it, was to head off the "prospect of a nasty congressional investigation."[18] He arrived in Honolulu on a Navy flying boat on 11 December, the day that Hitler did Roosevelt a political favor by declaring war on the United States, thereby saving the president a possible bruising battle with Congress.

Knox's thirty-two-hour visit to Pearl Harbor was a profound shock for the secretary of the Navy, who was appalled and moved by the extent of the destruction and the heavy casualties. He repeatedly questioned Kimmel's staff about the war warning he was convinced had been sent them "on the sixth," making it clear he was not confusing the Saturday warning with the one sent on 27 November or Marshall's alert of the one P.M. deadline that had not reached Kimmel or Short until Sunday afternoon.[19] Knox also interviewed Short because the plane carrying the Army's fact-finding mission had crashed in a snowstorm over the High Sierras. Arriving back in Washington on the Sunday following the attack, Knox first found that the Republicans in the Senate were demanding to know why the president had not yet made a full statement on the causes of the Pearl Harbor disaster. A row was also brewing between the War and Navy departments' staffs over which service bore the greater responsibility for the disaster.

"There is bitterness on both sides over the failure at Hawaii," Stimson noted in his diary, which records that "the younger, less responsible—and some of the irresponsible older men—are all trying to throw the burden on the other Department."[20] Despite his affection for the Navy, Knox was first and foremost a politician who understood the need to move swiftly to deflect public and congressional anger away from the administration. The twenty-nine page report he delivered to Roosevelt on 14 December, while evenhanded, concluded that Japan had succeeded because of the "lack of a state of readiness against such an air attack by both branches of the service."[21] This unreadiness the secretary of the Navy attributed principally to the denial of MAGIC to the Hawaiian commanders and also to the inadequate numbers of long-range patrol aircraft and antiaircraft batteries on Oahu. His report did not exonerate Kimmel and Short from any blame, but raised the question of whether they should be charged with dereliction of duty for their unpreparedness.

To satisfy the need for public reassurance and to repair morale in the Navy, Knox proposed a presidential inquiry to investigate the Pearl Harbor attack. He expressed reservations about the desirability of removing Admiral Kimmel from command of his Pacific Fleet before the investigation was completed and while he was responsible for the operation to reinforce the garrison at Wake, where the U.S. Marines had beaten off the first Japanese attempt to capture the island on 11 December. He did concede, however, that such a step might be necessary since Kimmel's name was linked with the disaster. What Knox called for was a dramatic shake-up of the Navy Department that would bring in Rear Admiral Ernest J. King, one of the most able organizers in the Navy and the uncompromising commander of the Atlantic Fleet. He was appointed to assume the new position of commander in chief, U.S. Fleet, with broad operational responsibilities that diminished Admiral Stark's authority. Knox believed Stark should remain as chief of Naval Operations for the time being, because to have replaced him too peremptorily would have made it appear that he was to blame for the events that led up to the 7 December disaster. This would have drawn attention to Washington's role in the debacle, which would have been politically unwise with the rumblings of congressional criticism of the administration already making themselves heard.

"Knox agrees with me that there had been remissness in both branches of the service," Stimson noted, on 15 December, after discussing with the secretary of the Navy how to deal with the difficult issue of accountability. His diary entry emphasized that they were both "very anxious not to get into any interdepartmental scraps, but to keep the thing on a basis of no recrimination, but inflexible responsibility and punishment."[22] Knox, that Tuesday, had made selected sections of his report public at a press conference, at which he admitted only that the battleship *Arizona* had been sunk along with three destroyers, an auxiliary, and the demilitarized dreadnought *Utah*, which was the Pacific Fleet's gunnery target. He announced that the president would be setting up a "formal investigation" to ascertain if there had been "any dereliction of duty."[23] Because no mention could be made of the part played by MAGIC, his statement that the "services were not on the alert against surprise attack" gave the impression that the Hawaiian commanders were to be investigated for dereliction of duty.[24]

Knox, at his press conference, had declared, however, that action against the Hawaiian commanders must await "the facts and recommendations made by the investigating board."[25] Roosevelt, however, was to force his hand by announcing the following day a presidential investigation commission "consisting of two army and two navy officers and a civilian to investigate responsibility for the loss and to make recommendations."[26] To have a full-blown investigation of two senior officers critically involved in conducting the war would not inspire public confidence.

In reality, the subsequent failure of the expedition to reinforce the garrison at Wake Island revealed that it was political expediency, rather than operational efficiency, that had prompted the removal of Admiral Kimmel as commander in chief of the Pacific Fleet. The announcement was made on 16 December, after a White House meeting at which the president approved the appointment of Rear Admiral Chester W. Nimitz as the new commander in chief of the Pacific Fleet. The secretary of war simultaneously announced that General Short and his air commander, General Martin, were also to be relieved because "a situation where officials who were charged with responsibility of the vital naval base would otherwise in this critical hour also be involved in the searching investigation ordered yesterday by the President."[27] The recall of the Hawaiian commanders reinforced the presumption of their guilt.

Roosevelt, however, knew that he had to move swiftly to sustain popular opinion and satisfy congressional criticism after the traumatic shock that the nation had suffered. He therefore selected an associate justice of the Supreme Court, who he hoped would inspire confidence and trust in his commission. He named Owen J. Roberts as its chairman, a prominent judge who had made his reputation in 1923 as the special prosecutor in the celebrated Teapot Dome scandals involving the fraudulent transfer of federal oil reserves. Roberts was also a leading supporter of the pro-interventionist *Committee to Aid America by Aiding the Allies*, so Roosevelt had every reason to be confident that he would pay due attention to the need for preserving national unity.

The president was also concerned about scotching isolationist claims that he had maneuvered Japan into attacking in order to get the United States into the war against Hitler "by the back door." The rumors gained a certain credence when Churchill arrived in Washington on 22 December to set up camp in the White House. The British chiefs of staff held the U.S. chiefs of staff to the Europe First strategy that gave priority to the defeat of Hitler before crushing Japan. The so-called Arcadia conference endorsed the decision to stand on the defensive in the Pacific, while making the Atlantic the main theater of operations for 1942. This did not please Admiral King, who in March was to replace Admiral Stark as chief of Naval Operations. When Wake Island was captured by the Japanese on 23 December after a gallant hold-out by the Marines, King gave voice to the "Remember Pearl Harbor" sentiments of many Americans by calling for resources to launch an immediate naval counteroffensive against Japan.

General MacArthur was also calling for the "diversion here of the entire output" of U.S. military resources. "If the western Pacific is to be saved, it has to be saved here and now," he warned General Marshall.[28] His demands fell on deaf ears in Washington because King lost out to the Navy and Army chiefs who sided with the British by sticking to the Atlantic strategy. The decision not to commit major resources to the Pacific sealed the fate of the Philippines, despite the succession of hollow promises from Washington that help was on its way. MacArthur pulled off a military coup that was celebrated at the time as "a Far East Dunkirk" when General Wainwright managed to pull back his Luzon army to Bataan, which was compared to the miraculous evacuation of the British Expeditionary Force from the Channel coast when they had been trapped by the German army eighteen months earlier.

The skillfully executed fighting retreat to Bataan, however, was ultimately doomed by the loss of the ammunition, food, and medical supplies that had been abandoned in the forward positions. Nor were there enough warships, transports, or aircraft in the Pacific theater to fight reinforcements through the Japanese blockade of the Philippines. The convoy carrying aircraft and troops that had been en route to Manila when war broke out had to be redirected to Australia after the Asiatic Fleet commander, Admiral Hart, evacuated his staff and the remainder of his warships and submarines to the temporary refuge of the ports of the Dutch East Indies. His departure did not endear the U.S. Navy to MacArthur, who now complained that he had been abandoned in his hour of greatest need. He contradicted Admiral Hart's contention that the overwhelming strength of the Japanese navy had effectively cut off the Philippines by describing it as no more than a "paper blockade."[29]

"I hope you will tell the people outside what we have done and protect my reputation as a fighter," MacArthur told General Brereton when he bade him farewell on Christmas Eve.[30] With all but a handful of his fighters shot down and the surviving bombers flown to safety in Australia, there was nothing to keep Brereton's Far East Air Force in the Philippines. With his aides, his wife and son, and President Quezon, MacArthur then boarded a small steamer that ferried them out across a moonlit Manila Bay to Corregidor. For the next ten weeks he directed the retreat to Bataan and the bloody battle for the peninsula from the Malinta tunnel, an underground cavern blasted out of the heart of the rocky fortress island, where his headquarters were protected from frequent Japanese air raids. For two and a half months, as the tide of Japanese victory in the Far East rose to its high point, only the Philippines held out against the cataract of military disaster that engulfed the Allied forces in Malaya, Singapore, and the Dutch East Indies.

At a time when American hope and American heroes were both in short supply, General Douglas MacArthur, by an accident of history and astute self-promotion, became the symbolic embodiment of the American fighting spirit during the darkest hours of World War II. His heroic stature made him indispensable to the Roosevelt administration, which had to portray itself as militarily competent to run a war after the trauma of initial defeat. The Hawaiian commanders were, by comparison, dispensable. MacArthur was able to become a national hero because Kimmel and Short were made the lightning rods for public resentment over the disasters of 7 December. By making Pearl Harbor the focus of its investigation, the administration succeeded in heading off the "nasty congressional investigation" that might otherwise have delved into the Philippine debacle. This would have uncovered how MacArthur had helped Washington set the stage for the Japanese attack on Pearl Harbor by embarking on a hopelessly flawed Far East deterrent strategy with the British. The transfer to the Philippines of the B-17s had stripped the Hawaiian commands of their intended long-range air reconnaissance and interdiction capability in order to build up American forces in the Philippines. Political priorities required that the blame be fixed on Kimmel and Short, whose obvious unreadiness to meet a surprise attack made them convenient scapegoats.

The terms of reference for the Roberts Commission were restricted to only investigating Pearl Harbor. Its members were steered away from investigating Washington's role too deeply. This was evident from the informal meeting Knox and Stimson held with Justice Roberts to give him guidance that was clearly prejudicial to the objectivity of investigation. With the exception of Rear Admiral William H. Standley—a retired former chief of naval operations—the other members of the commission were not truly impartial. They were instead beholden to those who appointed them, who had a vested interest in concealing their own roles in the events leading up to 7 December. Stimson's nominees were Major General Frank B. McCoy, one of Marshall's most trusted aides, and Brigadier General Joseph T. MacNarney, a ranking Army Air Force officer who had also been recommended by the U.S. Army chief of staff. Roberts himself was a friend and supporter of the president. Rear Admiral Joseph Reeves, whom Knox nominated, had been called out of retirement to take charge of the naval end of the Lend-Lease program.

One indication of the extent to which the Roberts Commission had been "packed" to support the interests of the War and Navy departments was that when it began its hearings on 17 December in Stimson's office, it did not wait for the one outsider, Admiral Standley, to arrive. Proceedings were conducted in a manner more appropriate to a mess discussion than a courtroom. Standley was disturbed to find that none of the initial witnesses had been sworn and that General Marshall and his chief of war plans, General Gerow, had prepped the commission with all the war warnings they had sent to the Hawaiian commanders.

In 1984, clear indication of the partiality of the Roberts Commission emerged from the discovery of the verbatim notes of Admiral Wilkinson, the chief of the Office of Naval Intelligence, detailing the second day of officially unsworn and unrecorded testimony. His memorandum disclosed that the commission was deflected from the truth by the emphasis that both naval and military intelligence officers put on the intelligence that had been sent to the Hawaiian Commands. Although the commission was not formally given access to MAGIC, a contemporary report addressed to the chief of Naval Operations by Wilkinson recorded that "the meeting was discussing MAGIC freely." In it he said he had told the commission "that all this information had either passed through the CinC Asiatic Fleets or, if not, it had been furnished them from the Navy Department."[31] Although not given under oath, Wilkinson's declaration to Justice Roberts that Kimmel "had as much information as we had" was so misleading as to be a deliberate lie. The commission, moreover, was not given the details of the MAGIC that had been denied the Pacific Fleet command, nor informed about such critical intercepts as the Honolulu consulate's "bomb-plot" message.

The presidential commission therefore proceeded under the clear impression that Kimmel did indeed have all the information that was available to Washington. But according to the official record, Roberts did not know anything about the Purple decrypts because their security was considered too vital to reveal even to the secret deliberations presided over by Justice Roberts. "The MAGIC was not shown to us. I would not have bothered to read it if it had been shown to us," Roberts himself was to testify to the congressional hearings. "All I wanted to know was whether the commanders had been advised of the criticalness of the situation."[32] But it is now clear from Wilkinson's memorandum that Roberts did know—at least in general terms—about MAGIC intelligence. The briefing Roberts had received in Washington from Wilkinson, in which Wilkinson left the impression that Kimmel and Short had received the Purple intercepts, clearly contributed to Roberts's conclusion that the Hawaiian commanders "had ample warning." Roberts and the majority of his fellow commission members were convinced, even before they arrived in Pearl Harbor to depose Kimmel and Short, that the Hawaiian commanders were guilty of dereliction.

"I felt that, with all the information available to them in Washington, Admiral Stark and General Marshall were equally culpable," Admiral Standley wrote.[33] But when the commission members arrived at the Royal Hawaiian Hotel three days later to hear Kimmel and Short, their unpreparedness on 7 December took on a much more serious aspect because of Roberts's assumption that they had been receiving MAGIC and therefore had the whole intelligence picture from Washington. It is also significant that at this point both of the Hawaiian commanders were still unaware of the extent of the MAGIC intelligence that they had been denied. So the assumption that ample warnings of Tokyo's move toward belligerency had been received by the Pacific Fleet command led Roberts to take a dim view of Kimmel's actions. He was especially critical of the Pacific Fleet commander's belief that his battleships were safe from torpedo attack in the anchorage. His failure to order round-the-compass air patrols together with his failure to react to the report of code burning at the local Japanese consulate were taken as evidence of a major dereliction of duty.

"The findings as to the sins of commission presented true enough statements," Admiral Standley would later write of the misapprehension under which the commission labored, "but the many sins of omission in the picture were omitted from our findings because the President in his executive order setting up the Commission had specifically limited its jurisdiction."[34] Standley noted how he was highly critical of the majority view of the commission that the local Hawaiian commanders were principally to blame for the disaster. He said he was dissuaded from submitting a minority report at the time because a divisive opinion would have threatened the war effort.

Justice Roberts, who submitted his report to the president on 24 January 1942, concluded that "in the light of the warnings and directions to take appropriate action," the Hawaiian commanders in chief were "in dereliction of duty" for not conferring with each other "respecting the meaning and intent of the warnings and appropriate means of defense required by the imminence of hostilities." He also found that they had "demonstrated a lack of appreciation of responsibilities vested in them and their inherent positions" by their failure "to make suitable dispositions to meet such an attack." According to the commission report, it was the local Hawaiian commanders and not Washington who "failed to properly evaluate the seriousness of the situation." Kimmel and Short were therefore judged to have committed these "errors of judgment" that were "the effective causes for the success of the attack."[35]

If the Roberts Commission had been briefed on the amount of MAGIC intelligence that had been denied to the Hawaiian commanders, their conclusions might have been reversed and Washington found guilty of dereliction. The deliberate distortion of the truth by the intelligence directors of the War and Navy departments, therefore, undermined the findings of the presidential commission, which carefully omitted any mention of MAGIC intelligence. The impression that Kimmel and Short had received every vital piece of intelligence available in Washington had shifted any responsibility for the disaster from the War and Navy departments. Roberts's conclusions exonerated the secretaries of war, state, and navy, who were found to have "fulfilled their obligations." Only the mildest of criticism was attached to the War Department for not having responded in "reply to the anti-sabotage measures." Otherwise the chiefs of staff were held to have discharged their "command responsibility" by properly warning the Hawaiian commanders.

The whitewashing evidence given to the commission by the senior members of the Navy and War departments to cover up their failures also enabled Roberts to absolve Roosevelt and his aides from any culpability for the Pearl Harbor disaster. The president rushed the commission's findings to the press, who drew the inevitable conclusion that Admiral Kimmel and General Short were almost entirely to blame for the disaster: a verdict that was welcomed by all but a handful of the president's die-hard isolationist opponents—and the Hawaiian commanders themselves. Without access to the secret intelligence record, there was little that Kimmel and Short could do to challenge the report, or escape the pillory of public scorn. Letters poured in condemning them and some demanding that they be executed for treason. Short submitted his resignation from the Army immediately, but Kimmel held out until 28 January for the reassignment of duty he had been promised by

Knox on his fact-finding trip to Pearl Harbor before Christmas. When this was not forthcoming, he, too, offered to retire.

The president directed that it was to be announced simultaneously that both officers had applied for retirement and that their requests had been granted "without condonation of any offense or prejudice to future disciplinary proceedings."[36] This carried with it the implicit threat of court-martial proceedings when the demands of war were less pressing. It prompted Kimmel to protest "my crucifixion before the public" to Admiral Stark. Many of his fellow admirals sympathized, but as long as the demands of wartime required national unity and public confidence in the Navy, they kept their counsel. After the war even the hardheaded Admiral King conceded that the Roberts Commission had unfairly assigned the responsibility for the disaster.

"It seems to me that this committee did not get into the real meat of the matter, but merely selected a 'scapegoat' to satisfy the popular demand for fixing the responsibility of the Pearl Harbor debacle," King wrote, noting how "Admiral Kimmel was not asked the important questions, nor was he given the proper chance to speak for himself. In fact he and General Short were 'sold down the river' as a political expedient."[37] His views were also endorsed by Admiral Raymond Spruance, the victor of Midway, who observed, "I have always felt that Kimmel and Short were held responsible for Pearl Harbor in order that the American people might have no reason to lose confidence in their government in Washington."[38]

Until the United States was on the road to final victory, Kimmel and Short had to endure in painful isolation the disgrace that fate and political necessity had dealt them. It was not until 13 July 1944 that an act of Congress directed the secretaries of Navy and War to reopen the investigation into the Pearl Harbor disaster. The Army Pearl Harbor board met from July to October 1944, examining 151 witnesses under oath. It also took account of MAGIC for the first time, during the final stage of deliberations, and this resulted in a report severely critical of General Marshall and his staff for not keeping the Hawaiian Department properly informed.

General Short did not escape criticism for not placing his forces on a higher state of alert. The naval court of inquiry, meeting simultaneously, also took account of MAGIC. It, too, exonerated Admiral Kimmel from the charges for which he had been found derelict by the Roberts Commission. Admiral Stark was severely censured for denying the Pacific Fleet vital intelligence and for sending out a war warning that "standing alone could not convey to the commanders in the field the picture as it was seen in Washington."[39] The secretaries of war and navy were understandably shaken by these findings, which reversed so many of the Roberts Commission's findings and called into question Washington's role and accountability for the Pearl Harbor disaster.

Stimson and Knox promptly ordered their own investigations by Colonel Henry Clausen and Rear Admiral Kent Hewitt in a bid to discover new information that would overturn the politically damaging finds of the Army and Navy inquiries. Their reports were never published, nor was the investigation by Colonel Carter W. Clarke, who conducted a secret inquiry into the handling of top-secret communications by the military intelligence division. But a record of the findings, however, was taken into account in the congressional investigation that began public hearings on 15 November 1945 and lasted six months, through 31 May 1946.

Established by a joint resolution of the House and Senate, the congressional hearings were conducted by a committee of six Democrats and four Republicans under the chairmanship of Senator Alben W. Barkeley of Kentucky. The principal surviving participants were called and examined, with the exception of the former secretary of war, Henry Stimson, who was by then too ill to testify. The death of Roosevelt six months earlier inevitably cast a long political shadow over the hearing. The Democratic majority sought to divert and discount Republican criticism of the late president. MAGIC was discussed exhaustively, but any mention of the penetration of Japanese naval code systems was severely curtailed and the Navy withheld two critical studies on its intelligence failures.

The Democratic majority discharged its political mission in a report that concluded, first and foremost, that there was no evidence that Roosevelt or his administration had provoked the Japanese attack. The primary cause of the disaster at Pearl Harbor was attributed to the failure of the Hawaiian commanders to conduct air reconnaissance and maintain a high enough state of readiness. In contrast to the conclusions of the Roberts Commission, Kimmel and Short's failure to make dispositions commensurate with the warnings they had received were held to be errors of judgment, not derelictions of duty. The War and Navy departments were also criticized for their failures, notably for failing to warn that a sabotage alert was an inadequate state of readiness and for not properly evaluating the significance of the "bomb-plot" and the one o'clock P.M. delivery messages. The minority report, issued by two Republican members of the investigating committee, censured Roosevelt for not taking "quick and instant executive action on Saturday night, December 6th and Sunday morning." They also concluded that Stimson, Knox, Marshall, Gerow, Stark—and the two Hawaiian commanders—had failed to properly discharge their duties.[40]

While Admiral Kimmel and General Short were subjected to no fewer than eight secret wartime investigations and the congressional hearings, which made them the public scapegoats for the disaster at Pearl Harbor, MacArthur was never once called to account. History may never, therefore, be able to determine for certain what the cause was of MacArthur's astonishing failure to respond to his war directives in the nine hours after Pearl Harbor was attacked. He had been forewarned and therefore had no excuse for unpreparedness. Moreover his failure to put his war plan into operation, with the subsequent loss of so many heavy bombers, was a far more serious dereliction than the "omissions" for which the Hawaiian commanders were effectively cashiered. The loss of the five Pacific Fleet battleships had no direct strategic impact on the course of the war in the Pacific, whereas the loss of the Philippines removed the principal barrier to Japan's military conquest of Southeast Asia.

MacArthur's intimate knowledge of the fatal Anglo-American deterrent gamble in the Far East, and the degree to which commitments had been given to the British and Dutch of armed support in the days before the war broke out in the Pacific, was reason enough for the Roosevelt administration not to open the Philippines debacle to isolationist criticism. But by so completely concealing their own role in the strategic and diplomatic miscalculations preceding Japan's attack, the senior service chiefs and the policy makers in Washington protected the president and themselves by sacrificing Admiral Kimmel and General Short.

If MacArthur had been called to account for the disaster that overtook him in the Philippines, he would not have been able to offer Kimmel and Short's defense that they had been denied vital MAGIC intelligence. MacArthur had no excuse for his astonishing unpreparedness when the Japanese bombers arrived to catch his air force on the ground nine hours after the attack on Pearl Harbor. But he was protected from criticism by his political status, which made him a write-in presidential champion for the Republicans in 1944. This made him too dangerous for Roosevelt to move against, and after the president's death, the Democratic administration in 1945 did not find it expedient for Congress to extend its investigation of Pearl Harbor into examining the Philippine debacle. MacArthur, as supreme allied commander in the Far East, was by then installed as the American proconsul charged by the Allies with governing the defeated Japanese. The prominent role he was playing in global foreign policy, however, did not prevent the investigating committee from taking a symbolic political shot at the general who had vaulted from defeat to become the American Caesar.

12

"NOTHING TO FEAR AT ALL"

MacArthur's Dereliction, Payoff, and Rewriting
of History to Escape Investigation

G eneral MacArthur, having the MAGIC intercepts, was in
a better position to judge the situation than was Admiral
Kimmel," the minority report of the joint congressional committee pointedly states.[1] In apparent deference to MacArthur,
who was then supreme commander Allied Powers in Japan,
the Republican congressmen noted that the attack on the Philippines "bears no relationship to the disaster at Pearl Harbor."
The debacle at Clark Field was safely beyond the remit of its
investigations. What is a matter of record is that MacArthur
himself had already denied under oath to Colonel Clausen that
he had access to MAGIC intelligence.[2]

"I have no recollection of seeing any of these before," Mac-
Arthur swore in his affidavit for Colonel Clausen, who had trav-
eled to Manila in the summer of 1945 to show him a selection
of the key MAGIC intercepts of November and December 1941.
"I did not see the messages described in the 'Winds Code,' nor
any activating or implementing message," he added, claiming
ignorance of the process by which Japan's Purple diplomatic
traffic was obtained. "The Navy had facilities, not possessed
by the Army for such processing of intelligence," MacArthur
stated. "All messages were transmitted by the Navy to the

Army."[3] These were "damning words" according to Clausen, who had believed from the onset of investigation that there were many contributing factors in the chain of events leading to the disaster at Pearl Harbor, one of the "major problems being the Navy's arrogant hoarding of secret information and doling it out when and how they pleased."[4] MacArthur's sworn statement was further ammunition for Clausen, as was that of his chief of staff, who told the same story.

General Sutherland attested that "to the best of his recollection" he also had not seen any of the Purple intercepts that Clausen showed him. The only ones he had any recollection of were the intelligence reports relayed to Tokyo by Japan's consul general in the Philippines, which Clausen had not selected as significant.[5] Major General Charles A. Willoughby, who had been acting chief of staff, G-2 (intelligence), for the Philippine command in 1941, expressly denied seeing the intercepts of Tokyo's instruction to their embassies to destroy their code machines.[6] "It was customary for the Navy," Willoughby explained, to send MacArthur's headquarters only a "portion of the total sum of this intelligence," which only amounted to what "the Navy considered necessary to the functions of the Army."[7] He said that he had not seen anything other than "isolated fragments" of diplomatic messages, recalling in particular only exchanges between Tokyo and its Manila consulate on shipping movements.

The denial by MacArthur and his headquarters staff that they had no direct access to MAGIC but for the crumbs of relatively insignificant intelligence relayed to them by the Navy is flatly contradicted by the affidavit of other intelligence officers serving with the Philippines command. "The Army and the Navy each had facilities for intercepting and decrypting and translating Japanese radio messages which were given the classification known as Purple," Colonel Joseph K. Evans stated. He attested to "very close liaison and exchange of intelligence information between the Army and the Navy at Manila."[8] The Purple machine at Station CAST, which in November had been moved from the 16th Naval District headquarters at the Cavite Naval Base to the safety of the Malinta tunnel on Corregidor, was not only in operation, but there was an established routine for relaying the Purple decrypts to Army headquarters in Manila. Lieutenant Colonel Howard W. Brown, who was then operations officer of the Army Signals Corp intercept station at Fort McKinley in the Philippines, was the officer who acted as the MAGIC courier between CAST and

MacArthur. The official account that he later wrote for the Army records notes that while awaiting delivery of their own Purple decoding machine, they had established a procedure for exchanging with the Navy "raw and derived radio intelligence information."[9] Since July, when MacArthur has assumed command of the USAFFE, Brown had the responsibility for collecting the decrypts from the Navy and taking them to the Calle Victoria headquarters, where he first had to show the folder of Purple intercepts to General Sutherland.

"If it contained anything which he thought might be of interest to General MacArthur (which it frequently did), he would ask us to take it in to the General," Brown wrote, observing that "some of the General's comments were classics."[10] It was Brown who came to Sutherland's office shortly after ten on the day that war broke out and handed Sutherland the MAGIC folder, which contained, among other translations, the ten-day-old Purple intercept that Tokyo sent to all its embassies setting up the emergency plain-language "hidden-word" code for warning when Japan's relations with the United States and Britain were in danger of breaking down.

"Very interesting and very timely!" Sutherland snapped, according to Brown. He recalled that the chief of staff's "sarcasm could not have been cut with a bolo" as Sutherland demanded to know whether an actual coded message to that effect had been picked up. Brown said that one had just come in indicating that "Japan was at war [sic] with Britain and the United States."[11] In response to Sutherland's question about why such an important piece of intelligence had been "delayed to the point of uselessness," Brown had said that the Navy had only just received the intercept. Washington had alerted them to listen for the message of 6 December, but they had omitted "to give any information as to what the message might mean." Brown's opinion was that the Navy might have translated the actual message that morning, several hours before Pearl Harbor had been attacked, but that they had not yet circulated the information. Sutherland directed Brown to take the message in to his commander in chief, MacArthur.

"I waited in General MacArthur's office for about five minutes before I got to talk to him," recounted Brown, who remembered, "It seems he was having his own troubles at the time—Clark Field was under attack by some 150 Jap planes, and the General had the Commanding Officer on the telephone giving him hell."[12] When his turn came to speak, Brown explained the intercept's significance. MacArthur "never moved a muscle or changed his expression" and simply waved him out with a curt "Thank you, son."[13]

Colonel Brown was not interviewed by Clausen, nor did Stimson's investigator question anyone about MAGIC except MacArthur and his closest aides, who had a vested interest in denying that they or the general ever saw MAGIC intelligence on a regular basis. It was not part of Clausen's remit to investigate the general's "terrible defeat."[14] But MacArthur did not miss the opportunity to roundly blame the Hawaiian commanders for being caught by surprise.

"Dispatches from the War Department," MacArthur declared, "gave me ample and complete information and advice for the purpose of alerting the Army Command in the Philippines on a war basis, which was done prior to 7 December 1941."[15] Considering that his command was taken by surprise nine hours after the attack on Pearl Harbor, MacArthur's declaration was self-serving and a gratuitous denigration of the Hawaiian commanders. When it came to recasting the historical record to conceal and deny responsibility for the disaster in the Philippines, MacArthur and his aides not only lied under oath about receiving MAGIC intelligence but twisted the record to make the general appear an innocent victim of events, rather than of his own folly. Their distortions of the record were facilitated by the destruction and subsequent loss, two weeks after the debacle at Clark Field, of most of the contemporary documentation relating to the opening days of the war. But none of MacArthur's explanations was more self-serving than his assertion that the "ultimate usefulness of our air arm in the Philippines had become academic because of the crippling of the American's at fleet at Pearl Harbor."[16]

"Our air forces in the Philippines, containing many antiquated models were hardly more than a token force with insufficient equipment, incomplete fields and inadequate maintenance," was the claim that MacArthur made. Although he had the biggest concentration of heavy bombers and fighter strength outside the continental United States, he contended that his "hopelessly outnumbered" air force had been "completely overwhelmed by the enemy's superior forces."[17] Asserting that they had done "everything possible within their limited resources," he chivalrously declined to blame General Brereton "for the incidents of battle" because "nothing could have saved the day for them."[18] By blaming Washington for putting the Philippines in the front line against Japan with inadequate forces, MacArthur avoided having to explain why he had not at least saved his air force from the ignominy of destruction on the ground, by authorizing the preemptive raid on Formosa that was a specific requirement of his war plan.

General Brereton, his air commander, had repeatedly tried to get permission to send the B-17s to bomb Formosa on the morning war broke out in the Pacific but could not get permission from USAFFE headquarters. MacArthur later denied that any such request had reached him. In his posthumously published memoir, he denies any discussion about a preemptive strike with his air commander, who "never at any time recommended or suggested an attack on Formosa to me."[19] He offered a number of explanations for the paralysis that apparently mired his command, and each is contradictory.

Accusing Brereton of putting a "most nebulous and superficial" proposal to his chief of staff when it ought to have been made "to me in person," MacArthur declared he would have vetoed a mission that he considered "suicidal."[20] This suggests that while Sutherland had taken it upon himself to block Brereton's access to MacArthur for five hours, his chief of staff was correctly presuming MacArthur's refusal to approve the raid. But by eleven that morning Sutherland, for reasons he never explained, *did sanction* a photoreconnaissance for the raid that was authorized to take off late that afternoon, *whether or not* the preliminary reconnaissance mission was completed. Then there is the question raised by MacArthur's radiogram to the War Department, sent *after* Clark Field had been devastated, informing Marshall that he had ordered a heavy bomber raid on Formosa for the following morning. MacArthur, as he later stated, would have considered a raid on Formosa to be suicidal that morning *before* more than half his bomber force had been wiped out. Would it not surely have been even more of a disaster to attempt it the next day?

"The exact location of enemy targets was not known," was another justification for his chief of staff's refusal to approve the strike on Formosa that MacArthur gave the Army's official historian.[21] This adds another dimension to the pattern of inconsistency in the general's excuses. If photoreconnaissance was needed, why did Sutherland wait until eleven before authorizing the mission and why did he not approve it at first light when Brereton made his first trip to USAFFE headquarters? Sutherland put the blame on the Far East Air Force commander in a 1945 interview in which he admitted "there was some plan to bomb Formosa, but Brereton said he had to have the photos first. That there was no sense in going up there to bomb without knowing what they were going after."[22]

The claims of MacArthur's chief of staff are contradicted both by surviving contemporary records and the testimony of surviving Army Air Force officers who said that they had conducted reconnaissance missions over Formosa before 7 December.[23] The entry in Brereton's diary referring to his request that morning for "missions previously assigned" indicates that plans for attacking Formosa had already been formulated.[24] MacArthur had received a directive from the War Department ordering the overflying of Formosa—even at the risk of Japanese retaliation—as an essential preliminary for the execution of his war plan, which called for "raids against enemy forces and installations within tactical operations radius."[25]

There is convincing evidence that these flights were made. Captain Gary Anloff, one of the B-17 Bombardment Force pilots, said he had taken part in what he referred to as a "recon flight to Formosa," during which their plane had approached to within "five miles," and he "personally saw over 100 twin engined bombers on each of two fields."[26] Anloff's was not the only confirmation that U.S. reconnaissance of the Japanese airfields and port of Takao had been conducted *before* that Monday morning. A Purple intercept dated 3 December from Tokyo—to which MacArthur would have had access—requested the Japanese ambassadors in Washington make a formal protest that "On 20th of last month a U.S. plane made a reconnaissance flight over Garaspi in Southern Formosa."[27] It is unlikely that MacArthur would not have been informed of these flights, especially since they risked provoking the Japanese, who took them seriously enough for their command at Takao to order all their aircrews to stand by for an American raid when fog grounded their dawn strike against Clark Field, which had been timed to take off shortly after the attack on Pearl Harbor.

The U.S. Army Air Force may have overrated the capabilities of the Flying Fortress as a strike aircraft, but its long-range reconnaissance capabilities were proven. No one was more enthusiastic about the B-17 than MacArthur himself, who referred to the Flying Fortresses of his Bombardment Force as his "ace units." By mid-November half of all the heavy bombers in the United States arsenal and a sixth of the U.S. Army Air Force fighter strength was in the Philippines, and MacArthur was calling for target maps to bomb Tokyo.

"Nothing would please me better than if they would give

me three months and then attack here," MacArthur had told Admiral Phillips at their conference just seventy-two hours before war broke out.[28] He assured the British commander in chief in the Far East that he had "nothing to fear at all" in the event of an earlier attack by Japan.[29] MacArthur's bombastic window dressing may have been intended to impress his potential British ally, but considering the emphasis that MacArthur had put on his "ace units," it is inexplicable that he refused to sanction their deployment when he learned three days later that war had broken out. No less astounding was his decision to execute a key part of his war plan only *after* half his force of B-17s had been wiped out at Clark Field.

MacArthur would later complain that the "weakness of our air force precluded any chance of success for such an operation" and that "our fighters from our airfields in Luzon were too far away from Formosa to protect our bombers."[30] Once again this was distorting the facts to rewrite history. On 5 December at the meeting with the British he had cast himself as another Churchill when it came to defending the beaches of the Philippines—though plane for plane, he certainly faced better odds countering the Japanese air assault than the RAF had a year earlier during the Battle of Britain. MacArthur's excuse that his fighters lacked both the range and numbers to escort the bombers overlooked the fact that the Flying Fortress was heavily armed with machine guns to make long-range bombing attacks independent of fighter cover. Despite his ex post facto rationalization that it would have been "suicidal" to mount a preemptive strike on Formosa, it could not have been any more disastrous than having the seventeen B-17s destroyed on the ground. Military logic and his war plan called for sending them into the attack when war broke out. Astonishingly, MacArthur held them back, later claiming that it was "in defiance of my basic directive" to launch a preemptive strike against the Japanese bases in Formosa.[31]

"My orders were explicit not to initiate hostilities against the Japanese," MacArthur assured the official army historian, but the attack on Pearl Harbor and the telephone calls received from Washington explicitly called for action. Although the alert of 27 November stated that Japan should be allowed to commit the first "overt act," MacArthur was directed that this "SHOULD NOT REPEAT SHOULD NOT, BE CONSTRUED AS RESTRICTING THE SUCCESSFUL DEFENSE OF THE PHILIPPINES."[32] In response to a War Department dispatch the next day instructing him to extend air reconnaissance to Formosa, MacArthur had replied in the affirmative, confidently stating that "everything is in readiness for the conduct of a successful defense."[33]

MacArthur also knew that newly operational radar at Iba Field had been tracking "forces of strange aircraft estimated at 9 to 27 bombers" flying in over the west coast of Luzon for four days before war broke out. "Presumably, they were making trial navigation flights to familiarize themselves with the air route," Brereton had noted in his diary on 3 December, after the fourth consecutive early morning Japanese reconnaissance flight had flown over the beachheads of Lingayen Gulf.[34] After so many Japanese violations of Philippine air space and the specific directives from Washington, MacArthur should have had little hesitation in dispatching his "ace units" of B-17s to bomb the enemy bases in Formosa.

Eight hours after MacArthur learned about the attack on Pearl Harbor, six hours after he was told to initiate his war plan, and two full hours after USAFFE headquarters received reports that Japan had bombed the port of Davao on Mindanao, along with half-a-dozen towns on Luzon, action was still being withheld. Apologists for MacArthur blame Brereton or Sutherland for the command indecision that resulted in so many aircraft being wiped out on the ground. It has even been suggested that the general was so shocked by the news of Japan's attack on Pearl Harbor that he lapsed into a catatonic state of indecision, which his sycophantic aides concealed from subordinate commanders.[35] The account of Colonel Brown, who was able to see MacArthur and discuss MAGIC intercepts with him that morning, does not suggest a commander paralyzed by a profound psychological shock. The contradictions and controversy multiplied over the years, but among the conflicting statements it is significant that it was MacArthur himself who offered a pointer to what could be the real explanation for his otherwise inexplicable failure to act.

"The Philippines while a possession of the U.S. had, so far as war was concerned, a somewhat indeterminate international position in many minds, especially the Filipinos and their government," MacArthur contended, by way of explaining the difficulties his command faced.[36] The point he raised appears to indicate that he faced a conflict of interests. That a commanding general of the United States should have thought that the interests of the Philippines had priority after he had been directed to go to war is surprising. But there is documentation in archives in America and the Philippines that provides evidence that MacArthur might have experienced a conflict of loyalties that fateful morning. They suggest that the paralysis that gripped his command in the aftermath of the Pearl Harbor attack was the result of his indecision over obeying the orders of the War Department and those he received from the president of the Philippine Commonwealth. To understand how this dilemma arose, it is necessary to appreciate the degree to which MacArthur was bound to the Philippines by family, professional, and emotional ties.

General Arthur MacArthur, Jr., a Union army hero of the Civil War, had been appointed in 1898 the first U.S. military governor of the Philippines. Five years later his son Douglas, as a young lieutenant, had been posted to Manila. Thirty-two years on, after stepping down as chief of staff of the U.S. Army, following a dazzling military career that had begun as the cadet captain at West Point and included front-line service as an infantry colonel in the trenches of World War I, Douglas MacArthur received a hero's welcome when he returned to the Philippines in 1935 as the official American military adviser to President Manuel Quezon. In semiretirement, he fretted in a post whose honorary nature was rendered more impotent by the decision that the Philippines would shortly become independent of the United States.

Ambitious to keep what he believed was a special appointment with destiny, a year later MacArthur had retired from the U.S. Army to become field marshall of the Philippines. His comic-opera command consisted of only four thousand Filipino regulars, for which MacArthur received the decidedly untheatrical salary and expenses of $33,000—the equivalent of over a third of a million dollars in current values—which with his U.S. Army pension made him the highest paid military officer in the world. MacArthur's autocratic charisma was driven by a self-important theatricality, which was observed at close quarters by Dwight D. Eisenhower, his longtime chief of staff, who had returned from Manila to claim that he "had studied dramatics under him for five years in Washington and four in Manila."[37]

MacArthur may have been a field marshall without a real army, but he was lionized in the Philippines, where he became a prominent member of the Masonic lodge and lived in isolated splendor with his young second wife and infant son in the air-conditioned luxury of a seven-room custom-built penthouse in Manila's most luxurious hotel. MacArthur had also accumulated considerable wealth by July 1941, when he had to take a big drop in income after he was recalled to the colors as a mere lieutenant general. After five years of reaping the material benefits of serving a venal and patriarchal colonial administration, MacArthur continued to maintain close ties with the Philippine president. Quezon was his patron, *compadre*, and principal benefactor. He was not the first—or last—Philippine president to exploit the national treasury as a personal bank to fund his patronage.

Records that came to light a decade after MacArthur's death in 1964 reveal the extent to which the general had become one of the beneficiaries of Quezon's largesse before war broke out, and they appear to indicate that he was not averse to accepting substantial inducements to promote the interests of the Philippines over those of the United States. The most bizarre element of his long relationship with Quezon was the documentation that shows that MacArthur became considerably richer when the Philippines were engulfed by the military disaster for which the general bore a large measure of responsibility.

Among the private papers of MacArthur's former chief of staff that were deposited in the National Archives after Sutherland's death can be found the only surviving copy of *Executive Order No. 1 of the President of the Philippines*. Executed on 3 January 1942, the day after the Japanese entered Manila and a week after Quezon and MacArthur had evacuated their government and military staff to Corregidor, it authorized the transfer to the general and his closest aides of $640,000 from the Philippine Treasury "in recompense and reward, however inadequate, for distinguished service rendered between November 15, 1935 and December 30, 1941."[38]

The principal beneficiary was General Douglas MacArthur, who received $500,000—nearly $5 million in current values! General Sutherland received a paltry $75,000 and two other aides split the balance between them. The recipients, as serving officers of the U.S. Army, were forbidden by regulations to accept "a substantial loan or gift or emolument from a person or firm with whom it is the officer's duty as an agent of the government to carry out negotiations."[39] Possibly because the payment was illegal, neither MacArthur nor any of the other officers who shared in this huge financial windfall ever mentioned the payment, or offered any justification for accepting it.[40]

MacArthur had already been handsomely paid for his services as a field marshall of the Philippines, and before he rejoined the U.S. Army in July, he had taken care to extract a promise from Quezon that he could be reappointed to the commonwealth army with the same pay and allowances.[41] Large payoffs for services rendered were part of the fabric of the Filipino social order. It is also significant that Eisenhower's diary entry for 19 July 1942 records Quezon offered him "an honorarium for services rendered . . . as MacArthur's chief of staff in Manila."

The impropriety of such an offer prompted Eisenhower to decline any "material reward" as "inadvisable and impossible."[42] But MacArthur, it seems, had no such qualms about accepting the $500,000. Not only did this make a considerable depletion in the national treasury of an impoverished commonwealth, but it was singularly inappropriate for the general to have accepted such a huge sum at a time when the Philippines were being overrun as result of his military blunder three weeks earlier. MacArthur also insisted on special arrangements with Manuel Roxas, who was then in charge of the Philippine Treasury, for his share to be held for him in the account of the Commonwealth of the Philippines, which was with the Chase National Bank in New York.[43]

The transaction was so unusual that before it was put through on 15 February, the instructions radiogrammed from Roxas to the New York bank were circulated to Secretary of War Stimson and President Roosevelt by Harold Ickes, the secretary of the interior, whose department was responsible for the Philippines. For reasons that are not explained on any of this paperwork, they were prepared to turn a blind eye to such a questionable financial transaction. This in itself is further indication of how important the commander in chief of U.S. armed forces in the Far East had become for the Roosevelt administration, despite his initial defeat, as a symbol of the American war effort against Japan. Nor, it turns out, was the half-million-dollar transfer the only financial deal that preoccupied MacArthur as he supposedly concentrated all his energies on battling the Japanese invasion from the fastness of his Corregidor headquarters.

In the papers of Jorge Vargas, Quezon's deputy, can be found MacArthur's demand for $35,000 in expenses, which he submitted on 28 December. In the midst of the chaos overtaking Manila and in complete disregard of the difficulties, he insisted that Vargas personally arrange to purchase New York stock certificates in the amount of his claim. The purchase was arranged in MacArthur's name by Vargas, who records that he completed the transaction with the assistance of the New York manager of the Philippine National Bank.

"After the war MacArthur became a millionaire on account of that last-minute purchase," Vargas noted of the deal.[44] That an American commanding general should have been playing the U.S. stock market with funds extracted from the commonwealth treasury as the Japanese occupied Manila is not in keeping with MacArthur's heroic image as the savior of the Philippines. Yet neither was his dereliction of duty during the opening hours of the war. The contradictions are so startling as to suggest there was a connection that resulted from the conflict between MacArthur's military duty and a personal obligation to his financial patron, Quezon. This could explain the curious justification he gave for his inaction that the Philippines had "so far as the war was concerned, a somewhat indeterminate international position in many minds, especially the Filipinos and their government." What MacArthur seems to have been alluding to was more significant than his disclaimer that while he himself "had not the slightest doubt we would be attacked, great local hope existed that this would not be the case."[45]

The explanation that MacArthur offered in suspiciously elliptical language indicates that the Philippine president and some members of the Philippine government had entertained the hope that the Japanese would not attack if they were not attacked first by MacArthur's forces. Unrealistic though this expectation was, it could have had a decisive influence on Quezon if the possibility of maintaining neutrality had been forcefully argued by those members of the ruling clique in Manila who were later to collaborate with Japan's occupation. The idea was to be put forward again in February 1942, during the fighting retreat in Bataan, when, with MacArthur's implicit support, the president cabled Roosevelt proposing that they jointly issue a declaration of neutrality to spare the Philippine population further agony.

An angry Roosevelt rejected such a declaration, which would be tantamount to the United States' surrendering the Philippines. Marshall himself admonished MacArthur for supporting the idea in the strongest terms.[46] It is possible, therefore, that Quezon had prevailed upon MacArthur to put on hold Washington's orders to attack the Japanese airfields on Formosa to test whether a de facto neutrality would forestall a Japanese attack on the Philippines. If so, it would explain why MacArthur refused to sanction the preemptive bombing raid and issued caveats about not firing upon Japanese aircraft unless they committed hostile acts by dropping bombs.

"Some of MacArthur's reactions and behavior in early 1942 are hard to comprehend apart from the context of his personal ties and devotion to the Philippine president, Quezon," was the view expressed by Clayton James in his biography, which cites a number of occasions when the general put Filipino interests before the military requirements of the United States. "MacArthur yielded to Quezon on several critical occasions," he wrote, citing as examples the refusal to transfer Army food dumps from central Luzon back to Bataan before the retreat and instructions against shelling of Japanese occupied towns to spare the local population.[47] MacArthur's deference to Quezon suggests that he put his emotional sympathy for the Philippines above his duty to the United States by stalling an attack on the Japanese until they had committed overt acts of hostility against the Philippines.

History may be denied a definitive answer, but there is circumstantial evidence to support this explanation for the "uncertain sound" of MacArthur's trumpet call to action during the opening hours of the war. It had sufficient credence for General Eisenhower to offer it to the head of The *New York Times* foreign service as an explanation for MacArthur's extraordinary inaction. In 1951, the then Republican presidential candidate told C. L. Sulzberger that Quezon had informed him that "when the Japanese attacked Pearl Harbor, MacArthur was convinced for some strange reason that the Philippines would remain neutral and would not be attacked by the Japanese."[48]

MacArthur may have twisted the truth when it came to protecting his reputation, but he was not an incompetent military strategist. Yet the only credible excuse he gave for his refusal to sound a call to action was that the "Filipinos and their government" had "great local hope" that the Japanese would spare the Philippines "if they made no overt hostile act."[49] But there could have been no doubt in MacArthur's mind that the attack on Pearl Harbor was an "overt and hostile act" against the United States and all American territories in the Pacific over which the Stars and Stripes flew. That MacArthur held back offensive action that morning under pressure from his patron Quezon—who then compensated him with the equivalent of a five-million-dollar payoff—is a more credible explanation than that he was in a state of catatonic paralysis. Whatever the reason for his failure to act in accordance with his war plan, MacArthur has to be held accountable, as commander in chief, for a spectacular tactical defeat that doomed the Philippines to Japanese occupation.

The enormity of the disaster that overtook Pearl Harbor as a result of the miscalculations concerning the Philippines was concealed to protect the Roosevelt administration. This facilitated MacArthur's cover-up of his direct responsibility for the debacle at Clark Field. He explained his failure as the result of a "Second Pearl Harbor," in which he had been the victim of another "sneak attack."

"I prepared my *meager* forces," MacArthur wrote in his memoir, "to counter as best I might the attack that I knew was coming from the north, swiftly, fiercely and *without warning* [emphasis added]."[50] His claims, however, are as unhistorical as they were self-justificatory. Clark Field was not a second Pearl Harbor. In stark contrast to Pearl Harbor, where the Japanese attack took place without prior warning, at dawn on a Sunday while the military routine was still on a peacetime footing, the raid on Clark Field occurred after warnings had been received at midday, on what was a Monday across the international date line, nine hours after war had erupted in the Pacific. Not only had MacArthur been alerted by continuous access to the MAGIC intelligence of Japan's move toward belligerency, which the Hawaiian commanders had been denied, but he had been specifically and repeatedly warned by Washington—which Kimmel and Short were not—that the Philippines was a probable target for Japanese attack. He had also received direct telephone calls that morning from Washington specifically telling him not to get caught, as the Hawaiian command had been, with his air force on the ground.

MacArthur's *Reminiscences,* a memoir he wrote for publication only after his death, set out his definitive and final effort to absolve himself for posterity. In it he stated, "Our sky defense died with our battleships in the waves off Pearl Harbor." This false epitaph that MacArthur erected to explain his failure went even further in rewriting history. "Actually, the ultimate usefulness of our air arm in the Philippines had become academic because of the crippling of the American Fleet at Pearl Harbor," MacArthur wrote, declaring, "the stroke at Pearl Harbor not only damaged our Pacific Fleet, but destroyed any possibility of future Philippine air power." His claim that the raid five thousand miles away had "cancelled Rainbow 5, and sealed our doom" was as breathtaking a distortion as it was self-serving.[51] To claim the destruction of his airpower was "academic" when Japan's attack should have been taken as the

signal for him to unleash his force of heavy bombers against
Formosa as called for by his war plan was a shameful attempt
to burden the Hawaiian commanders with responsibility for
the Philippines disaster.

The strategic equation for the United States in the Pacific
theater by December 1941, as MacArthur was well aware, since
he had helped to formulate it, was that it was his command
and not that of Admiral Kimmel and General Short that had
the prime military responsibility for defending the United
States interests in the Pacific. It was not the Pacific Fleet but
the force of B-17 bombers that Washington had counted on as
the principal United States deterrent against Japan. MacArthur's blinding self-confidence had mislead the chiefs of staff
in Washington into believing in a fatally flawed high-risk military gamble in the Philippines. It was MacArthur who had
been given command of an aerial deterrent force that proved
neither awesome nor potent enough to deter. If he had been
called to account, MacArthur could have exposed how he had
been given an impossible mission by an administration in
Washington that had rushed into economic warfare with Japan without having the military capacity to enforce an oil and
trade embargo.

Any investigation of the subsequent debacle in the Philippines would have revealed how this deterrent strategy had
been founded on wishful thinking and how a secret pact with
the British had drawn away from Pearl Harbor the air defenses
that were essential to guarding against a Japanese carrier attack. Unlike Kimmel and Short, whose unpreparedness was
the result of being deprived of intelligence and adequate numbers of long-range aircraft, MacArthur had been given first-
call on the production of B-17 bombers and direct access to
MAGIC intelligence. He had also received repeated and very
specific warnings that his forces could be subjected to Japanese attack. Tokyo refused to be cowed by an inadequate "big
stick" of American military power in the Philippines and called
in this diplomatic and military bluff long before the American
force of heavy bombers and British battleships in Singapore
could be built up to the point that it threatened their strategic plans.

The ill-fated Anglo-American deterrent had, therefore, invited Japan's preemptive strike, which is precisely what a policy based on deterrence must not do. The dimension of the
American strategic miscalculation was to be magnified by the
speed and ease with which the Japanese disposed of the B-17

heavy bombers in Pearl Harbor. After the emptiness of their
Far East military gamble had been exposed, it is not surprising
that it was deliberately disowned in Washington and buried
by all those who had been party to it, as the "Pearl Harbor
Syndrome" took its toll on the truth about the culpability of
senior officers in the War and Navy departments. MacArthur
bore a special responsibility for its eventual tactical destruction. He was not to be called to account for fear of exposing
that the final responsibility rested with the military strategists
and diplomatic policy makers in Washington, and therefore,
ultimately, with the president.

"The ultimate responsibility for the attack and its results
rests upon Japan," the 1945 congressional investigation concluded, acknowledging that it had been "an attack that was
well planned and executed."[52] The skill and execution of the
Japanese attack has never been in dispute. All the attempts
made so far to fix the responsibility at the receiving end have
failed to take into account the role played by the Philippines.
Instead, the debate has been restricted to whether the high
command in Washington or the commanders in Hawaii bore
a greater share of the blame.

This central issue by 1945 had become hopelessly mired in
the contemporary partisan politics of the congressional committee. The Democratic majority sought to protect the wartime Roosevelt administration by ignoring the flaws in the
original Roberts Commission report and its findings that Admiral Kimmel and General Short were more culpable than the
president or his advisers. On the other side of the political
divide were the Republican minority, determined to blame
Roosevelt, who concluded that Washington deserved as much
if not an even greater share of the blame. The one finding on
which both sides agreed was that the investigation had exposed a weakness in the American command systems that was
highlighted by the breakdown of the intelligence process. This
lesson was not lost. It resulted in the postwar establishment
of the unified Department of Defense and the Central Intelligence Agency.

It has taken much longer to learn the lesson that one of
the underlying factors leading to the United States' general
unpreparedness to deal with the Japanese was its tendency to
discount the Asian nation's resolve and military capabilities,
which stemmed from ingrained Western institutional beliefs
and cultural factors. This underestimation fatally influenced
the policy makers and high command in Washington as much

as it did the individual commanders in Hawaii and the Philippines. The Pearl Harbor attack, because of the tendency to discount an Asian nation's abilities, was such a national outrage to American pride that inevitably the idea that someone in charge must have committed a monumental blunder exercised the public imagination and fired the continuing search for the "real" culprit.

The neglect of the Philippines factor by the congressional committee and all the other investigations concealed its central role in setting the stage for Pearl Harbor. This prevented there being a full picture against which the issue of who was responsible could be more fairly decided. No account was taken of MacArthur's role in the overall Pacific debacle by the Roosevelt administration, for whom it had been a matter of wartime expediency to conceal its own blame and make Kimmel and Short the principal scapegoats. The historical injustice that was done to the two Hawaiian commanders pales into insignificance when measured against the charges of gross dereliction that can be now documented against General MacArthur. Although they were caught less prepared for war than Washington believed they should have been, their reputations deserve a posthumous rehabilitation if only because of the monstrous unfairness with which they were dealt by an administration that let the culpable Philippine commander escape all retribution.

Out of the small mountain of documentation that has come to light in the half-century since the end of World War II that argues for justice to be done to Admiral Kimmel and General Short, no portion is more persuasive than those files that show how they were deliberately denied not only long-range aircraft but also vital intelligence, because by the fall of 1941 Washington regarded the Philippines and not Pearl Harbor as the American front line in the Pacific. It was this tragic mindset and the consequent denial of MAGIC intelligence and its diplomatic context to the Hawaiian commanders that left them so ill-prepared to meet the Japanese attack.

The full extent to which Admiral Kimmel had been denied the information that could have saved the Pacific Fleet battleships and the lives of thousands of American servicemen was not to become apparent until fifty years later. The discovery of privately held ultrasecret U.S. Navy documentation was followed by the declassification of a 1946 naval intelligence analysis of the pre–Pearl Harbor intercepts of Japanese naval communications that had been largely unreadable in 1941.

This report's conclusions were so potentially explosive that it appears to have been deliberately concealed from the congressional investigating committee—which had statutory authority over all the Pearl Harbor records—and it remained a classified secret for nearly half a century.

13

"WE JUST DID NOT HAVE IT!"

The U.S. Navy Conceals for Fifty Years that the
Unread Intercepted Japanese Naval Traffic
Contained the Clues to Pearl Harbor

The role that General Douglas MacArthur and the Philippines deterrent played in the twin disasters on 7 December 1941 was not the only issue that went unprobed in the six-month-long hearings before the joint committee of Congress. By 1945 it was a matter of record that by breaking the Japanese naval codes, the numerically inferior Pacific Fleet had ambushed the Combined Fleet at the Battle of Midway, six months after war broke out. Yet for all the thousands of references to the Purple *diplomatic* cipher and the "East Wind Rain" code, there are only three references to the Japanese *naval* ciphers in the entire forty-volume congressional report.

"If we could have solved the Flag Officers system, Admiral Kimmel would probably have known of the Japanese plans and the Pacific Fleet would not have been surprised on 7 December," was the statement in a memorandum on the penetration of Japanese naval ciphers by Captain Safford, who throughout 1941 had been head of OP-20-G, the section of the Office of Naval Communications responsible for intercepting and breaking the radio traffic of foreign navies.[1] According to Safford, "neither the U.S. Navy nor the British cryptanalysts ever succeeded in cracking this system," and he also stated

278

that the Combined Fleet's general-purpose cipher, known to the Americans as JN-25, "yielded no information which would have aroused even a suspicion of the Pearl Harbor raid, *either before or afterward* [emphasis added]."[2]

Safford's testimony may explain why in their quest for the truth about Pearl Harbor the congressional investigators completely overlooked the Japanese naval codes and instead focused on the missing "East Wind Rain" execute message. But even as this wild-goose chase was diverting their attention, it is now apparent that the Navy Department was secretly conducting its own review of the Japanese naval codes that proved that Safford's assertion had been wrong.

An eight-month-long study of thousands of Japanese naval signals picked up in 1941 that had remained unbroken or only fragmentarily read at the time was to reveal the shocking fact: the U.S. Navy had possessed all along the intercepts containing all the pieces of the Pearl Harbor puzzle that would have revealed the Combined Fleet's plan to attack the Pacific Fleet anchorage. They had remained unread because of a bureaucratic blunder made by the Navy Department in the spring of 1941 that had given priority to breaking the wrong Japanese naval cipher system. Had this explosive evidence leaked out during the hearings, the congressional committee might have reached a very different conclusion about the true extent of the intelligence failure in Washington.

Pre–Pearl Harbor Japanese Naval Dispatches is the deceptively innocuous title of a report of stunning implication that was delivered to the chief of naval operations early in 1946. So potentially damaging were its conclusions that it was to remain a closely guarded secret for the next forty-five years![3] Its ULTRA security classification and advisory note that "the very knowledge of the existence of this publication identified by the long title must be regarded as TOP SECRET" are a measure of the sensitivity of what proved to be an indictment of the Navy Department's failure to rate the Japanese fleet cipher as a source of potentially vital intelligence when it came to allocating priorities for the limited resources of the code-breaking section of the Office of Naval Communication.

In 1941 Safford was in charge of the naval code-breaking section of OP-20-G known as NEGAT. His most important asset was the remarkable female cryptanalyst, Mrs. Agnes Meyer Driscoll, who had been instrumental in breaking the so-called Red Book Imperial Navy code in 1926 and the Blue Book "A" Code system, which succeeded it. It was an article of faith for

"Miss Aggie," as she was respectfully known by a generati
of naval intelligence officers, that no code invented by mz
could not be broken by a woman. It was thanks to her effort,
that the U.S. Navy was able to intercept and read the most
secure Japanese naval communications until the new Fleet
Code cipher was introduced on 1 June 1939.[4]

Japan's new naval cipher was identified at the time as the
"5-numeral code" or "AN" system. It is better known as JN-25
(Japanese Navy code number 25), which in 1942 became the
Navy's shorthand for what was officially designated as the Imperial Navy's General Purpose Fleet Code. It was a two-part
system that had an encode book in which the "plain text" was
alphabetized for ready reference with its equivalent scrambled
or "randomized code value"—a five-digit number group, in the
case of JN-25. There was also a decode book in which, for ready
reference, those code values were in sequence. The separate
key book (pad, table, sheet) in the case of JN-25 consisted of
five-digit "additive tables" that were used to super-encipher
the code value by "false," i.e. non-carrying arithmetic. These
were applied by encoder—and removed by the decoder—using
a duplicate of the key book, *after* which the code value could
be looked up in the decode book. The starting point in the
additive book was determined according to a key that changed
daily, and to enhance the security of the system additive books
were replaced with new ones after an average period of six
months.

JN-25 was not a particularly difficult cipher to crack in
principle, but to penetrate the system to the extent of reading
the traffic transmitted in the Japanese Fleet Code required intercepting and decoding thousands of messages in order to
reconstruct the dictionary book. But before this could be done
it was necessary to assemble the sequences of numbers in the
additive book that had first to be stripped away to reveal the
underlying code. The U.S. Navy cryptanalysts under Mrs. Driscoll had broken into the "A" version by September 1939, but
by the time they had begun to penetrate the system, it was
discontinued at the end of 1940, when an entirely new "B"
version of the code book was introduced in conjunction with
a more sophisticated set of additive tables.

To reconstruct the 33,333 five-digit groups in the new code
book that was to remain in use until May 1942, while simultaneously recovering the values of the new additive books
demanded cryptanalytic resources beyond those that were
available to the U.S. Navy in 1991. This "bookbreaking" pro-

cess, as the Americans termed it, was a time-consuming operation. The equivalent British term, "bookbuilding," more descriptively sums up the painstaking analysis of thousands of intercepts needed to reconstruct the additive tables and the underlying code book. To add to this travail, 27,500 of the potential code groups in the "B" version dictionary book were assigned two meanings, and by January 1941 only some 2,000, or about four percent, of these had been recovered, mostly consisting of numbers 000 through 999.[5] To break JN-25B to the extent of being able to read more than routine ship-movement reports demanded far more code-breaking effort than Safford had available in OP-20-G, whose time and attention in 1941 was increasingly focused on the Purple cipher.

The task of penetrating JN-25 was assigned by Safford to the CAST code-breaking team at the Philippines because the Asiatic Fleet was in closer proximity to the Japanese than the Pacific Fleet. Some backup was provided by the cryptanalysts in the Navy Department, known as Station NEGAT, but what effort they provided focused on analysis of past traffic rather than current messages. The consensus of the postwar testimony and later interviews with some of the code breakers and analysts involved is that the U.S. Navy was able to penetrate only an average of ten percent of the intercepted Japanese fleet code traffic by December 1941. This proved not to be sufficient penetration for any meaningful intelligence to be extracted from the current JN-25B traffic before 7 December 1941. Precisely what information was gleaned before war broke out is still impossible to gauge because no decrypts have ever come to light showing what was read before 7 December 1941. All that has been officially admitted was that these consisted only of "ship-movement reports: arrivals and departures, together with some fragmentary schedules."[6]

The reason so little information is available on JN-25 is evident from the analysis of the intercepts themselves, which is contained in *Pre–Pearl Harbor Japanese Naval Dispatches*. This shows that if the full story had emerged in 1945, it would have undermined confidence in the Navy Department and damaged the reputations of the senior officers involved. They were already hard-pressed by Congress to account for the intelligence failures four years earlier, so every effort was made to conceal the true significance of JN-25. No hint of the contents of the report reached any outside investigator, and it was destined to remain a classified secret for nearly half a century. Its very existence remained unrecorded until it was discovered in a warehouse used to store naval records in Crane, Indiana, by historians from the National Security Agency, the super-secret organization set up to conduct United States electronic surveillance and code breaking during the Cold War.[7]

The 1946 Navy report on what was in Japanese naval traffic shows that the Navy Department could have provided Admiral Kimmel with specific advance warning of the attack if JN-25 had been read to any great extent in the fall of 1941. In contrast to the indirect indications that Pearl Harbor was the focus of an extensive espionage operation, which appear in the intercepted Purple diplomatic traffic that Washington denied Admiral Kimmel, the intelligence in the Fleet Code intercepts reveals all the elements of Japan's Hawaiian Operation. They are obvious and unmistakable even without the advantage of the hindsight that was required to interpret the "bomb-plot" message.

That the JN-25 intelligence was not broken out in time was not the result of a sinister conspiracy, but a simple bureaucratic miscalculation. The failure to give priority to the Fleet Code would, nonetheless, turn out to be a monumental blunder. This explains why the Navy Department carried out a meticulous postwar "housecleaning operation," which removed from the official record all traces of the pre–Pearl Harbor JN-25 decrypts, which in 1946 amounted to a file of 26,581 Japanese naval messages intercepted between September and December 1941.

According to the report, none of the seven crypto-systems in which these messages had been transmitted could be understood, except fragmentarily, at the time when their unread intelligence could have had a vital impact on the course of events. The value of this lost intelligence was destined not to be realized until four years later. Then it became an embarrassment that had to be concealed.

This was appreciated only after the thousands of JN-25 intercepts that had been gathering dust in Navy Department files since 1941, but which have since vanished, were comprehensively analyzed in a process that began in September 1945 and continued through to May 1946. By winnowing out those signals whose addresses indicated that they contained only low-grade administrative traffic, some ninety percent of the intercepts were quickly put aside as unimportant. This left 2,413 Japanese naval messages that had been transmitted and picked up before 7 December that were considered "of sufficient interest for translation." Of these, 188 were found to contain vital intelligence clues to the Japanese intention to attack Pearl Harbor.

"All of the important dispatches were encrypted in JN-25B, the Japanese Fleet General Purpose System," according to the investigator's report. It noted that the "B" version introduced on 1 December 1940 with the new encipherment code book remained in use until May 1941. The six-month changes of the additive books, however, meant that by 1 December, when the eighth change in the additives was introduced, there had been ample opportunity to penetrate the code system that carried all the major operational details of Japan's naval war plan. But the U.S. Navy had committed too little manpower to breaking the Fleet Code to be able to read the JN-25B "7" version in the critical months running up to the outbreak of war. If they had, it is clear from the 1946 analysis that it would have revealed enough detail about the Japanese Hawaiian Operation for the Americans to have a precise warning of the attack on Pearl Harbor.

"The U.S. Navy's communications analysts in Corregidor, Hawaii and Washington would have made that prediction if they had been able to read them at the time," was the unequivocal verdict of Frederick Parker of the National Security Agency, the first historian to study the 1946 report. In accordance with the NSA's ongoing concern for preserving the secrecy of the operations and methodology of American cryptanalytic process, some items were censored out of the report, including all references to the actual JN designation of the signal messages cited.

What does emerge very clearly from the 1946 Naval Intelligence report was that while the "B" version of JN-25 was not yielding meaningful current intelligence during the fall of 1941, the U.S. Navy, after more than a decade of reading Japanese naval communications, had assembled a remarkably accurate picture of the command structure of the Combined Fleet and its associated air units. Although the U.S. Navy at the time was blind to the content of the intercepts, the Japanese naval radio signal continued to provide important intelligence from direction finding and traffic analysis, which did not require the solution of the Fleet Code since the originator and addressee were not enciphered in JN-25.

The composition of the task forces of the Combined Fleet, and in some cases even their targets, could be deduced and their movements tracked by the call signs of the individual warships and force commanders. The transmissions were picked up by skilled operators who manned the network of listening posts ringing the Pacific and who were known as the "On the Roof Gang"—from the location of their original training center, which was a hut built on the roof of the Navy Department in Washington. Sometimes it was possible to identify the warships sending the signals from the individual "fist" signatures of the Japanese radio operators as they tapped out the enciphered messages in the seventy-three dot-dash combinations of the Morse code used to transmit. This was converted directly to the kana version of the Japanese language by the listeners, using specially modified typewriters.[8]

The best efforts of the "On the Roof Gang," while revealing an accurate picture of the steady buildup and southward movement of Japanese naval forces in November 1941, had not been able to provide advance warning of the strike on Pearl Harbor because the carrier task force that carried out the Hawaiian Operation had maintained strict radio silence while they assembled and during the passage across the northern Pacific. But the contents of 188 signals intercepted during their training exercises and the orders relayed to the silent task force as it sailed to keep its rendezvous with destiny provided all the pieces necessary to assemble a complete picture of the Pearl Harbor attack plan.

The picture that could have been assembled piece by piece in 1941, as it was in 1946, establishes that the Fleet Code intercepts from September 1941 onward slotted together reveal the timetable and targets of the Hawaiian Operation, and they could have been pieced together had their contents been read by the U.S. Navy at the time. In order to emphasize that the picture could have been completed without the advantage of hindsight, the giveaway clues are underlined in the Navy's report on *Pre–Pearl Harbor Japanese Naval Dispatches*.

"A state of complete readiness for battle operations must be achieved by the first of November," the commander of the 2nd Fleet signaled on 5 September. This first clue to the timing of the Japanese war plan was followed four days later by another, as the chief of staff of the Combined Fleet sent a dispatch to all units: "As conditions become more and more critical, each and every ship and all units will aim at being prepared for commencing war operations by the *first week of November* [emphasis added]."[9] During the next month, the term "Striking Force" and "Advance Expeditionary Force" began appearing regularly in the instructions transmitted by Japan's Combined Fleet headquarters. On 13 October there was a dispatch calling for communications drills. Orders were transmitted four days later to Japanese naval yards to paint "friendly recognition markings" on all submarines by "*the end of October* [emphasis added]."[10] Then on 18 October the Imperial Navy minister signaled to all ships that "conditions today, both abroad and at home, have truly become so critical as to decide the rise or fall of our Empire."[11]

The first clues to the composition of the Striking Force appeared in signals detailing operating procedures that were transmitted on 24 October by the chief of staff of the 1st Air Fleet to Battleship Division 3, Cruiser Division 8, Destroyer Squadron 1, and Carrier Division 4. Corroboration that he was the commander came two days later in a signal in which he ordered that "all ships (units) scheduled to be assigned to the Striking Force (?) [indicating the American translator's informed guess] have all torpedoes adjusted by *18 November* [emphasis added]." The mission for which the Striking Force was being equipped had started to become evident.

The three signals from the 1st Air Fleet chief of staff intercepted on 28 October referred to specially modified torpedoes. One particularly revealing signal instructed that "on 30 October, this fleet will pick up five to ten near surface (?) torpedoes at Sasebo Military Stores Department. Classes on this torpedo will be held at Kanoya for about five days." Simultaneously, a signal addressed to the commanders of Carrier Division 1 ordered, "Send personnel and workers to carry out instructions on Type 91 torpedoes *(equipped with stabilizers)* [emphasis added]." The same day the 1st Air Fleet requested 60 additional torpedo technicians be assigned "between the end of October and *20 November*" [emphasis added] to Carrier Divisions 1, 2, and 5, where the "lack of personnel is causing grave delays."[12]

The first indications of the target for which these shallow-running torpedoes were being specially modified emerged the following week, after the 1st Air Fleet commander had informed the local naval air station on 3 November that "in 3rd Special Drill *in ambushing*, [emphasis added] 54 shipboard bombers will carry out bombing and strafing attack in sight of the Saeki Base." That it was battleships the Japanese pilots were practicing to attack was confirmed the next day by a dispatch from the commander of Carrier Division 2 ordering the destroyer *Yuzuki* to "pick up and take to Kagoshima the torpedoes (total of 4) which Cardivs 1 and 2 are to fire *against anchored capital ships on the morning in question* [emphasis added]."[13]

If the U.S. Navy had been reading JN-25B, the intercepts already received by early November would have disclosed that a Japanese carrier Striking Force was being equipped and trained to attack anchored battleships with bombs and torpedoes modified for running in the shallow waters of a harbor. Since it was less than a year since the British had successfully mounted a surprise raid by carrier aircraft on the Italian Fleet in its Taranto anchorage in November 1940, it would have been obvious to any naval intelligence officer worthy of the name that the Japanese were preparing to mount a copycat attack.[14] If there had been any doubt that it was American capital ships that were the intended target of all this intensive activity, then the Japanese helpfully confirmed their intention in a 1 November signal referring to the continuing drill maneuvers to "*ambush* and completely destroy *the U.S. enemy* [emphasis added]."[15]

The number of heavy units and carriers in the Striking Force was made clear in a signal that the commander in chief of the 1st Air Fleet sent on 9 November, addressed to the *Akagi*, the flagship of Carrier Division 1, which was copied to Carrier Division 2 and 5 together with Battleship Division 3, Cruiser Division 8, and Destroyer Division 1. This suggested that these were the units that would operate as a single Striking Force. Three of the five carrier divisions in the Japanese navy constituted such a formidable commitment of Japanese naval power that the question of its intended target would have caused considerable concern had the U.S. Navy been able to read this signal at the time.

More clues about the operation began emerging in intercepted signals to the oiler attached to the carriers that "will complete all preparations for action at Kure and Sasebo, and after taking on fuel and secret supplies will carry out training exercises in fuelling at sea."[16] That the Striking Force intended to sail a considerable distance from Japan came to light in a series of dispatches to the carriers giving specific instructions "regarding the load of drums and fuel oil" aboard warships of the Striking Force that had also been issued to the 1st Air Fleet commander. Of particular concern was the way the heavy containers were to be stored aboard the carriers *Akagi*, *Sooryuu*, and *Hiryuu*, "as it will affect the strength of the hull and the ships performance."[17] Other signals ordered additional fueling hoses and one of the escorting destroyers on 9 November requested permission to disembark inessential equipment "in view of the fact that it is absolutely essential to carry additional oil and ammunition . . . to effectively carry out future assignment."[18]

Further evidence that the Striking Force would be heading deep into the Pacific came on 14 November when naval headquarters in Tokyo radioed that it was assigning an additional oiler named *Shirya* to the 1st Air Fleet. Previous maneuvers by the Japanese navy had revealed that the disposition of oilers in the fleet train presaged the movement of the major units. Four days later another intercept disclosed that this particular tanker was ordered to be supplied with a copy of the Striking Force Secret Operational Order. So by mid-November the JN-25 intercepts pointed to a carrier raid on an American fleet anchorage. Even if it was not yet clear whether the target was Pearl Harbor or a naval base on the West Coast, there could be no mistaking the accelerating pace of Japan's preparations as evidenced by the orders transmitted to put their naval communication networks on a war footing.

"Maintain wartime radio silence on shortwave commencing 0000 November 11," the 6th Submarine Fleet was directed on 10 November; four days later "Wartime Recognition Signals for Japanese Merchant Shipping" were ordered into effect on 1 December. Two days later the first "Striking Force Operational Order" was issued for "Commencing 0000 on 19 November 'Battle Control' effective for short wave radio frequencies."[19] On 16 November the Combined Fleet headquarters ordered that "new forms for making dispatch reports regarding the type of enemy formation will be placed in effect on 20 November." The Southern Expeditionary Fleet was also instructed four days later to "maintain precautionary radio silence" from that same date. Also on 20 November, Admiral Yamamoto sent the Combined Fleet a top-secret signal whose import was flagged by the instruction that it was to be decoded "only by an office."

"At 0000 on 21 November, repeat 21 November, carry out Second Phase of preparations for opening hostilities."[20] This was an unmistakable indication that the Combined Fleet was henceforth operating under war conditions and was confirmed the next day when the radio call sign lists, which had only come into effect on 1 November and which would normally have been in effect for six months, were ordered to be changed again on 1 December. An intercept of 25 November ordered, "From 26 November, ships of the Combined Fleet will observe radio communication procedure as follows: Except in emergency the Main Force and its attached force will cease communications." This effectively blacked out transmissions of the operational forces of the Combined Fleet and prevented their being tracked by radio direction finding, a clear sign that the Japanese war plan was preparing to unfold.

The intercepted JN-25 traffic had yet to disclose any mention of the target of the Striking Force. But dispatches of 16 and 24 November contained the revised intercepts of the new call signs lists which contained six-letter designator codes for the operations. In addition, alphabetic identifiers were given to an E, H, M, and "N Force" in addition to a "Southern Force," a "Northern Force," an "AA Occupation Force," a "G Occupation Force," and an "AF Destruction Unit."[21] Not until 1942 was the geographic designator of "AF" established as Midway, with "AA" as Wake and "G" as Guam. But in 1941 any naval intelligence analyst armed with a map and the information on the disposition of the buildup of the naval forces obtained from traffic analysis and direction finding, would have been able to mark off the obvious Japanese targets. The alphabetic designators for the principal bases of European and American power in the western Pacific and Far East had by an oversight been selected with scant regard for security.

So it was that "E" (English) stood for the British territory of Malaya, "H" (Holland) was Dutch possessions in Borneo, Java, and Sumatra. "M" (Manila) was the Philippines, the principal bastion of the United States in the Far East, which commanded the sea route between Japan and the oil fields of the Indonesian archipelago. The N (Nippon) Force was the Combined Fleet battleships guarding the Japanese home islands. The area of operation of the "Northern" and "Southern" forces was also self-evident from their descriptive designation.

Only the Striking Force was conspicuously missing any link to a geographic target designator. But a numerical count off of the call signs for the forces, against the map of the Far East, would have revealed that the British, American, and Dutch bases had been covered. This fact, taken together with the indicators that the Striking Force had been practicing for a long-range Taranto-style raid against anchored capital ships, pointed incontrovertibly to Pearl Harbor. It was the only base in the entire Pacific where there was a lineup of battleships that would have justified the commitment of a six-carrier task force.

Even if this had not been immediately obvious, it could

have been clear from further clues contained in a series of intercepted orders transmitted from naval headquarters in Tokyo to Carrier Divisions 1, 2, and 5, which constituted the punch of the Striking Force, after the force began observing strict radio silence from 26 November. By then it would have been possible to establish from the intercepts that Carrier Divisions 3 and 4 were not part of the Striking Force. None of their call signs had been linked to the Operational Order Number 1 addressed to the warships under the overall command of the 1st Air Fleet. That the remaining two carrier divisions were part of the Southern Force operation could have been confirmed by a 22 November signal ordering a seaplane tender attached to Carrier Division 4 to transport planes from Sasebo to Palau "as quickly as possible." On 26 November a signal from the commander of Carrier Division 3 requested a refueling rendezvous with the oiler *San Clemente Maru* at noon on 4 December, putting the light carriers in the vicinity of Palau to the west of the Caroline Islands.[22]

Lacking this vital information in the unread JN-25 intercepts, traffic analysis and direction finding alone could not locate the recipient, only the source of a radio transmission. It could not, therefore, reveal the whereabouts of the Japanese carriers after transmissions addressed to their call signs ceased. The last radio fixes obtained by the U.S. Navy direction finders on the three divisions, made up of the six largest Japanese carriers, put them in the Sakei Wan anchorage in the Inland Sea. Then all reporting from them ceased. When even their call signs vanished from intercepted transmissions, the issue of the precise location of these carriers caused increasing concern to the U.S. Navy's traffic analysts at Pearl Harbor.

"There was great unease in all of our minds because of the lack of traffic," admitted Commander Rochefort, the head of the Combat Intelligence Unit at Pearl Harbor. From the information that he and his cryptanalysts at HYPO had at their disposal, it was not clear whether the carriers had put to sea again. As he explained it, "The inability to locate more battleships and carriers was not considered in itself as a bad sign by reason of the fact that up until that time we had generally been unsuccessful in locating a majority of the larger ships."[23] He was inclined to attribute at least part of this failure to the inadequacies of HYPO's main source of radio intelligence, the mid-Pacific direction finder network. According to Rochefort, it was "not as efficient or as productive of results as it might have been . . . due to the type of equipment, lack of trained operators and the long distance involved."[24] He allowed that the "missing carriers" might have been at sea and were observing radio silence or had just not been picked up. Rochefort was inclined to believe that their call signs had vanished because the carriers were swinging around their moorings and communicating with Combined Fleet headquarters by telephone line.

"The estimate submitted on 26 November consisted of the opinion that the Japanese were concentrating to the south of Japan, one force proceeding toward Indochina; the direction of the other force not known," was Rochefort's conclusion. "An additional force of some strength and containing at least one carrier division was placed quite definitely in the Marshalls area."[25] His actual "Priority" estimate for that Wednesday put the main focus of Japanese naval activity in the waters south of Formosa, where "for the past month Commander Second Fleet has been organizing a task force."[26] This was the intelligence picture that he personally elaborated the next day, 27 November, when Admiral Kimmel visited the dungeonlike offices of HYPO in the basement of the Submarine Base at Pearl Harbor. The Pacific Fleet commander was accompanied by Admiral Bloch, the commander of the 16th Naval District, who had direct authority for HYPO. According to Rochefort they spent "an hour and a half" discussing the "Communication Intelligence Summary," which concluded most of the Japanese carriers "are still located in home waters."[27]

If HYPO had been able to read JN-25, Rochefort would have been able to tell Kimmel that the six carriers were not in home waters, but that very morning had put to sea from the Kurile Islands, as the Striking Force ploughed eastward into the heavy gray swells of the north Pacific toward the Hawaiian Islands. The keys of all the shipborne radio transmitters had been sealed off to ensure there was no accidental breaking of the Striking Force's radio silence.[28] Yet despite these precautions, the course that it steered toward Pearl Harbor was betrayed by a string of orders and weather forecasts flashed out to the Striking Force by Imperial General Headquarters both before and during its dash across the stormy waters of the north Pacific.

Confirmation is provided by the intercepted JN-25 signals translated by the U.S. Navy investigators in 1946, two of which in particular could have revealed that the "missing" Japanese carrier divisions were assembling in Hittokapu Wan, a windswept bay on the west coast of Etorofu, the southernmost island of the Kurile chain, off the northernmost tip of Hokkaido. The clues were contained in a seemingly cryptic message of 17 November from the Naval General Staff in Tokyo addressed to the commanders of the 1st Air Fleet and Battleship Division 3, informing them that "Suzuki (1776) *is being sent to your headquarters on board the [battleship] Hiei to report on inspection results* [emphasis added]." The following day the Ominato Guard District in the north of Honshu was instructed to "please arrange to have Suzuki (1776) picked up about 23 or 24 November at Hittokapu Wan by ——— (unidentified ship) of your command."[29]

Only after the end of the war could it be established that Lieutenant Commander Suguru Suzuki was a Japanese intelligence officer who had just returned from a surveillance voyage to Honolulu as a passenger aboard the liner *Taiyo Maru*. But this knowledge was not necessary for the U.S. Navy to have deduced that Battleship Division 3 and the 1st Air Fleet—and therefore the main force of Japanese carriers to which they were assigned—were gathered in the Kuriles a thousand miles away from their home ports. Additional confirmation that the Striking Force was in the high north preparing to sail on a major offensive operation was provided by a 19 November signal from a submarine unit, which reported its passage northward from the Yokuska Communications Zone to Ominato (on Hokkaido) on 22 November and "*thereafter, 1st Air Fleet Flagship Communication Zone* [emphasis added]"—putting the carriers in the Kuriles.[30]

The actual sailing order transmitted to the Striking Force was not intercepted by any of the U.S. Navy listening posts, but even without the interception of the sailing order, if the U.S. Navy code breakers had been able to read JN-25, the intercepts would have revealed that the Striking Force was heading on an easterly course across the Northern Pacific. The analysis made in 1946 identified "two of the most significant dispatches of this period" as a shipping advisory and a weather report. The first was sent on 30 November to inform Admiral Nagumo, the Striking Force commander, "Although there are indications of several U.S. ships *operating in the Aleutians area*, the ships *in the northern Pacific* [emphasis added] appear chiefly to be Russian vessels. Known Russian ships are *Uzbekistan* (about 3,000 tons and an estimated speed of 12 knots) and *Azerbaidjan* (6,114 tons and an estimated speed of 10 knots). The former left San Francisco on 12th, and the latter on 14th, and both are westbound."[31]

The second was a two-part message sent the next day containing the weather update: "The low pressure center of 740mm which was near 'N RI 0 NA' at noon today is advancing at a speed of 45 kilometers. Wind speed is over 15 meters within 1000 kilometers to the southwestward of the center, and about 26 meters near the center. The high pressure in 'RU' area continues to proceed eastward at 45 kilometers. Line of discontinuity ——— ——— ———." Attached to it was a good-luck message from Prince Hiroyasu Fushimi, an admiral and former chief of the Imperial Naval General Staff from 1932 to 10 April 1941, for Commander in Chief Nagumo, "I pray for your long and lasting battle fortunes."[32]

Separately or together, these two dispatches were confirmation that the Striking Force was heading eastward. The Russian freighters carrying Lend-Lease supplies to Vladivostok were known to take the northern route west.[33]

The alert about American ships in the vicinity of the Aleutians was also an indication of the general location of the Striking Force, whose position could have been pinpointed more precisely from the barometric pressure given in the weather forecast. Although the superenciphered geographic grid coordinates would not be broken out even in 1946, they would have offered no concealment of the Striking Force track since this would have been revealed by comparing the readings with the current U.S. barometric weather map of the northern Pacific Ocean. Investigators in 1946 were unable to find a contemporary forecast, but they noted that "a skilled weather observer has stated that it would have been possible to break the grid on the above and following weather dispatches by means of information then available, particularly that of the Pan Am Airways weather service."[34]

Once it had been established that the Striking Force was steaming eastward just to the north of the thirtieth line of latitude, a simple navigational calculation based on an estimated average speed of the oilers accompanying the Japanese carriers would have shown that it would come within air-strike range of Pearl Harbor during the weekend of 6/7 December. Confirmation that the Pacific Fleet anchorage was the target would have been provided on 1 December by the intercept of the report radioed by the tanker *Shirya* that she was "proceeding to position 30.00N, 154,20E. Expect to arrive at that point on 3 December. Thereafter will proceed eastward along 30 degree north latitude at speed 7 knots."[35] Since this oiler had already been identified as part of the Striking

Force's supply train, it could have been deduced that the *Shirya* was standing by to the west of the Hawaiian chain to refuel the task force as it headed west after raiding Pearl Harbor. The actual timing of the raid on Pearl Harbor was revealed in the intercept of Yamamoto's celebrated attack order transmitted on 2 December: "This dispatch is Top Secret. This order is effective 1730 on 2 December. Combined Fleet serial #10. Climb Niitakayama 1208, repeat 1208."[36]

A high-school atlas would have revealed that Korean Mount Niitaka was the highest peak in the Japanese Empire. Any competent naval intelligence officer would not have needed any special insight to have guessed that this was the prearranged "GO" code signal to commence hostilities on the eighth day of the twelfth month in Japan, or 7 December across the international date line in Hawaii. As the naval analysts pointed out in their 1946 report, this was the last dispatch intercepted before the eighth version of the JN-25 "B" version of the additive book came into use on 4 December. The new random-digit encipherment tables would have blacked out further reading of the system until the values of thousands of fresh additives had been recovered. Even had it been possible to read the Fleet Code to that point, the necessary bookbuilding process would have taken days, if not weeks, to accomplish, making it most unlikely that any useful intelligence would have been recorded from the JN-25 B-8 version in the remaining seventy-two hours before Japan's prearranged schedule of attacks plunged the Pacific into war on 7 December 1941.

Pre–Pearl Harbor Japanese Naval Dispatches is a remarkable historic document because its belated declassification confirms what many conspiracy theorists have long contended: the U.S. Navy had indeed intercepted Japanese signals that *could have forewarned* Admiral Kimmel of the impending attack on Pearl Harbor. But the unread JN-25 intercepts do not amount to the long-sought-after "smoking gun" that revisionists looked for to try to incriminate Roosevelt in a plot to withhold the warning from the Pacific Fleet. The vital intelligence these JN-25 intercepts contained was locked in a cipher system that could not be read at the time by the United States Navy. If the Fleet Code had been broken to the point of current readability up to 4 December 1941, then as the U.S. Navy's 1946 analysis demonstrates, it would almost certainly have provided, in the view of one of the veteran naval cryptanalysts, a clear and unequivocal warning of Japan's bold Hawaiian Operation.

"Any knowledgeable intelligence analyst who would not have come to the conclusion that Pearl Harbor was not about to be attacked would have lost his job," was the considered judgment of Commander Prescott Currier, a member of the OP-20-G cryptanalytic staff in Washington at the time, after closely studying the report on *Pre–Pearl Harbor Japanese Naval Dispatches*. "I know I would have," he added, recalling that it was a matter of great shame and regret that in November 1941 "we just did not have it!"[37] According to testimony given in 1944 by his former boss, Safford, the combined efforts of the CAST and NEGAT cryptographic teams at Cavite and Washington resulted in JN-25B becoming only "partly readable in November 1941."

This was confirmed to the author by the authoritative judgment given shortly before their deaths in 1984, by both Captain Thomas H. Dyer and Captain Wesley A. "Ham" Wright. They were members of Rochefort's HYPO team, which finally gained access to all the JN-25B code book and additive recoveries on 17 December, and from their recollections they agreed that their opposite numbers in Cavite and Washington could not have been deciphering more than about ten percent of the traffic in the Fleet Code messages up until the beginning of December 1941.

Yet precisely what intelligence, if any, the U.S. Navy derived from the JN-25 intercepts before 7 December 1941 still cannot be established. The contemporary worksheets all disappeared in what appears to have been a very thorough "housecleaning" of all the pre–Pearl Harbor JN-25 message worksheets and partial decrypts by the Navy Department in the wake of the revelations in the 1946 report.[38] This postwar analysis shows that the failure to discern and pass on the warning was the result not of a deliberate conspiracy but of a breakdown of analysis that stemmed from a decision made nine months earlier in Washington to give the Fleet Code a low priority when it came to assigning the Navy's limited cryptanalytic resources.

"Due to the lack of personnel during 1941, none of the above systems was read currently," was the only reason given by the investigating team that wrote the 1946 report for the breakdowns that occurred in the intelligence process before Pearl Harbor was attacked. Inadvertently the report itself drew attention to the magnitude of the failure by noting that "neither the basic code book nor the cipher was captured, hence the translations used are the result of cryptanalysis."[39]

This self-congratulatory statement and a bundle of yellowing U.S. Navy documents in a black tin trunk in the attic of a private home in Orange County, California, unlocked another long-concealed secret in the Pearl Harbor saga.

On the other side of the United States, thousands of miles from the orderly rows of official government records housed in the dimly lit stacks of the National Archives on Pennsylvania Avenue in Washington, D.C., the top-secret ultra reports bequeathed to his daughter by Joseph Rochefort revealed how he had made a unique contribution to the American victory over Japan that was not officially recognized by his country for over four decades. On 30 May 1986, fourteen years after the death of Commander Joseph J. Rochefort, at a unique White House ceremony held on the eve of the forty-fourth anniversary of the Battle of Midway, Rochefort's son and daughter received from President Ronald Reagan, on behalf of their father, the Distinguished Service Medal. The citation for his posthumous award recorded Rochefort's singular contribution to the breaking of the Japanese naval codes that had made it possible for the Pacific Fleet to achieve their Midway victory over Japan's Combined Fleet, which turned the tide in the Pacific War.

Official recognition for the singular service that Rochefort had rendered was the result of a long campaign waged by some of his brother officers from HYPO ever since his original recommendation for the medal, made by Admiral Nimitz, the commander in chief of the Pacific Fleet, had been turned down, not once but twice. The Navy Department had finally reversed itself "on the merits of the case" shortly before the publication in Admiral Layton's memoir, *And I Was There—Pearl Harbor and Midway, Breaking the Secrets*, after its findings had been the subject of a paper given at the 1985 Naval History Symposium at the U.S. Naval Academy. The book was to make public many of the documents Rochefort had preserved in his trunk that had never been released by the Navy to the National Archives. Drawing on his experience as the Pacific Fleet's intelligence officer before and after the attack on Pearl Harbor, Layton's account revealed the extent to which feuding senior officers in the Navy Department had covered up the bureaucratic failures that contributed to the Pearl Harbor disaster. Not only had they blamed Rochefort for supposedly allowing himself to be taken in by Japanese deception before war broke out, but they denied him credit for correctly piecing together details of Admiral Yamamoto's Midway operation six months later. This was done to conceal their embarrassment that their own analysts in Washington had misinterpreted the intelligence information gained from reading the Japanese Fleet Code messages preceding the action.[40]

"If we had listened to Washington, we would all have ended up prisoners of war of the Japanese," was how one of Rochefort's officers at Pearl Harbor summed up the awesome stakes in what was revealed to have been a fiercely fought secret battle over the Midway intelligence evaluations.[41] Fortunately for the United States, the estimates of Japan's intentions made by Rochefort were accepted by Nimitz in time for him to concentrate the numerically inferior Pacific Fleet carriers and ambush the Combined Fleet in the waters of Midway Island on 2 June.

A powerful clique of ambitious officers running the offices of naval communications and intelligence in Washington—who had so nearly blundered once again by wrongly assessing Japan's intentions—blocked Rochefort's decoration because his correct evaluation of the JN-25 information had proved them mistaken. They conspired to deny him the award for which the commander in chief of the Pacific Fleet had put in a strong personal recommendation and had then engineered Rochefort's recall from the front line of the intelligence war in the Pacific four months after the Battle of Midway had been won. Rochefort's unique talents were squandered for the next three years by his assignment to command a floating dock at the Tiburon naval base on the West Coast. According to Layton, his colleague was "speared like a frog and hung out to dry for the rest of the war" to save the careers and vanities of ambitious Washington staff officers whose intelligence estimates had proved wrong before Pearl Harbor and Midway.[42]

Rewriting this important page in the United States history of World War II had been made possible only because Rochefort had taken it upon himself to save for posterity copies of reports that might otherwise have been lost to historians. The original documents were suppressed by the Navy Department after the war in order to consolidate their "official" version of events and protect the reputations of senior officers. Defying security regulations, Rochefort made it his business, after he had returned to intelligence work in Washington in 1944, to search out and preserve copies of the signal logs and summaries from the 1941 and 1942 wartime intelligence files.

"DUE SPECIAL QUALIFICATIONS NECESSARY EMPLOY LTCOM JOSEPH J. ROCHEFORT IMPORTANT ASSIGN-

MENT FOURTEENTH NAVAL DISTRICT JUNE X REQUEST YOU NOMINATE RELIEF," reads one of the yellowing documents in Rochefort's black tin box.[43] It is a page from the incoming 15 March 1941 signal log of the *Indianapolis*, the heavy cruiser on which he was then serving and which was the flagship of the Pacific Fleet Scouting Force. The communication received from the Navy Department sheds new light on a sequence of miscalculations that nine months later was to deny the U.S. Navy access to the vital information about the attack contained in the Japanese Fleet Code.

Lieutenant Commander Rochefort must have received the news of his reassignment ashore with regret. His posting as intelligence officer aboard the *Indianapolis* had been the first seagoing duty he had drawn in over a decade. He was a lean, intense personality, whose superficial calm and unassuming courteous manner concealed a fierce tenacity that had been forged by his hard-won promotion to lieutenant after joining the U.S. Navy in World War I as an enlisted man. "Joe" Rochefort's postwar career as a signals intelligence specialist had taken him to Tokyo, where he had learned Japanese after demonstrating an aptitude for the language and for intelligence work that made him one of the pioneers in the arcane and secret specialty of code breaking. Since 1926, when he had worked under Mrs. Driscoll to effect the first penetration of the Japanese naval ciphers, Rochefort had been considered one of the best cryptanalysts in the U.S. Navy. These were the "special qualifications" noted in the 21 March order that had led to his recall ashore to head the crack team of code breakers at HYPO, the Pearl Harbor Combat Intelligence Unit.

"KNUTZ!!" is the facetious comment that Rochefort scribbled on the copy of the 15 March 1941 order. Just when he penned his jaundiced reaction to his transfer is not clear. But according to his daughter, the favored expletive used by her father was unlikely to have been made at the time when his posting ashore promised a promotion. It is more likely that it was added after he returned to Washington in 1944, to work the Naval Communications Annex at Nebraska Avenue, where he was able to ferret out the signals that disclosed it was originally intended that he would lead HYPO's assault on the Japanese Fleet Code. Other contemporary documentation shows that the decision to recall Rochefort was taken a week after the British had sent to Asiatic Fleet headquarters at Cavite all the JN-25 code recoveries made by their Far East Combined Bureau in Singapore. This was reported to Washington by Admiral Hart, the Asiatic Fleet commander, on 5 March 1941, who proposed that the local code-breaking team at CAST should concentrate on the Fleet Code.[44]

Initially the Navy Department had turned down the Asiatic Fleet commander's proposal in a negative response cabled to Hart the next day, which informed him that the cryptanalytic unit of the 16th Naval District at Cavite lacked the "necessary statistical machinery" and manpower. HYPO had just been equipped with the latest IBM tabulating machines to speed up the laborious process of bookbuilding. Hart was therefore advised to forward the British JN-25 material to HYPO since the "present plan [is] to transfer this attack to Pearl Harbor in July."[45]

If the Navy Department had adhered to its original plan, then Rochefort and his crack code-breaking team at HYPO would have had five months to work on the main Fleet Code system before the Japanese attack. Since it later took them only four months, after they were finally given permission to work on JN-25 on 17 December, to break the cipher to the extent necessary to uncover Japan's Midway operation, there would have been a good chance of their penetrating the main Fleet Code before the attack on Pearl Harbor.[46] Whether Rochefort could have succeeded in cracking JN-25B in time to have warned of the raid was never to be known because the Navy Department changed its plans for HYPO and decided to assign the task to the code breakers at CAST after all. On 24 April a signal was sent to Hart granting his original request because the "project will not be transferred to Fourteenth [Naval District] as previously planned."[47]

When Rochefort took over HYPO two months later, in June 1941, he found that his team had been ordered to concentrate all its efforts toward breaking the "NL" cryptographic system that had been introduced the previous December for communications with Imperial Navy flag officers. This was a four-character code with a complex transposition superencipherment that made it a much tougher system to crack than JN-25, not least because it was employed so infrequently in 1941 that only two hundred messages had been intercepted by 7 December. This proved to be an inadequate number to make any meaningful penetration of the so-called Flag Officers cipher.[48] As they had fewer than three intercepts a day on which to work, the recalcitrant cipher was to consume virtually the entire code-breaking effort of Rochefort's team of cryptanalysts for six months to no avail—a complete waste of effort that would have justified Rochefort's dismissive "KNUTZ!"

What is also clear from the records Rochefort uncovered is that the British JN-25 recoveries ultimately proved to be a poisonous gift. The extent to which the code breakers at the Far East Combined Bureau in Singapore had penetrated the Japanese Fleet Code cipher still remains a matter of speculation, but the partially compiled code book that they gave the Americans in March 1941 evidently persuaded the Navy Department that the code breakers at Station CAST in the Philippines would have a head start with breaking the system.[49] This resulted in the reversal of the decision to concentrate this effort at HYPO. Instead Rochefort's better equipped and staffed unit at Pearl Harbor was ordered to concentrate on the more complex Flag Officers code because in the past tapping the communications traffic between the Japanese admirals had proved the most valuable source of intercepted operational information.

If the Japanese Fleet General Purpose Code messages could have been read at the time they were received, they would at the very least have revealed the "missing" Japanese carriers by identifying them as part of the 1st Air Fleet's Strike Force. It is also very probable that its Hawaiian objective would also have been revealed by analysis of its training exercises, composition, and northward movement to the Kuriles before it sailed to attack Pearl Harbor on 26 November. The failure to assign either priority or the resources needed to build the JN-25B code book, which could have averted the disaster that overtook the Pacific Fleet, was the result of bureaucratic mismanagement in the Navy Department. Of the eighty officer cryptanalysts in the U.S. Navy, no fewer than fifty-three were assigned to the Navy Department, whereas only twenty-one were assigned to the Pacific theater. Of these, only the six in the Philippines had any capability to work on the Japanese Fleet Code. Twice that number were at Pearl Harbor under Rochefort, but they had no capability in either the Fleet Code or the Japanese diplomatic ciphers. They squandered their efforts on the impenetrable Japanese Flag Officers codes, while over twenty-five thousand intercepts in JN-25 and the other Japanese naval systems had poured into Washington from the intercept stations in Pearl Harbor, Guam, and Corregidor. These went unread, because the efforts to recover the JN-25B code book values were restricted to the four U.S. officer-linguists at Corregidor who worked in unofficial liaison with the British codebreakers at the FECB in Singapore. Not until after August 1941 did Op-20G commence assisting with the JN-25B code recovery, but progress in building an underlying code book to make the intercepts readable was hampered by lack of manpower. Instead of focusing on the Japanese naval traffic, which was clearly what the worsening strategic situation in the Pacific demanded, the limited cryptanalytic resources at the Washington center were overwhelmed to the point where little effort could be spared to work on JN-25B. Higher priorities had been given to monitoring the German U-boat radio traffic from the Atlantic and the Purple diplomatic traffic.[50]

The Purple decrypts became synonymous with MAGIC, which was so hedged about with secrecy that the restrictions imposed on access to the information eventually ended up eroding its value as intelligence, by preventing a proper analysis and dissemination of the translated messages. MAGIC was kept so secret that it encouraged the belief, among the restricted circle in Washington receiving the decrypts of Tokyo's most secret diplomatic communications, that it provided an inside track on Japan's policy making and military intentions. This created a false sense of security in Washington.

The Purple machine did not prove to be the magic wand that revealed either Japan's decision to go to war, as popularly believed, or any clue to the operational attack plans of their armed forces. What MAGIC did reveal was advance warning of Tokyo's negotiating ploys, not her military intentions. But U.S. service chiefs had so fallen under the spell of MAGIC that by the spring of 1941 they neglected other more vital sources of military and naval intelligence. Purple was allowed to absorb a disproportionate share of the cryptographic resources that might otherwise have been devoted to penetrating the operational systems of the Japanese armed forces. As a result the JN-25B Fleet Code remained unread until 1942 and the Japanese Army cipher systems did not begin to yield until a year later. This was to prove a particularly sore point for Rochefort, who discovered that his team was denied access to Purple because the decoding machine that was originally built for HYPO was shipped to Britain. He was also not given the code recoveries for lower-grade Japanese diplomatic ciphers that could have allowed him to monitor the espionage reports that the Honolulu consulate was making to Tokyo about the disposition of the warships in the Pacific Fleet anchorage.

Much was to be made at the congressional investigations of Washington's decision to deny HYPO access to the diplomatic traffic and to send its Purple decoding machine to the British. But the questions of JN-25 remained unexamined and the explosive findings of the *Pre–Pearl Harbor Japanese Naval Dispatches* report took half a century before they came to light to show that Washington had intercepted, but had *not* been able to recover, all the data needed to have uncovered the Japanese attack on Pearl Harbor. This report could have proved political dynamite for the U.S. Navy if it had surfaced during the congressional hearings. Why the contents of such a large number of intercepted Japanese naval messages had been left unread as the result of a bureaucratic blunder would not easily have been explained. It would have shifted to the Navy Department the question of ultimate blame for the intelligence failures that led to the Pacific Fleet being caught by surprise.

The conclusions reached in the long-concealed 1946 U.S. Navy report raise the question of what the British had made of the pre–Pearl Harbor Japanese naval intercepts at the time. There has been growing speculation in recent years that Churchill learned from British code breaking in late November 1941 what the Americans did not discover until five years later: a Japanese striking force was heading out across the Pacific to attack Pearl Harbor. How much the British knew from their own interception of Japanese diplomatic and naval traffic remained a closely guarded official secret. Shortly before the fifty-second anniversary of Japan's attack in November 1993, the British government began releasing the files that contain the final secrets of Pearl Harbor.

14

THE FINAL SECRETS OF
PEARL HARBOR

**What Did Churchill Really Know About
Japanese Plans from British Code Breaking?**

"THIS BOX IS ONLY TO BE OPENED BY THE PRIME MIN-
ISTER IN PERSON" was the notice on the locked yellow
boxes containing the "most-secret" output of Britain's wartime
code breakers.[1] After reading these intercepts of enemy communications and the diplomatic cables of friendly, as well as
hostile, foreign powers, they were returned in the same sealed
box by special courier to Broadway Buildings, the headquarters of the Secret Intelligence Service. Churchill acknowledged
the army of unarmed warriors who helped win the battles
without firing a single shot as the "geese who laid the golden
eggs but never cackled."[2] Just how avidly he consumed the
"golden eggs" has now been revealed, after more than fifty
years, by the release of the reports that constituted his daily
wartime diet of intelligence. By the fall of 1941 the menu in
the prime minister's locked box might include a dozen or more
German military dispatches from the North African and Eastern fronts, half a dozen U-boat signals, and the translations of
a dozen or more diplomatic messages, including those of Japan, in addition to half a dozen other nations—including the
United States.

Churchill's unique direct access to Britain's most secret

302

intelligence had been established four months after he came to office, in a letter of 27 September 1940 to the director of the Foreign Office's Secret Intelligence Service (SIS), popularly known as M16. This instructed "C," as the director was customarily addressed, that henceforth the prime minister "wishes you to send him all the ENIGMA messages."[3] Brigadier Stewart Menzies, whose anonymity was established by the alphabetic label, was responsible not only for directing Britain's global espionage operations but also for the Government Code and Cipher School, the Foreign Office's secret code-breaking establishment, referred to as GC&CS as for short.[4]

Established after World War I as part of MI6 with the overt responsibility for maintaining a secure British cipher system, but with the covert mission to break the diplomatic codes of foreign powers, GC&CS had expanded rapidly after the demands of the war in an operation that centralized the cryptanalysis on military as well as diplomatic cipher systems. The key that unlocked the secrets of the Enigma enciphering machines used by the German armed services to encrypt their radioed command traffic had been inherited in 1940 from the Polish and French intelligence services. The complex mathematical process of unraveling Enigma resulted in a rapid expansion in the forces under Foreign Office command who fought the signals intelligence war. The compliment of code breakers, analysts, and translators at GC&CS had risen in two years from one hundred in 1939 to over eighteen hundred by the beginning of 1941, as the best academic brains in Britain were enlisted into this shadow army.

This formidable concentration of brainpower was put to work in a heavily guarded complex of wooden huts that had been hastily erected in the wooded grounds of a requisitioned red-brick Victorian millionaire's mansion known as Bletchley Park. It was fortuitously located midway between the ancient ivy-covered colleges of Oxford and Cambridge universities, from which the majority of these scholars-turned-code breakers were recruited. War Station X, as the establishment was referred to in official communications, was also known as "Room 47 Foreign Office," or Government Communications Headquarters. But it was as Bletchley Park that it became synonymous with one of the most extraordinarily successful code-breaking efforts in military history.

Churchill had served as first lord of the Admiralty at the beginning of the first war with Germany. Since 1916, when the Royal Navy code breaks of the radio transmissions of the

Kaiser's High Seas Fleet had sent Britain's Grand Fleet steaming into the Battle of Jutland, he had been keenly attuned to signals intelligence as a weapon in modern warfare. The disposition of the fleets and armies on the oceans and battlefields depended on enciphered radio orders, which could be intercepted and broken. When he moved from the Admiralty into Downing Street, Churchill had instructed Major Desmond Morton, his comrade-in-arms from the Western Front and trusted adviser, to organize a system to ensure that he could continue to have access to the intelligence being produced by the code breakers at Bletchley Park.[5] It was Morton who set up the locked-box delivery system a month after Churchill had personally directed "C" that "I do not wish such reports as received to be sifted and digested by the various intelligence authorities." Morton, he insisted, was "to be shown everything," from which the major would then select "what he considers of major importance" and then "submit authentic documents to me in their original form."[6] The locked boxes containing the "golden eggs" from GC&CS were delivered by special courier to Downing Street several times each day, depending on the amount of intercepted traffic. The cover name BONIFACE had originally been employed to conceal the source of this SIGINT, under the pretext that the intelligence in the intercepted communications originated from a spy in the Axis high command. Later ULTRA became the generic designation for intelligence derived from intercepted signal traffic, or SIGINT, after it was found that senior military officers cleared to receive the BONIFACE reports discounted its "absolutely reliable" attribution because of the disbelief that any individual spy had such wide-ranging access to enemy operational orders.

Churchill shared with Stalin, in contrast to Roosevelt, an obsession for raw intelligence data. Both enjoyed acting as the final arbiters of intelligence and did not hesitate to second-guess their military chiefs rather than relying on the predigested summaries circulated by their respective intelligence services. The declassified records reveal how the prime minister interfered directly in the conduct of military operations. A typical instance arose on 24 August 1941 when Churchill read an Italian naval decrypt disclosing a supply convoy that was heading to North Africa. He passed it on to the Admiralty with instructions that the commander in chief Mediterranean should be directed to send surface warships to intercept the Italian freighters. "Please ask specifically what if anything he is going to do," Churchill minuted the first sea lord, testily reminding him, "We are still at war." Long-suffering Admiral Pound responded to the handwritten injunction on the decrypt by reminding the prime minister of the "danger of compromising our source of information, which can easily be done if we send a surface ship to intercept a ship in an area which our forces do not normally operate. It is unnecessary to stress what the loss of this information would mean to us."[7]

Preserving the security of the ULTRA code breaking was the paramount preoccupation of the British chief of staff. Only six weeks earlier, on 24 June 1941, "C" had been obliged to warn the prime minister against "divulging to the President the informations regarding U.S. Naval Units being chased by U. Boats."[8] The German navy's Enigma system was finally beginning to yield intelligence after a year of effort, and Menzies advised Churchill that it would not be possible to "devise any safe means of wrapping up the information in a manner which would not imperil this source, which should, without fail play a vital part in the Battle of the Atlantic."[9] The Americans "were not as security minded as one would wish," he told the prime minister, reminding him of the chiefs of staff's decision that "information from this Most Secret source should only be communicated to the US naval and military authorities *when we were satisfied that the source was not endangered* [emphasis added]."[10]

"It is true that the American experts who visited the United Kingdom gave us a very valuable insight into Japanese cryptographic methods," Menzies conceded, adding, "but they themselves, impressed upon me how cautious they were in passing the results to the State Department."[11] This was a gross understatement. In January 1941 Bletchley Park had received two of the American Purple decoding machines, the pair originally constructed for the HYPO Combat Intelligence Unit at Pearl Harbor. This gift had provided the GC&CS code breakers with far more than just "very valuable insight" into Japan's cipher systems. Without these two hand-built decoding machines Churchill could not have had the direct access to Tokyo's diplomatic communications that he would later so vigorously deny! His denials were no less a fiction than the postwar claim that the U.S. Navy had bitterly condemned General Marshall for authorizing a one-sided exchange even though the British allegedly reneged on their promise to supply the United States with a German Enigma in return for the Purple machines.

An exchange in kind was not the basis of the original deal,

according to Prescott Currier, the senior Navy member of the American team. He escorted the crates containing the two Purple machines to Bletchley Park in January 1941, where he and his three countrymen worked for two months instructing the British in their operation. "Although we were not given an Enigma machine to take back to Washington (which I don't believe any of the four of us expected), we were thoroughly briefed in the latest techniques applied to its solution and in the operations of the 'bombes.'"[12] These were the primitive computers developed by the Cambridge mathematician Alan Turing to sift through thousands of combinations to establish the solution to the daily Enigma cipher key settings. Their secrets were fully explained to the American cryptanalysts. Since their only experience was of Japanese code breaking, they spent much of their time at Bletchley Park "becoming familiar with German and Italian materials," according to Currier, who noted they were given "ample opportunity to take as many notes as we wanted and watch first-hand all the operations involved."[13] While they may not have carried back with them an actual Enigma machine, when they left Bletchley Park on 18 March 1941 for the transatlantic crossing aboard the battleship *Revenge*, they did bring a comprehensive understanding of the inner workings of the German system and how to break the cipher. Lieutenant Robert H. Weeks, who had also been part of the American cryptanalytic team, said that they took back to Washington a "paper analogue" of the Enigma that gave the U.S. Navy a head start on setting up OP-20-G's own Atlantic U-boat tracking operation.[14]

The British, however, had received from the Americans the ability to begin to penetrate the Japanese diplomatic system immediately. By the end of February 1941, the two Purple machines at Bletchley Park were spewing out decrypts of Tokyo's most secret communications to its consulates and embassies worldwide. This is not apparent from the declassified British records, which contain no Japanese intercepts earlier than August 1941, although several dating from May turned up in a War Office intelligence file.[15] What is evident from an early Bletchley Park Purple intercept is that hitherto undocumented exchanges about the contents of the Japanese traffic were taking place between London and Washington four months before the attack on Pearl Harbor.

"In view of the fact that the Americans themselves gave us the key to the Japanese messages it seems probable the President knows this already," was the note Churchill appended to

a 23 August 1941 translation of the cable that Japan's ambassador in Berlin dispatched on 15 August to Tokyo.[16] Since it reported that "Hitler had declared that in the event of a collision
between Japan and the United States, Germany would at once
open hostilities with America," the prime minister instructed
"C" that it was "desirable" that the president be made aware
of this. "Propose me action please," he noted on the copy, which
was returned by Menzies the next day with the comment, "The
Americans have had this message."[17]

Since "C" could have established that the president had
seen this particular intercept only by direct contact with the
U.S. Army or Navy, who were responsible for circulating
MAGIC, he must have resorted to a secure telegraphic and
cipher channel to relay a question on such sensitive ULTRA to
Washington. From similar instructions Churchill appended to
Japanese cables in March 1942 and two other Purple decrypts
which arrived at Downing Street with an attached note indicating that "President Roosevelt has requested that you should
see attached B.J. report," there clearly was an established direct channel between MI6 headquarters and the headquarters
of the U.S. armed services that had been functioning before
the United States entered the war.[18] In view of the secrecy with
which both ULTRA and MAGIC were guarded, "C" could only
have communicated with Washington via the secure channel
MI6 maintained with its Rockefeller headquarters in New York
using the British Typex cipher machine.[19]

Churchill did not discuss ULTRA information directly with
Roosevelt during their transatlantic telephone conversations
or refer to it in the cables he sent to the White House via the
U.S. embassy in London. His declassified SIGINT file reveals
the reason: he was well aware of just how insecure the State
Department codes were because he was receiving decrypts of
high-level U.S. diplomatic traffic from Bletchley Park. How
much intercepted American cipher traffic was being read by
Bletchley Park before Pearl Harbor cannot be established with
any precision, but most of it has been retained by the Foreign
Office. Although no cables from the U.S. embassy in London
have surfaced among the "golden eggs" Churchill received in
1941, three American diplomatic intercepts slipped past the
Foreign Office weeders. An intercept of an 8 September report
from the American ambassador to Turkey and two 18 November telegrams to Secretary of State Hull from the American
legation in Dublin appear among the prime minister's SIGINT.
This suggests that these three cables are not the sole examples

of Bletchley Park's ability to eavesdrop on U.S. diplomatic communications.[20] (The files belatedly released in 1992 on the subject of the 22 May flight to Scotland of Hitler's deputy, Rudolf Hess, also include a BJ decrypt of a report on the affair made to Washington from the U.S. legation in Berne, Switzerland.[21]) By the end of December 1941 the BJ serial numbers, which the Foreign Office assigned sequentially, regardless of the country of origin, for the diplomatic intercepts circulated to the prime minister had reached ten thousand.

It is therefore likely that among the documents represented by the gaps in the numerical sequence in the released copies there are many more State Department cables, which are still being withheld in the vast secret archives of the Government Communications Headquarters (the Foreign Office's successor code-breaking organization to GC&CS), which inherited all the wartime Bletchley Park records. Without access to the originals, it is impossible to ascertain what percentage of the missing BJ numbers represent U.S., Spanish, Italian, Turkish, Vichy, or Japanese diplomatic intercepts.[22] Churchill made an unpublicized and secret visit to Bletchley Park in October 1941 to spur the code breakers on to even greater efforts, and this would have included their work on the U.S. cipher systems, which had been carefully concealed from the American team of cryptanalysts when they worked at Bletchley Park.

Churchill appears to have found it so useful to be able to monitor high-level U.S. communications that he waited almost three months after the attack on Pearl Harbor had made the United States an official ally before he alerted Roosevelt that "our experts claimed to have discovered the system and constructed some tables used by your Diplomatic Corps" in his letter of 25 February 1942.[23] "From the moment we became Allies, I gave instructions that this work should cease," the prime minister assured the president, elliptically warning him that "the danger of our enemies having achieved success cannot, I am advised, be dismissed."[24] Reports three months later from "C" about a German penetration of the American cipher system give reason to believe that GC&CS code breakers continued to monitor United States traffic despite the prime minister's assurance.[25]

Japanese decrypts that are missing from Churchill's ULTRA reports are in the American MAGIC records. That is important, because the earliest Japanese decrypt to appear in the prime minister's SIGINT file is a 28 August report of the Japanese chargé d'affaires in London giving a summary of the press coverage of the Churchill-Roosevelt Atlantic summit meeting. That so many of the earlier Tokyo intercepts are "missing" is curious given the prime minister's appetite for the Black Jumbos, which Bletchley Park's Purple machine began spewing out in April 1941. Before leaving for his summit meeting with the president five months later, Churchill issued specific instructions that his aide Major Morton and *not* the Foreign Office was to select the diplomatic decrypts to be sent to him while aboard the *Prince of Wales*.[26] There was also a standing arrangement with Bletchley Park that when a particularly significant message was decrypted, the prime minister was couriered a copy hot off the teleprinter, rather than waiting until the following day for "C" to circulate a typed-up copy headed by a one-line summary of its contents.

No fewer than eighty-seven of these advance intercepts are missing. The first one to appear in the declassified series is a 4 December teleprinter sheet marked "Advance Diplomatic BJ 88" that alerted Churchill that Tokyo had ordered its embassies to begin destroying their cipher machines and burn their secret codes.[27] None of the preceding intercepts, which were considered so important that they were sent to Downing Street as soon as they were translated, have been released. Among the most significant of these unreleased Purple intercepts are the "East Wind Rain" setup of 19 November and Tokyo's fourteen-part message to Washington of 6 December, together with the one P.M. deadline instruction sent the following day.

The mere absence of a document, however, does not establish that one once existed and was later weeded out. In this case, there can be no doubt about the contents of these missing Japanese diplomatic messages because they are in the American MAGICs in the National Archives. Some of the Bletchley Park decrypts were supplied to Colonel Clausen in 1945 and are in the record of the congressional investigation into Pearl Harbor.[28] Not only does a comparison of the extant British and American versions reveal differences in translation that indicate that any exchange between London and Washington on their contents was the exception rather than the rule, but in some instances the date on which the intercept was broken out of the Japanese cipher is markedly different. A particularly important example is an "East Wind Rain" setup message that is not in Churchill's SIGINT file but is part of the Clausen investigation exhibit. Yet another copy of it exists in the Australian National Archives.[29] The notation on the Bletchley Park version indicates that it was circulated on 25 November 1941 as BJ 098127. This, as can be confirmed from the American version, was *three full days* before the U.S. Navy translation set the alarm bells ringing in Washington on 28 November.[30]

In the light of the flap that the "Winds" setup message caused three days later in Washington, with American radio operators alerted to listen for the Tokyo weather forecast of "East Wind Rain," the fact that Churchill read it on 25 November suggests that it could have played a crucial part in his last-minute intervention over the American modus vivendi proposal. The prime minister, as we have seen in Chapter 6, distanced himself with vigorous denials and outright dissimulation from any suggestion that he could have influenced Roosevelt's decision the next day to drop the attempt to reach a temporary accommodation with Japan. The coincidence of timing and consequence suggests that the "Winds" intercept was part of the "specific evidence of the Japanese intention to wage offensive war against Great Britain" that the U.S. Army Pearl Harbor board concluded reached Roosevelt on the morning of 26 November 1941.[31] The clue pointing to Churchill as the source of that war warning is the secret message for the prime minister from the president carried that morning by his eldest son, Colonel James D. Roosevelt, to the New York headquarters of Britain's Secret Intelligence Service.

"NEGOTIATIONS OFF. SERVICES EXPECT ACTION WITHIN TWO WEEKS,"[32] was the message relayed to London by Sir William Stephenson, the self-styled "quiet Canadian" millionaire who was the wartime head of the MI6 network in the United States. His telegraphic address, "Intrepid, New York," was later to be appropriated by Stephenson as his code name, although it was actually that of the head of the MI6 front organization known as "British Security Coordination," which was headquartered in Suite 303 at 630 Rockefeller Plaza.[33] Roosevelt's cryptic message appears to have been the response to one from Churchill received via the secure Typex cipher to "C" from London the night before. This was the same channel he had used in August to question whether the president had seen the 25 August Purple decrypt, so it was logical that Roosevelt would have used the same channel to send back a response to an intelligence-derived war warning from Churchill. He could hardly have risked sending through the State Department such a blunt declaration as "NEGOTIATIONS OFF," which, had it leaked out, would have been misconstrued by his isolationist opponents as a casting down of the military gauntlet to Tokyo.[34]

A further indication that the prime minister first sent word of Japanese treachery to the White House via secret-service channels and then dispatched to the president his "thin diet" cable via the U.S. embassy as cover is that the accompanying note from the Downing Street secretary apologized for "the lateness of the hour" of its delivery to the U.S. embassy. Yet there was nothing in Churchill's message that justified the urgency of sending it over to Grosvenor Square at three A.M. in the morning.[35] Washington was five hours behind London time, and Churchill's cable could have been dispatched to the U.S. embassy at nine that morning and *still* have reached the White House before the president arose. That a more urgent message of a very different character was sent from London to Roosevelt that night is indicated by Lord Halifax's diary entry. It notes that on Tuesday 25 November "in the evening" he received word from the prime minister via the Foreign Office instructing him to request Secretary Hull "to stay his hand *until Winston had sent a message* to the President [emphasis added]."[36] Moreover, his "thin diet" cable, as Churchill himself insisted, was not strongly worded because he *never* intended it to be taken as a veto on the American modus vivendi proposals. The secretary of state himself characterized it as a "lukewarm" response to terms to be offered Japan, which were communicated to the British ambassador the previous day. So this cable is therefore inconsistent with the call on the ambassador to intervene with Hull that evening, unless Churchill was preparing to send Roosevelt a more substantive reason for staying the secretary of state's hand.[37]

The British translation of the "Winds" alert setup, if it was sent to the president that night, in itself could have constituted the evidence of Japan's intention "to wage an offensive war on Britain and the United States."[38] Although it is captioned innocuously—"Japanese Code Phrases for Broadcasting in the Event of an Emergency"—its wording, and possibly Churchill's paraphrasing of it for Roosevelt, confirms that Tokyo was preparing for war. Many Americans who saw it three days later thought that an "East Wind Rain" broadcast would be the final warning of war. Yet its absence from the declassified Churchill SIGINT raises a suspicion that it amounted to a war warning either on its own, or possibly when read in the context of some other piece of intelligence sent to Downing Street that Tuesday. Only three of the six boxes of ULTRA intelligence that the prime minister received on Tuesday, 25 November, have been released. The others are being withheld by the Foreign Office.[39]

One clue to the contents of that "missing" intelligence emerged during the Clausen investigation in 1945. He uncovered in the Bletchley Park archive a copy of the cable that "C" had sent that same Tuesday to Major Gerald Wilkinson in Manila,[40] alerting the MI6 station chief:

> Secret source (usually reliable) reports that
> A. Japanese will attack Kra Isthmus from Sea on Dec. 1, repeat Dec. 1, without any ultimatum or declaration of break, with a view to getting back between Bangkok and Singapore.
> B. Attacking forces will proceed directly from Hainan and Formosa. Main landing point likely to be in Songkhala area. Valuation for the above is No. 3, repeat # (i.e., only about 55 to 60 per cent probable accuracy).
> American Military and Naval Intelligence informed.[41]

This warning, which the congressional investigators concluded had also been sent to Washington by 26 November, was evidently based on information received by "C" from one of the MI6 undercover agents working for British intelligence in the Far East. Wilkinson could not recall the source when he was interviewed by Colonel Clausen in New York in 1945, where as a lieutenant colonel in MI6 he was attached to Stephenson's BSC headquarters in Rockefeller Plaza. For all the scornful comments that Wilkinson in Manila had run "a horse trading operation, pure and simple" in the affidavit taken from General Willoughby, MacArthur's intelligence chief, Clausen, testified that he believed "Wilkinson could be relied on."[42] Moreover, despite the less-than-perfect reliability accorded to the 25 November MI6 report, the probability of Japan's launching an attack without warning on the Kra Isthmus, as a prelude to an invasion of Malaya, was discussed three days later by the British war cabinet's Joint Intelligence Committee.[43]

When the minutes of the wartime JIC meetings were finally declassified by the Foreign Office in 1993, excisions were made to protect Secret Intelligence Service operations and agents. The historic records of MI6 and its agents' reports are still protected by Britain's draconian Official Secrets Act, which makes it impossible to establish the precise source and nature of the MI6 alert of 25 November. But in addition to SIGINT, Churchill also had direct access to the intelligence that "C" received from the MI6 global network of stations through the daily communications identified as "Agents' Reports."[44] None of the MI6 reports that constituted this file have been released, except inadvertently, as in the case of the Clausen investigation, which was made part of the public record by the U.S. Congress. In this context, it should also be noted that a whole section of the prime minister's secret office file relating to Japan is marked "closed for 75 years."[45] Since the documents preceding the withheld section deal with Japanese naval intelligence in the fall of 1941, the presumption is that the "missing" reports also contain intelligence that could have been a warning of Tokyo's impending aggression. But repeated requests for the release of this particular file by this author and other historians are still being met with denials that "it would not be in the national interest at this time."[46]

What information can be so sensitive after fifty years that it is not in the "national interest" for the British government to release documents about the Japanese navy in 1941 that might resolve an important gap in the historical record? Whatever the nature of the information in the still-secret MI6 records and in the "missing" section of Churchill's intelligence file, it is clear that at the time the stakes riding on its interpretation were high for both the prime minister and the president. It's also clear that Churchill would not have intervened with Roosevelt over the modus vivendi unless he had received some very specific and absolutely irrefutable intelligence that indicated Japan's determination to resort to hostilities. While the decryption of the "Winds" message, together with the MI6 report that the Japanese invasion convoys assembling at Hainan Island and Formosa would land troops on the shores of the Kra Peninsula by 1 December, might have been specific enough to prompt Churchill to issue a warning to the president, would it have provided the irrefutable evidence needed by Roosevelt to turn his back on the pleas of his Army and Navy chiefs of staff for three more months to complete the reinforcement of the Philippines? Possibly, if the source had been identified as a direct leak of part of the Japanese war plan via an agent of the British or Dutch secret services, who worked closely together in the Far East.

With seven hundred copies of Yamamoto's *Operational Order No.: 1* in circulation by 25 November and many more copies of the Army orders for their invasion operations distributed, the chances of a leak as the source of the war warning cannot be ruled out. But in more than half a century, no spy has surfaced to claim credit for this coup and no indication emerges that Britain obtained a more detailed forewarning of Japan's attack plan than the Americans. Nor has there been any public acknowledgment by Russian sources that one of their many agents in China and Japan obtained access to all or part of the Japanese war plan. The Soviet intelligence services had, however, established a very productive espionage network in Tokyo. Richard Sorge, a Russian-born German journalist who had won the confidence of Eugen Ott, Hitler's ambassador in Tokyo, had also cultivated extensive diplomatic contacts and recruited thirty-five Japanese subagents. They included Hotsumi Ozaki, an ardent Marxist with family connections to high-level officials in the Japanese government.[47] From his sources Sorge had been able to provide the GRU (Soviet military intelligence) with confirmation that Japan would move south and not attack Siberia, shortly before he was arrested on 18 October 1941, along with many members of his network. Japan's security police, the Kempentai, succeeded in rolling up the Sorge ring before the promulgation of the detailed Army and Navy war plans. But although this removed Stalin's masterspy in Tokyo, it did not put an end to Soviet espionage operations in Japan since other members of his network—including Prince Saionji, a cousin of the emperor—remained above suspicion and presumably operational.[48]

Colonel Boris Goodze, a retired Soviet military intelligence officer who at the time had been involved in running the Tokyo GRU networks from Moscow, later recalled how difficult it had been to convince Stalin to accept Sorge's reports until the Soviet leader was shown the confirmation in intercepted Japanese diplomatic cables.[49] Confirmation that the Soviets did have access to these was provided by Arkady Baidakov, a KGB officer who in 1989 authored an article in *Pravda* that quoted in full four Berlin-Tokyo Japanese cablegrams. They included the 27 November 1941 instruction to Baron Hiroshi Oshima, Japan's ambassador in Berlin to "Explain to Hitler that the main Japanese efforts will be concentrated in the south and that we propose to refrain from deliberate operations in the north (i.e., Siberia)."[50] Whether this cable had been intercepted and decrypted or was obtained by a Soviet penetration of Tokyo's embassy in Moscow, to which it had been copied, is not explained. Yuri Rasturov, a KGB Far East specialist since the thirties who defected to the CIA in Tokyo in

1954, maintained that the so-called Research Section of NKGB's Fifth Directorate, which had been established in February 1941 with responsibility for ciphers and cryptanalysis, had achieved considerable successes monitoring Japanese traffic.[51]

Stalin's insight into Tokyo's military intentions, whether from intelligence obtained from decrypted Japanese cipher communication or from that produced by spying, was remarkably well informed, according to General Wladislaw Sikorski, the exiled Polish leader, who visited the Kremlin on 4 December. Sikorski's diary records that the Soviet leader had precisely predicted the date of Japan's attack on Malaya. There is also an intriguing remark made by General Marshall, in his testimony before the congressional committee in 1945, that made an oblique allusion to intelligence that the British obtained from the Soviets.[52] This cryptic reference of the U.S. Army chief of staff could indicate why it was no coincidence that on 3 December "C" issued a very specific war warning whose final paragraph stated: "Our considered opinion concludes that Japan envisages early hostilities with Britain and the United States. *Japan does not repeat not intend to attack Russia at Present but will act in South* [emphasis added]."[53]

Whatever the warning's source, the MI6 station chief in Manila, Major Gerald H. Wilkinson, promptly forwarded this cable to Harry Dawson, the British vice-consul in Honolulu, who was the British secret service man in Hawaii. He in turn provided copies to the local FBI chief as well as to U.S. Navy and Army intelligence officers. Clausen, who established in the course of his investigation that the American recipients of this warning discounted its reliability, but that John E. Russell, the British president of the Theo H. Davies trading firm, took the warning at face value. Russell promptly canceled shipments to Manila and thereby saved his firm a considerable sum of money.[54] In August 1945 Clausen was able to obtain confirmation in a cable from London headquarters of Britain's Secret Intelligence Service that the information in the final paragraph of the 3 November warning had been *"based on BJ,"* i.e. intercepted diplomatic communications. The director of MI6 also cautioned the "security of ULTRA is at stake if this evidence made public."[55] Since none of the Japanese diplomatic Purple intercepts, even with the advantage of hindsight, can be pinpointed as the BJ that gave rise to "C"'s warning, the possibility exists that his reference could have been to an ULTRA decrypt of a Soviet cable.

Yet another possible source was the Dutch code breakers, who maintained a small but effective SIGINT facility attached to their military headquarters on Java. Under the direction of the cryptanalyst Colonel J. A. Verkuyl and his no less talented deputy, Captain J. W. Henning, Kamer 14, the Dutch code-breaking unit at Bandoeng, had penetrated the so-called Red diplomatic machine code and the Japanese consular code systems. General Hein ter Poorten, the commander in chief of the Netherlands East Indies forces, cooperated fully with the British, and the intercepts of Purple his unit made were forwarded to their ally for decrypting.[56] Kamer 14 was also working on the Japanese naval systems, but there is no evidence that they broke into the main fleet cipher. General ter Poorten did go so far as to claim, in 1965, that *his* cryptanalysts had indeed circulated intelligence reports that "showed Japanese naval concentrations near the Kuriles."[57] None of the Kamer 14 records survived the destruction in March 1942 before the Dutch surrender on Java. But twenty years later Captain Henning did note in a memorandum for the Netherlands Military Archives that "from analysis of Japanese radio traffic, it was possible to conclude from the last week of November 1941, that there were large fleet concentrations near the Kuriles." The former head of Kamer 14 was careful to note that only "later it appeared" that it was the islands off the northern coast of Hokkaido from whence the Striking Force had steamed forth to raid Pearl Harbor.[58]

"That war was imminent was clear to us," Captain Henning recorded in his memorandum, "but I am sure there has never been talked [*sic*] directly about an attack on Pearl Harbor."[59] This would explain why, according to General ter Poorten's account, his staff assumed that the Japanese warship concentration in the Kuriles was poised for an attack on Vladivostok in a repeat of their 1904 surprise assault on Port Arthur. What Henning's 1960 report for the Military Archives of the Netherlands does indicate is that his assessment was the result of traffic analysis and radio direction finding, *not* the breaking of the Japanese fleet cipher. Henning makes no reference to Kamer 14 having decoded any JN-25 naval traffic or picked up any sailing instructions to the Striking Force, as some have claimed happened.[60] Moreover, the Dutch intelligence reports of the Combined Fleet concentrations in the Kuriles, in addition to the buildup Kamer 14 also detected in the area of the Pescadores and Hainan Island in the South China Sea, were immediately passed to the British at Singapore. Such intelligence assessments could have provided the confirmation of imminent Japanese naval operations.[61]

Churchill would have regarded the intelligence reports from the Far East as clear evidence that Tokyo was using negotiations with the United States as cover for its preparations for an attack on Malaya.

There is still another possible source of intelligence for this warning. The two major gaps in the serial numbers on "C"'s covering letters that he sent to the prime minister on 25 November indicate that these batches of SIGINT are still considered too secret by the British government to release. Such concerns would not apply to the "missing" intercept of the "Winds" message, but to some Japanese naval SIGINT that could have given the prime minister irrefutable evidence that Tokyo really was hell-bent on hostilities. Conspicuous by its complete absence from Churchill's most secret intelligence file is any report on Japanese naval movements. This is a most surprising omission since the declassified files contain regular summary reports that he was receiving on German, Italian, and even Spanish naval intercepts. It is difficult to believe that the former first lord of the Admiralty, who was accustomed to taking a direct hand in naval operations in two wars, would not have insisted on being kept abreast of the latest intelligence on the disposition of Japan's Combined Fleet when the *Prince of Wales* task force—which he believed could "catch and kill anything"—was heading for Singapore. What was there in the intelligence the prime minister received about Japanese naval movements in the final months of 1941 that still not a single item can be released? The absence of *any* report gives reasonable grounds for suspecting that all traces of the Japanese naval intelligence summaries have been withheld because their release would reveal the extent to which the British code breakers had succeeded—where the U.S. Navy had failed—in penetrating the Japanese navy ciphers. But there is such an intercept that, even if only partially decrypted, could have provided Churchill with the warning that war was imminent with Japan.

"AT 0000 ON 21 NOVEMBER CARRY OUT SECOND PHASE OF PREPARATIONS FOR OPENING HOSTILITIES," was the order flashed out to all ships from the Imperial Navy's powerful transmitter at Owada outside Tokyo.[62] Could the decryption of all or part of this message, which put the Combined

Fleet on a war footing, have been the "dog that did not bark" in this case? The U.S. Navy records confirm both the interception and text of this signal, which the Royal Navy could not have missed picking up at their Hong Kong listening post on Stonecutters Island. Even if the decrypt of this preliminary war order had been so fragmentary that only the two final words could be broken out in the five days after its transmission, this still would have provided an absolutely reliable indication on 25 November for Churchill to pass to Roosevelt that Japan was actually about to embark on hostile operations.

The Japanese Striking Force also put to sea the next day, so if a sailing signal had been intercepted and broken out of the JN-25 cipher that day, it, too, would provide a vital piece of intelligence. Despite the claims that such a dispatch was sent, it was not picked up by the U.S. Navy.[63] Even without any interception of a sailing order, the ominous import of the "OPENING HOSTILITIES" decrypt would have been obvious.

The question of whether the main Japanese Fleet Code cipher in which this message was transmitted could have been broken by the British before December 1941 is, therefore, an important historical issue. The 1946 analysis *Pre–Pearl Harbor Japanese Naval Dispatches* provided conclusive proof that the U.S. Navy had not made sufficient progress in recovering the meanings of the 33,333 five-digit groups to achieve a "meaningful penetration" of the JN-25B cipher system.[64] What the British code breakers were making of the Japanese naval traffic can only be surmised through the mist of conflicting personal recollection, a tantalizingly few official references, and a complete lack of documentary record. Not a single signal in the Japanese Fleet Code that was intercepted either before or after 7 December has been declassified in Britain.

What can be established is that the British assault on the Japanese naval cipher systems was conducted by the cryptanalysts of the so-called Far East Combined Bureau in the Singapore naval base, whose principal radio listening outpost until 7 December 1941 was at the FECB's original base on Stonecutters Island in Hong Kong Harbor. According to a former senior historian of the National Security Agency who had access to classified British history, work on the JN-25 system had been transferred in December 1939 from Bletchley Park to the mainly naval cryptanalytic team at the outstation at the Singapore naval base at Changhi. One of the few acknowledgments of FECB code-breaking achievement appears in the first volume of the officially sanctioned history *British Intelligence in the Second World War.* This states that in September 1939 "beginning with the fleet cypher, the new cyphers began to yield."[65] This reference together with a footnote in the second volume that records that the FECB was able "to keep track of her main naval movements" could indicate that the British penetration of the Combined Fleet's main cypher was continuous and unbroken throughout 1941.[66]

This was the impression given by the late Captain Eric Nave, the veteran cryptanalyst of the Australian Navy who had made a major contribution to FECB's successful breakthrough into the "A" version of JN-25 Fleet Code in 1939.[67] But in neither the original manuscript of his memoir nor *Betrayal at Pearl Harbor,* which Nave coauthored with James Rusbridger, does he discuss the problems that the FECB cryptanalysts must have encountered recovering and compiling the "B" version of the JN-25 cipher. This new version was introduced nine months after Nave left Singapore, in February 1940, to join the Royal Australian Navy's newly established code breaking unit at Melbourne. The American records suggest that the more complex "B" variant which came into use in December 1940 required completely rebuilding the code book. Difficulties were encountered, according to another FECB veteran, Commander Raymond Mortimer, a former Yangtse river pilot and lieutenant commander in the Royal Navy Reserve who served as an analyst with the FECB throughout the war.[68]

"Lots of the intercepts were so vague that they never reached me," Mortimer recounted of his work in the fall of 1941 as an analyst in the Operational Intelligence Center, which was known as the "Loony Bin" by its staff, who had put up the notice "YOU DON'T HAVE TO BE MAD TO WORK HERE, BUT IT HELPS." Mortimer depended on the traffic analysis and code breaks produced by the eight-strong team of Japanese cryptanalysts under Paymaster Captain Arthur P. Shaw, who had honed his code-breaking skills, like the other naval officers, on assignment to the secret GC&CS code-breaking establishment.[69] Mortimer's task was to keep track of Japanese shipping and general naval movement by analyzing the SIGINT in the context of the intelligence relayed from MI6 agents operating in the Far East. ZYMOTIC, as the Japanese naval intercepts were referred to at FECB, could not provide Mortimer with the whole picture in the fall months of 1941 because "lots of stuff coming in before Pearl was difficult to interpret." He did maintain, however, that it provided him with sufficient information to keep an accurate track of all

Japanese shipping movements. The steady disappearance of all Japan's merchant vessels as they were recalled to their home ports, which was plotted by Mortimer, was a clear indication that war was about to break out.

In interviews and correspondence extending over many years, Mortimer always insisted that FECB *did* continue penetration of the Japanese fleet cipher in the period preceding 7 December.[70] This was also the recollection of Mrs. Mary Burnett, the widow of one of the Royal Navy's leading Japanese cryptanalysts, who had flown with her husband to Singapore in December 1939. Commander Malcolm Burnett carried with him all the recoveries Bletchley Park had made into the "A" version JN-25 and with which Nave had produced the solution to this first version of the fleet cipher. Their work enabled FECB to read Japanese fleet traffic on a current basis until the following December when the JN-25 codebook was replaced.

"Bouncer" Burnett, as he was known to Mortimer, then applied his skills to penetrating the "B" version of JN-25, which the Japanese navy introduced at the end of the following year. Mary Burnett was recruited, along with the wives of the other "Loony Bin" naval officers as TWAs (Temporary Women Assistants) to assist with running the Hollerith punch-card machines used by the cryptanalytic section to speed up the laborious and time-consuming task of rebuilding the dictionary code book and recovering the random additive table books, the seventh of which came into use on 1 August.[71] Although Burnett never made any public statement about his work on the Japanese Fleet Code, his wife knew about his progress because she worked alongside him. She also knew that shortly before his death from a fatal stroke in 1984, her husband had unburdened himself of his secret knowledge to Dr. Andrew Gordon, a government historian who was a close family friend in Scotland. According to Gordon, Burnett told him that FECB *had* succeeded in breaking into the Japanese Fleet Code again in 1941 and had continued to read parts of the traffic until the introduction of the eighth additive book on 4 December.[72] Burnett also related how the Singapore station had read certain transmissions from Combined Fleet headquarters that had convinced him that Pearl Harbor was to be a target of Japan's attack. Speaking publicly of her husband's prediction for the first time, for a television documentary made for the fiftieth anniversary of the Pearl Harbor attack, Mrs. Burnett vividly recalled his astonishment at learning the U.S. Navy had been caught by surprise on 7 December 1941.

"The night before Pearl Harbor, my husband had to make a prediction as to the date it would happen, but owing to bad atmospherics, the intercepted Japanese signals hadn't been very clear," Mrs. Burnett recalled. "I knew that he was expecting an attack on Pearl Harbor and when finally the news came through on the radio he was so relieved that he just said 'Thank God I got it right.'" According to his wife, Burnett "at that time was convinced" that a warning had been sent to Pacific Fleet."[73]

So, too, was Commander Mortimer. "There were lots of leads passed over to the Americans, all our signals were directed to Director Naval Intelligence, repeated to CinC Pacific Fleet," he insisted, noting how all his reports on Japanese shipping had also been relayed to Pearl Harbor. He recalled that on the morning after Japan's attack, Commander Tom Wisden, his boss, had appeared in a "great state" and instructed him to "check all our information had gone to CINCPAC (Commander in Chief Pacific Fleet)."[74] His review of the signal logs proved that they had, but fifty years later when shown the American records that showed they had not been received, Mortimer declared, "Something bloody well went wrong!"[75]

The lack of FECB records or *any* related signal logs in the British Public Records Office made it impossible to confirm the accounts given by Mrs. Burnett and Commander Mortimer. At the end of the war, according to Mortimer, who was then serving with FECB in Ceylon, their order was received at the Colombo headquarters to "destroy every signal that we held." The wry comment circulated among the staff at the time was "Churchill does not want anyone to ever write the story apart from himself!"[76] Mortimer also noted that he and Commander Wisden were "asked for at the first Pearl Harbor enquiry," but that the Admiralty refused to let any British officer go to the United States to testify. It remains a matter of debate how much Japanese naval traffic Burnett and the team of code breakers at FECB really were reading in the period prior to the attack on the Pacific Fleet and whether they succeeded in breaking sufficient intercepts to reach the same conclusion as that made by the U.S. Navy in 1945: that JN-25 contained clues that pointed specifically to Japan's Pearl Harbor operation.

The detailed documentary record essential to establishing precisely how little, or much, of the Japanese naval communications the British really were reading in 1941 still remains classified. But in May 1994, a request for still-closed World War II Admiralty intelligence records resulted in one of these volumes on "Special Intelligence in the Far East and Pacific" slipping through the computerized ordering system. It contained a series of wartime memoranda on the operational history of FECB that were written by some of the naval officers who were its members, including Mortimer.[77]

This collection of reports sheds important new light on the hotly debated issue of how much of the Japanese naval ciphers were being read by the British before Pearl Harbor was attacked. One report on JN-25, dated July 1942, contains the following revealing paragraph:

"In May 1940 the book [i.e., the JN-25 A code book] had been sufficiently built for simple messages to be translated, provided the depth of the subtracter table was enough for stripping" and in October the Japanese introduced a new code book [JN-25B] but unfortunately for them, [they] retained in use the current recyphering table and indicating system during the months of October and November. These had been solved in some positions and new code groups were discovered immediately. It may be explained here that but for this mistake on the part of the Japanese, the form of the new [code] book from which, as is known, *intelligence from a wide field was produced in November 1941* and from March 1942 until its supersession in June 1942 [emphasis added]."[78]

What the tantalizing "intelligence from a wide field was" is not specified in this report, but in another memorandum in the same file can be found the remarkable statement that FECB did obtain "besides routine intelligence, the following results of outstanding importance:

1. *Ample warning* that Japan was going to war in 1941

2. Intelligence that the "Prince of Wales" and "Repulse" had been spotted and would be attacked from the air, *four hours* before the attack was launched. By the time that *the Japanese signals had been decoded* and got to FECB and then transmitted to the "Prince of Wales" the disaster had occurred [emphasis added]."[79]

While still lacking specific detail, and certainly providing no indication that the British might have been penetrating the Japanese fleet ciphers to the depth necessary to have broken out the clues to Pearl Harbor, these reports nonetheless appear to confirm that the British were able to penetrate JN-25B and other Japanese naval cipher systems to a significant extent. It is also of note that the report headed "Collaboration of British and U.S. Radio Intelligence" also states that "in May 1941 the policy of complete exchange of Radio Intelligence with the U.S. was decided on. An exchange of visits between the U.S. Unit at Corregidor and the British Unit at Singapore showed that the British were well ahead with JN-25 results, and the U.S. began a program of expansion. From then until Japan entered the war, the Singapore and Corregidor units worked in close cooperation."[80]

Yet we can be certain from the U.S. Navy records that if the British cryptanalysts at Singapore were obtaining meaningful intelligence from the Japanese Fleet Code, it was not communicated to the U.S. Navy at Station CAST in the Philippines. The FECB at Singapore had been secretly exchanging information with the Americans, according to Duane L. Whitlock, a U.S. naval intercept operator and traffic analyst who was a member of that team on Corregidor. "I can attest from first-hand experience that as of 1 December 1941 the recovery of the JN-25B had not progressed to the point that it was productive of any appreciable intelligence—not even enough to be pieced together by traffic analysis," Whitlock emphatically wrote. "The reason that *not one single* JN-25 decrypt made prior to Pearl Harbor has ever been found or declassified is that no such decrypt ever existed. It simply was not within the realm of *our combined* cryptologic capability to produce a usable decrypt at that particular time [emphasis added]."[81] But Whitlock's categorical declaration that "not one single" decrypt was broken out has to be measured against the authoritative statement by former NSA senior historian Donald M. Gish that "current JN-25 messages read by U.S. analysts on Corregidor during this period *were few in number* and were invariably ship movement reports: arrivals and departures together with some fragmentary schedules." While this may not have amounted to "meaningful intelligence" that forecast an attack on the U.S. Pacific Fleet, the former NSA historian, who acknowledged that he was writing with access to still-classified U.S. Navy records, suggests there was some success in penetrating the Fleet Code. He also asserted that "In view of the collaboration and exchange with FECB, Singapore, there is no reason to believe that the British exceeded these accomplishments."[82]

However limited were the U.S. Navy's "accomplishments," they are significant because of the complete absence of contemporary American or British records of what either made of JN-25B in November 1941.[83] Despite years of search it has been publicly stated that the NSA authorities have yet to positively identify or declassify a single pre–Pearl Harbor JN-25B decrypt, whether it was a ship arrival or departure schedule.[84] The FECB was presumably also doing no worse than the Americans in its penetration. But the records of what the Singapore station may have gleaned from the Japanese naval ciphers, before or after 7 December, if not destroyed, have not been declassified. The official history of Britain's wartime intelligence operations categorically stresses there is "nothing in the British archives that is not in the American records."[85] Such a blanket assertion has no historical credibility in the light of the Naval Intelligence summaries about JN-25 and the revelations in Churchill's SIGINT file shows that Bletchley Park eavesdropped on Japanese diplomatic traffic that was not being monitored by the Americans. There also exist differences in the wording of the translations that distort the true sense of some of the Japanese diplomatic cables as they were decrypted in Bletchley Park and Washington.[86]

Indeed it is the very lack of *any* intelligence about Japanese fleet movements in the prime minister's declassified SIGINT file that raises the issue of why those records are being withheld and why the section of the prime minister's secret office file containing information on Japanese naval dispositions cannot be released for seventy-five years. The concealment of this information has lent credibility to the claim that Britain's prime minister deliberately withheld from the president intelligence that indicated that the Japanese intended to attack United States territory in the Pacific. Rusbridger, who liberally interpreted what he had been told by the Australian cryptanalyst, Captain Nave, concluded that "Churchill was aware that a task force had sailed from northern Japan in late November 1941, and that one of its likely targets was Pearl Harbor." Their book declares, with a certainty that far exceeds the evidence they present, that "Churchill deliberately kept this vital information from Roosevelt, because he realized an attack of this nature, whether on the U.S. Pacific Fleet or the Philippines, was a means of fulfilling his publicly proclaimed desire to get America into the war at any cost."[87]

It is significant that *Betrayal at Pearl Harbor*, because it claimed that the U.S. Navy was also part of the conspiracy to deny intelligence, provoked veteran NSA officials to excoriate Rusbridger for his "flagrant perversion of fact" which "in its libel of Churchill reaches a new depth of scurrility." It is a reflection on the sensitivity that surrounds even fifty-year-old SIGINT revelations that it took the NSA nearly two years to declassify the critique made by one of its own senior historians. For all the inflamed passions of the surviving American cryptanalysts, they do not explain the gaps in the British record that do raise suspicions that Churchill knew more about the Japanese intentions than the British government has chosen to make public. This possibility was first documented by this author's comprehensive history, *The Pacific War*, published in 1981. This raised the issue of what intelligence of Japanese treachery Churchill might have sent to Roosevelt to persuade him to abandon the modus vivendi. Ten more years of research and further declassification of documents on both sides of the Atlantic reinforce rather than diminish this conclusion:

> If Churchill was indeed forewarned it might explain his extreme touchiness over the subject of the Pearl Harbor attack and his repeated denials that Britain was privy to Japan's diplomatic communications. It would also explain the continued reluctance of the British government to release so far any of their Japanese ULTRA intelligence files— and why key reports dealing with Japan in the Prime Minister's records have been removed and remain closed for seventy-five years.[88]

In contrast to the claim that Churchill had foreknowledge of the attack on Pearl Harbor, the additional evidence that has now come to light raises the strong possibility that FECB's fragmentary readings of the JN-25 Fleet Code was what convinced the prime minister on 25 November that the Japanese military machine was irrevocably committed to an attack on Thailand, followed by Malaya, and the Dutch East Indies. By the following week, this picture became a certainty. But there is still no indication that the pieces of the intelligence jigsaw assembled by the British revealed anything more than a *possibility* of a simultaneous attack on the United States territories in the Far East. There is no evidence that Churchill received a positive forewarning from SIGINT sources that Japan was *committed* to invading the Philippines and no evidence of even a hint of any attack on Pearl Harbor. If there had been, he surely would not have needed to make the frantic diplomatic efforts to secure Roosevelt's guarantees of U.S. "armed support" in the event the Japanese only attacked Malaya. Nor is there any logical reason why the prime minister, had he been forewarned, would have withheld from the president intelligence that the Pacific was targeted for attack. Such a disclosure could only have helped him secure United States armed support for Britain in the Pacific.

If so vital a piece of intelligence as Japan's intention to attack the United States had been supplied by FECB, it would certainly have been made available to the British chiefs of staff. In their records, there is not only no evidence of it but instead continuing doubt about Tokyo's intentions even after the Japanese convoys had been sighted by the RAF on 6 December steaming south toward the Kra Isthmus. But the British chiefs of staff could not decide whether the "Japanese mean business" and were really going to attack Thailand and Malaya or were "bluffing in order to discover our reactions."[89] After their meeting at six that evening they communicated their concerns to the prime minister about the American commitment in a memo signed by First Sea Lord Dudley Pound, Chief of Air Staff Sir Charles Portal, and Alan Brook, the newly appointed chief of the Imperial General Staff.

"From the military point of view it would pay us to attack these convoys at sea, but our present political instructions prevent us from doing this," Churchill was told. "Unless we are absolutely assured that an attack delivered in these circumstances would have the armed support of the United States, we ought not to make the first move."[90] If the chiefs of staff had been aware of an absolutely reliable piece of SIGINT intelligence that Japan would also attack Pearl Harbor or the Philippines, the prime minister would not have hesitated to order the *Prince of Wales* task force out from Singapore to intercept the convoy at sea and to simultaneously set in motion the planned Matador advance of British troops across the Malayan border, to forestall an invasion of Thailand. But both Churchill and his chiefs of staff had to await confirmation from the president that his promise of "armed support" given two days earlier could be extended to cover these preemptive British moves against Japan.

"President has informed Ambassador that U.S. authorities are publishing what information they have regarding threatening moves of Japanese troops and ships off Indo-China in order to prepare the public mind for possible development," was the only crumb of reassurance from Roosevelt that was received by the morning of 7 December.[91] The cable that Churchill then drafted to satisfy the conditions the president had set for moving against the Japanese convoys was never sent. It was made redundant by the news of the attack on Pearl Harbor.[92] A further indication that FECB intelligence at Singapore had not broken into enough of the Japanese Fleet Code to be able to even forecast the true intention of the convoys in the South China sea is contained in the dispatch from Singapore received at 1:15 P.M. London time on 7 December.

"During last 24 hours majority of signals originated by CinC Combined Fleet *whereabouts unknown to me* [emphasis added]," the commander in chief reported to the Admiralty, in a signal that he copied simultaneously to the Dutch commander in chief and Washington.[93] His report provided the latest estimates of the Singapore Operational Intelligence Centre that the battleship "*Kongoo* [sic]" and seven cruisers, along with the fourth and seventh destroyer squadrons, had been identified from the "W[ireless]/T[elegraphy] traffic" as the cover for the twenty-two-ship convoy. No identification at all could be made of the warships escorting the second twenty-one-ship convoy, and only one cruiser was believed to be guarding a third convoy of three ten-thousand-ton merchant vessels.[94] Such a sketchy report made only hours before the simultaneous blows fell on the Kra Isthmus, Malaya, and Pearl Harbor does not suggest that the FECB code breakers and analysts had come up with a precise estimate of the details of Japan's attack plan. If there had been any indication at the eleventh hour from intercepted Japanese naval communications that a striking force was about to attack Pearl Harbor, the prime minister would have been the first to know of it.

During the tense ten-day wait for Japan to strike the first blow, Churchill had been on the telephone to Bletchley Park "at all hours of the day and night." According to the diary of Commander Malcolm Kennedy, a naval Japanese linguist working on Purple at Bletchley Park, there was no letup in Churchill's calls "asking for the 'latest information and indications of Japan's intentions.'"[95] By 7 December the prime minister did not need SIGINT to confirm that the Japanese would probably attack on Thailand and then, in short order, on Malaya. Nor would Tokyo's fourteen-part message or the instructions for its 1 P.M. delivery that Sunday have reached Churchill in time to have forewarned him. Comparison of the time taken by the U.S. Army and Navy decryption of Purple intercepts with that of the Bletchley Park's code-breaking team reveals

that during the first week of December, the delay from interception to delivery of the translation to the president was just
under two days. It was taking *twice as long* for the same Japanese cable to be translated for the prime minister because the
American code breakers had given priority to the Purple intercepts of Tokyo's exchanges with their Washington envoys. By
6 December the translated intercepts were circulated to Roosevelt and his chiefs of staff within a matter of hours. But no
such sense of urgency spurred the efforts the Bletchley Park
code breakers, who were still taking two to three days to process the Purple traffic between Tokyo and its embassies in London and Washington.[96] On this schedule Churchill could not
have received the "missing" fourteen-part message and the
deadline intercept until the day after war broke out. The decrypts that have been released also confirm that there were no
other "advance BJ" deliveries made to Downing Street between BJ/90, the 2 December code-destruct intercept, and BJ/
91, the 7 December plain-language alert sent out by Tokyo to
all their embassies.

"Relations with Japan and Great Britain and the United
States are extremely critical," was the warning cable in the
hidden-word code whose solution had been given in an earlier
Purple decrypt.[97] This clear indication of the imminence of
war was intercepted just before midday on Sunday morning.
The advance translation would therefore have been sent to
Churchill by motorcycle courier from Bletchley Park within
the hour. This appears to have prompted him to finally tele-
graph the Thai prime minister at 1:20 P.M. a warning of the
"possibility of imminent Japanese invasion" and that Britain
would "regard an attack on you as an attack upon ourselves."[98]
The prime minister happened to be on weekend retreat at
the Chequers estate in Buckinghamshire, not many miles
from Bletchley Park. By another coincidence that can be construed as either fortuitous, or suspicious, Churchill was also
entertaining two of Roosevelt's trusted confidants as house
guests: the American ambassador, John Winant, and Averell
Harriman.

Ambassador Winant recorded in his memoir that Churchill
had retired that afternoon after luncheon, explaining that he
had not had much sleep the previous night.[99] When Churchill
reappeared at around eight that evening before dinner, he
"seemed tired and depressed" according to Harriman. "He
didn't have much to say throughout dinner and was immersed
in his thoughts, with his head on his hands."[100] Nor did his

mood lighten as they listened to the BBC nine o'clock news, missing the initial announcement of Japan's attack on Pearl Harbor as they waited for the tube receiver to warm up. It was only when Sawyers, the butler, confirmed that he had heard on the radio outside that the Japanese were attacking the Americans that Churchill and his dinner guest "all sat up." Within a matter of minutes a telephone call had been put through to the White House.

"It is quite true," Roosevelt told Churchill. "They have attacked us at Pearl Harbor. We are all in the same boat now."[101] Unless the prime minister had conducted an elaborate charade for the benefit of American guests, these firsthand accounts of his behavior are consistent with his having been just as surprised as the president by the news of the raid on Pearl Harbor. The only reason for doubting Churchill is that the attack began at 7:30 A.M. in Hawaii, which was 7:00 P.M. in London. This allowed just over two hours during which the news that war had broken out in the Pacific could have been conveyed to Churchill *before* he heard it on the radio. The British ambassador in Washington did record in his diary that the president telephoned at 2:15 P.M. "to say that the Japanese were bombing Hawai [*sic*], and asked me to pass it on as quickly as possible."[102] Lord Halifax could, therefore, have telephoned Churchill during the next forty-five minutes, catching the prime minister before he went down to dinner. But the delays attendant in transatlantic calling through an operator that were in force at the time would have delayed the ambassador's call to London, and it would then have had to be routed through the Foreign Office. So it is equally plausible that Churchill remained in ignorance. Had he known, he would hardly have been in the depressed mood observed by his American guests, who make no mention of any call interrupting their gloomy dinner.

The prime minister's despondency might well have been brought on by the news that the Japanese landings had commenced on the north coast of Malaya two hours earlier, plunging Britain into war with Japan with no certainty of United States armed support. But there was a delay in reporting to London as a result of tardy reporting by local commanders on the north coast of Malaya and further confusion at Britain's Far East Command headquarters in Singapore. There is no indication that word of any Japanese attack reached Churchill before he learned of Pearl Harbor.

What is certain is that as long as the suspicious gaps remain in Churchill's files and Britain's SIGINT intelligence remains so glaringly incomplete, the "missing" documentation will continue to suggest that the final secrets of Pearl Harbor are still being kept locked away by the British government in the closet of official secrecy.

WHO WAS REALLY TO BLAME?

H istory is not merely what happened but rather what happened in the context of what could have happened" is the guiding axiom for interpreting historical evidence.[1] It has a particular relevance when it comes to the weighing of historical evidence in order to determine where the burden of responsibility should be placed for the United States's getting taken so badly by surprise on those grim days of infamy when the defenses of the Philippines and Hawaii were overwhelmed by the unprovoked attacks with which Japan plunged into war.

Who was really to blame? is the question that has exercised three generations of historians and writers, and produced a hundred or more books and studies—many charged with the fiercely partisan political emotions that have shed more heat than light on the central issue of whether the Roosevelt administration or the Hawaiian commanders were the more culpable. To determine the question of responsibility for critical failures at the nexus points in a complex progress of decision making and command functioning requires taking into account the "what-ifs" and "what-might-have-beens" that lead to speculation and second-guessing with the advantage of hindsight. But "what happened in the context of what could have happened" is critical to determining the question of accountability.

One of the most important lessons to be learned from the Pearl Harbor disaster is a guiding principle that in a military command chain "he who withholds information shares the blame for any disaster that follows."[2] The facts as they had been set forth make it difficult not to conclude that the local commands in Hawaii and the Philippines would have been more prepared had their superior commanders in Washington provided—or at least not withheld—information that could have given a more accurate warning of the direction and timing of Japan's plunge into war. But was the intelligence picture sufficiently clear to have averted disaster had it been communicated to Pearl Harbor? At the same time it can be argued that since it was the policy makers and military planners in Washington who had set the stage for the twin disasters, there is a prima facie presumption that the Roosevelt administration bore the ultimate responsibility for the strategic surprise that overtook the United States during those days of infamy in December 1941. These are the two fundamental issues that have to be addressed when weighing the historical evidence presented in the preceding chapters in determining the balance of culpability for both the strategic surprise and the tactical unpreparedness that led to the twin disasters at Pearl Harbor and Clark Field. The accounting has to be made on the basis of the larger strategic context of United States military and diplomatic policy in the Pacific, not the narrow "Pearl Harbor Syndrome" focus that blinkered the wartime inquiries and that continues to permeate the postwar analyses that have sustained the guilt of the Hawaiian commanders—most recently Prange's monumental work and Clausen's attempt to extend the validity of his 1944 inquiry, which set out to exonerate the U.S. Army chief of staff, and by implication Roosevelt, from any blame.

Since the future can only be perceived "through a glass, dimly" and the past is seen with 20/20 vision, assigning accountability is at best an exercise of imperfect historical deduction in which the criteria on which the "final judgment" is reached may be more subjective than objective. Within the limitations of this caveat, an assessment of the responsibility for the twin disasters that overtook the United States in the Pacific in December 1941 can be made by conflating the complexity of the "what if" factor into three fundamental questions:

1. Were the resources and the disposition of United States military power in the Pacific compatible with supporting an American policy of economic warfare against Japan?

2. Were the decision makers in Washington fully aware,

from the information available at the time, that the confrontation with Japan had reached the brink of war?

3. Were the local commands in Hawaii and the Philippines adequately made aware of the degree of Washington's concerns to the extent that they could reasonably have been expected to be on the alert for a possible Japanese attack?

There can be no simple, single answer to the first question, which raises the issue of the overall accountability of the Roosevelt administration for creating the scenario in the Pacific that resulted in the strategic and tactical disasters. What the record shows is that by the fall of 1941 three decades of sound military planning based on the presence of the Pacific Fleet in Hawaii had been overturned in favor of a high-risk Philippine deterrent strategy based on airpower that lacked the means of immediate implementation. It was driven by foreign policy, not military considerations, and required reversing the strategic priorities in the Pacific to enforce an American oil embargo to check further Japanese aggression in the Far East. It was founded on the unproven potential of a strategic bomber force whose very ability to deter depended on Washington's babying of Tokyo for the nine months that would be needed to complete the reinforcement of the Philippines. Attempting a military buildup on the doorstep of a potential enemy took no account of the provocative invitation to the military leaders in Tokyo to accelerate their plans to make a preemptive strike before the Americans had assembled sufficient power to interfere with strategic ambitions while Japan's oil reserves were still sufficient to sustain a large-scale operation. The aerial reinforcement of the Philippines could be carried out only at the expense of the defenses of the Hawaiian command and with the cooperation of the British, who were offered a secret defense pact in return for giving up their allocation of the B-17 bomber production.

While the President and his military advisers cannot be held to have acted with prudence or foresight when they embarked on what amounted to a colossal strategic gamble, allowance has to be made for constraints under which the decision to confront Japan was taken. Until the previous year Congress had dragged its feet on military appropriations, and with Britain on the ropes again the U-boat war, the President was seduced by War Department wishful thinking into accepting their premise that the B-17 bombers were the solution to an intractable strategic dilemma: how to reinforce the United States military presence in the Pacific quickly when military and naval resources were inadequate for preparing to fight a two-ocean war. But once the gamble had been taken to build up MacArthur's air force as the primary deterrent to Japanese aggression in the Pacific, Washington succumbed to the mindset that Hawaii was therefore no longer a prime target for Japanese attack. MAGIC intelligence that provided Washington with the ability to eavesdrop in Japan's diplomatic maneuvering reinforced this false sense of security. The presumption was that the Purple machine would provide plenty of advance warning of any warlike moves by Japan as the United States embarked on a confrontation strategy of economic warfare.

A deterrent strategy conceived in response to a foreign policy initiative that was beyond the limits of the United States military to support or sustain was a recipe for disaster. From the most senior echelons in the War and Navy Departments, which provided the rationale for the Philippines deterrent; to the Secretaries of War, Navy, and State who eagerly endorsed it, and the president who gave the plan his blessing; all must share in the collective responsibility for setting the United States on a course in the Pacific that was to lead to a major strategic disaster. But for allowing diplomatic events to get out of hand in November 1941, when six months more were needed to complete the buildup of MacArthur's air force, on which the deterrent strategy depended, the president and secretary of state were principally to blame.

When it comes to assessing whether the White House and the American high command was aware by 6 December that Japan was about to go to war, the historical record is incontrovertible. The MAGIC intercepts of Tokyo's diplomatic intercepts had by 26 November made it very clear that "things were automatically going to happen" if an accommodation could not be reached by the end of the month. At the White House cabinet meeting that afternoon in which it was decided to offer the modus vivendi to Japan's ambassador next day, the president himself had fretted that the slim concessions to be offered would not be sufficient to satisfy the hard-liners in Tokyo. He predicted that the United States was "likely to be attacked perhaps as soon as next Monday morning, because the Japanese are notorious for attacking without warning."[3] But his unilateral decision to abandon the attempt at a temporary accommodation the following morning made this outcome more certain. Whether Roosevelt's decision was prompted by intelligence—received overnight from Churchill—of Japan's preparations for hostilities, or whether it was simply bowing to "hysterical" protests from the China lobby, as the official record maintained, it is self-evident that the dramatic diplomatic U-turn by the United States was taken by Tokyo to amount to the ultimatum that made war in the Pacific inevitable.

In the countdown to 7 December, a ten-day-long paper trail confirms, in Washington, an awareness of the looming possibility of imminent war with Japan. The anticipation was that the logical *point d'appui* for the initial attack would be MacArthur's forces in the Philippines, not the Pacific Fleet in its Hawaiian anchorage. Successive MAGIC intelligence intercepts reinforced the Washington mindset with the result that the significance of the Pearl Harbor warship reports of Japan's consul general in Honolulu were overlooked, because they pointed to the possibility of an air raid on the fleet, which was five thousand miles away from the Philippines, the anticipated target of the Japanese attack.

Despite Washington's confidence in MAGIC intelligence, it could not reveal the targets of Japan's war plan, because they were never communicated to Tokyo's Foreign Ministry. The "Winds Code Setup" and the "codes destruct" intercepts, although pointers to the Japanese preparations for hostilities, did not give away their timetable for war. Even the decryption of Tokyo's fourteen-part message in the final hours of 6 December did not provide any more indication either that war was only hours away. It was not until receipt of the one-o'clock delivery instructions the Japanese ambassadors in Washington were read on Sunday morning that it finally began to dawn on senior officers in the War and Navy Departments that this might be a significant pointer to imminence of an impending attack somewhere in the Pacific. But where? The Washington mindset was so fixed on the Philippines that it was read only in the context of a probable predawn invasion of Luzon—not a carrier-plane attack to be launched at first light against the Pacific Fleet base on Hawaii. As every reader of Walter Lord's classic account of *Day of Infamy* knows, even this vital last-minute intelligence was fated to lose its value as a war warning in a communications fiasco that could have been scripted by the Marx brothers.

The most specific pointers to the Pearl Harbor attack, it has only recently been disclosed, had been available to the

Navy Department in Washington and to the British FECB code breakers at Singapore and the U.S. Navy crypto unit, with whom they were in an unofficial liaison. But their value as intelligence was lost in 1941, because the missing pieces of the Pearl Harbor intelligence jigsaw were locked in intercepts of Japanese naval communications in the JN-2B ciphers that were only partially readable. Had the necessary cryptographic resources been available to Washington, there were 188 JN-2B intercepts that could have been broken out in time to have averted the Pearl Harbor disaster. Although the U.S. Navy was not to unlock their secrets until 1946, they are historically important, because their information was important in addressing the issue of "what happened in the context of what *could* have happened" in the context of the overall breakdown of the intelligence process in Washington. The shortsighted bureaucratic miscalculation that denied Rochefort's elite code breaking the opportunity to begin their assault on the Japanese Fleet code in July 1941 can now be seen to have cost the U.S. Navy the best chance it ever had of alerting Pearl Harbor. It is also of historical significance that the top-secret report on *Pre–Pearl Harbor Japanese Naval Dispatches* was never disclosed to the Congressional Investigating Committee, who had been invested with a constitutional authority to examine all extant records pertinent to the disaster at Pearl Harbor. The disappearance of that 1946 report for nearly fifty years, and the continued failure to uncover any contemporary JN-25 records, can be construed as a further manifestation of the "Pearl Harbor Syndrome" that led the Navy Department to bury the whole issue of JN-25, because it was potentially very embarrassing evidence of the failure in the handling of intelligence.

The unread JN-25 intercepts add a new "what-if" factor in determining whether the Hawaiian command received enough intelligence from Washington to enable them to guard against Japanese air attacks. Had the information that was broken out of the Japanese naval communications in 1946 been available in Washington four years earlier, only the most die-hard of Roosevelt-hating revisionists would claim that they would not have been relayed to the Pacific Fleet, because the president would have conspired with the Navy Department to deny them to the Pacific Fleet to ensure that the Japanese attack would bring the United States into the war. But what is certain is that if Kimmel and Short received the intercepts listed in *Pre–Pearl Harbor Japanese Naval Dispatches*, they would not have needed

20/20 hindsight to realize that there was a Japanese carrier force heading in to attack on or about 7 December.

Whatever the JN-25 issue adds to the dimension of the intelligence breakdown, Washington cannot be held guilty on the basis of denying the Hawaiian commanders intelligence that it did not possess in an intelligible form. But what Kimmel and Short were denied, however, were the so-called bomb-plot intercepts from the Japanese consulate that contained abstract indications, but not *conclusive* evidence, that Tokyo would have required only such detailed information about where the American warships were at anchor, *if* an air raid on Pearl Harbor was being planned. As a potential threat indicator, if not a specific warning, Kimmel had justification in maintaining that had he received the so-called bomb-plot intercepts in the context of the full MAGIC intelligence picture, he *would* have raised the level of their alert and therefore not have been caught unprepared. But his assertions have to be considered in the context of another "what-if"—namely that the warning and intelligence that the Hawaiian command *did* receive from Washington *should* have prompted a higher state of defensive readiness that was ordered.

The Congressional investigating committee came to the conclusion that Kimmel and Short did have all the information needed to order higher levels of war alert. Their failure to do so was a result, not so much of a lack of intelligence— they had, after all, been sent a war warning and alerted to be ready for "surprise aggressive movements in any direction"— but of failing to have the foresight that was expected of commanders in chief. The committee held that even with a more-limited access to the intelligence picture than Washington, had Kimmel and Short liaised and consulted properly, they could, for example, have correctly interpreted the intelligence significance of the "codes-destruct" message in the context of the Honolulu FBI reports of the burning of secret papers at the local Japanese consulate. This interpretation placed the greater measure of blame on the Hawaiian commanders. But this assessment was prejudiced not just by the "Pearl Harbor Syndrome" and hindsight, it neglected to take into account Washington's failure to appreciate one of the cardinal rules of intelligence: that in the absence of specific direction on what action to take, the "mindset" of the local commander, especially background perceptions against which incoming information of threat are evaluated, plays a critical role in determining his response.

"Command decisions as to the conduct of surveillance and the initiation of operational responses deemed to be prudent in the light of operational experience must be understood by those who judge as being a dynamic, continuing process, highly dependent on timely, complete intelligence."[4] This important factor was neglected by investigators from the Congressional committee in 1945—Prange and Clausen, according to Vice Admiral David C. Richardson, a distinguished intelligence specialist who had served at Pearl Harbor until 1941. "The initiatives available to a commander, given twelve or more hours' warning, are relatively many; given an hour, very few," Richardson contends. "Not understanding this basic and most vital point is where Washington was irresponsible."[5]

The record, moreover, shows that not only did the War and Navy departments—specifically Admiral Turner—fail to pass all relevant intelligence to Kimmel, but in the absence of specific directives as to how he was to respond, the war warnings of 27 November were misleading, because they had been framed for the command in the Philippines, not for the commanders on Hawaii. The simultaneous order to Kimmel to dispatch his two carriers with marine fighter reinforcements for Wake and Midway reinforced the mind-set at Pearl Harbor that Washington did not perceive any imminent Japanese threat to the Hawaiian Islands. Moreover, since Short had communicated his low state of war readiness to the War Department, required by his war warning, but had not received any countermanding instruction, is conclusive evidence that Washington not only shared, but reinforced the Hawaiian command's unpreparedness to meet a surprise attack.

The commander in chief in the Philippines, by contrast, was the recipient of a very specific war warning from Washington that implied a very real and immediate threat. MacArthur's prima facie dereliction was therefore magnified not only by the alerts he received from the War Department, but also from his own MAGIC intelligence. He had received the full diplomatic picture of Japan's march toward belligerence. Even if he, like Washington, did not know precisely when the attack would come, still, given the news of the raid on Pearl Harbor, it is astonishing that a commander of his stature and experience should not have realized that an air attack from Formosa was not just probable, but a near certainty. That he ignored both war warnings and intelligence indicated that his mind-set that morning reflected the wait-and-see attitude of the government of the Philippines rather than his duty as an American commander to order an immediate execution of his war plan, which called for a preemptive bombing strike against Japanese bases in Formosa. MacArthur's imperiousness in refusing to make himself accessible to his air commander in the hours of crisis that followed the outbreak of war with Japan reveals an amazing denial of the lessons to be drawn from a vast body of military history of which he was an ardent scholar.

An astute military commander adjusts his state of readiness according to the dictates of intelligence, and combat effectiveness requires a proper delegation of authority from commanding general to field corporal. Neither of these qualities was demonstrated by General Douglas MacArthur during the ten and a half hours that passed from the time his bedside phone rang and he received news of Pearl Harbor to the time when the Japanese bombers arrived to blast his air force on Clark Field into a blazing shambles. Seldom can a commander in chief have been caught with his military pants down as dramatically or so totally as was the American Caesar on 8 December 1941.

History shows that defeat can prove fatal to a military commander who fails to discharge his duty at the outbreak of war. But it was not MacArthur, but Kimmel and Short, whose execution for treason was suggested in letters received by the White House. Had it been two centuries earlier, the Hawaiian commanders might well have paid the ultimate penalty as did Admiral Sir John Byng, who, in 1757, had received his orders from the Admiralty to sail in his fleet to secure Minorca. He sailed off across the Mediterranean only to discover that the French navy had beaten him to the island and his force was not powerful enough to dislodge their siege. On his return he was charged with neglect of duty, court-martialed, and shot on his own quarterdeck. The unfortunate Byng was made a scapegoat who paid with his life for the ministerial bungling in the British Admiralty at the start of the Seven Years War with France. His execution was the butt of Voltaire's celebrated taunt in *Candide* about the idiosyncrasies of the English, who "thought well to kill an admiral from time to time to encourage the others."[6]

The penalty that the Hawaiian commanders were to pay for getting taken by surprise on 7 December was no less opprobrious for a more civilized age than that faced by the unfortunate British admiral nearly two centuries earlier. Fear of political fallout prompted the president to move swiftly to make the Hawaiian commanders the scapegoats for the disasters of the days of infamy as the "Pearl Harbor Syndrome" began to manifest itself. By restricting the wartime investigations to the examination of only the circumstances leading up to the attack on Pearl Harbor, the administration concealed the secret bargain Roosevelt had struck with Churchill for the Anglo-American Far East defense pact that resulted in the ill-conceived Philippines deterrent gamble that set the stage for the December disasters. The sacrifice of Kimmel and Short to satisfy American indignation of Japan's terrible humiliation of the United States, while it may have been justified by the demands of wartime, was to do a great personal injustice as well as distort the popular interpretation of history.

The smoke of the controversy that later erupted over who was really to blame for the disaster only served to camouflage responsibility for the far greater strategic calamity that had overtaken MacArthur's armed forces in the Philippines. Kimmel and Short were the ones who were cashiered and found guilty of dereliction by a secret presidential commission that served them up as the public scapegoats for the Roosevelt administration's flawed deterrent strategy against Japan. But their unpreparedness would have paled into insignificance had the dereliction of MacArthur's command in the Philippines ever been investigated. Admiral Byng had at least been tried by a court-martial of his peers, but the Hawaiian commanders were judged in secret and convicted in the court of public opinion by a misguided presidential commission and a politically charged Congressional hearing. They were portrayed as two sentries on guard duty who were caught asleep when the enemy attacked and were therefore ipso facto guilty. But the record shows that they were really more like two guards who had been blindfolded by the lack of intelligence, told to face the wrong direction, and inadequately armed to fend off an enemy air attack. Nor does the sentry theory of their culpability account for why MacArthur, who was on guard in Manila with none of the handicaps, escaped any retribution for a far more egregious dereliction of duty after being warned of the nature and proximity of an impending air attack.

It has taken half a century for the documentation to become available that reveals that the disaster at Pearl Harbor and the debacle of the Philippines were *not* simply the result of the unpreparedness of the local commanders, or a breakdown in the intelligence process. The chain of defeats that overwhelmed the United States in the Pacific on the days of infamy in December 1941 were the direct consequence of a major failure in military strategy and foreign policy by the Roosevelt administration. An equitable accounting of responsibility for the strategic and tactical disasters may have been inappropriate in the midst of war, when the "Pearl Harbor Syndrome" enabled the president and the high command in Washington to shield themselves from blame during the hour of supreme national crisis. But such considerations can no longer justify burdening the Hawaiian commanders unfairly with all the responsibility. Whatever the omissions of Kimmel and Short, they paid a far higher penalty than the mitigating circumstances of their unpreparedness warranted. Their command shortcomings pale into relative insignificance before the far more egregious dereliction of MacArthur.

History shows that Kimmel and Short did their nation a profound service, even if not willingly, by shouldering the burden of blame for the Roosevelt administration's diplomatic and military blunders in addition to those of MacArthur. He was permitted to redeem himself by making a substantial contribution to the Allied victory, but the Hawaiian commanders were never to be given that chance. The record, therefore, ought now to be set straight—as it should have been soon after the war, when they were alive and could have appreciated that an unjust and unjustified burden of blame had finally been lifted.

History shows that they were more victims of the "Pearl Harbor Syndrome" than the culprits responsible for that disaster. It may be too late for Admiral Kimmel and General Short, but there is now a compelling case to be made for putting the public record straight with a posthumous restoration to the full ranks that the two Hawaiian commanders would have attained had not they been forced to retire in disgrace.

THE JAPANESE ATTACK ON THE PHILIPPINES

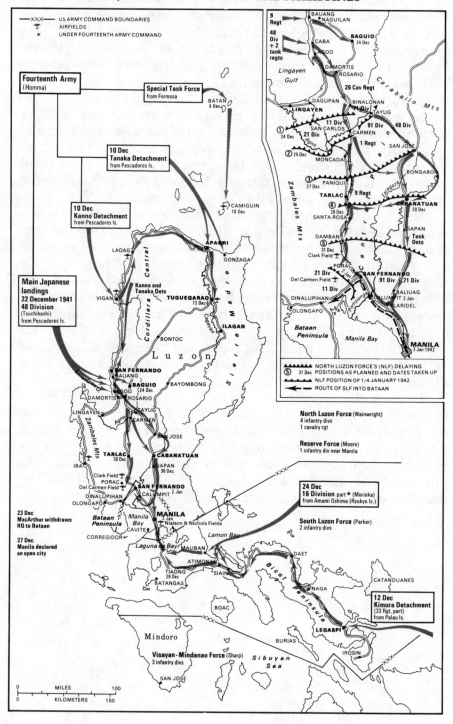

THE JAPANESE AIR RAID ON PEARL HARBOR

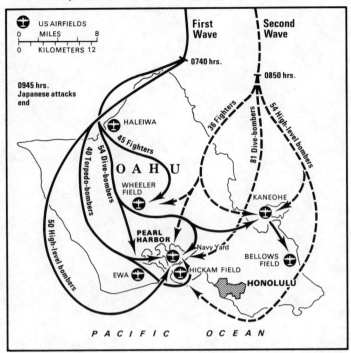

US AIRFIELDS
0 MILES 8
0 KILOMETERS 12

First Wave
Second Wave

0740 hrs.
0850 hrs.

0945 hrs.
Japanese attacks end

HALEIWA
45 Fighters
36 Fighters
54 High-level bombers
54 Dive-bombers
40 Torpedo-bombers
81 Dive-bombers

O A H U

WHEELER FIELD
KANEOHE

PEARL HARBOR
Navy Yard
BELLOWS FIELD

50 High-level bombers
EWA
HICKAM FIELD
HONOLULU

P A C I F I C   O C E A N

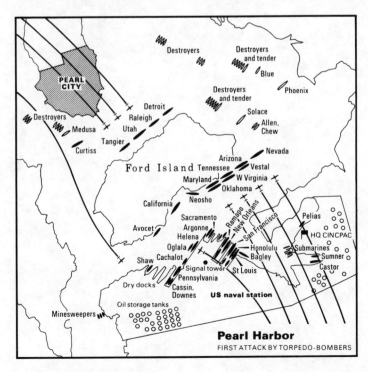

Destroyers
Destroyers and tender
Blue
Phoenix

PEARL CITY

Destroyers and tender
Solace
Allen, Chew

Destroyers
Detroit
Raleigh
Medusa
Utah
Tangier
Curtiss

Nevada
Arizona
Ford Island   Tennessee   Vestal
Maryland   W Virginia
Oklahoma
California   Neosho
Sacramento
Avocet   Argonne   Rampao   New Orleans   San Francisco   Pelias
Helena
Oglala   Honolulu   Submarines   Sumner
Shaw   Cachalot   Bagley   Castor
Signal tower   St Louis
Dry docks   Pennsylvania
Cassin, Downes   US naval station
Oil storage tanks
Minesweepers

HQ CINCPAC

Pearl Harbor
FIRST ATTACK BY TORPEDO-BOMBERS

APPENDIX I

THE "EAST WIND RAIN" CONTROVERSY

The "Red Herring" at the Congressional Hearings

The issue of whether a genuine "East Wind Rain" alert had been transmitted by Tokyo radio and picked up before 7 December 1941 became a cause célèbre at the 1945 congressional hearings. At the time the assumption was made that if such a message had been picked up, it would have been a clear indication that Japan was about to go to war. The actual "Winds" setup, however, was intended only as an alert to Japan's legations worldwide that diplomatic relations with the United States, Britain, and Russia were in danger of being ruptured. Pearl Harbor historians such as Roberta Wholstetter and Gordon Prange sidestepped the issue by pointing out that the 2 December codes-destruct intercepts, which had been sent to the Pacific Fleet command, were a more accurate indication that war would break out.

Yet the importance attached to the "Winds" alert in Washington at the time, the plethora of false alerts received, and the fact that *no* actual "Winds" execute warning reached the Hawaiian commands ensured that the dispute over whether a *Higashi No Kaze Ame* execute had been intercepted became a focus of the fiercely partisan debate. Conflicting testimony was given about its receipt in the eight secret wartime investigations. The controversy intensified when postwar interrogations of Japanese officials failed to establish conclusively, one way or the other, whether a "Winds" alert had ever been transmitted. Debate over the "Winds" code distracted attention then, and ever since, from the investigation of more significant issues, such as what was contained in the JN-25 naval intercepts. Because of the controversy it generated along with volumes of official denials, it provides insight into the vigorous efforts made by Washington to deny and cover up its own culpability for failing to pass intelligence on to the Hawaiian commanders.

Commander Safford was convinced that a genuine alert had been received. Given his authority as the chief of OP-20-G he was taken seriously. It was his discovery, made in the fall of 1943, that the "East Wind Rain" message was missing from the office log in which all intercepts were recorded that prompted his campaign to "expose the people who had framed Admiral Kimmel and General Short."[1] Up until that time Safford, as he explained in letters exchanged with Lieutenant Commander Kramer, who was then stationed at Pearl Harbor, had been unable to understand why Admiral Kimmel had been caught by surprise. It was not until he discovered the receipt of what Safford claimed had been a genuine "East Wind Rain" execute that the logs showed had *not* been passed on to Pearl Harbor that he realized the Pacific Fleet had been denied vital MAGIC intelligence. He then began to collect information from Kramer and others to prove the point. In May 1945 Safford provided extensive testimony to Admiral Kent Hewitt, who was charged with investigating the intelligence background to the conclusions of the 1944 naval court of inquiry.

The Navy Department subsequently went to great lengths to contradict Safford's claims. Witnesses were produced and affidavits collected from scores of "On the Roof Gang" radio operators denying that any genuine *Higashi No Kaze Ame* ("East Wind Rain") intercept had been picked up. Many of their statements were suspiciously uniform in their echoing of what appeared to be a formulated denial.[2] The declassified OP-20-G records also support Safford's contention that the incoming OP-20-G signal log had been tampered with. The entry line on 4 December for "# 7001" in the "J[apanese] D[iplomatic]" sequence of numbers is blank. According to Safford's testimony, when he turned over the records in the weeks after the Pearl Harbor attack, it originally contained the missing "Winds" execute intercept.

If this intercept, even if not genuine, could have been produced at the congressional hearings, it would have provided dramatic and irrefutable evidence of the Navy Department's failure to pass on critical intelligence to the Pacific Fleet. As Safford and Kramer were to discover, the attempt to prove that an "East Wind Rain" intercept had been picked up challenged the integrity and institutional authority of the Navy Department, which closed ranks to deny that it had ever been received. Safford's claim rested on the blank page in the run of serial numbers, where he claimed the typed-up message had originally been filed. But since the surviving record indicated "7001-Cancelled," he could not prove what he repeatedly attested there had been, a genuine "Winds" execute intercepted from Station M, the Navy's listening post at Cheltenham in Maryland, which was received at OP-20-G on the morning of either 4 or 5 December.

Safford's case was not helped by his uncertainty over the date, although his recollection of the missing intercept was impressively precise. He described it as "a Teletype copy (typed on yellow paper) of the entire Japanese broadcast, about two hundred or three hundred words long. Three significant words *(Kita, Higashi,* and *Nishi)* appeared and they were in Japanese. Kramer's translation appeared in pencil or colored crayon at the bottom of the sheet. There was very little chance of confusion."[3]

In Kramer's December 1943 response to Safford's letter of inquiry, he stated that he had only a "hazy recollection of being called down to the office" to see the "East Wind Rain" intercept, which he attributed to the "arrangements to handle it expeditiously."[4] Since Safford's "My dear Kramer-san" letter predated the first official investigation of the "Winds" alert, Safford had proposed in it that Kramer be "guarded as to what you state" and relay information by using a cryptic series of numbers and letters to refer to the MAGIC intercepts. A year later, at the 1944 Navy court of inquiry, Kramer unhesitatingly agreed that he had indeed seen the yellow teleprinter sheet that Safford claimed was now missing.

"'Higashi no kaze ame,' I am quite certain," was how Kramer testified to its "East Wind Rain" contents. "The sense of that, however, meant strained relations or a break in relations, possibly implying war with a nation to the eastward, the United States."[5] In 1945, Kramer "was less positive" in his testimony at Admiral Hewitt's inquiry. He was now only "under the impression that the message referred to England and possibly the Dutch, rather than the United States." By February 1945, when he was questioned at the congressional hearings, his recollection was that it had been "a false alarm in the winds system" that at the time was thought to be authentic and which turned out to refer not to the United States but "to the best of my recollection, it was England."[6]

It was alleged by a number of his colleagues that Kramer had changed his testimony under pressure. They included Mrs. Eunice Willson Rice, a longtime OP-20-G staff member whose job was to type up the Japanese diplomatic messages. In correspondence with the author in 1945 she wrote that the denial by her former boss was the result of his "being instructed on orders from above to deny delivering the message."[7] Rear Admiral Robert H. Weeks, Kramer's friend and Arlington neighbor at the time, also recalled to the author having been told at the time that the former head of the Translation Section had been told to "speak right or undergo more mental treatment."[8] Weeks pointed out that Kramer had been admitted to the neuropsychiatric ward of the Naval Hospital at Bethesda in November 1945, suffering from mental distress. This was just two months before he was due to testify at the congressional hearings. The story made newspaper headlines at the time after Representative O'Keefe charged at the hearings that Kramer was being held at the Bethesda psychiatric facility "under orders" and that his uniform had been taken away. When his turn came to testify, Kramer denied that he had been "beset and beleaguered" to change his story.[9]

Safford, who stuck to his original account of the "East Wind Rain" execute having been picked up, believed that Kramer had changed his testimony under duress to support the Navy Department's contention that no genuine alert had been received. Another witness who later surfaced to claim that he, too, saw the missing intercept and was forbidden by his commanding officer to testify before the congressional hearings was Ralph T. Briggs. In a 1977 deposition to the Naval Security Group Command, Briggs asserted that he had been the radio operator at Cheltenham Station M who had intercepted the disputed *"Higashi No Kaze Ame"* message. In 1960 when he was a warrant officer on the staff of Naval Security Group Command headquarters in Washington, Briggs had searched through the microfilm records trying to locate the missing intercept. Unable to find it, he appended to the duty personnel log sheet of 2 December a handwritten statement noting that "all transmissions intercepted by me between 0500 thru 1300 on the above date are missing from the files and that these intercepts contained the "Winds' message warning code."[10]

The notation of Briggs, who a former classmate confirms was "hardly the sort to have made up a tale," conflicts with Safford's testimony in that he puts the receipt of the "East Wind Rain" message to 2 December, two days earlier than 4 December. This lends credence to the official claims made at the 1945 hearings that Safford was confused by what Kramer testified were "reams, yards of Teletype paper covering the plain language broadcasts of the Japanese" "Winds" alert messages.[11] It was claimed that a "North Wind Clear" weather alert picked up on 4 December appeared initially to be so similar to the three messages on the prompt cards that it had triggered a false alert.[12] According to a deposition filed with the Naval Security Group Command by Captain George W. Linn, another watch officer in Kramer's translation section, "this episode established that an execute order had not been received prior to late on December 4."[13] Linn asserted that when he was on watch that day, he did not see any genuine "Winds" alerts.[14] But it could have arrived when he was off duty, the following morning of 5 December. This was Safford's alternative date, which coincided with the testimony that Colonel Sadtler gave to the 1944 Army Pearl Harbor board about the Navy's receiving an "East Wind Rain" intercept that was later claimed to be another false alert.[15]

Corroborative testimony, but no documentary evidence, that a genuine "East Wind Rain" message was transmitted by Tokyo was provided by Brigadier General R. Thorpe, who in 1941 was the U.S. Lend-Lease commissioner and military observer at the Netherlands East Indies headquarters in Java. Thorpe, who was also not called upon to testify at the congressional hearings, claimed that the Dutch commander in chief, General Hein Ter Poorten, had shown him the "Winds" execute. According to his recollection, it was not intercepted in a weather forecast broadcast by Tokyo radio, but in a decrypt of "an intercepted and decoded dispatch from the Foreign Office in Tokyo addressed to the Japanese ambassador in Bangkok."[16] Thorpe had then taken it to Dr. Walter Foote, the American counsul general in Batavia, who forwarded it to Washington with questions about its reliability. He also showed it to the senior U.S. naval attaché, Commander Paul S. Slawson, who also relayed it to Washington. But when the message was produced at the 1945 hearings, it referred only to the details of the "Winds" code setup, but did *not* contain an actual "East Wind Rain" message.[17] In a postwar written recollection, Ter Poorten claimed that he had also advised the British and American liaison officers of a "Winds" execute message and had sent it by Teletype to the Dutch embassy in Washington.[18] He claimed that the Dutch consulate in Hawaii also received a copy of his message warning of "an imminent attack somewhere in the Pacific," which he took care to emphasize "did not specifically mention Pearl Harbor."[19]

According to the written recollection of the chief cryptanalyst of Kamer 14 at Bandoeng, Captain J. W. Henning, also in the Royal Netherland Army Archives, both the "Winds" code setup and a genuine alert had been intercepted. But Henning provided no dates, only the declaration that "from a deciphered Teletype of the beginning of December 1941, we concluded that a Japanese attack was to be expected at short notice."[20] Although John Toland was to inflate Henning's assertion in *Infamy*, as part of his claim that Washington had received a *specific* warning from the Dutch sources that Pearl Harbor was to be attacked, Henning's letter categorically denied it: "When and where the Japanese attack would explode could not be concluded from the telegram."[21]

British sources also provided secondhand corroboration, but no definite proof, that an "East Wind Rain" message was intercepted. This came from an interview conducted with Lieutenant Commander Cedric Brown by the late James Rusbridger, who coauthored *Betrayal at Pearl Harbor* with Captain Eric Nave, a code breaker who served in the Royal Australian Navy. During Brown's internment in a Japanese prisoner of war camp, Brown said that he had encountered a New Zealand naval officer, Lieutenant H. C. Dixon, who had worked for Britain's Far East Combined Bureau's code-breaking establishments at Hong Kong and then Singapore. According to Brown, Dixon told him that he had not been able to comprehend how the Americans had been taken by surprise because he knew the British intercept station at Stonecutters Island in Hong Kong Harbor had picked up the "East Wind Rain" execute in a Tokyo weather broadcast "a few days before the attack on Pearl Harbor."[22] But there is no such intercepted message in the declassified Prime Ministerial SIGINT file. There are, however, suspicious gaps in the original serial numbers that reveal that many of the 1941 intercepts sent directly to Churchill are still being withheld.

Without the release of all the products of Britain's 1941 codebreaking of Japanese traffic, the proof is still lacking that a genuine "East Wind Rain" execute message was broadcast by Tokyo Radio. Without such a contemporary file message, there can be no final corroboration that Safford and Sadtler were correct in their assertions that a *Higashi No Kaze Ame* phrase was picked up sometime before 7 December. The missing page of the OP-20-G diplomatic signal log, together with a large volume of official paper denying Safford's testimony, together with the eyewitness accounts, provide grounds for presuming that either a genuine alert, or something that was taken at the time to be one, was received and later removed from the record in a Navy Department cover-up.

APPENDIX II

SMOKING GUNS OR EMPTY HOLSTERS?

Revisionist Theories

After the congressional hearings of 1945 failed to exonerate the Hawaiian commanders, it was inevitable that the campaign that Kimmel and his supporters continued to wage to clear his name would become entangled with the Roosevelt-hating Republicans and their conviction that the late-president and his advisers had conspired to get the United States into the war in order to save Britain from Hitler. The accusation that Roosevelt had "wanted to provoke Japan to attack" was first publicly made by John T. Flynn in his privately printed 1944 pamphlet *The Truth About Pearl Harbor*, although in it he had been careful to state that the president "certainly never looked for an attack that would kill 3,000 Americans and knock the American Navy and Army out of the war that day."[1] His thesis was to be echoed by George Morgenstern in *Pearl Harbor: The Story of the Secret War*, published in 1947. But it was not until 1948 that the case was argued authoritatively by Charles Beard, a respected and widely read American historian, who published in 1948 an articulate and reasoned indictment, *President Roosevelt and the Coming of the War, 1941*.[2]

The thesis that the United States had been deliberately steered into the war against the Axis powers by Roosevelt became an article of faith of the so-called revisionist historians. It was to be taken a stage further in 1952 by Charles C. Tansill in *Back Door to War: The Roosevelt Foreign Policy 1933–1941*, which argued that it was the president's confrontational diplomacy that had precipitated a clash with Japan in the Pacific. This led the "revisionist" historians to multiplying and inflating all manner of accusations against Roosevelt, from diplomatic manipulation to the Machiavellian charge that he had deliberately conspired to withhold from the Hawaiian commanders intelligence information of the impending attack in order to get the United States into the war. The leading advocate of the Roosevelt-conspiracy revisionists was Harry Elmer Barnes, a one-time colleague of Beard's at The New School. In 1953 he edited another assault on the late-president's reputation titled *Perpetual War for Perpetual Peace.*[3]

"Steps were taken to insure that the Hawaiian commanders . . . would not be warned" was Barnes's explanation for the way in which Kimmel and Short were denied information of the impending Japanese attack.[4] This contention became the driving theme of *The Final Secret of Pearl Harbor,* which was written in 1954 by Rear Admiral Robert A. Theobald, a zealous champion of Admiral Kimmel. Although Barnes remained the principal animator of revisionism, who inspired many postwar investigators with his belief that Roosevelt had conspired to get the United States into the war with Germany by the back door of Japan, neither he nor Theobald was ever able to produce any hard evidence to support their contention that specific intelligence revealing Japan's plan to attack Pearl Harbor had been deliberately withheld from Kimmel and Short on Roosevelt's orders. There was, however, more ammunition to support their assertion that the Hawaiian commanders had been made scapegoats by a conspiracy orchestrated by the administration in Washington. In a 1972 publication published shortly before his death, Barnes was finally obliged to concede that "there is no definitive documentary evidence which has thus far been revealed and fully proves that Roosevelt had been informed" of Japan's plans to attack Pearl Harbor.

The search for the evidence that would provide confirmation of the Roosevelt plot continued. It eluded Bruce Bartlett, whose 1978 investigation *Cover Up* revealed that in all his efforts the author had not uncovered any evidence of the president's having suppressed intelligence useful to the Hawaiian commanders. It was not until 1982, when Pulitzer Prize-winner John Toland published *Infamy,* that Toland claimed to have found the "smoking gun" that had eluded all the other the revisionists for nearly forty years. But Toland's "evidence," far from providing the proof that Roosevelt was a war criminal, turned out, on close examination, to be less than an empty holster.

The main weight of the neorevisionist case argued in *Infamy* turns on mysterious radio signals intercepted from the north Pacific that Toland asserted emanated from the Striking Force. This flew in the face of the Japanese record that Admiral Nagumo's radio operators had orders to seal their transmitters and was directly contradicted by no less an authority than Admiral Genda.[5] No radio signals that were identified as emanating from the *Strike Force* were recorded by the U.S. Navy in any of the declassified official reports. But faint signals were picked up, according to the radio operator's log of the Matson liner *Lurline*, during the first days of December as it headed on its regular run from the West Coast to Hawaii.

"The Japs are blasting away on the lower Marine Radio frequency—it is all in Japanese code, and continues for several hours," noted Leslie E. Grogan, the first assistant radio operator of the liner, on the evening of 1 December. He claimed to have detected the call letters JCS—a Yokohama station—that was "rebroadcast simultaneously" for what he and Chief Operator Rudy Asplund assumed were the "crafts with small antennas" somewhere in the Pacific. The "main body of signals came from a Northwest by West area." Their *Lurline*'s direction finding "from our second night from Los Angeles bound for Honolulu was, according to the log, "North and West of Honolulu."[6] Grogan's journal asserts that as soon as the SS *Lurline* docked at Honolulu on the morning of 3 December, he and Asplund reported the radio contacts to an officer at the 14th Naval District headquarters who "showed little outward reflection as to what we believe was a mighty serious situation."[7]

One explanation for the Navy's apparent lack of alarm was that radio direction finding by the *Lurline*'s operators could not pinpoint the source of the mysterious radio signals. Grogan could only assume they were transmissions being made from Japanese vessels in the mid-Pacific, since he had only been able to establish their general direction as northwest by west of Honolulu. They could, therefore, have originated from any point along a line reaching from the Hawaiian Islands to the Kurile chain at the other side of the Pacific or have emanated by skip reflections from the ionosphere. Toland could only speculate, based on the ex post facto rationalization of Grogan, that these coded radio messages came from a "bunched up" Japanese Striking Force as it steamed in to attack Pearl Harbor.

In another speculative leap, Toland claimed that these radio signals were the same as those picked up by commercial wire services and reported to the 12th Naval District Intelligence Office. He cited this sensational new information to "Seaman First Class Z," an electronics expert on the Intelligence Office staff who wished to remain anonymous, who claimed he had obtained "cross bearings on the mysterious signals," which he had identified as "possibly the missing carrier force" to his boss, Lieutenant Ellsworth A. Hosner.[8] Begging the question of how a radio operator in San Francisco would have known that the "missing carriers" were a striking force approaching Pearl Harbor, Toland then invited his reader to accept his presumption that the president would immediately have been informed that a hostile force was approaching Hawaii. His tenuous case rested on the fact that the chief of the 12th Naval District Intelligence Office, Captain Richard T. McCollough, "was Roosevelt's personal friend and had access to him through Harry Hopkins's telephone at the White House."[9]

There is no evidence that Roosevelt was informed, or would have been informed, by the 12th Navy District, nor is there any reason to suppose that the White House would have been made aware of the *Lurline*'s radio operator's log. The president was not called upon to evaluate such raw information, and there is no recorded evidence that these reports reached the Office of Naval Intelligence either. The reason for this is clear from the lengthy deposition that "Seaman Z," who identified himself as James D. Ogg in 1984, gave for the record to an officer of Naval Security Group Command. His recollections were neither as specific nor as sensational as Toland had made them out to be. According to Ogg's deposition, the radio transmissions that had been picked up by RCA and other commercial radio companies from 3 to 5 December contained "no reference that it was a carrier force, rather than a fishing force."[10]

Contradicting the certainty implicit in Toland's version of his story, Ogg conceded that he "could not be sure" that the transmissions in Morse were Japanese. They were on "odd frequencies" at a far lower end of the spectrum than normally used by Japan's navy. Far from pinpointing the sources as northwest of Hawaii, as Toland had categorically claimed, Ogg recalled it had been possible to establish only approximate triangulations from the shore stations, which put the transmissions on 2 December into "an area *east* of the International Dateline [emphasis added]."[11] This was also the area of the Pacific being traversed by the two Soviet freighters *Kazakhstan* and *Azerbaidjan*, and it seems likely that it was their radio transmissions that were the source of Ogg's recollection, and the mysterious signals were picked up by the *Lurline*'s radio operator.

Toland's other sensational piece of "new" evidence that Washington was aware of the incoming attack on Pearl Harbor is another leap of speculative faith over the historical record. This was his interpretation of diary entries of Captain Johann E. M. Ranneft, who since 1938 had been the naval attaché of the Netherlands in Washington. On 2 December Ranneft recorded that he had paid a visit to Admiral Wilkinson at the Office of Naval Intelligence, where he talked with Captain McCollum and Lieutenant Commander Kramer about the situation in the Pacific.

In the reproduction of this diary page that appeared in the original edition of *Infamy*, Toland incorrectly translated Ranneft's Dutch diary note. Ranneft had written that he was given the "position of two carriers . . . of Honolulu."[12] But Toland translated that to read that there was a carrier force approaching "just NORTHWEST" of Honolulu, and he asserts that his translation was endorsed by the ailing former Dutch naval attaché in an interview shortly before his death.[13] However, it is clear that what Ranneft had been told by McCollum and Kramer referred not to the Striking Force, but to one, or possibly two, carriers that HYPO and CAST traffic analysts believed might be heading for the Marshall Islands, which lay west by southwest of Hawaii. Toland's assertion would make McCollum and Kramer part of the conspiracy to deny specific intelligence of an incoming Japanese attack to the Pacific Fleet. This is at odds with McCollum's testimony that he had tried to initiate a warning, one based on a much more general assessment.

"What novelist could persuade a reader to accept the incredible activities during those two days by America's military and civilian leaders?" Toland demands rhetorically at the culmination of his revisionist thesis.[14] Basing his argument on the hearsay misreading of the radio intercepts and the mistranslation of the Dutch naval attaché's diary, he confidently asserts that the president, his closest aides, and the Office of Naval Intelligence were all aware that a Japanese task force was bearing down on Pearl Harbor on 4 December. Roosevelt, he argues, then faced "three options": to announce the fact to the world in anticipation that Japan would be forced to call off the operation; to alert the Hawaiian commanders to send out long-range patrols to "discover" this force, with the same probable result, or let the Japanese attack, in anticipation that only by keeping the Pacific Fleet in ignorance could he achieve his goal of bringing the United States into the war. The president, he argues, took a "calculated risk" by gambling that the Japanese raid would be beaten off with relatively little damage or casualties.

It stretches credibility beyond the breaking point to argue that Roosevelt's intense affection for the Navy would have allowed him to make the Pacific Fleet a tethered goat for a Japanese attack by ordering senior naval officers to withhold an unequivocal warning. Apart from the historical records being suspended and distorted to brace up the web of conspiracies in *Infamy*, there is no evidence, which can be verified, to support Toland's central theme that the president had actually been informed that a Japanese carrier task force was bearing down on Pearl Harbor. Without that essential strut, his edifice of theory, buttressed by speculation and hearsay recollection, comes tumbling down.

A similar missing dimension of historical credibility deconstructs two other key elements that Toland and other revisionists have cited in their argument that Roosevelt and his aides received advance intelligence of a Japanese attack on Pearl Harbor. They are the postwar assertions made by Duskov Popov, a Yugoslav in the pay of the German intelligence service who was acting as a British double agent, and Kilsoo Haan, an activist with the Sino-Korean People's League. Both claimed after the event that they had supplied specific information of the plan to high officials in Washington.

Popov, who was code-named "Tricycle" by the British Secret Intelligence Service—allegedly for his sexual athleticism with double female partners—was ordered by his German *Abwehr* controller to travel to the United States in the summer of 1941 to set up an espionage network. One of the questionnaires he had been given involved making a detailed survey of Pearl Harbor. His British controller flew Popov over to the United States by Pan Am Clipper at the beginning of August. He then spent a generous portion of the substantial funds the Germans had provided for his espionage mission on a succession of mistresses, whom he entertained in extravagant style in New York and Miami while he awaited American approval for a trip to Hawaii. This did nothing to recommend "Tricycle" to the fastidious director of the FBI, who, when he was finally persuaded to interview Popov, discounted him as an untrustworthy playboy.

When Popov wrote his swashbuckling memoir *Spy/Counterspy*

thirty years later, he greatly exaggerated the significance of his questionnaire as an indicator of Japan's intention to make a Taranto-style raid on Pearl Harbor.[15] Its actual wording indicates a typical espionage agent's shopping list of questions about the United States' Pacific Fortress rather than giving any specific indication that Pearl Harbor was a Japanese target. According to the declassified FBI records, it was not simply the distaste that J. Edgar Hoover personally had for Popov that led to his discounting the significance of Popov's Hawaiian mission. The director was far more interested in the "microdots" that "Tricycle" could make by photographically shrinking documents to the size of dots. The new German espionage technique rather than the contents of the message was what Hoover reported to the president in great detail. In his memorandum to the White House, he omitted any mention of Popov's Pearl Harbor questionnaire, but *did* pass it on to the Office of Naval Intelligence. They supplied the FBI with this information to feed to the Germans via Popov about fictitious "anti-torpedo" net defenses at Pearl Harbor, but did not see fit to warn Admiral Kimmel about the German espionage.[16]

Similarly in the case of Kilsoo Haan, the information that the Korean claimed to have passed to the State Department about Japan's intention to attack Pearl Harbor was more speculative than factual at the time. Haan claimed that in the fall of 1941 he had learned from contacts in the Korean underground of a source who had seen at the Japanese consulate in Honolulu blueprints of dockyard installations. Haan concluded that this meant that the Japanese intended to attack the Pacific Fleet base before Christmas. After failing to get his report taken seriously by the State Department, at the end of October 1941, Haan managed to persuade Senator Guy Gillette of Iowa of its plausibility. The senator alerted the State Department and Army and Navy intelligence of the report that the Japanese were planning an attack not only on Pearl Harbor but on the Philippines and other American bases in the Pacific.

After receiving another tip-off from the Korean underground, Haan telephoned Maxwell Hamilton of the State Department on 4 December with a warning about an attack on Pearl Harbor. He followed it up with a written report that "Japan may suddenly move against Hawaii this coming weekend." He drew this inference, it would appear, not from any specific intelligence, but from a November report of U.S. Army Air Corps maneuvers on the Hawaiian Islands due to take place "every day except Sundays and Holidays" that had appeared in a Japanese newspaper. His second source was equally indirect, an Italian newspaper forecast of war breaking out in the Pacific with a Japanese attack on Hawaii. This was pure speculation made in a Japanese book, *The Three Power Alliance and the U.S.-Japan War*, published the previous year, which alluded to the probability that war would break out with a surprise attack "aimed at Hawaii, perhaps the first Sunday of December."[17]

This was not the only Japanese or American book published before the war to predict that an attack on Pearl Harbor would be the probable opening gambit of a war in the Pacific. It had been a staple of fictional accounts and serious strategic analyses published on both sides of the Pacific. So despite postwar claims and the credence given Haan by Toland and the other revisionists, his account was neither specific nor unusual. Haan had no solid intelligence on which to base his claims, only the fragmentary and ambiguous sources in the Korean underground who were never established to have had any knowledge of the Japanese war plan. Only 20/20 hindsight lent credibility to Haan's so-called warning, which at the time was considered to be speculation based on circumstantial theorizing. Contrary to Toland's resurrection of his claim, Haan did not have anything remotely resembling "proof positive" that Japan would attack Pearl Harbor on 7 December 1941.

Appendix III

U.S. Army/Navy Organization for Signals Intelligence Nov. 1941

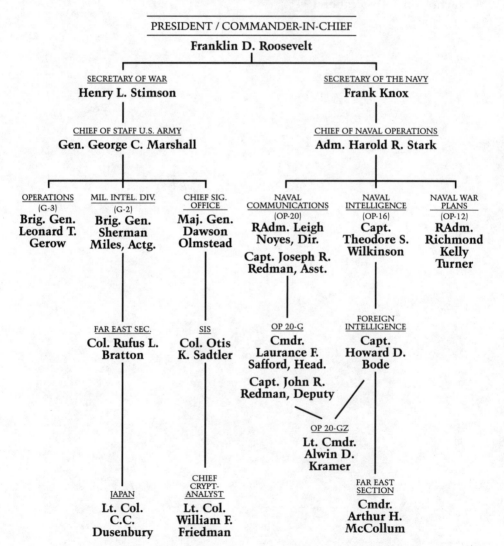

PRESIDENT / COMMANDER-IN-CHIEF
Franklin D. Roosevelt

SECRETARY OF WAR
Henry L. Stimson

SECRETARY OF THE NAVY
Frank Knox

CHIEF OF STAFF U.S. ARMY
Gen. George C. Marshall

CHIEF OF NAVAL OPERATIONS
Adm. Harold R. Stark

OPERATIONS (G-3)
Brig. Gen. Leonard T. Gerow

MIL. INTEL. DIV. (G-2)
Brig. Gen. Sherman Miles, Actg.

CHIEF SIG. OFFICE
Maj. Gen. Dawson Olmstead

NAVAL COMMUNICATIONS (OP-20)
RAdm. Leigh Noyes, Dir.
Capt. Joseph R. Redman, Asst.

NAVAL INTELLIGENCE (OP-16)
Capt. Theodore S. Wilkinson

NAVAL WAR PLANS (OP-12)
RAdm. Richmond Kelly Turner

FAR EAST SEC.
Col. Rufus L. Bratton

SIS
Col. Otis K. Sadtler

OP 20-G
Cmdr. Laurance F. Safford, Head.
Capt. John R. Redman, Deputy

FOREIGN INTELLIGENCE
Capt. Howard D. Bode

OP 20-GZ
Lt. Cmdr. Alwin D. Kramer

JAPAN
Lt. Col. C.C. Dusenbury

CHIEF CRYPT-ANALYST
Lt. Col. William F. Friedman

FAR EAST SECTION
Cmdr. Arthur H. McCollum

358

APPENDIX IV

U.S.-JAPAN STRATEGIC BALANCE OF FORCES AND TACTICAL BALANCE SHEET

NAVAL FORCES

PACIFIC FLEET	U.S.	JAPAN COMBINED FLEET
Carriers	3	10
Battleships	9	12
Cruisers	21	35
Destroyers	53	110
Submarines	23	65

THE HAWAIIAN OPERATION
7 DECEMBER

JAPANESE STRIKING FORCE
1st, 2nd, and 5th Carrier Divisions

6 Carriers
2 Battleships
3 Cruisers
9 Destroyers
3 Submarines

FIRST AIR FLEET
  1st Attack Wave
    Kate   High-level bombers   49
    Kate   Torpedo bombers   40
    Val   Dive bombers   51
    Zero   Fighters   45

  2nd Attack Wave
    Kate   High-level bombers   54
    Val   Dive bombers   80
    Zero   Fighters   36

SIXTH FLEET

                                                        25 Submarines
                                                         5 Midgets

LOSSES AND CASUALTIES

	U.S.-SUNK	DAMAGED	JAPAN-SUNK
1. SHIPS			
Battleships	4	4	1 Submarine
Cruisers		3	5 Midgets
Destroyers		3	
Others	2	2	
2. AIRCRAFT			
		165	29

	AMERICAN	JAPANESE
3. CASUALTIES		
Killed	2,403	185
Wounded	1,178	

THE PHILIPPINES

FORCES	U.S. (MACARTHUR)	JAPAN
GROUND		
Troops	11,988 Filipino	
	19,116 American	
Tanks	54	
Antiaircraft	1 Regiment	
AIR		
Fighters	175	72 Army 108 Navy
Four-engine bombers	35	
Twin-engine bombers	39	71 Army 117 Navy
Reconnaissance, etc.	58	39 Army 32 Navy
		182 257
	307	439

NAVAL	ASIATIC FLEET (HART)	
Carriers-Light		3
Cruisers	3	75 Aircraft
Destroyers	13	
Submarines	29	

JAPANESE AIR ATTACKS
8 DECEMBER

TARGET	ELEVENTH AIR FLEET (NAVY)
Clark Field	54 bombers 54 fighters
Iba Field	54 bombers 36 fighters
General Raids Luzon	FIFTH AIR GROUP (ARMY)
	71 bombers 72 fighters
Coastal Raids	75 carrier aircraft

LOSSES AND CASUALTIES

	U.S.	JAPAN
1. AIRCRAFT		
Bombers, four-engine	18	
Fighters	55	7
Others	33	
2. CASUALTIES		
Killed	80	7
Wounded	150	

GLOSSARY OF ABBREVIATIONS
AND TERMS

Adm	Admiralty (U.K.)
AAF	Army Air Forces (U.S.)
AGO	Adjutant General's Office (U.S. Army)
ALNAV	All Navy
A/CNO	Assistant Chief of Naval Operations
BatDiv	Battleship Division
BB	Battleship
BJ	Black Jumbo—decrypted SIGINT (U.K.)
BP	Bletchley Park (U.K.-GC&CS)
BUNAV	Bureau of the Navy
CA	Heavy Cruiser
CAB	Cabinet (U.K.)
CAST	Operational Intelligence Center (Naval Code-breaking Unit) Cavite/Corregidor, Philippines
CarDiv	Carrier Division
CCA	Churchill College Archive (Cambridge)
Cdr	Commander

CINCAF	Commander in Chief, Asiatic Fleet
CINCPAC	Commander in Chief, Pacific Fleet
CINCAF	Commander in Chief, Atlantic Fleet
CINCUS	Commander in Chief, U.S. Fleet
CL	Light Cruiser
CNO	Chief of Naval Operations, OPNAV
COMINT	Communications Intelligence
COM-14	Commandant, 14th Naval District (Honolulu, Hawaii)
COM-16	Commandant, 16th Naval District (Cavite, Philippines)
COS	Chief of Staff (U.S. and U.K.)
COSCombined	Chief of Staff, Combined Fleet (Japanese)
COMSCOR	Commander, Scouting Forces (Pacific Fleet)
CruDiv	Cruiser Division
CV	Fleet Carrier
CL	Light Carrier
DD	Destroyer Division
DesRon	Destroyer Division
D/F	Direction Finding
DNC	Director of Naval Communications (Op-20)
DNI	Director of Naval Intelligence (Op-16)
ENIGMA	German Encoding Machine
ECM	M-134 Encoding Machine (U.S. Navy)
FBI	Federal Bureau of Investigation
FECB	Far East Combined Bureau (U.K.)
FDRL	Franklin D. Roosevelt Memorial Library, Hyde Park, New York
FEAF	Far East Air Force (USAAFE)
FO	Foreign Office, London
FOIA	Freedom of Information Act
G-2	Director of Military Intelligence

GC&CS	Government Code and Cipher School (U.K.—Bletchley Park)
GCHQ	Government Communications Headquarters (U.K.—counterpart to NSA)
INFO	Information
HM	His/Her Majesty('s) (U.K.)
HW	Prime Minister's SIGINT Records
HYPO	Operational Intelligence Center (Naval Codebreaking Unit, Pearl Harbor, Hawaii)
JD	Japanese Diplomatic (SIGINT)
JN-25	General Purpose Fleet Code (Japanese)
LA	U.S. designation for Japanese Consular Code
MAGIC	Translations of SIGINT (U.S.)
MDLOC	Manuscript Division, Library of Congress
MI	Military Intelligence
MI6	Secret Intelligence Service (U.K.)
ND	Naval District
NEGAT	Operational Intelligence Center (Naval Codebreaking Unit, Washington, D.C.) Op-20-G
NAW	National Archives, Washington, D.C.
NSA	National Security Agency
OCS	Office of Chief of Staff (U.S. Army)
OIC	Office in Charge
OTRG	On the Roof Gang
PBY	Amphibious Patrol Aircraft *(Catalina)*
PAK-2	U.S. designation for Japanese Consular Cipher
P.H.	Pearl Harbor
PHH	Pearl Harbor Hearings (Records of Joint Congressional Investigating Committee)
PHLO	Pearl Harbor Liaison Office (Records)
PREM	Premier (Prime Ministerial Records—U.K.)
PRO	Public Records Office, Kew, England

PURPLE	American nomenclature for Japanese Diplomatic Machine Cipher
PSF	President's Secretary's File
RAdm	Rear Admiral
RAF	Royal Air Force
RG	Record Group
RI	Radio Intelligence (Includes SIGINT, D/F and T/A)
SECNAV	Secretary of the Navy
SIGABA	M-34 encoding machine U.S. Army
SIGINT	Signals Intelligence (COMINT)
SIS	Signals Intelligence Service (U.S. Army)
SIS	Secret Intelligence Service—MI6 (U.K.)
SRDJ	SIGINT Records, Diplomatic Japanese
SRH	Special Research History (SIGINT)
SRN	SIGINT Records Naval
T/A	Traffic Analysis
TYPEX	British Encoding Machine
ULTRA	TOP SECRET (U.S.), MOST SECRET (U.K.) (Security Classification for SIGINT)
USAF	U.S. Army Air Force
USAAFE	U.S. Army Air Force, Far East (FEAF)
WPD	U.S. Army War Plans Division
V/Adm	Vice Admiral

ACKNOWLEDGMENTS

Days of Infamy will certainly not be the final book about the Japanese attack on Pearl Harbor and the Philippines, but it may well be the last to be written by an author who had direct access to one of its central figures. Rear Admiral Edwin T. Layton was the Pacific Fleet intelligence officer 7 December 1941 and he was never able to recall the terrible hours of the Sunday morning without choking up. In 1981 I had already written my first account of the attack in *The Pacific War* and I was offered an introduction to the admiral by Captain Roger Pineau, who had been impressed enough by the fresh analysis I had developed from recently declassified documentation to spring to my defense after a dismissive critique of my book in the *New York Times*.

Roger, as I quickly came to appreciate, knew the Pearl Harbor story inside out. A wartime Japanese linguist with the Navy, he had become a distinguished naval historian after serving as assistant to Rear Admiral Samuel Eliot Morison during his research and writing of the official history of the U.S. Navy's operations in World War II. As our mutual respect and friendship developed, the admiral was encouraged to break forty years of silence and commit to telling his full story for the first time, which Roger and I brought to publication—after the admiral's sudden death in 1984—under the title *And I Was There: Pearl Harbor and Midway—Breaking the Secrets*.

I was not at Pearl Harbor on 7 December 1941, but in the course of researching and writing three books, as well as lecturing on its many intriguing facets, I have come to appreciate very keenly the emotive impact and fascination it still exercises on the American psyche. Serving my apprenticeship in naval intelligence alongside two such experts, I was introduced to many of their wartime colleagues, whose firsthand knowledge of code breaking and traffic analysis in the U.S. Navy during World War II helped interpret many arcane notations on the wartime decrypts of Japanese naval communications. In addition to Admiral Layton and Roger Pineau, among those veterans of the secret war of intelligence whose insights I have once more been able to draw upon are Captain Thomas H. Dyer, Captain Wesley A. Wright, Rear Admiral Robert H. R. Weeks, and Fred Woodrough.

Regrettably, since my initiation into this privileged circle twelve years ago, there have been too many somber visits to Arlington National Cemetery—including the one on a bright November day last fall to join the large and distinguished gathering who came to pay their final respects to Roger Pineau. The depth of his knowledge of the history of the United States Navy and Japan's was matched only by his profound sense of humor and fascination with the peculiarities of the English language. As a friend, mentor, collaborator, and trusty navigator for my voyage of exploration into the records of the naval war in the Pacific, Roger will be irreplaceable. It was with his encouragement that I embarked on this book—and we spent many hours testing my new theories. I can only hope that it will measure up to the standard of scholarship and integrity of the primary sources that he passed on to me from his mentor, Admiral Morison. At least he will be able to rest easy that I have remembered not to put "howevers" at the beginning of sentences as lazy conjunctions! In dedicating this work to Roger's memory, I should like to express my sincerest gratitude to Maxine Pineau, whose marvellous hospitality and charming encouragement contributed so much to the memories I have of the happy days working alongside her late husband in our quest for the ever-elusive historical truth.

Days of Infamy had its genesis in two papers on the intelligence background to the Japanese attacks on Pearl Harbor and the Philippines that I delivered to the "Gathering Storm" conference in May 1991 at Austin, Texas, and the "Storm Unleashed" conference in Honolulu that marked the fiftieth anniversary that December in Honolulu. These memorable gatherings of veterans, scholars, and the public were organized by the Admiral Nimitz Museum in conjunction with the USS *Arizona* Memorial. I owe a great debt of gratitude to Helen Macdonald, the ever-gracious and always indefatigable dynamo of the Admiral Nimitz Museum. And also to Rear Admiral D. D. Grojean, the Executive Director of the Admiral Nimitz Foundation; Bruce Smith, the Superintendent; Jerry R. Kelley, M.D.; Doug and Fran Hubbard; and all the museum staff at Fredericksburg, Texas—not least for sparking the project, but for their exceptional hospitality and for giving me access to the historical collection. The documentation assembled for the writing of this book will be donated to the Pacific Historical Studies Center for Pacific War Studies at the Nimitz Museum, and a portion of the royalties from this book will make a contribution to the George Bush Gallery of the Pacific War and the Hall of Presidents that is to be inaugurated by the former president next year, on the occasion of the fiftieth anniversary of the signing of the peace treaty with Japan.

This book could not have been written without nearly twenty years of delving into the mountain of World War II documentation in archives on both sides of the Atlantic, but at the same time I acknowledge the contribution drawn from the published and unpublished works cited in the source notes. Three generations of Pearl Harbor researchers have received the advice and assistance of John Taylor of the National Archives in Washington—and my consultations with him span more than two decades. It is a tribute to his patience and sagacity, which have always kept me abreast of each new "discovery" and every fresh "theory," and over the years have sent me down many productive paper trails. Edward R. Reese, his colleague in the Modern Military Reference Division of the Archives, has contributed much to my knowledge of MacArthur and Richard von Doenhoff and to my quest for naval documentation. To them especially, but also to Wilbur S. Mahoney, Sally Nicastro, Terri Hammet, Harry Black, and all the staff of that formidable institution on Pennsylvania Avenue in Washington, my indebtedness is great.

The staff at the Public Records Office at Kew have made a more anonymous, but equally essential, contribution, especially Dr. Andrew Macdonald and the team who manage the reprographic section and reading room. Richard D. Bone of the Foreign Office Library in London; Pat Andrews of the Cabinet Office; Norman Hopkinsson at GCHQ; and David A. Hatch, Director of the NSA's Center for Cryptologic History, have all contributed to opening doors a little wider into the still sensitive vaults of the World War II SIGINT records. The Director of the Franklin D. Roosevelt Presidential Library, Vernon Newton, and his team at Hyde Park have been generous with assistance, as has the Archives of Churchill College, Cambridge. Primary source material has also been obtained from the Naval Historical Center, Washington D.C.; the Yale University Stirling Library; Georgetown University Library; Harvard University's Houghton Library; the Library of the University of Hawaii; the Australian National War Memorial; and the Military History Section of the Royal Netherlands Army. Published records have been provided with their customary courtesy and promptness by the New York Public Library, the Library of Congress, the New York Public Library, and the Miami Beach Public Library.

Days of Infamy has benefited from the close scrutiny of former members of the intelligence community: Vice Admiral David C. Richardson; Rear Admiral Kemp Tolley; Rear Admiral Donald M. Showers; Captain Raymond P. Schmidt; Captain Thomas K. Kimmel; and David W. Gaddy, former chief historian of the NSA. My debt to them is considerable, as it also is to Professor Timothy J. Naftali; Professor Warren F. Kimball; David Khan; and Captain A. L. Beach, the noted naval historian who is currently completing *Scapegoats: The Ordeal of Admiral Kimmel and General Short*. Their constructive comments and detailed critiques have made a unique contribution to the final manuscript—and the author takes full responsibility for any irritating errors of fact or judgment.

Daniel A. Martinez, park historian at the USS *Arizona* Memorial, has been generous with his encyclopedic knowledge not only of Pearl Harbor itself, but also of the many attack sites on Oahu that provide the "feel" for time and place. Over the years that I have been honing my theories, guidance and encouragement have also been given by many scholars, but I owe a special thank-you to Professor Arthur M. Schlesinger Jr., Professor Michael J. Gannon, Dr. John W. Chapman, Dr. David G. Reynolds, Dr. D. Clayton James, Professor A. N. Yakolev, Dr. Martin Gilbert, and Dr. John Charmley. Many others have contributed to my steady accumulation of fact and anecdote about Pearl Harbor. Among those I would single out are Edward R. Kimmel and Tom K. Kimmel Jr., Dr. Dean Allard, B. F. Cavalcante, Mrs. Miriam Layton, Paul M. Stillwell, Admiral Pete W. Dillingham, Captain Prescot W. Currier, Henry P. Schorreck, Gerry Coates, the late James Rusbridger, Louis D. Tordella, Hayden B. Peak, Walter Pforzheimer, Robert T. Crowley, Peter L. Bull, Hodding Carter, Dr. Ruth Harris, John Crossland, Robert Harris, David Irving, Robert Haslach, Ned P. Schnurman, Rupert Allason, James O'Shea Wade, Bruce Lee, Commodore Bruce Loxton, Commander Raymond Mortimer, Michael Montgomery, Gervase Cowell, Ray S. Cline, Daniel J. Mulvenna, Edward B. Hanify, Dr. Bill Evans, Edward S. Miller, Frederick W. Parker, Mrs. J. Rochefort Elerding, and Richard Natkiel.

My thanks also to Oleg Tsarev in Moscow, Harald Ketzer in Frankfurt, Hans-Rudolf Zellweger in Zurich, and Jasper Wight at Cambridge University for their various contributions to the research effort—and to Felix for his knowledge of the cases of Sherlock Holmes. Matthew D. Anderson in New York and Craig Trenticosta in Miami contributed their assistance with word processing and administrative backup, for which I am indebted. For their continuing logistical support and hospitality, I extend my gratitude to Robin Wight, Kenneth Nichols, Laurence Pratt, Gary Lazarus, and Gerald P. Jantzi—with a very special thanks to Julia Wight, who makes my home away from home. To my agent, John Hawkins, of nearly two decades, I offer a unique accolade—and also to my tirelessly supportive new editor, Paul D. McCarthy; his diligent assistant, Eric Tobias; and Cecelia Hunt, whose copyediting contributed so much to the process of transforming a raw manuscript into this finely produced book. Thank you all.

Miami Beach, July 1994

_ SOURCES AND NOTES _

INTRODUCTION

1. Roosevelt's speech to Congress, 8 December 1941. Sammuel I. Rosenman, ed., *The Public Papers and Addresses of Franklin Delano Roosevelt*, 13 vols. (New York: Macmillan, 1939–1952).

2. Ibid.

3. Accounts differ about the precise timing of the Japanese air raids on Clark and Iba Fields, but there is general concurrence that they began shortly after 12:30 P.M. Philippines time and that the last attacking plan flew off from Iba some forty-five minutes later, around 12:15 A.M. Washington time on 8 December. The raid on the Philippines occurred some ten and a half hours after the attack on Pearl Harbor. The exigencies of the international date line, therefore, carried Japan's opening round of attack into a second day of infamy for the United States command in Washington.

4. A detailed analysis of Japan's belated realization of the strategic necessity for neutralizing the strategic outpost of American naval power in the central Pacific is given by John J. Spalding in *Hawaii Under the Rising Sun: Japan's Plans for Conquest After Pearl Harbor* (Honolulu: University of Hawaii Press, 1984).

5. Rainbow 5 War Plan as revised 19 November 1941. Louis Morton, *Strategy and Command: The First Two Years* (Washington: Office of the Chief of Military History, Department of the Army, 1943) 67.

6. Francis B. Sayre, *Glad Adventure* (New York: Macmillan, 1957) 223.

7. Claire L. Chennault, *Way of a Fighter: The Memoirs of Claire Lee Chennault*, Robert Hotz, ed. (New York: G.P. Putnam's Sons, 1949) 124.

8. Interview with Whitcomb, *Escape from Corregidor* (Chicago: Henry Regnery, 1958) 23 (hereafter Whitcomb, *Corregidor*).

9. *Report of the Joint Committee on the Investigation of the Pearl Harbor Attack, 79th Congress, 2nd Session, 1946. Hearings before the Joint Committee on the Investigation of the Pearl Harbor Attack Congress of the United States, 1st Ses-*

sion, 39 Vols. (Washington, D.C.: U.S. Government Printing Office, 1946) [hereafter PHH Vol. No.]

10. Edward H. Carr, *What Is History* (New York: Vintage Books, 1961) 35.

11. Edward S. Miller, *War Plan Orange: The U.S. Strategy to Defeat Japan 1897–1945* (Annapolis: U.S. Naval Institute Press, 1991) 279.

12. Maurice Matloof and Edwin M. Snell, *Strategic Planning for Coalition Warfare: 1941–1942* (Washington, D.C.: Office of the Chief of History, U.S. Army, 1953) 75.

CHAPTER ONE

1. Quoted in John J. Beck, *MacArthur and Wainwright* (Albuquerque: University of New Mexico, 1974), 11 (hereafter Beck, *MacArthur*).

2. Quoted in Stanley Weintraub, *Long Day's Journey into War: 7 December 1941* (New York: Dutton, 1991), 277 (hereafter Weintraub, *War*).

3. Diary entry, 7 December 1941 "War Diary of Rear Admiral Thomas C. Hart," CinC Asiatic Fleet, U.S. Navy Historical Center, Navy Yard, Washington, D.C.

4. Ibid.

5. 1 Cor. 14:8, Holy Bible, King James Version.

6. *Hearings Before the Joint Committee on the Investigation of the Pearl Harbor Attack*, 79th Cong. (Washington, D.C.: U.S. Government Printing Office, 1946) 8:3829 (hereafter PHH vol:p).

7. Handwritten note on diary page, 7 December 1941 and typed memorandum of events, Folder 19, Box 6, Papers of Harry H. Hopkins, Georgetown University Library, Washington, D.C.

8. Louis Morton, "The Fall of the Philippines," *United States Army in World War II: The War in the Pacific* (Washington, D.C.: Office of Military of History, Department of the Army, 1953), 80–82 (hereafter Morton, *Philippines*). Original radiogram #737 signed by General Marshall, in War Plans Division, "General Correspondence 1920–1942," WPD 4557/4, Box 254, Record Group 165, National Archives, Washington, D.C. (hereafter RG NAW).

9. D. Clayton James, *The Years of MacArthur 1880–1964*, 3 vols. (Boston: Houghton Mifflin, 1970), 1:619 (hereafter James, *MacArthur 1*).

10. Record of telephone conversation between Gerow and MacArthur, 7 December 1941, War Plans Division Records, WPD 4622, quoted in Forrest C. Pogue, *Ordeal and Hope 1939–1942*, vol. 2 of *George C. Marshall* (New York: Viking, 1966) 233 (hereafter Pogue, *Marshall 2*).

11. Douglas MacArthur, *Reminiscences* (New York: McGraw Hill, 1964), 117.

12. WPD 4622, quoted in Pogue, *Marshall*, Vol. 2, 233.

13. Ibid.

14. Chief of Staff letter to Commanding Generals USAFFE dealing with War Plan Rainbow 5, WPD 4402–112, cited in Morton, *Philippines*, 82.

15. Lewis H. Brereton, *The Brereton Diaries: The War in the Air in the Pacific, Middle East and Europe 3 October 1941–8 May 1945* (New York: William Morrow, 1946), 38. Entries for 8 December and 7 December. The diaries were written up some time after the events they describe and cannot be regarded as entirely objective since their author was an interested party to the dispute over the command decision to hold back the Formosan bombing raid.

16. Captain Takahashi Chihaya, interviewed 20 October 1945, no. 74, "Interrogations of Japanese Officials by Naval Analysis Division, "*United States Strategic Bombing Survey (Pacific)*, vol. 1 (Washington, D.C.: U.S. Government Printing Office, 1946), 74–76 (hereafter USSBS 1).

17. Wesley Frank Craven and James Lea Cate, vol. 1 of *The Army Air Forces in World War II Plans and Early Operations—January 1939 to August 1942*, (Chicago: Office of Air Force History, University of Chicago Press, 1948), 204 (hereafter Craven and Cate, *USAAF 1*).

18. Ibid.

19. Ibid.

20. Colonel Eubank quoted in Walter D. Edmonds, "What Happened at Clark Field," *The Atlantic Monthly* (July 1951):19.

21. Ibid.

22. Koichi Shimada quoted in Weintraub, *War*, 453.

23. Brereton, *Diaries*, 38.

24. Sutherland interview, 12 November 1946, quoted in Morton, *Philippines*, 83.

25. Ibid., 39.

26. Ibid.

27. Allison Ind, *Bataan, the Judgement Seat: The Saga of the Philippine Command of the United States Army Air Force, May 1941 to May 1942* (New York: Macmillan 1944), 91 (hereafter Ind, *Bataan*).

28. Colonel Eade interview, 6 April 1944, quoted in Craven and Cate, *USAAF* 1: 687n.

29. Ibid.

30. War Warning of 27 November, Marshall to MacArthur, Radiogram, No.: 624 General Correspondence of War Department 1941, WPD 4544–13 RG 165 NAW.

31. Brereton, *Diaries*, 34–35.

32. Sutherland, quoted in Morton, *Philippines*, 83.

33. Ibid.

34. Ind, *Bataan* 92.

35. Brereton, *Diaries*, 35.

36. Ibid.

37. Notes of Mrs. Henry R. Luce's interview with Major General Lewis Brereton, April 1942 Center for Military History, Ft. McNair Washington. Quoted in James, *MacArthur* 2:831.

38. Reconstructed Journals of 24th Pursuit Group and 19th Bomber Group, as they appear in "Papers of General Sutherland," Box 1, RG 200, NAW.

39. Morton, *Philippines*, 84–5.

40. Clayton James, "MacArthur 1941–1945," 95.

41. General Moore, interview, May 1991 *"The Hunt for the Pearl Harbor Files,"* hosted by Hodding Carter III, The Discovery Channel, broadcast on 7 December 1991. TV documentary.

42. General MacArthur's answers to questionnaire submitted by Dr. Louis Morton, 18 February 1954, Morton Papers, Misc. 201, Center for Military History, Ft. McNair Washington, D.C. (hereafter CMH). Quoted in full in James, *MacArthur* 2:11.

43. *New York Times*, 28 September 1946.

44. Morton, *Philippines*, 89.

45. Sutherland, quoted in Morton, *Philippines*, 89.

46. Summary of Activities quoted by Craven and Cate, *USAAF* 1:206. This notes that the *FEAF HQ Summary* appears to have been typed up a month or so after the attack and there are certain discrepancies in dating (the entries for 8, 9, 10 December are given as 1942 not 1941). Its cover notes that it was "General Brereton's Headquarters Diary 8 December 41–24 February 1942. "According to the U.S. Army Air Force historians, it probably represents a "compilation taken from available records for assistance in the preparation of such a report as is understood to have been made by General Brereton in late January or early February 1942" for General Arnold, which subsequently disappeared. "Whatever the case, the fullness and exactness of detail given, together with the fact that at so many points independent corroboration can be had," led the official historians to conclude that "the document represents a valuable record compiled closer to the events described than any other known source of comparable scope."

47. Commander Ryosuke Nomura, 1:28 November 1945, no. 601, and Captain Takahashi Chihaya, 20 October 1945, no. 74, USSBS 1:74–5; 2:531.

48. Morton, *Philippines*, 83, citing 5th Air Group and 11 Air Fleet operational records.

49. Captain Gary Anloff, interview, in Weintraub, *War, 345*.

50. *FEAF HQ Summary*, Craven and Cate, *USAAF* 1:207–8.

51. Ibid.

52. Henry H. Arnold, *Global Mission* (New York: Harper Bros., 1946), 272.

53. Beck, *MacArthur*, 13.

54. Brereton, *Diaries*, 40.

55. *FEAF HQ Summary*, op. cit.

56. Ibid.

57. *FEAF HQ Summary*, op. cit.

58. Arnold to MacArthur, Radiogram #749, Adjutant General Office, "FAR EAST," Radiograms 11-27-41–12-10-41," Box 648, RG 407, NAW.

59. *FEAF HQ Summary*, op. cit.

60. Brereton *Diaries* p. 40. Sutherland, when interviewed by Morton, denied any direct exchanges had taken place between Brereton and MacArthur.

61. *FEAF HQ Summary*, op. cit.

62. Brereton, *Diaries*, 41.

63. *FEAF HQ Summary*, op. cit.

64. Ibid.

65. Ibid.

66. Ibid.

67. Reconstructed Group Journals 1941–2, 24 Pursuit Group & 19th Bombardment Group, Sutherland Papers, Box 1 of 36, RG 200, NAW.

68. Interviews quoted in Weintraub, *War*, 519.

69. Ibid.

70. William Manchester, *An American Caesar: General Douglas MacArthur 1880–1964* (Boston: Little Brown, 1978), 211.

71. E.B. Miller, *Bataan Uncensored* (Boston: Houghton and Mifflin, 1949), 66.

72. Quoted from firsthand account of seeing his friend in hospital after the raid in "Reminiscences of Lieutenant Colonel Howard W. Brown," prepared under Direction of Chief of Signal Office, 4 August 1945, Special Research History 106 RG 457 NAW.

73. Ibid.

74. Ind, *Bataan*, 100–1.

75. Interview quoted in Weintraub, *War*, 521.

76. Ibid., and interview of Saburo Sakai, Oral History Program for Pacific Studies Center, Admiral Nimitz Museum, Fredericksburg, Texas (hereafter Nimitz Museum).

77. Victor Mapes, letter, in Weintraub, *War*, 520.

78. Anton Bilek, letter, in Weintraub, *War*, 521.

79. Whitcomb, *Corregidor*, 20.

80. Quoted in Weintraub, *War*, 526.

81. Jonathan M. Wainright, *General Wainwright's Story* (Doubleday: New York, 1946), 23.

82. Samuel Grashio interview in Weintraub, *War*, 527.

83. Miller, *Bataan Uncensored*, 71.

84. Colonel Eugene L. Eubank, quoted in Weintraub, *War*, 529.

85. The official casualty list given by MacArthur's headquarters to the War Department at the time reported 55 dead and 110 wounded. But these figures do not agree with those given by eyewitnesses. General Wainright wrote that "ninety-three were killed at Clark" and an airman at Iba recorded that 45 died at this airfield.

86. Brereton, *Diaries*, 64.

87. Press Release, 8 December 1941, 9:00 P.M., Sutherland Papers, RG 200, NAW.

88. Radiogram #1133, Manila to Adjutant General's Office War Department, received 1:10 A.M. EST, 8 December 1941, AGO 381, Box 648, RG 407, NAW.

89. Radiogram #1135, Manila to AGO, 9 December 1941, AGO 381, Box 648, RG 407, NAW.

90. Ibid.; quoted in full in Arnold, *Global Mission*, 272.

91. Ibid.

92. Colonel Constant, interview, Morton Papers, CHM; quoted in Weintraub, *War*, 574.

93. *Triumph in the Philippines*, quoted in Weintraub, *War*, 577.

94. Ibid.

95. Arnold, *Global Mission*, 272. Brereton, *Diaries*, 50.

96. Brereton, *Diaries*, 50.

97. Ibid.

98. Lt. General Richard K. Sutherland, interview with Walter D. Edmonds, Manila, 4 June 1945, as quoted in Craven and Cate, *USAAF* 1, 204.

99. Brereton, *Diaries*, 64.

100. Ibid.

101. Ibid.

102. Ibid.

103. Arnold, *Global Mission*, 272.

104. Ibid.

105. Chihaya interview, USSBS 1:74.

106. 27 November 1941, Warning, AGO 381, Box 648, RG 407, NAW.

107. *Diaries*, Colonel Harold H. George quoted in Weintraub *War*, 240.

108. Morton, *Philippines*, 88.

109. Ibid., 90.

110. Ibid., 84–5.

111. Manchester, *Caesar*, 156. Manchester draws a comparison between MacArthur's paralysis during the opening hours of the war with a computer overload.

CHAPTER TWO

1. PHH 14:943.
2. PHH 1:282.
3. Ibid.
4. PHH 1:305–6.
5. Ibid.
6. George C. Dyer, *On the Treadmill to Pearl Harbor: The Memoirs of Admiral James O. Richardson* (Washington, D.C.: Naval History Division, Dept of Navy, 1973), 435.
7. PHH 24:1363.
8. Ibid.
9. Ibid.
10. PHH 14:1042.
11. Ibid.
12. Testimony of Captain Roscoe E. Schuirmann, naval liaison officer, to State Department, PHH 26:450–1.
13. Ibid. Letter, CNO to CINPAC, 1 February 1941. No connection has ever been found to substantiate that the rumor was anything more than cocktail party gossip. There was nothing particularly surprising or authoritative about Grew's report. There had been many fictionalized accounts in the interwar years that if Japan went to war with the United States, it would be launched by a surprise attack on Pearl Harbor. Admiral Layton recalled translating such an account by Shigeru Hata, *Warera moshi tatkawaba* [*When We Fight*] (Tokyo: Kodansha, 1933). It is significant that the War Plans Division was simultaneously exercised by a concern that "if war eventuates with Japan, it is believed easily possible that hostilities would be preceded by a surprise attack on the Pacific Fleet naval base at Pearl Harbor." This from a January 1941 memo: Secretary of Navy to Secretary of War, ref A–7–2(2)FF1, U.S. Navy Operational Archives, Strategic Plans Records, Navy Yard, Washington, D.C.
14. PHH 33:683.
15. Maurice Matloff and Edwin M. Snell, *Strategic Planning for Coalition Warfare: 1941–1942* (Washington, D.C.: Office of the Chief of Military History, U.S. Army, 1953), 75 (hereafter Matloff and Snell, *Coalition Warfare*).
16. General Council Meeting memo, 19 February 1941, Box 888, Records of Office of Chief of Staff, RG 165, NAW. Quoted in Jonathan G. Utley, *Going to War with Japan* (Knoxville: Tennessee University, 1985), 112.
17. Hornbeck memorandum, 6 June 1940, State Department Records, U.S.-Japan 1940–1941, 711.94/1564, RG 59, NAW.
18. Loomis memorandum, 6 October 1940, WPD, 3251–37, RG 165, NAW.
19. Memorandum to Army Chief of Staff from Chief of Staff War Plans Division, 20 November 1940, WPD 3251–39, RG 165, NAW.
20. Ibid.
21. MacArthur letter to Steve Early, 21 March 1941, 400, Franklin D. Roosevelt Library, Hyde Park N.Y. (hereafter FDRL).
22. James, *MacArthur* 1:585.

23. Marshall to MacArthur, 20 June 1941, OCS 20850–15, quoted in James, *MacArthur* 1:592–3.

24. Nobutake Ike (Ed) *Japan's Decision for War: Records of 1941 Foreign Policy Conferences* (Stanford: Stanford University Press, 1967), 77–90.

25. Preliminary Historical Report on the Solution of the 'B' Machine," by William F. Friedman, December 1945, SRH 159, RG457, NAW. The first detailed and authoritative account of how Purple was broken was provided by David Kahn in his seminal history of cryptology, *The Codebreakers* (New York, Macmillan, 1967), 18–23.

26. Theodore M. Hannah, "Frank B. Rowlett," *Cryptologic Spectrum* (Spring 1981), 16.

27. Tokyo to Berlin 7 July 1941 SRDJ12727, RG457, NAW.

28. PHH 14:1398.

29. PHH 5:2384.

30. PHH 14:1398.

31. Roosevelt, quoted in James M. Burns, *Roosevelt: The Soldier of Freedom 1940–1945* (New York: Harcourt Brace Jovanovich, 1970), 107.

32. Harold L. Ickes, *The Lowering Clouds 1939–1941*, vol. II of *The Secret Diary of Harold L. Ickes* (New York: Simon & Schuster, 1954), 583–4.

33. PHH 14:1398.

34. Ibid.

35. PHH 6:2512.

36. PHH 16:2173.

37. PHH 14:1399.

38. Analysis of call signs and Combined Fleet radio traffic in April 1941 had established the formation of the 1st Air Fleet as a new command under Admiral Chuichi Nagumo linked with the Carrier Division 1—Flagship *Akagi*, Japan's biggest thirty-thousand-ton carriers—and Carrier Division 2 made up of the newer *Sooryu* and *Hiryu*. The light carriers *Ryujo* and *Hosho* had been established as comprising Carrier Division 3. Carrier Division 4 contained the new twenty-thousand-ton *Shokaku* and *Zuikaku*, while Carrier Division 5 was made up of the auxiliary carriers converted from two merchant ships. The battleships and cruisers of the Combined Fleet were known to operate as the 1st Fleet, or main battle force, and the 2nd Fleet, a scouting force, while a 3rd Fleet of light cruisers, destroyers, and transports operated as a blockade and transport force.

39. Interrogations of Japanese prisoners after the war confirmed that Carrier Division 2 had provided the covering force for the Indochina operation. What was not discovered at the time was that on their trip back to Japan they had rendezvoused with Carrier Division 1 to practice combat maneuvers that were crucial in the planning of the Pearl Harbor attack.

40. PHH 7:7130.

41. For a detailed analysis of the respective roles by Acheson and Ickes in engineering the total embargo, see Utley, *Going to War with Japan*, 151–3.

42. *The New York Times*, 27 July 1941.

43. Frazier Hunt, *The Untold Story of Douglas MacArthur* (New York: Scribners, 1954), 210.

44. Secretary of War to President, 20 June 1941, formerly Top Secret Correspondence of Secretary of War—July 1940–September 1945 ("Safe File"), Box 11 "Philippines," RG 107, NAW (hereafter Stimson, "Safe File").

45. Quoted in James, *MacArthur* 1:591.

46. Ibid.

47. Letter, 6 October 1941, from MacArthur to John Callan O'Laughlin, editor, *Army & Navy Journal*, O'Loughlin Papers, Manuscript Division, Library of Congress, Washington, D.C. (hereafter MDLOC).

48. Radiogram #1712, 28 July 1941, quoted in Morton *Philippines* p. 31.

49. James, *MacArthur* 1:609.

50. Conclusions of the Majority, *Report of Joint Committee on the Investigation of the Pearl Harbor Attack, 79th Congress of the United States* (Washington D.C.: US Government Printing Office, 1946), 96.

Chapter Three

1. Minutes of the session of British and American chiefs of staff, 11 August 1941, aboard *Prince of Wales*, Records of U.S. Army Air Forces 1939–42, Classified, Central Decimal File, "Conference," 293, RG 18, NAW.

2. Author interview in 1973 with Admiral of the Fleet Sir Bruce Fraser, who in 1940 had been director of naval construction at the British Admiralty.

3. Minutes of 11 August 1941, Session of U.S. and British chiefs of staff, op. cit.

4. British Chiefs of Staff Report, COS (40) 592, 31 July 1940 Cab 66/10, Public Records Office, Kew, UK (hereafter PRO).

5. The British archives contain no record of the loss of the cabinet papers when the *Automedon* was captured. The documentation is in the captured German naval records: telegrams and war diary of Rear Admiral Paul Wenneker, German naval attaché in Tokyo, "T" series, Microfilms, NAW.

6. Telegrams from Wenneker to Berlin, 7 December 1940, SRNA 0020, RG 457, NAW. The Wenneker diary has been translated by Professor J.M.W. Chapman and quoted in "Forty Years On—The Imperial Japanese Navy, The European War and the Tripartite Pact" in 1980 *Proceedings of British American Japan Society*, vol. 1, part 1. See also "The Sinking of the *Nanking* and the Capture of the *Automedon*," James Rusbridger, *Encounter* 64, no. 5 (1985).

7. Telegram for President from Naval Person (Churchill), 15 May 1940, in Warren Kimball, ed. *Churchill & Roosevelt: The Complete Correspondence*, vol. 1 (Princeton: Princeton University, 1984), 37–8 (hereafter Kimball, *Churchill & Roosevelt*).

8. Telegram for President from Former Naval Person, 8 October 1940, ibid., 74.

9. Cited in J.R.M. Butler, *September 1939–June 1941*, vol. 2 of *Grand Strategy*, (London: HM Stationery Office, 1957), 493.

10. Cable to Prime Minister John Curtin, December 1940, Cab 65/22 or 23, PRO.

11. For President from Mr. Churchill, 15 February 1941, Kimball, *Churchill & Roosevelt*, 136.

12. Referred to in a note to the Prime Minister of Defense on "Control of the United States Air Force," 14 October 1941, Prem 3/156/6, PRO.

13. Reference to telegram 2727, 21 May 1941, in the memorandum on the chronological record of the U.S.-Japanese discussions, FO 371/2794, PRO.

14. Ibid.

15. War Cabinet 72nd Meeting, 21 July 1941, Conclusions to Minute 10, Confidential Annex, CAB 65/23, PRO.

16. Confidential Annex, 28 July 1941, Cab 65/23, PRO.

17. Ibid.

18. Confidential Annex, 28 July 1941, Cab 65/23, PRO.

19. Ibid.

20. Note for the Prime Minister on "Reinforcement of the Philippines" from General Ismay, 14 October 1941, Prem 3/156/6, PRO.

21. "Notes on Chiefs of Staff Conference," 11–12 August 1941, p. 4, Memo for Chief of Staff Records of the Army Air Forces, RG 18, NAW.

22. Arnold, *Global Mission*, p. 261.

23. The B-17 "C" models supplied to Britain were equipped with only four handheld guns, not the ten to twelve .50 caliber machine guns, including the underbelly and tail turrets, built into the later versions. They were also fitted with inferior Sperry bombsights, which were less accurate than the top-secret Norden model. Mechanical and aerodynamic fixes, including more extensive armor and a redesigned tail were being incorporated by Boeing in the B-17 "D" version that came off the production lines at its Seattle plant by the late summer of 1941.

24. Memorandum for Chief of Army Air Forces, 27 July 1941, File 451.1 Foreign Files, Philippines Islands, AIR AG, Central Decimal File, AAF Records, RG 18, NAW.

25. Brief of Information and Decisions at War Council Meeting, 28 July 1941, Secretary War Conferences, Chief of Staff Secretariat 1938–2, War Department Staff Records, RG 165, NAW.

26. "Afterthoughts of dinner—highlights of Churchill's speech 10 August 1941," Arnold Diary Notes 1941, Papers of General Henry H. Arnold, MDLOC.

27. Handwritten entry for 9 August in manuscript of the private diary of Sir Alexander Cadogan, ACAD 1/10, Churchill College Archives, Cambridge University, (hereafter CCAC).

28. Most Secret dispatch, Prime Minister to Deputy Prime Minister, 11 August 1941, Prem 3/485/1, PRO.

29. 19 August 84 Meeting, Confidential Annex, Cab 65/13, PRO.

30. Cadogan diary, 11 August, ACAD 1/10, CCAC.

31. It was an issue pursued by the congressional investigators in their questioning of Secretary Hull. He had not been present at the Atlantic Charter summit, but his assistant secretary of state, Sumner Welles, had been there and came in for a searching examination. Welles hewed to the line that no formal arrangements had been made but admitted that he had not been party to the private meetings between Roosevelt and Churchill, when what amounted to a "gentlemen's agreement" of U.S. support in the Far East was given to Churchill by Roosevelt. PHH 1:458–553.

32. General Arnold's Diary Notes, 12 August 1941.

33. Ibid.

34. "Notes on Staff Conference," 11–12 August 1941.

35. Initialed note to the Prime Minister from Anthony Eden, 2 August 1941, Prem 3/156/6, PRO.

36. Ibid.

37. Arnold diary note, 14 August 1941, op. cit.

38. Confidential Annex 108th War Cabinet Meeting, 3 November 1941, Cab 65/24 PRO.

39. Ibid.

40. Exchange of cables with British ambassador in Washington 1–7 December 1941, Prem 3/158/6, PRO.

41. *Japan 1941*, vol. 2 of *Papers Relating to the Foreign Policy of the United States* (Washington, DC: U.S. Government Printing Office, 1946) 355 (hereafter PRFPUS Japan 2).

42. Record of Parliamentary Debates—House of Commons, 27 January 1941, *Hansard*, (London, HMSO 1941), 607.

43. Ibid.

44. Ibid.

45. Memo 21 January 1941, Hopkins Papers FDRL.

46. Minutes of Meeting 4 September 1941. Records of Joint Army and Navy Boards and Committees, RG 225, NAW (hereafter Joint Board).

47. Joint Board Minutes 3 November 1941.

48. In reference to this meeting, Stark was asked by Senator Lucas, "While you discussed, from time to time matters with the British and Dutch and about what should be done in the event you all got into war, at no time was any formal agreement drawn up by the President of the United States?" The chief of naval operations rejoined, "And on which would be predicated a forecast that if the British or Netherlands East Indies were attacked we could come in?" PHH 5:2469.

49. Quoted in Roger Pineau "Admiral Yamamoto," *The War Lords: Military Commanders of the Twentieth Century*, ed. Field Marshal Lord Carver (Boston: Little Brown, 1976), 396–7.

50. Washington to Tokyo, 8 August 1941, SIS 21151, SRDJ 014152, RG 457, NAW.

51. Takushiro Hattori, *Dai-Toa Senso Zenshi: A Complete History of the Greater East Asia War* (Tokyo: Haro, Shoko, 1953), vol. 1, 178; Translations made of U.S. Army Military Intelligence in 1953, Document 77510, 500th Military Intelligence Group, AF-8-5.1, vol. 1.

52. Quoted in Nobutake Ike, ed., *Japan's Decision for War: Records of the 1941 Policy Conferences* (Stanford: Stanford University, 1961) 95–6.

53. Quoted in Robert J.C. Butow, *Tojo and the Coming of War* (Stanford: Stanford University, 1961), 258.

54. Ibid.

55. Ike, *Japan's Decision for War*, 133.

56. COS Memorandum, "Reinforcement of the Philippines," 14 August 1941, from Brigadier General L.T. Gerow, COS, File, "The Philippines," RG 165, NAW.

57. Pogue, *Marshall* 2:186.

58. Pogue, *Marshall* 2:187.

59. Memorandum for Secretary of War, from COS War Plans General Gerow, 8 October 1941, Stimson "Safe File," Philippines Folder, Box 11, RG 107, NAW.

60. PHH 14:1031.

61. Memorandum "Aircraft Requirements for Defences of the Western Hemisphere and American Interests in Asia," 26 August 1941, Entry 93, Series II, Central Decimal Files 1939–1942 381.D, "War Plans 1941," RG 18, NAW.

62. PHH 3:1120.

63. PHH 3:1119.

64. PHH 3:1120.

65. Memorandum "Aircraft Requirements for Defences of the Western Hemisphere" op. cit.

66. Joint Board Minutes, 19 September 1941, RG 225, NAW.

67. PHH 3:1119.

CHAPTER FOUR

1. "There is a homely adage: 'Speak softly and carry a big stick; you will go far.' If the American nation will speak softly and yet build and keep at a pitch of the highest training a thoroughly efficient Navy, the Monroe Doctrine will go far." Theodore Roosevelt, speaking in Chicago, 3 April 1903, reported in the *New York Times*, 4 April 1903.

2. Letter to the President of 21 October 1941 White House Box 11, RG 107, NAW.

3. Ibid.

4. Stimson's 21 October 1941 letter to the President, "Safe File," Box 11, RG 107, NAW.

5. Ibid.

6. Memorandum for Harry Hopkins "Please speak to me about this. I am a bit bewildered, FDR," 25 October 1941, Private Secretary's File, FDRL (hereafter PSF FDRL).

7. "Strategic Concept of the Philippine Islands," 8 October 1941, Army Chief of Staff, Memorandum for Secretary of War from Acting Assistant Chief of Staff, RG 165, NAW.

8. Roosevelt from Churchill, 5 November 1941, Kimball, *Churchill & Roosevelt*, 266.

9. Ibid.

10. Ibid.

11. Roosevelt to Churchill, 7 November 1941, Kimball, *Churchill & Roosevelt*, 267.

12. Stimson Diary, 7 November 1941. There are two typewritten drafts of the so-called Stimson diary in the "Pearl Harbor Liaison Office Files" in the National Archives. The first is a running, abbreviated chronology and a fuller version similar to the version in the Yale collection of the Stimson Papers. The gist is the same, although the wording sometimes differs. The citations in "Stimson Diary" are from the longer version unless otherwise stated. (PHLO) RG 80, NAW. A copy of the short version can also be found in The Pearl Harbor Investigation Records "Joint Committee File," Box 333, RG 128, NAW.

13. MacArthur's cable to Marshall, 30 August, as relayed to the President on 9 September James MacArthur, II p.612–3.

14. Ibid.

15. Philippines memo, "Air Offensive Against Japan," prepared for General Staff, 6 November 1941, by Brigadier General Laurence S. Kuter, COS, Decimal File 1941–3, RG 165, NAW.

16. Memorandum written by Robert Sherrod, one of the reporters who attended the conference, in the possession of the George C. Marshall Foundation, Lexington, Va. Quoted in Michael S. Sherry, *The Rise of American Air Powers: The Creation of Armageddon* (New Haven: Yale University, 1991), 109.

17. Ibid.

18. Ibid.

19. "Status of incendiary bombs for the Philippines," 5 September 1941, Diary Chief of Air Staff, File 336, Central Decimal 1939–42, AAF Records, RG 165, NAW.

20. *New York Times*, 15 November 1941.

21. Kuter Memorandum op. cit.

22. Ibid.

23. Admiral Hart War Diary entries 15–30 September 1941, U.S. Navy Operational Archives, Washington Navy Yard (hereafter NOA); Copy of memorandum "Control of Air Operations Over Water" to CinC U.S. Asiatic Fleet, 7 November 1941, AG381, COS Files, RG 165, NAW.

24. PHH 3:1167.

25. Ibid.

26. Secretary of War to President, 21 October 1941, PSF FDRL.

27. Robert J.C. Butow, *Tojo and the Coming of War*, 263.

28. PHH 14:1402.

29. PHH 16:2212.

30. PHH 16:2212.

31. PHH 14:1402.

32. PHH 16:2219.

33. Ibid., 2215.

34. PHH 32:191.

35. PHH 18:3197–8.

36. PHH 14:1402.

37. Ibid.

38. Entry for 23 November 1941 in the typewritten "Confidential" version of manuscript diary of Lord Halifax, Borthwick Institute, Garrowby Hall, Yorkshire (hereafter Halifax "Confidential" Diary). Halifax had a second version prepared that was nonconfidential.

39. Ibid.

40. Starting on 5 November with a message containing the telltale phrase "it is absolutely necessary that all arrangements for the signing of this agreement be completed by 25th of this month," the instructions to the Japanese embassy in Washington indicated Tokyo's timetable. An 11 November dispatch urged the ambassador that because "time was becoming short," he had to "redouble" his already "strenuous efforts" to meet the "absolutely immovable" and "definite deadline" for a settlement on terms dictated by Tokyo. On 15 November the ambassador was reminded that the 25 November deadline was "an absolutely immovable one" and that he had to "make the United States see the light." The very next day the ambassador was urged to "fight harder than you ever did before" because "there will be no change" in the deadline because of the necessity for "an immediate solution." In response to Nomura's plea for more time, they were told on 22 November "there are reasons beyond your ability to guess why we wanted to settle Japanese-American relations by the 25th," that if they could have four more days after that "things are automatically going to happen." Forty-eight hours later the emissaries declared that the "new time limit" of 29 November referred to Tokyo time, 28 November in Washington. PHH 12:100–65 passim.

41. SRDJ 011563, JD-09. Tokyo-Washington, 5 May 1941. Copies of this and associated signals can also be found in U.S. Navy Department Pearl Harbor Liai-

son Office, Box 62, RG 80, NAW (hereafter PHLO). Precisely what codes were vulnerable was not clear, but it is clear from the subsequent intercepted messages that the source of this warning was Berlin. It appears that the Germans had intercepted a reference to a conversation Admiral Nomura had in Washington when it was relayed in a report that the British embassy sent to London by mistake; it was in a low-grade diplomatic cipher, which the Germans had broken. Since the exchanges about security were sent in Purple, it was clear that the Japanese still believed that this cipher system remained secure. For a full analysis of this theory see Dr. Ruth Harris, "The Magic Leak of 1941 and Japanese-American Relations," *Pacific Quarterly*, 61 (February 1981), 77–96.

42. "Signal Intelligence Disclosures in the Pearl Harbor Investigations," SRH 154, RG 457, NAW.

43. PHH 11:5475.

44. PHH 11:5476.

45. Quoted in Hiroyuki Agawa, *The Reluctant Admiral: Yamamoto and the Imperial Navy* (New York: Kodansha International, 1979), 235.

46. Ibid., 237.

47. Hattori *Dai-Toa* 1, 197.

48. PHH 14:1052.

49. Joint Board Minutes, 3 November 1941, RG 225, NAW.

50. Ibid.

51. Ibid.

52. Ibid.

53. Ibid.

54. PHH 16:2222.

55. Memo to First Sea Lord, 29 August 1941, Prem 3 183/2, PRO.

56. Telegram from Prime Minister to President, 2 November 1941, Kimball, *Churchill & Roosevelt*, 265.

57. Churchill telegram from Smuts, 16 November 1941, Prem 3 163/3, PRO.

58. PHH 12:97.

59. PHH 12:94.

60. PHH 12:98.

61. Ibid., 99–100.

62. PHH 2:429.

63. Ibid.

64. Tokyo-Washington, 11 November 1941, SRDJ 016641, RG 407, NAW.

65. Tokyo-Washington, 15 November 1941, SRDJ 016576, RG 457, NAW.

66. Washington-Tokyo, 17 November 1941, SRDJ 016844, RG 457, NAW.

67. Ibid.

68. Cable from John Hay Whitney to Donovan, #5392, 12 November 1941, PSF Donovan, FDRL.

69. Washington-Tokyo, 17 November 1941, SRDJ 016844, RG 457, NAW.

70. Halifax to Foreign Office, 17 November 1941, #12475, FO 371/27913, PRO.

71. PRFPUS Japan 1941 Vol 4, pp 606-13.

72. Conversation reported in Washington-Tokyo, 18 November 1941, SRDJ 016777, RG 457, NAW.

73. Tokyo-Washington, 22 November 1941 SRDJ 016816, RG 457, NAW.

74. Washington-Tokyo, 24 November 1941, SRDJ 016855, RG 457, NAW.

75. Tokyo-Washington, 22 November 1941, SRDJ 016816, RG 457, NAW.

76. Ibid.

77. Hull, written testimony, PHH 2:404, and oral examination, PHH 2:554.

78. PRFPUS Japan Vol 2 1941 p. 755.

79. Hull to Hornbeck letter, 27 November, in response to Hornbeck to Hull memorandum of the same date. The text of the exchange was supplied to Ambassador Joseph C. Grew in a letter dated 14 October 1955 from Max Bishop. He was a career State Department official who had been at the U.S. embassy in Tokyo until 1941, when he returned to Washington and was the aide who "kept the files of all American-Japanese conversations during the summer and fall of 1941." Bishop told Grew that after 7 December he was "directed" to "return to Hornbeck his 'personal memoranda.'" The 27 November exchange with Hull was "included in that category. However, because of their historical significance I felt they should not go into the incinerator. Virginia Collins, who you will recall used to be with us in Tokyo, was in the Department at the time and made copies for me. The original [sic] were given to Hornbeck and are either in his files or destroyed. They were seen by Max Hamilton, by Joe Ballantine and myself, in addition to, of course Hornbeck and Secretary Hull." There is no reason not to believe Bishop, whose integrity and ability resulted in his appointment as U.S. ambassador to Thailand. Copies of Bishop letters in Kimmell Papers. Copies supplied by Captain Thomas Kincaid Kimmell.

80. Ibid.

81. Ibid.

82. President to Prime Minister, 24 November 1941, Kimball, *Churchill & Roosevelt*, 275–6.

83. Stimson Diary, 25 November 1941 short version op. cit.

84. Ibid.

85. It reflected his concern that whatever the outcome, "it was desirable to make sure that the Japanese be the ones to do this so that there should be no doubt in anyone's mind as to who were the aggressors." Stimson Diary, 25 November 1941, op. cit.

86. PHH 14:1194.

87. Memorandum of Secretary of State of Conversation with Chinese Ambassador, 25 November 1941, 711.94 2479, RG 59, NAW.

88. Stimson Diary, 26 November 1941.

89. Washington-Tokyo, 26 November 1941, SRDJ 017036, RG 457, NAW.

CHAPTER FIVE

.1 Hull's written testimony PHH 2:435. On being questioned about when the decision was made, the former secretary of state stated that they had decided that it, the modus vivendi, "would not be feasible to present "to the Japanese" until, perhaps, the afternoon of 25 November." PHH 2:452.

2. Ibid., 454.

3. Cordell Hull, *The Memoirs of Cordell Hull* (New York: Macmillan, 1948). Assistant Secretary of State Sumner Welles, in a conversation with Lord Halifax, the British ambassador, put the blame on the British and Chinese opposition to the modus vivendi for the American decision to abandon the proposal. This took Halifax by surprise, and he, too, branded Chiang Kai-shek's reaction as "hysteri-

cal." Memo, 27 November 1941, by assistant secretary of state, DS 711.94/2560, RG 59, NAW.

4. Telegram for president from prime minister, 26 November 1941, Kimball, *Churchill & Roosevelt*, 277–8.

5. Ibid.

6. Halifax "Confidential" Diary, 26 November 1941.

7. Ibid.

8. Minute to Foreign Secretary, 23 November 1941, Prem 3 156/6, PRO.

9. Day to Day Diary of Far East Fleet—Part I, ADM 199/1185, PRO.

10. Halifax "Confidential" Diary, 26 November 1941.

11. Ibid.

12. Winston Churchill, *The Second World War: The Grand Alliance* (Boston: Houghton Mifflin, 1950), 502.

13. Ibid.

14. Ibid., 504.

15. The decision to exchange information on codes was an extension of the sharing of technical secrets, including radar, which had been arranged during the August 1940 trip of a British mission led by the Oxford scientist Sir Henry Tizard.

16. The party, together with the crated and closely guarded Purple machines, sailed for England aboard the battleship *King George V*. (Letter in author's possession from Captain Prescott Currier, November 1991). The claim was made that a Purple decoding machine was sent to FECB Singapore by James Rusbridger and Captain Eric Nave in *Betrayal at Pearl Harbor: How Churchill Lured Roosevelt into World War II* (Touchstone: New York, 1992), 260. The British did not send one of the Purple machines received at GC&CS out to the code breakers of the Far East Combined Bureau at Singapore, according to still-classified NSA records seen by Donald M. Gish "Cryptologic Analysis" in *International Journal of Intelligence and Counterintelligence* 6:3 (Fall 1993), 387.

17. Ibid.

18. Clausen Report Exhibit, PHH 35:686.

19. The archive "Dir/C" is the source for the ULTRA declassified by GCHQ, the successor organization to Bletchley Park, which has been designated HW by the Public Record Office. For more details see Chapter 14.

20. No mention of the pre–Pearl Harbor code breaking of the Japanese diplomatic traffic appears in the five-volume official history of British Intelligence in World War II or any of the other government-sponsored histories. Even as late as the summer of 1993 the editors of a collection of essays on Bletchley Park were told to omit all references to the use of the American Purple machines. See Chapter 14 for details.

21. Quoted by Warren Kimball in a firsthand recollection by Anthony Montague Brown, *"Churchill and Roosevelt"* in *Churchill: A Major New Assessment of His Life in Peace and War*, Edited by Robert Blake and Wm. Roger Louis (New York: Norton, 1993), 294 and note.

22. Sir Robert Craigie's Report, 22 August 1943, File 35957, FO 371, PRO. This is the amended version in which his criticism was toned in response to Churchill's complaint.

23. Ibid.

24. Ibid.

25. Handwritten minute to Lord Halifax and Sir Ronald Campbell, 7 October 1941, Records of the British Embassy in Washington, FO 115/3425, PRO.

26. 112th War Cabinet Conclusions, 12 November 1941, Confidential Annex, CAB 65/24, PRO.

27. Winston S. Churchill, "The Second World War," Vol. 3, "The Grand Alliance" (Boston, Houghton Mifflin, 1950), 594.

28. War Cabinet Conclusions 12 November 1941, op. cit.

29. The commitment of the secretary of state to the modus vivendi is given by Robert Sherrod, quoting Hopkins's notes: "It is true that Hull told the Secretaries of War and Navy that he believed Japan might attack at any moment. On the other hand, up to the very last day, he undoubtedly had hopes that something could be worked out at the last moment. Hull had always been willing to work a deal with Japan. . . . Hull wanted peace above everything because he had set his heart on making an adjustment with the Japanese and had worked day and night on it for weeks. There is no question that up until the last ten days before the outbreak of war he was in hopes that some adjustment could be worked out." Robert Sherwood *Roosevelt and Hopkins*, (New York, Harper Bros., 1948), 428.

30. The information was given to Max Bishop by Harrison, a former second secretary at the U.S. embassy in Berlin, shortly before Bishop wrote to Grew in October 1955. "It was just a day or so before November 26 when Harrison was in Mr. Hull's office and Hull was summoned by private telephone to the White House. He asked Mr. Harrison to wait in the office for he, Secretary Hull, expected to return immediately. The Secretary was gone only 15 minutes or so and came back in a very agitated frame of mind. He said something like this: 'Those madmen over there (White House—he may have used the term "madmen" but Harrison doesn't want to go that far) do not believe me when I tell them the Japanese will attack us. You cannot give an ultimatum to a powerful and proud people and not expect them to react violently.'" Bishop-Grew letter, 14 October 1955, Kimmell Papers, op. cit.

31. Hornbeck-Hull letter, 27 November 1941, quoted by Bishop in his 14 October 1955 letter to Grew, op. cit.

32. Ibid.

33. Ibid.

34. Halifax "Confidential" Diary, 27 November 1941.

35. Ibid., 29 November 1941.

36. Ibid.

37. Ibid.

38. Ibid.

39. Ibid.

40. Cable 5474, Halifax to the Foreign Office, 29 November 1941, FO 371/27913, PRO.

41. Ibid.

42. Ibid.

43. Minute by Sir Ronald Campbell on his conversation with Dr. Hornbeck, 28 November 1941, FO 115/3437, PRO.

44. Ibid.

45. It took a week for the full text of the ten-point message to be communicated to the British. Much to the annoyance of the Foreign Office, it was not transmitted to London until 2 December 1941.

46. Minute by Sir Ronald Campbell, op. cit.

CHAPTER SIX

1. Stimson Diary, short version.
2. Stimson Diary, short version.
3. Stimson Diary, short version.
4. Letter and enclosures, 25 November 1941, Stimson "Safe File," Philippines Folder, Box 11 RG, 107, NAW.
5. Stimson Diary, long version.
6. Letter and enclosures, Stimson "Safe File," op. cit.
7. Ibid.
8. Ibid.
9. Halifax to Foreign Office, "War Cabinet Distribution," Telegram No. 5418, 26 November 1941, FO 371/27913, PRO.
10. Pencil notes, Stimson "Safe File," Folder "Far East Before 7 December 1941," Box 4, RG 107, NAW.
11. Carbon copy of 26 November 1941 letter, Stimson "Safe File," White House Folder, with note that it was "hand delivered by Sergeant Quick 1225 Nov. 26 1941," Box 11, RG 107, NAW. The original is in the Stimson Correspondence file at the FDR Library.
12. Diary of Treasury Secretary Henry Morgenthau, 26 November 1941, Morgenthau Papers FDRL.
13. PHH 3:1444.
14. Ibid.
15. PHH 32:732.
16. Ibid.
17. Ibid.
18. PHH 3:1404.
19. PHH 5:23044.
20. PHH 3:144.
21. Stimson Diary, 25 November 1941, long version.
22. Minute by Sir Ashley Clarke on the chronological record of the U.S.-Japanese discussions, 4 January 1942, FO 371/27914, PRO.
23. Minutes of the Conference in the Office of the Chief of Staff, 10:40 A.M., 28 November 1941, WDCSA/381, RG 165, NAW.
24. Minutes of 10:40 A.M. Conference, 26 November 1941, COS U.S. ARMY, 1941–3 "Philippines," Box 11, RG 165, NAW.
25. Hart War Diary, 26 November 1941, NOA.
26. Ibid.
27. Dispatch OPNAV 271441 to CINCAF, 27 November 1941, PHLO, Box 45, RG 80, NAW.
28. Memorandum for the president, "The Far Eastern Situation," 27 November 1941, COS U.S. Army 1941–3, "Philippines," RG 165, NAW.
29. Stimson Diary, 25 November 1941.
30. Foreign Secretary to Lord Halifax, 29 November 1941, Prem 3 156/5, PRO.
31. Telegram to Halifax Washington, 28 November 1941, FO 371/27913, PRO.
32. Halifax "Confidential" Diary, 29 November 1941.

33. Ibid.

34. Halifax to Foreign Office, Telegram No. 5494, 30 November 1941, FO 371/27913, PRO.

35. War Cabinet Conclusions 122nd Meeting, Confidential Annex, 1 December 1941. CAB 65/24, PRO.

36. Ibid.

37. Ibid.

38. Ibid.

39. Halifax to Foreign Office, Telegram No. 5519, 1 December 1941, FO 371/27913, PRO.

40. Ibid.

41. Ibid.

42. Undated drafts of proposals for president's speech to Congress from Stimson, Knox and Hull, received "about 27 November 1941" by Secretary of State, 711.94 2540–590, RG 59, NAW.

43. Halifax "Confidential" Diary, 2 December 1941.

44. Prime Minister's Minute for Foreign Secretary, 2 December 1941, FO 371/27913, PRO.

45. Ibid.

46. War Cabinet 124th Meeting, Confidential Annex, 4 December 1941, CAB 65/24, PRO.

47. Halifax to Foreign Office, Telegram No. 5577, 4 December 1941, FO 371/27914, PRO.

48. Foreign Office to Halifax, Telegram No. 6710, 5 December 1941, FO 371/27914, PRO.

49. Ibid.

50. Ibid.

51. Halifax to Foreign Office, Telegram No. 5503, 5 December 1941, FO 371/27914, PRO.

52. Prime Minister to Prime Minister of Australia, T 923, 5 December 1941, Prem3/158/6, PRO.

53. Halifax to Foreign Office, Telegram No. 5363, 6 December 1941, Prem3/158/6, PRO.

54. Draft telegram to Lord Halifax for transmission to the President with note by J. M. Martin, 7 December 1941, Prem3/158/6, PRO. "PM approved of draft of this telegram 8:30 p.m. 7.12.41. Subsequently in view of Japanese commencement of hostilities instructions were given to cancel it."

55. Unsent Churchill to Roosevelt cable, 7 December 1941, confirming Halifax's 5 December telegram reporting Roosevelt's assurances of conditions under which Britain could count on U.S. armed support, Prem 3/158/6, PRO.

56. OPNAV to CINCAF, 1 December 1941, PHLO, BOX 45, RG 80, NAW.

57. Foreign Office to Halifax, Telegram No. 6711, 6 December 1941. FO 371/27914, PRO.

58. CINCAF to OPNAV, 6 December 1941. Signal reproduced in Kemp Tolley, *The Cruise of the Lanikai* (Annapolis: U.S. Naval Institute, 1973), 265.

59. Day to Day War Diary Far Eastern Fleet, ADM 199/1185, PRO.

60. Verbatim minutes of Manila conference of 6 December 1941 with Admiral Phillips and General MacArthur, typed up for Admiral Hart, December 1941, NOA Hart Papers.

61. Ibid.
62. Ibid.
63. Ibid.

CHAPTER SEVEN

1. CNO Dispatch #727337, War Warning, 27 November 1941, Box 1, Folder 6, PHLO, RG 80, NAW.

2. Ibid.

3. PHH 32:51.

4. "Our people are growing impatient" and "unfortunate results will ensure" if a "speedy" settlement of Japanese-American relations is not reached.—2 November. The "situation does not permit delays," and a "second formula is advanced with the idea of making a last effort to prevent something happening."—4 November. "Our domestic political situation will permit no further delays . . . as far as we are concerned this is the final phase."—11 November. "In view of the fact that the crisis is fast approaching, no subsidiary complications can be countenanced."—15 November. "We here in Japan, in view of the extremely critical situation, only hope most earnestly for a speedy settlement."—24 November. "We are advised by the military that we are to have a reply from the United States on the 25th."—25 November. "The situation is momentarily becoming more tense and telegrams take too long," was followed by instructions for the ambassadors to make their reports by telephone using code words relating to the crisis.—26 November. "If the negotiations turn out to be a failure, cannot tell but what a lamentable situation will occur." "If, unfortunately, the United States refuses to accept those terms, it would be useless to continue negotiations."—11 November. "Should negotiations collapse, the international situation in which the Empire will find herself will be one of tremendous crisis."—14 November. "If the U.S. consent to this cannot be secured, the negotiations will have to be broken off." "The negotiations will be de facto ruptured"—28 November. PHH 12:110–204 passim.

5. *New York Times*, 10 November 1941.

6. PHH 16:2220.

7. PHH 16:2223.

8. Ibid., 2253.

9. Ibid.

10. Ibid.

11. PHH 10:4886.

12. PHH 14:1405.

13. Ibid.

14. Ibid.

15. PHH 32:49.

16. PHH 32:51.

17. Husband E. Kimmel, *Admiral Kimmel's Story* (Chicago: Henry Regenery, 1955).

18. Edwin T. Layton, Roger Pineau, and John Costello, *"And I Was There": Pearl Harbor and Midway—Breaking the Secrets* (New York: William Morrow, 1985), 183 (hereafter Layton, *"And I Was There"*).

19. PHH 32:234.

20. Layton, *"And I Was There,"* 215.

21. Ibid.

22. Ibid.

23. Flimsy of Original War Department warning dispatch, 27 November 1941, Radiograms, General Correspondence, WPD 4544–9, WPD RG 165, NAW.

24. Copy in AGO 381, 11-27-41–12-10-41, Box 648, RG 407, NAW. The War Department planners in Washington were apparently unaware that in July 1941 Short had rewritten the alert procedure, reversing the original order of readiness, so that the maximum readiness requiring "occupation of all field positions by all units, preparing for the maximum defense of Oahu and the Army installations on outlying islands" became the third, rather than first, state of readiness. The intermediate level, 2, called for "security against attacks from hostile subsurface, surface, and air-craft, in addition to defense against acts of sabotage and uprisings." In Henry Clausen and Bruce Lee, *Pearl Harbor: Final Judgement* (New York: Crown, 1992), 55–88 (hereafter Clausen and Lee, *Final Judgement*) the charge is made that Short was therefore derelict in this regard. But there could have been little confusion in Washington over the precise state of readiness since Short *did not* report his state of readiness by number but spelled out that his alert was "to prevent sabotage." Moreover, given that his war warning was couched in less urgent terms than the Navy's and he was cautioned against alarming the civilian population, he could hardly have been expected to proceed at once to the highest stage of alert. It should also be noted that the Navy had not gone onto its Number 1 full alert and therefore it is surprising to find that so many members of the naval staff at Pearl Harbor assumed that the Army had adopted the highest state of readiness.

25. PHH 14:1330.

26. Radiogram, Hawaiian Department to War Department, 28 November 1941, AGO 381 RG 407 NAW.

27. PHH 36:4176.

28. PHH 14:1331.

29. PHH 14:1328.

30. PHH 3:1421.

31. Ibid.

32. Clausen and Lee, *Final Judgement*, 90.

33. Ibid. Clausen's memoir, written with the help of Bruce Lee, relies heavily on verbatim recollections of conversations that took place almost half a century ago. The historical value of its conclusions is therefore open to question.

34. Ibid.

35. Ibid.

36. PHH 32:151.

37. Ibid.

38. Adm. William F. Halsey and Lt. Cmdr. Joseph Bryan II, *Admiral Halsey's Story* (New York: McGraw-Hill, 1947), 75–6.

39. PHH 16:2276.

40. PHH 26:280.

41. PHH 8:3598–3621. The reports from Consul General Foote and General Thorpe both specifically referred to an "intercepted and decoded" message from the Japanese Ministry of Foreign Affairs. Kamer 14, the code-breaking unit attached to the NEI Armed Forces at Bandoeng, had achieved considerable success penetrating the Japanese cipher systems. The precise details of what codes

they were able to break and how much traffic they intercepted is not clear because so many of the records were destroyed during the evacuation in the face of the Japanese invasion of Java, in February 1942. Most of the surviving officers were faithful to their oath and took their secrets to their graves. For a published background of the Dutch efforts before Pearl Harbor, see Robert D. Haslach, *Nishi no Kaze Hare (West Wind Clear)* (Netherlands: Unieboek, 1985). The background on Dutch intelligence operations in 1941 is given in a letter by Captain J. W. Henning, chief cryptanalyst at Kamer 14, Bandoeng, dated 11 March 1965, Royal Netherlands Army Archives.

42. Clausen made much of his failure. But once again in his rush to condemn (Clausen and Lee, *Final Judgement*, 233–4), Clausen ignores the fact that the significance of the whole "Winds" code setup was grossly exaggerated by Washington. In the absence of the context of the MAGIC intelligence about the rapidly deteriorating diplomatic relations with Japan, its apparent importance as a war warning would have been far from obvious. Clausen and Lee, *Final Judgement*, 76.

43. PHH 6:2543.

44. Kimmel, *Kimmel's Story*.

45. PHH 6:2543.

46. PHH 17:2659.

47. Ibid.

48. Layton, *"And I Was There,"* 243.

49. Ibid.

50. Professor Roberta Wholstetter mistakenly states that Kimmel made his remarks "jokingly" to Layton, on p. 62 of her 1963 ground-breaking study, *Pearl Harbor: Warning and Decision* (Stanford: Stanford University, 1963). Clausen also ignored the context given in Layton's account, to suggest that Kimmel simply made a "sarcastic remark" without having any regard for the intelligence danger of knowing where the carriers were. Clausen and Lee, *Final Judgement*, 296.

51. Layton, *"And I Was There,"* 183.

52. Summary for 23 November 1941 in original copies of Layton's CINPAC summaries and reports in boxes 40, 41, 42, 48, 49, and 63 of the "Navy Pearl Harbor Liaison Office Records," RH 80, NAW.

53. PHH 17:2623.

54. Ibid. Rochefort was quoted in the anonymous memorandum that was circulated to counter the charges made in *Black Magic in Communications*, the Navy Department assessment, CSP 149A, 15 April 1942, under the signature of Vice Admiral F. J. Horne.

55. *Black Magic in Communications* and anonymous memorandum.

56. Layton, *"And I Was There,"* 228.

57. Ibid.

58. PHH 10:4838.

59. PHH 36:149. See also the 1 December 1941 Communications Summary made by Commander Rochefort of HYPO. Copy in Papers of Joseph J. Rochefort, private collection held by his daughter.

60. The Pacific Fleet's move was an important element of the so-called Orange War Plan, which called for the fleet to move into the Marshalls and Carolines in order to fulfill its primary mission of battling its way westward to relieve the U.S. Army garrison in the Philippines. Plan Orange had projected a "long and exhausting struggle of up to two years," a duration which had taxed American planners for three decades. WPL 46 is included in Pearl Harbor Hear-

ing, vol. 16, p. 226. For a thorough and detailed analysis of the evolution of the U.S. strategic planning in the Pacific, see Edward S. Miller, *War Plan Orange* (Annapolis: U.S. Naval Institute Press, 1991).

61. Layton, *"And I Was There,"* 223.

62. AAF Telegram to MacArthur, 26 November 1941, WPD 4544–9, General Correspondence 1920–42, RG 165, NAW.

63. PHH 14:1407.

64. Ibid. "Circular twenty four forty four from Tokyo on 1 December ordered London, Hong Kong, Singapore, and Manila to destroy Purple machines. Batavia machine already sent to Tokyo. December second Washington also directed destroy Purple. All but one copy of other systems. And all secret documents. British Admiralty today reports Embassy London has complied." It is significant that by identifying the Admiralty as the source of the intelligence, this dispatch OPNAV to the U.S. Pacific Fleet commands provided confirmation not only that the British were also breaking Purple (with the two machines that should have gone to Pearl Harbor), but that they were also exchanging their intelligence with the United States. This contradicts Churchill's denial that during 1941 he was having to rely on the Americans for Japanese MAGIC.

65. Layton, *"And I Was There,"* 250.

66. At the time it indicated to me, in conjunction with the other messages I had, that Japan was taking precautionary measures preparatory to going into Thai, and because they thought that the British or the Americans, or both of them might jump on them and seize their codes and ciphers after they went into Thailand." PHH 6:2764.

67. PHH 1:1520.

68. Rochefort's HYPO "Running Chronology," 4 December 1941, Rochefort Papers.

69. "One of the reasons that they authorized this was because they found my communications set-up had given them [the islands] some very secret codes and they wanted them destroyed right away because they never should have had them." PHH 6:2765. OPNAV to CINCPAC, #042017, reproduced in "Diplomatic Background to Pearl Harbor," SRH 012 p. 184, NAW.

70. Signals reproduced in Appendix 1, "Diplomatic Background to Pearl Harbor," SRH 012 p. 184, NAW.

71. OPNAV to CINCPAC Info CINCAF, on 6 December, 1941, SRH 012, NAW.

72. PHH 35:43.

73. "Believe local consul has destroyed all but one system although presumably not included in your eighteen double five of third" [the Japanese codes destruct message sent three days earlier]. PHH 14:1409.

74. PHH 6:2765.

75. This was according to the testimony of his assistant G-2, Captain George W. Bicknell, to whom Rochefort had shown the codes-destruct message shortly after its receipt on 3 December. But Bicknell waited for three days before he passed the information on. This was despite having received, that same evening, intelligence from Harry Dawson, the British Special Intelligence Service officer in Honolulu, which had just arrived by cable from Lieutenant Colonel Gerald Wilkinson, the M16 officer in Manila. It reported on accelerating Japanese troop movements and preparations at their bases in Indochina, and included the highly significant prediction: "Our considered opinion concludes that Japan envisages early hostilities with Britain and U.S. Japan does not, repeat not, intend to attack

Russia at present but will attack south." The distribution list shows that in addition to Bicknell's receiving it, Captain Mayfield and the FBI had each received copies of this report. It was not until Saturday, after he had received confirmation from the FBI that the local consulate was burning its papers, that Bicknell reported this intelligence to Short. "I told those assembled, which included the Chief of Staff what I had learned concerning the destruction of their important papers by Japanese consuls," Bicknell was to testify. But although, he admitted, he made no specific reference to code machines being destroyed at the 6 December staff conference, Bicknell made it clear that "because of this concurrent information which I had from proven reliable sources that the destruction of such papers had a very serious intent and that something warlike by Japan was about to happen." PHH 25:30. Bicknell, who did not have the Top Secret clearance to receive MAGIC, sought in his testimony to the early Pearl Harbor investigations to protect Rochefort as his source. Clausen and Lee, *Final Judgement*, 95–7 and 113.

76. PHH 35:274.
77. PHH 31:3188–9.
78. PHH 28:1542; 27:738.
79. Radiogram report to Manila, 5 December 1941, AGO 381, RG 407 NAW.
80. PHH 36:141.
81. Ibid.
82. Layton, *"And I Was There,"* 274.

CHAPTER EIGHT

1. Portion of signal #25 underlined by Navy analysts that was intercepted on 6 December but not translated until 8 December 1941, reproduced in full, SRH 012, pp. 200–201, RG 457, NAW.
2. #254, ibid.
3. #123, ibid.
4. Handwritten "memo," 2 December 1941, from Yale Maxon, Rochefort Papers.
5. PHH 36:350.
6. Kuehn was a Nazi who had been a member of the secret police of the German navy from 1928–30. He had contracted with the Japanese navy as a spy in 1935. Kuehn and his wife arrived in Honolulu ostensibly to study Japanese at the University of Hawaii. In 1939 he was given a radio transmitter by the Japanese for communicating with submarines. The German couple had come to the attention of the District Intelligence Office of the 14th Naval District as a possible German agent in 1939, but his activities, including meeting with Takeo Yoskikawa, the undercover Japanese intelligence agent at the Honolulu consulate, had not been closely monitored. The FBI arrested Kuehn immediately after the Japanese attack. He was tried for espionage and sentenced to death, although this was later commuted. "Investigation Report Japanese Consulate Honolulu—Espionage Activities," 6 and 9 February 1942, Records of 14th Naval District, RG 181, National Archives, San Bruno, California. See also Gordon Prange with Donald M. Goldstein and Kate Dillon, *At Dawn We Slept* (New York: McGraw Hill, 1981), 310–2, 423–4, 450–1,650, passim.

7. Signal reproduced in full in "Diplomatic Background to Pearl Harbor," SRH 012, RG 457, NAW.

8. #128, 6 December 1941, p. 199 SRH 012, RG 457, NAW.

9. #83, 24 September 1941, SRH 012, RG457, NAW.

10. See analysis in SRH 012.

11. #041, 29 September 1941, SRH 012, RG 457, NAW.

12. PHH 5:2175.

13. PHH 4:1922.

14. PHH 9:4541.

15. PHH 2:785.

16. Bratton testified that he was "told on innumerable occasions by my opposite in ONI that they were giving all this stuff to the Army." PHH 9:4541.

17. PHH 2:896.

18. PHH 2:911.

19. PHH 14:1378.

20. PHH 2:795.

21. Ibid., and PHH 9:4534.

22. Tokyo-Washington, 2 September 1941, translated on 4 September 1941, SRDJ 014545, RG 457, NAW.

23. SHR 012, p. 141.

24. Honolulu-Tokyo, 4 September 1941, translated 26 September 1941, SRDJ 015132, SIS #22697, RG 457, NAW.

25. Tokyo-Honolulu, 18 November 1941, translated 3 December 1941, SRDJ 017188, RG 457, NAW.

26. Honolulu-Tokyo, 15 November 1941, translated 6 December 1941, SRDJ 017305, RG 457, NAW.

27. Tokyo-Honolulu, 18 November 1941, translated, 3 December 1941, SRDJ 017188 SRD, RG 457, NAW.

28. Tokyo-Honolulu, 20 November 1941, translated 4 December 1941, SRDJ 017270, RG 457, NAW.

29. Tokyo-Honolulu, 29 November 1941, translated 29 November 1941, SRDJ 107311, RG 457, NAW.

30. PHH 4:1748; 5:2174.

31. PHH 2:859.

32. Diplomatic Background at Pearl Harbor, SRH 012, p. 186–7, op. cit. The full importance of the Japanese consulate messages as potentially vital intelligence was not apparent to Professor Roberta Wholstetter when she produced her groundbreaking study *Pearl Harbor: Warning and Decision*, published in 1963. Although her work was, and is still, respected for its comprehensiveness and impartial examination of all aspects of the contentious issues, she may not have seen the "Diplomatic Background to Pearl Harbor" in 1942 because it was not released to the congressional inquiry and not declassified until 1982.

33. Layton, *"And I Was There,"* 167.

34. PHH 6:2543.

35. "I do not know that we have missed anything," Kimmel wrote to the chief of naval operations in February, "but if there is any doubt as to whose responsibility it is to keep the Commander-in-Chief fully informed with pertinent reports on subjects that should be of interest to the Fleet, will you kindly fix that responsibility so that there will be no misunderstanding." CINPAC to CNO letter, 18 February 1941, PHH 16:2229. His postscript specifically reminded Stark to

ensure that he received "information of a secret nature." Stark's vague and all-embracing reply the following month that "ONI is fully aware of its responsibility in keeping you adequately informed" (CNO to CINPAC letter, 22 March 1941, PHH 16:2160) left Kimmel uneasy. This according to Layton, who on 11 March sent to his old friend Commander McCollum, who was then head of the Far East Section of ONI, a personal plea that the Pacific Fleet receive intercepted Japanese traffic. The response that "the material you mention can necessarily have but passing and transient interest as action in the political sphere is determined by the government as a whole and not by the forces afloat" was not encouraging. PHH 10:4846. The apparent belief in ONI that diplomatic intelligence was, in effect, none of the Pacific Fleet's business, prompted Kimmel to write to Stark again, reminding Stark that he was "far removed from the seat of government in a complex and rapidly changing situation" and that "full and authoritative knowledge of current policies and objectives" made it vital for the commander in chief of the Pacific Fleet to "be guided by broad policy and objectives rather than by categorical instructions." Accordingly he "suggested" to the chief of naval operations that it be made a "cardinal principle" that his command "be immediately informed of all important events as they occur and by the quickest means available." PHH 16:2238. Although Kimmel received no specific response from Stark, he took this as confirmation of the CNO's assurance that he would be kept abreast of all developments. His belief was reinforced by the new director of the Office of Naval Intelligence, Captain Wilkinson, who wrote on 19 August that "if you do not get as much information as you think you should get the answer probably is that the situation which is uppermost in your mind has just not jelled sufficiently for us to give you anything authoritative." PHH 4:1838.

36. Layton, "And I Was There," 168.

37. PHH 4:1771. The system of gathering pertinent information appears to have worked relatively well, although according to the testimony of Captain Wilkinson, Naval Intelligence was better informed about changes in Japanese diplomatic policy from MAGIC than it was about contemporaneous developments in the State Department and White House policy.

38. Turner's single-minded intelligence and assertiveness, which had made him a model midshipman at Annapolis, had also left him resentful at being graded five places below head of the class of 1908 at the U.S. Naval Academy.

39. Description of Turner by one of his junior officers, as cited in A. A. Hoehling, The Week Before Pearl Harbor (New York: Norton, 1963), 56.

40. Ibid.

41. The nickname arose from a hazing jibe by an upperclassman who had incorrectly recalled General John Stark's celebrated declaration to the Revolutionary troops before the Battle of Bennington: "We will win today, or Betty Stark will be a widow tonight." What he had actually said was "Tonight the American flag floats from yonder hill, or Molly Stark sleeps a widow." But "Betty" stuck, and thenceforth Harold Stark was familiarly known as Betty.

42. Stimson Diary, 6 May 1941.

43. Robert Sherrod, On to Westward (New York: Duell, Sloan and Pearce, 1944), 256.

44. PHH 4:1915.

45. PHH 4:1914.

46. PHH 4:1926.

47. "The Reminiscences of Rear Admiral Arthur H. McCollum, USN (Ret),

an Oral History," U.S. Naval Institute Oral History Program, Annapolis, Maryland (hereafter McCollum, Oral History).

48. Ibid., 310.
49. Ibid., 311.
50. Ibid.
51. PHH 4:1926.
52. Ibid.
53. Letter, Wilkinson to Rochefort, 19 November 1941, Rochefort Papers.
54. Captain Howard D. Bode, one of ONI's most experienced and conscientious analysts and acting head of the ONI Foreign Intelligence Section, drafted the message, according to "The Bomb Plot Revisited," an unpublished article prepared by Commander C. C. Hiles, based on information he obtained from Safford.
55. PHH 4:1747.
56. PHH 4:1772.
57. PHH 16:2163.
58. CNO War Warning, 27 November 1941, op. cit.
59. PHH 4:1754.
60. PHH 4:1963.
61. Hoehling, *Pearl Harbor*, ibid.
62. "U.S. Army Investigations into the Handling of Certain Communications Prior to the Attack on Pearl Harbor," SHR081, RG 457, NAW. Transcript of testimony of Colonel Otis K. Sadtler to the Clarke Investigation, 15 September 1944, PHH 10:4629.
63. PHH 10:3646.
64. PHH 10:4630.
65. PHH 15:1841. Because ONI had been regulated to evaluating only the less important information, his memorandum relied on drawing attention to such inescapable indications that Japan was on the brink of war as the report of her consul in Shanghai informing Tokyo that "all preparations are complete for taking over all physical property in China belonging to the British, American and other individuals." Another point McCollum made was that the Tokyo Imperial General Staff had sent urgent requests for information on "U.S. and Dutch troop and plane strengths and dispositions in the Philippines."
66. PHH 8:3385.
67. Ibid.
68. Ibid.
69. McCollum, Oral History, 131.
70. PHH 8:3388.
71. Ibid.
72. Ibid.
73. Layton, *"And I Was There,"* 20.
74. Ibid., 21.
75. Ibid.
76. PHH 33:883.
77. PHH 33:897.
78. PHH 33:898.
79. PHH 4:1976.
80. PHH 4:1975.
81. PHH 4:1976.

82. The portrayal of the Hawaiian commanders as sentries who had fallen asleep on duty was made the central theme of the case accusing Kimmel and Short of dereliction. It was resurrected by Clausen and Lee in *Final Judgement*. But such a simplistic metaphor was both inaccurate and inappropriate. The postwar record has shown that it was a convenient charge that Stimson invoked to cover up his and Washington's responsibility for the twin disasters of 7 December 1941. Not only had the front line of U.S. Pacific defenses shifted to the Philippines, but the "sentries" at Pearl Harbor had been denied both the weapons and the intelligence that was essential for Kimmel and Short to properly discharge their duty.

83. PHH 4:1911–2063.

84. 5 December estimate, WPD 544–9, RG 165, NAW.

85. PHH 14:1246.

86. Hart Diary, 6 December 1941, NOA.

CHAPTER NINE

1. PHH 36:303–4.

2. Fred Woodrough, interview with author, 8 June 1984.

3. Ibid.

4. PHH 36:303–4.

5. Ibid.

6. Fred Woodrough, op. cit.

7. PHH 9:4171.

8. Ibid.

9. Ibid.

10. Ibid.

11. Fred Woodrough, op. cit. "Kramer" could never give a short answer and would weigh all the pros and cons," according to Woodrough, who sometimes played an off-duty rubber of bridge with his boss. In the course of many games, he had noted how Kramer would always be the last to play his hand, trying the patience of his partner as he laid out his whole strategy in minute detail. "If everything went the way he figured, with everyone discarding as he allowed, he would play the next card," "Woodrough recalled. "But if there was the slightest variation he would have to go back into his trance again."

12. Ibid.

13. Ibid. It was obvious to Woodbrough that Kramer had been overstressed in the last months of 1941. He put in long hours, munching chocolate bars and dropping crumbs, which attracted mice. As Kramer became more overworked, he became increasingly obsessed with achieving perfect translations and would not authorize the release of any decrypt until he had personally satisfied himself that it was absolutely correct. This slowed up the whole process of translating the MAGICs.

14. Ibid.

15. PHH 12:195.

16. Tokyo to Washington, 6 December 1941, SRDJ 017330, RG 457, NAW.

17. Ibid.

18. Ibid.

19. PHH 29:2399. The previous day Safford, whose duty as OP-20-G also

gave him authority over the security of all naval codes and cipher, had reviewed the distribution of the Registered Publications Section. It revealed that Wake had copies of virtually every secret code and cipher system that the Navy possessed. Before he left for home in the early hours of Saturday morning, he had then drafted an urgent dispatch to this effect that he suggested should be sent to Wake.

20. PHH 29:2395–2400.

21. PHH 14:1407.

22. Vice Admiral Frank E. Beatty recalled the exchange in "The Background of the Secret Report," *National Review* (13 December 1966): 1261, *Pearl Harbor.*

23. Tokyo to Washington, 6 December 1941, SRDJ 017336, RG 457, NAW.

24. Ibid.

25. PHH 12:251.

26. PHH 10:4662.

27. Tokyo to Washington, 6 December 1941, SRDJ 017336, RG 457, NAW.

28. This Schulz was at pains to emphasize when he testified: "The President then turned toward Mr. Hopkins and said in substance—I am not sure of the exact words, but in substance—'This means war.'" PHH 10:4662. That there was no sinister intent is evident because the presence of the lieutenant, who had been on the White House staff for only a fortnight, did not inhibit Roosevelt from a discussion of what was going to happen. According to Schulz, Hopkins suggested that since war was inevitable, "it was too bad that we could not strike the first blow and prevent some sort of surprise." Roosevelt was adamant. "No we can't do that. We are a democracy and a peaceful people," the president said before reflecting, "But we have a good record." PHH 10:4663.

29. PHH 14:1243–45.

30. Kramer memo, Box 4, PHLO, RG 108, NAW.

31. PHH 8:3905.

32. PHH 8:3903.

33. Kramer memo, op. cit.

34. PHH 11:5545.

35. PHH 4:4026–30.

36. PHH 10:4608.

37. PHH 9:4473.

38. Clausen and Lee, *Final Judgement*, 158.

39. Ibid., 81–2.

40. Ibid., 171.

41. Clausen and Lee, *Final Judgement*, 170.

42. PHH 2:925.

43. Ibid., 926.

44. Clausen and Lee, *Final Judgement*, 242. Clausen challenged the credibility of Bratton's account by contending that he could not have discussed the thirteen-part message with Miles on the evening of 6 December, because he knew the general dined that evening with Admiral Wilkinson. But according to Kramer's account it was nearly 11:30 before he arrived at Wilkinson's home and found Miles there. There would therefore have been time for the director of military intelligence to have reached the Wilkinsons' Arlington residence *after* a discussion with Bratton in the War Department when the thirteenth part of Tokyo's final message was decrypted around nine o'clock. To further discredit the reliability of Bratton as a witness, Clausen had obtained sworn statements

from General John R. Deane, who had been the Assistant Secretary of the General Staff in 1941, that Bratton had arrived in his office, not at 7 A.M. on Sunday 7 December as he had testified to the Army Board, but sometime between nine and nine-thirty. This was corroborated by Lt. Colonel C. C. Dusenbury, G-2's Japan Desk officer. (Clausen and Lee, *Final Judgement*, 81–82). The length that Clausen went to brand Bratton a liar concealed the heart of the issue: that Miles *must have been aware of the contents of the thirteen-part message that evening*—either before he left the War Department or when it was brought by Kramer to Admiral Wilkinson at 11:30.

45. PHH 10:4616.

46. PHH 10:4612.

47. The source is "George Marshall's Action in the Pearl Harbor Attack December 7, 1941" signed "Certified a true copy of the original statement made by Colonel Raymond Orr USAF Ret" and dated 17 October 1961. The accuracy of some things that Orr recollected Bratton telling him appears to have been distorted somewhat by the years that passed before he committed them to writing. He claimed, for example, that Bratton told him about going up to Marshall's Fort Meyer quarters around nine o'clock that Saturday evening with the MAGIC pouch containing the full thirteen-part message only to be "ordered . . . from the house and severely reprimanded . . . for such a rude intrusion on a private dinner party." This contradicts Marshall's testimony and conflicts with a report in the *Washington Times Herald* that the U.S. Army chief of staff spent the evening at a veterans reunion dinner. There also appears to be a serious flaw in Orr's recollection of Bratton's account that "early the next morning" he had made the trip to Fort Meyer again. When informed that Marshall was "horseback riding in Rock Creek Park," Bratton drove there and found "Marshall on horseback and in company with a woman."

Marshall testified he was riding alone along the Virginia shore of the Potomac, which certainly makes more sense since it was within an easy ride of his quarters. There was never any other mention of his mystery female companion.

More reliance, however, may be placed in Orr's recollection of Bratton's account of Marshall's admitted, but nonetheless surprising, detachment from the final onrush of events: "Colonel Bratton, as Marshall's G-2 [*sic*] had numerous messages, especially on December 5 and 6, all pointing to an early Japanese attack on Hawaii. All this information was quickly given Marshall, along with reminders of General Short's request to be answered [for], giving General Short permission to move his forces into a defensive position, and allowing Admiral Kimmel permission to move his ships out of Pearl Harbor. Marshall promptly refused Bratton's suggestion. During the afternoon of Saturday, December 6, Marshall left the office, telling Colonel Bratton he was going to his quarters and did not want to be disturbed." Orr Memorandum in Kimmel Papers, University of Wisconsin.

48. PHH 2:968.

49. PHH 3:1429.

50. PHH 3:1430.

51. "Perjured testimony must be identified as such lest history be tainted," Clausen selfservingly contended in his memoir, complaining that "some historians and writers of Congressional reports have ignored this fact." Clausen and Lee, *Final Judgement*, 180. His investigation had been instituted to discredit Bratton, and he was only able to do so by obtaining a collective denial from those to

whom Bratton claimed he had made his deliveries on the night of Saturday, 6 December 1941. Clausen does not explain what motive the head of the Far East Section might have had for so deliberately lying in his earlier testimony. The only explanation alluded to is that his failure had denied Pearl Harbor the final war warning that Marshall would undoubtedly have sent out had he received the MAGIC pouch. But the glaring inconsistency here is that at least one of those who did see the thirteen-part message was General Miles, the director of military intelligence. Despite his own later assertion that he would have taken action had he received the MAGIC pouch, Miles *did* see the thirteen-part message at Admiral Wilkinson's house at eleven-thirty. He agreed with the director of naval intelligence that it did not warrant any action since it contained no new intelligence!

52. Clausen and Lee, *Final Judgement*, 164.

53. Given Miles's reaction it is unlikely that General Marshall would certainly have issued a final alert, as Clausen contended in his memoir. "Dusenbury's failure on December 6 to deliver the messages to Marshall kept the one man unalerted who, I believe, would have taken immediate action upon learning of the impending crisis," he wrote, echoing not only his oft-repeated admiration for the chief of staff, but also reflecting the prime objective of his 1944 investigation: to clear Marshall of the blame for not sending out a final warning after receiving the thirteen-part message, which it appeared, with the advantage of hindsight, to have warranted. Clausen and Lee, *Final Judgement*, 280.

54. Since Bratton was an army officer of unusual intelligence and diligence, it is difficult to conceive why he would have lied under oath to the Army board in 1944 about the delivery of the MAGIC pouches. An officer in his position must surely have anticipated that if General Marshall and his aides really had not seen the Japanese messages that Saturday, they would deny it vociferously. Nor is there any logic in the argument that Clausen put forward in his memoir that Bratton tried to escape his responsibility for a subordinate's failure to carry out an order by incriminating the U.S. Army chief. It makes no sense that an officer as conscientious and practiced in handling intelligence as the Far East Section chief undoubtedly was would have advised Dusenbury to await the arrival of the fourteenth part before distributing the MAGIC pouches that night. It was abundantly clear from the thirteen parts already received that Tokyo, as everyone in Washington anticipated, was in the process of rejecting further negotiations. So what was the point of waiting for what would surely be further confirmation that diplomatic relations were on the verge of rupture?

There was, moreover, no indication of when the final part of that message would be transmitted. Bratton knew better than most that timely delivery was a vital factor in handling intelligence, which was a highly perishable commodity. Furthermore, because of the unusually close liaison that afternoon with OP-20-G, he would have been aware that the Navy was proceeding with its distribution round. Since this included the White House, Bratton knew that the president might wish to consult the service chiefs, who expected to receive the same MAGIC pouches simultaneously. It appears to have escaped Clausen and the congressional investigators that Bratton did deliver the State Department pouch at about the same time that Kramer left the White House for the secretary of the navy's residence. Neither Clausen, for obvious reasons, nor the congressional investigators probed the inconsistencies in Bratton's "refreshed" version, the most glaring of which was the failure to explain why, if Bratton's revised testimony was the true version, he would have supplied the secretary of state the thirteen-part message but given his assistant instructions not to deliver it to the other recipients until the final part had come in.

55. According to a report in next day's *Washington Times Herald*, Marshall had attended a reunion of World War I vets who had "made a pilgrimage to Fort Meyer, Va., scene of part of their training . . . Later at a dinner in the University Club they honored their former 'CO,' Brigadier General Joseph A. Atkins, who came from San Antonio, Tex., for the celebrations. General George C. Marshall, Chief of Staff, attended and was given a vote of confidence." His presence at the reunion that night could explain why the general had been so anxious to leave the War Department that afternoon. But it was surprising that when he was cross-questioned quite intensively, Marshall testified that he could not recall attending the dinner at the University Club.

56. Letter, James G. Stahlman to Professor Preston Slosson, Vanderbilt University, 28 April 1975, Kimmel Papers. The credibility of Stahlman's firsthand account of his conversation with Knox is vouchsafed by his unique access to the secretary of the navy: "I was on duty in the Navy from 20 January '41, eleven months before Pearl until the war was practically over in 1945. I was in Naval Intelligence most of that time as Chief of the Navy Section of the Joint Intelligence Collection Agencies, embracing A-2, G-2, ONI, OSS, BEW and State Department Intelligence . . . Frank Knox was my close personal friend, by reason of our long service together in the newspaper business. I had *entrée* to his office as a junior reserve, which irritated the hell out of some of the regular USN boys."

57. Secretary of State Cordell Hull, for example, was not listed as present. According to Hopkins, Roosevelt blamed Hull for the "weakness of our policy," complaining to his closest confidante that Hull "always ducked the question" and "would never envisage the tough answer to the problem that would have to be faced if Japan attacked, for instance, either Singapore or the Netherlands East Indies." Robert E. Sherwood, *Roosevelt and Hopkins* (New York: Harper & Brothers, 1948), 428.

58. White House Ushers's Visitor Log, 6 December 1941, FDRL.

59. Entry of 6 December quoted in B. Berle and T. Jacobs, eds., *Navigating the Rapids: From the Papers of Adolf A. Berle* (New York: Harcourt Brace, 1973), 382.

60. Ibid.

61. PHH 2:584.

62. Clausen, in his report and memoir, makes much of the fact that his investigation disclosed that the fourteenth part had been received shortly after midnight in Washington (arriving in the Army Signals Section via a newly installed secure Teletype link). This was over three hours earlier than Bratton had originally testified. Clausen and Lee, *Final Judgement*, 81–2. According to Clausen, Dusenbury's statement that it arrived at "about 12 that night" was "shining forth like a beacon" in his affidavit. That Marshall had not been notified right away, Clausen asserts, "lost Washington a vital nine hours that could have been used to alert Hawaii *prevent* Pearl Harbor" [the emphasis is added to this glaring *non sequitur*]. "In the absence of some specific reference to Japan's intention to attack Pearl Harbor, which there was not in the fourteen-part message, there can be no certainty that the Hawaiian commander would have perceived the danger, nor did Clausen ever uncover any direct corroboration for assertion that Marshall would have sent out an additional alert based on the fourteen-part message

alone. This would surely have been most unlikely because his intelligence chief Miles testified repeatedly that it had "no military significance."

63. Wohlstetter, *Pearl Harbor*, 225. "No one really believed—in the sense of implying a course of action—that a diplomatic rupture firmly announced by Japan would mean immediate war initiated directly against the United States," Professor Wohlstetter emphasized in her landmark study *Pearl Harbor—Warning and Decision*. "There was absolutely nothing in MAGIC that established such a Japanese intent clearly and firmly. And even if there had been, there would still have been doubt as to whether Pearl Harbor was to be included in the Japanese plans of attack."

64. It was portrayed by Kimmel and Short as the culmination and the most damaging proof of the way in which Washington had deprived them of MAGIC and therefore of what they presumed would have been a vital last-minute warning of war. That was the presumption of the Army Pearl Harbor board's criticism of General Marshall. It was the same trap that Clausen also fell into as a result of his efforts to prove that the U.S. Army chief had not seen the Japanese fourteen-part message until Sunday morning.

CHAPTER TEN

1. PHH 12:248.
2. PHH 12:249.
3. Clausen in his memoir implies that had the radar been working around the clock, then the Pacific Fleet battleships could have been saved. Clausen and Lee, *Final Judgement*, 94.
4. Agawa, *Yamamoto*, 253.
5. PHH 8:3393.
6. McCollum, Oral History, 411.
7. PHH 11:5274.
8. PHH 8:3907–8; 9:4109.
9. Clausen and Lee, *Final Judgement*, 175, 179. Clausen admits that he neglected to question Bratton directly about the discrepancy when he took his affidavit in Paris. He apparently accepted Dusenbury's word because the later time of arrival got Marshall off the hook again.
10. PHH 9:4517, 4527.
11. Ibid., 4571, 4548.
12. Ibid., 4534; 3:114.
13. PHH 9:4595, 4524.
14. Ibid.
15. PHH 8:3910.
16. PHH 9:4048
17. PHH 8:3909.
18. McCollum, Oral History, 411.
19. Ibid.
20. PHH 9:4053.
21. PHH 9:4518.
22. PHH 14:1410.
23. PHH 9:4518.
24. PHH 14:1334.

25. PHH 9:4518.
26. PHH 5:2132.
27. PHH 9:4519.
28. PHH 5:2133.
29. PHH 9:4519.
30. PHH 29:2313.
31. PHH 9:4519.
32. PHH 9:4555, 14:1411.
33. PHH 34:33; 27:109, 114; 23:1103.
34. This popular myth was false in fact and as a metaphor. But it has been given additional credence by two recent books. *At Dawn We Slept, The Untold Story of Pearl Harbor* by Gordon W. Prange with Donald M. Goldster and Katherine V. Dillon (New York, McGraw-Hill, 1981), the enticing title given to the monolithic but anecdotal history of the attack and its aftermath, was compiled from thirty years of research of the late Professor Gordon W. Prange, for whom the investigation of the events leading up to 7 December 1941 became a lifelong obsession. The other recent work that harps on the same theme is Clausen's memoir, but his account is less than objective history since the purpose of his 1944 investigation was to show how Kimmel and Short were to blame for being caught "asleep at the switch" because they were like sentries who had failed to remain alert to a supposedly comprehensive war warning from Washington. This repeats the conclusion reached by Prange and his collaborators in their monumental compendium *At Dawn We Slept*, which Bruce Lee, Clausen's coauthor, also edited.
35. Confidential Letter, 2 CL-41, 15 February 194, revised 14 October 1941, PHH 33:1162.
36. Ibid.
37. PHH 15:1437; 22:350.
38. PHH 6:2535.
39. Ibid.
40. Ibid., 2536.
41. PHH 37:1299.
42. PHH 33:1162.
43. PHH 1:42.
44. PHH 32:444.
45. PHH 26:209–10.
46. PHH 23:1125, 1193.
47. PHH 28:499.
48. PHH 27:520.
49. PHH 27:531.
50. Ibid., 532.
51. Ibid.; PHH 27:569.
52. Mitsuo Fuchida, "I Led the Air Attack on Pearl Harbor," *U.S. Naval Institute Proceedings* 78, no. 9 (September 1952): 945.
53. Ibid., 950.
54. Copy of original signal in Rochefort Papers.
55. Interview of Kimmel quoted in Prange, *At Dawn We Slept*, 507.
56. Layton, *"And I Was There,"* 313.
57. PHH 8:3828–9.

58. Robert E. Sherwood, *Roosevelt and Hopkins* (New York: Harper Bros., 1941), *430–1*.

59. Cordell Hull, *The Memoirs of Cordell Hull* (New York: Macmillan, 1948), 106.

60. Ibid.

61. Hull oath quoted in John Toland, *The Rising Sun* (New York: Random House, 1970), *357*.

62. Typed memo of events on 7 December 1941, Hopkins Papers, Georgetown University Library.

63. Walter Karig and Wellborn Kelly, *Battle Report: Pearl Harbor to Coral Sea* (New York: Farrar and Rhinehart, 1944), 79.

64. PHH 23:899.

65. Layton, *"And I Was There,"* 316.

66. Ibid., 317.

67. PHH 37:1250.

68. Samuel Eliot Morison, *The Rising Sun in the Pacific*, vol 3 of *History of United States Naval Operations in World War II* (Boston: Little, Brown, 1948), 215.

69. Fuchida, "Air Attack," 952.

70. Interview quoted in Prange, *At Dawn We Slept*, 546.

71. PHH 6:2812.

72. Prange, *At Dawn We Slept*, 543.

73. Nimitz Speech to Bar Association of San Francisco, 8 November 1962, quoted in Clausen and Lee, *Final Judgement*, 240.

CHAPTER ELEVEN

1. A. M. Sperber, *Murrow: His Life and Times* (New York: Freundlich Books, 1986). Alexander Kendric, *Prime Time: The Life of Edward R. Murrow* (Boston: Little Brown, 1969), 240.

2. Murrow broadcast, 23 September 1945, quoted in Sperber, *Murrow*, 206.

3. John G. Winant, *A Letter from Grosvenor Square: An Account of A Stewardship* (London, Jonathan Cape, 1947), 196.

4. Churchill, *World War II*, vol. 3, 538–9.

5. Ibid., 2:608.

6. *The Reminiscence of France Perkins*, vol. 7 (1955), 35–98, Oral History Collection, Columbia University.

7. Ibid.

8. Ibid.

9. *Washington Post*, 9 December 1941.

10. Quoted in Weintraub, *War*, 463.

11. Quoted in Weintraub, *War*, 488.

12. Murrow broadcast, 23 September 1945, quoted in Sperber, *Murrow*, 206.

13. Ibid.

14. *New York Times*, 8 and 9 December 1941.

15. *New York Times*, 9 December 1941.

16. John Hershey, *Men on Bataan* (New York: Knopf, 1943), 48. Clark Lee, *They Call it Pacific* (New York: Henry Holt 1952), 71.

17. Hershey, *Bataan*, 39–40.

18. Letter, to Paul S. Mowrer, 18 December 1941, Knox Papers, Box 1, MDLOC.

19. According to the record kept by Knox's naval aide, Captain Frank E. Beatty, Secretary Knox asked Kimmel, "Did you get the Saturday night dispatch the Navy Department sent out?" When Kimmel denied receiving one, the secretary of the Navy said, "Well we certainly sent you one." Kimmel's chief of staff, Captain William Smith, also recalled Knox's insisting to him that a warning message was sent "on the Saturday preceding Pearl Harbor." PHH 7:3360. Layton, too, cites a similar exchange with Knox. PHH 7:33660. Several writers, including Prange (*At Dawn We Slept*, 5860), have asserted that the message that Knox was referring to was the one o'clock deadline warning that Marshall sent out at noon on 7 December. But all the respondents recall that Knox specifically mentioned that the message had been sent out on the night of the sixth. It also ties up with the account Stahlman said Knox had given him about the White House war council decision to send a war warning that night.

20. Stimson Diary, 11 December 1941.

21. PHH 6:2749–60.

22. Stimson Diary, 15 December 1941.

23. *New York Times*, 16 December 1941.

24. Report of Knox press conference, *New York Times*, 16 December 1941.

25. Ibid.

26. Ibid.

27. *New York Times*, 18 December 1941. General Martin, in contrast to Admiral Kimmel, was given an alternate command—of the naval air forces on the West Coast.

28. Quoted in James, *MacArthur*, 21–22.

29. Manchester, *American Caesar*, 213.

30. Brereton, *Diaries*, 61–2.

31. "Secret Memorandum for the Chief of Naval Operations: Subject: Proceedings of the Presidential Investigation Committee, 1000 to 1200, December 1941, Naval Operational Archives, Naval War Plans Division, NOA.

32. PHH 7:3280.

33. William H. Standley and Arthur A. Ageton, "The Pearl Harbor Debacle," unpublished manuscript, p. 84, Kimmel Papers.

34. Ibid., 88.

35. Roberts Commission report, PHH 39:1–21.

36. Admiral Kimmel's letter of resignation and letter of acknowledgment, 18 February 1942, Kimmel Papers, University of Wisconsin.

37. Ernest J. King Papers, MDLOC.

38. Letter, Spruance to Admiral Samuel Eliot Morison, 29 November 1961, Private Paper of Captain Roger Pineau.

39. PHH 39:317.

40. Report of the Joint Committee, PHH 40:495–7.

CHAPTER TWELVE

1. Minority Report of the Joint Committee, PHH 40:534.

2. MacArthur affidavit, Clausen Investigation Exhibits, PHH 35:35.

3. Ibid.

4. Clausen and Lee, *Final Judgement*, 142.

5. Sutherland affidavit, PHH 35:86.

6. As MacArthur's intelligence officer through the Pacific war, Willoughby had been in the thick of the feuding over control of ULTRA intelligence. He was therefore only too keen—with MacArthur's encouragement—to vent his long-standing grievance that the Navy "enjoyed an almost monopolistic privilege." What he told Clausen was music to the investigator's ears since it bolstered his case that the Navy's denial of information to the Army was a major contributory factor in bringing about the Pearl Harbor disaster. Willoughby explained how in the period preceding the war the Army signals intercept unit at Fort McKinley outside Manila was required to pass the traffic it intercepted to the Navy for decryption. The 16th Naval District combat intelligence unit, known as CAST, had been sent a Purple machine, whereas HYPO at Pearl Harbor was denied the ability to read this traffic. For a comprehensive review of MacArthur's use, misuse, and attempt to wrest control of ULTRA from Washington and the Navy during the Pacific Campaign, see Edward J. Drea, *MacArthur's Ultra: Codebreaking and the War Against Japan, 1942–1945* (San Francisco: Presidio, 1991).

7. Willoughby affidavit, PHH 35:87. Clausen and Lee, *Final Judgement*, 145.

8. Clausen appears to have discounted the affidavit he obtained on 22 March 1945 from Colonel Joseph K. Evans, who was G-2 of the Philippines Army command. MacArthur was a fellow Freemason, which Clausen appears to have taken as a guarantee of veracity during his investigation. Evans affidavit, PHH 35:44.

9. According to Brown, it was the Navy's responsibility to monitor the Tokyo-Berlin and Tokyo-Rome radio circuits. Brown "Reminiscences," op. cit.

10. Ibid.

11. The actual message read, "RELATIONS WITH JAPAN AND ENGLAND ARE NOT IN ACCORDANCE WITH EXPECTATIONS," and Brown was clearly referring to the inference to be made that this meant war.

12. Brown, "Reminiscences." His recollection of the timing appears to be astray, since he would have seen MacArthur's office around ten-thirty and Clark Field did not come under attack for another two hours.

13. Ibid.

14. It is also clear from Clausen's account that he was awed by MacArthur, no least because they shared high degrees in the Scottish rite of Freemasonry—as did MacArthur's intelligence officer, General Willoughby. This appears to have been an important factor in his belief that he was "in the presence of a great man, a general who had fought his way back after a terrible defeat to thrash the enemy all the way from Australia to the Philippines." (Clausen and Lee, *Final Judgment*.) The manner in which Clausen repeatedly identifies witnesses as especially reliable because they were Freemasons is another deeply disturbing element when it comes to weighing the contribution that his memoir rates as history. Freemasons have no monopoly on the truth, and the clannish way in which Clausen sought out other initiates in the secret lodges suggests that he was by no means the unbiased investigator after the truth that he makes himself out to be.

15. Clausen and Lee, *Final Judgement*, 142.

16. MacArthur, *Reminiscences*, 120.

17. *New York Times*, 28 September 1946.

18. Ibid.

19. MacArthur, *Reminiscences*, 120.

20. Ibid.

21. Morton cited in full in James, *MacArthur*, 2:11.

22. Quoted in Weintraub, *War*, 345.

23. General Moore, interview, *The Pearl Harbor Files*, broadcast on The Discovery Channel, 7 December 1991. TV documentary.

24. Brereton, *Diaries*, 37–9.

25. Ibid.

26. Anloff interview quoted in Weintraub, *War*, 345.

27. Tokyo-Washington, 3 December 1941, JD SRDJ 017419, RG 457, NAW.

28. Verbatim record of Conference of 5 December 1941, Hart Papers, NOA.

29. Ibid.

30. MacArthur's answers to questionnaire from Dr. Louis Morton, 18 February 1954, quoted in full in James, *MacArthur* 2:11.

31. Ibid.

32. PHH 14:1047.

33. MacArthur to Marshall, 28 November 1941, OCS 18136–118, AGO 381, Box 686, RG 407, NAW.

34. Brereton, *Diaries*.

35. Manchester, *American Caesar*, 231: "The puzzle may be explained by a bit of computer jargon: input overload."

36. MacArthur, *Reminiscences*, 117.

37. Dwight D. Eisenhower, interview, 1964, in Manchester, *American Caesar*, 166.

38. Executive Order 1, 2 January 1942, Box 4, Sutherland Papers, RG 200, NAW. The document was first uncovered by Dr. Carol M. Petillo, who discussed her research and its implications in an article, "Douglas MacArthur and Manuel Quezon: A Note on an Imperial Bond," *Pacific Historical Review* (1979):10.

39. Army Regulation 600–10 Part 2c(9), December 1938, War Department, Washington, D.C., NAW.

40. A 1935 regulation had permitted serving U.S. officers acting as military advisers to the Philippine Commonwealth, allowing them to accept additional compensation. But by December 1941 MacArthur, Sutherland, and his deputy Lt. Col. Richard Marshall and MacArthur's naval adviser Lt. Sidney L. Huff, the beneficiaries of the payout from the Philippine Treasury, were by then all in the pay of the U.S. Armed Forces.

41. James, *MacArthur*, 2:91.

42. Eisenhower Diary, 19 July 1942, Eisenhower Presidential Library, Abilene, Texas.

43. Document signed by Roxas on 19 February 1942, Sutherland Papers, Box 1, RG 200, NAW.

44. Vargas Papers, University of Philippines. Cited in Weintraub, *War*, 578.

45. James, *MacArthur*, 2:11.

46. For the cabled exchanges and a full analysis see James, *MacArthur*, 2, pp. 91–99.

47. Ibid., 91.

48. Journal entry, 25 September 1951, C. L. Sulzberger, *A Long Row of Candles: Memoirs and Diaries 1934–1954* (Macmillan: New York, 1969), 672.

49. MacArthur, *Reminiscences*, 111.

50. Ibid.

51. Ibid., 121.

52. Majority Report of the Joint Committee, PHH 40:251.

CHAPTER THIRTEEN

1. "Evaluation of Messages, 16 November 1941," memorandum for Admiral Hewitt's inquiry drawn up for Commander John F. Sonnet by Captain Laurence F. Safford, PHLO, Box 49, RG 80, NAW.

2. Ibid. Author interviews with former U.S. Navy Cryptanalysts Captain Thomas Dyer and Captain Wesley A. Wright in April 1984.

3. *Pre–Pearl Harbor Japanese Naval Dispatches*, declassified by the NSA on 21 October 1991 as SRH 406, RG 457, NAW.

4. See also the amplifying details provided in Donald C. Gish, "A Cryptologic Analysis," *International Journal of Intelligence and Counterintelligence* 6 no. 3 (Fall 1993): 369–88.

5. Ibid., 377.

6. Gish statement based on examination of still classified records in the NSA Archives.

7. Frederick D. Parker, "A New View to Pearl Harbor," unpublished paper, dated 16 May 1990. Copy in author's collection.

8. Examples cited by Admiral Layton. Although the Japanese believed that their complex language afforded them a measure of security against eavesdropping, its inherent weakness was the cumbersome *kana* system. This consisted of seventy-three ideographs developed as a shorthand way of representing the syllabary. *Kana* had been adapted to commercial Western telegraphic systems with the ideograph represented by roman letters know as *romanji*. But since a single kana ideograph might have several meanings, depending on whether it was spoken with a hard or soft inflection, the suffixes that had to be added to indicate the inflexion required an equally elaborate system of Morse code. Consequently, transmitted messages were far longer than they would have been in Western languages, which gave the intercepting operators more time to lock onto and transcribe the traffic. A special *kana* typewriter had been developed for the purpose by the Underwood Company in conjunction with U.S. Navy cryptanalyst Lieutenant Laurance F. Safford in 1924. The keys were printed with the *kana* Morse code's two-letter signature and the keys typed the Japanese ideograph equivalent.

9. *Pre–Pearl Harbor Japanese Naval Dispatches*, SRH 406, p. 9, NAW.

10. Ibid.

11. Ibid.

12. Ibid., 10.

13. Ibid., 12.

14. The British had also perfected a modified torpedo that could dive under the nets used to protect battleships in a shallow harbor. The attack had to be limited to the planes that could be flown off a single carrier and because the British *Swordfish* torpedo bombers were lumbering biplanes with poor defensive capability, the attack was mounted at night. Twenty-one *Swordfish* bombers were flown off the *Illustrious* in two waves shortly after 10 P.M. as the carrier approached to 170 miles from Taranto. The raid, which achieved complete surprise, crippled three out of five Italian battleships.

15. *Pre–Pearl Harbor Japanese Naval Dispatches*, SRH 406, p. 9, RG 457 NAW.

16. Ibid., 12.

17. Ibid.

18. Ibid., 12.

19. Ibid., 13.

20. Ibid., 15.

21. Ibid., 15.

22. Ibid., 16.

23. PHH 26:221.

24. Copies of official correspondence in the Rochefort Papers reveal that he had failed to persuade the Navy Department to remedy the deficiencies, although the 14th Naval District Command had been more sympathetic and agreed to set up receiving stations at Midway and the Palmyra atoll from the equipment available at Pearl Harbor. But as Rochefort pointed out, the output of the outstations' interceptions, along with those of the eastern Pacific direction finding network, was then put in the mail and carried to Honolulu by the transpacific Pan Am Clipper service. This service could often be delayed by days, if not weeks.

25. Report of intelligence estimate in Rochefort Papers.

26. Com 14 to CNO copied to COM 16, CINCAF INFO CINCPAC telegram 260110 26 November 1941 November, Rochefort Papers.

27. COMMUNICATIONS INTELLIGENCE SUMMARY for 27 November 1941, copy in Rochefort Papers.

28. "We kept absolute radio silence," wrote Admiral Minoru Genda, who had been one of the key planners of the Pearl Harbor attack, in a letter to *The New York Times* (13 March 1982). He was moved to respond by the claim made in John Toland's recently published *Infamy* that radio signals from the Japanese carriers had been picked up by a U.S. Navy listening station on the East Coast.

29. *Pre–Pearl Harbor Japanese Naval Dispatches*, SRH 406, p. 17, RG 457 NAW.

30. Ibid., 17.

31. Ibid., 18.

32. Ibid., 19.

33. While writing his memoir Admiral Layton noted a reference to this signal in the "Hawaiian Operation" *(Hawaii Sakusen)* which is volume 10 of the Japanese War History Series *(Senshi Sosho)*. On page 210 it records that Tokyo had radioed the Striking Force of its "concern that we might run into a Soviet merchant ship bound from San Francisco to the Far East." An examination of the sailing records in the *San Francisco Chronicle* for November 1941 led us to conclude—incorrectly—that the *Uritsky* was the vessel in question. Our error was correctly pointed out by Professor A. N. Yakolev, a Soviet historian, in his book *Pearl Harbor*, published in Moscow in 1985.

34. *Pre–Pearl Harbor Japanese Naval Dispatches*, SRH 406, p. 19, RG 457, NAW.

35. Ibid., 116.

36. Ibid., 114.

37. Prescott Currier, interview, November 1991, as broadcast in the television documentary *The Hunt for the Pearl Harbor Files*, hosted by Hodding Carter, IIIrd, and broadcast by the Discovery Channel on 7 Dec 1991.

38. According to the NSA's Center for Cryptologic History, microfilms were located in 1992 in a U.S. Navy warehouse facility at Crane, Indiana, that may

contain pre–Pearl Harbor JN-25 worksheets. The condition of the microfilm is so fragile that it has to be restored before declassification and release.

39. *Pre–Pearl Harbor Japanese Naval Dispatches*, SRH 406, RG 457, NAW.

40. The details of how Rochefort led the HYPO team at Pearl Harbor as they pieced together the Midway plan from the Japanese naval intercepts in the teeth of opposition from the Office of Naval Intelligence in Washington, whose analysts in NEGAT resisted this evaluation, were laid out for the first time by Admiral Layton in chapters 30 and 31 of his memoir, 405–430.

In Navy Department Secret Publication CSP 149A, dated 14 April 1942, written by Vice Admiral F.J. Horner, five pages entitled "Did the Japanese Paint Us a 'Picture'" sought to show that Rochefort was misled before Pearl Harbor by dummy Japanese messages. The running feud between HYPO and Captain Joseph R. Redman, then the director of the Office of Naval Communications, continued after the victory at Midway, with Rochefort being accused of insubordination and denied the decoration for which Admiral Chester W. Nimitz had recommended him. In Chapter 35 of *"And I Was There"* Layton described how the director of naval communications and his brother Captain John R. Redman, then head of OP-20-G, conspired to have Rochefort removed from the Cryptanalytic work for which he was uniquely qualified. Rochefort was recalled to the West Coast, where he was put in command of floating dock until 1944.

41. Captain Thomas H. Dyer, interview with author, June 1984.

42. Layton, *"And I Was There,"* 466.

43. BUNAV to COMSCOFOR, #151507, 15 March 1941, Rochefort Papers.

44. CINCAF to OPNAV, 5 March 1941, cited in a SECRET memorandum, "Assignment of Work on Various Naval Systems During the Year 1941," drawn up by OP-20-G (NCMG), 3 August 1944. A copy survives in the Rochefort Papers. (Hereafter "OP-20-G 1944 Report.")

45. OPNAV to CINCAF, #062134, 6 March 1941, Rochefort Papers.

46. In "A Cryptologic Analysis" Gish does not discuss this possibility. He makes the point that after December 1941 "there was a war going on, and that immense resources that were made available to deal with JN-25 were necessarily all focused on maximizing the production of current intelligence," op. cit.

47. OPNAV to CINCAF, 24 April 1941, Rochefort Papers.

48. Captain Thomas Dyer, interview with author, June 1984; undated 1944 Memorandum, written by Rochefort, Rochefort Papers; and also "A Cryptologic Analysis," Gish et al, op. cit.

49. This according to summaries of FECB's wartime history in Naval Intelligence Division, Vol. 42, "Far East and Pacific," ADM 223/297 PRO (see Chapter 14 for details).

50. Frederick D. Parker, "Pearl Harbor Revisited: United States Navy Communications Intelligence 1924–1941," U.S. Cryptologic History Series IV, World War II, Col. 6, 1994 (Maryland: Center for Cryptologic History, National Security Agency, 1994). This monograph is drawn from both published, declassified, and still-classified sources—the most significant is "History of Op-20-3-GYP," 2 Series IV.W.1.5.12,CCH History Collection.

CHAPTER FOURTEEN

1. MOST SECRET letter on 10 Downing Street notepaper addressed to "C" (Sir Stewart Menzies) from Major Desmond Morton, Churchill's intelligence aide,

dated 27 September 1940. He added the PS: "As there will be no check possible here would you please institute a check on the receipt of returned documents to see that you have got them all back." HW/1/1, PRO.

2. The boxes were yellow, according to Morton's assistant, Arthur Benson. Ronald Lewin, *Ultra Goes to War* (London: Hutchinson, 1971), 184–88.

3. HW/1/1, PRO.

4. "C" was the initial with which Captain—later Admiral—Sir Mansfield Cumming, the first head of Britain's overseas intelligence services signed himself in green ink. He bequeathed this tradition to his successors, although it is interesting to note that Menzies's covering letters to Churchill are signed "C" in red!

MI6 had been the overseas intelligence division of the War Office until after the First World War, when it was incorporated into the Secret Intelligence Service, an interservice organization under the Foreign Office. It continued to be referred to by outsiders as MI6, but to its members and Whitehall, it is SIS. The Government Code and Cipher School was ostensibly set up as part of SIS's fiefdom, charged with the overt responsibility for the devising and security of British government ciphers. The covert purpose of GC&CS, and its postwar successor GCHQ (Government Communications Headquarters), was, and is, the breaking and penetration of the cipher systems of foreign powers.

5. Morton had first encountered Churchill while they were both serving on the Western Front in 1916. From 1929 to 1939 Morton had been responsible for the Industrial Intelligence Centre, a government-sponsored agency that gathered intelligence on German industry. Morton had been given authority to keep Churchill abreast of this information during his years out of office when he was warned of the growing menace of Hitlerism.

6. Lewin, *Ultra Goes to War*, 268.

7. First Sea Lord from WSC 24, August 1941, HW 1/25, PRO.

8. Letter, C/7863 to Prime Minister, 24 June 1941, HW 1/6, PRO.

9. Ibid.

10. Ibid.

11. Ibid.

12. Reminiscence written by Captain Prescott H. Currier, supplied to the author in October 1991 in connection with his interview on the TV documentary *The Hunt for the Pearl Harbor Files*, op. cit.

13. Ibid.

14. Author interview with Admiral Weeks 1984 and written reminiscence by Captain Prescott Currier. In March 1941 the British were partially reading only the Luftwaffe Enigma. Bletchley Park did not succeed in penetrating the German naval Enigma system until four months after the American team had left. The breakthrough was made possible only after the deliberate seizure of a German trawler in May, the fortuitous capture of parts of a naval Enigma machine from a U-110 later that month, and the capture of a second trawler in June, which provided the naval machine key settings for the whole month of July 1941. This gave the Bletchley Park code breakers sufficient cribs for the naval system to become fully readable. The introduction of an entirely new key system blacked out all the U-boat traffic from British eavesdropping from February through December 1942. But once the solution had been found with the aid of electro-mechanical computing devices known as "Bombes." The main German naval cipher systems were to remain readable through the end of the war. F. H. Hinsley, "BP, Admiralty, and the Naval *Enigma*," in *Code Breakers—The Inside Story of*

Bletchley Park, ed. F. H. Hinsley and Alan Stripp (Oxford: Oxford University Press, 1993) 79–80. The most comprehensive account of the cracking of the German naval Enigma cipher system is given in David Khan, *Seizing Enigma* (Boston, Houghton & Mifflin, 1991).

15. These are summaries of the contents of the Berlin to Tokyo and Rome to Tokyo intercepts of BJ's 90502; 91601; 96741 for 2, 10, and 20 May 1941, in WO 208/882, which also contains BJ 96774 of 21 October 1941. The first Churchill Purple decrypt so far released is that sent to him on 28 August 1941 in HW1/30, PRO.

16. Japanese Ambassador in Berlin to Foreign Minister Tokyo, No. 1027, intercepted on 15 August 1941, BJ 09473 of 23 August 1941, HW 1/25, PRO.

17. Ibid.

18. Prime Minister's annotation on Foreign Ministry Tokyo cable to Bangkok and Saigon, BJ 102220, in C/8986 of 17 March 1942, in HW 1/420, and the President's request is noted on Japanese Ambassador in Berlin to Foreign Ministry Tokyo, 377 and 378, of 17 March 1942, BJ 102443, in C/9007, and and BJ 102473, in C/9011, of 21 March, in HW 1/429 and HW 1/431, PRO.

19. The British cipher system was a development of the original German commercial version of the rotary Enigma patented in 1927 by Arthur Scherbius. Two of these early models had been purchased by GC&CS, and they were replicated with modifications by the RAF seven years later in a cumbersome prototype, unlike the German version, which in illuminated lamps, spelled out the code, the British device printed out the cipher message and plain text simultaneously on paper tape. The RAF Engima Type-X was subsequently developed by Creed & Company as the Typex Mark 1, which came into use by the RAF in 1937. Its performance so impressed Britain's Cipher Committee that the later marks of the Typex system became the standard ciphering machine for both government and military communications. The Germans, as far as is known, never succeeded in breaking Typex. Convinced by their own misplaced confidence in the impenetrability of rotary cipher machines, they never mounted a serious assault on Type-X, of which their own Enigma system was the precursor.

The government-controlled Cable and Wireless Company controlled the transatlantic lines to maintain secure links with the United States. (Captured records, however, indicate that for a time in 1940 the Germans succeeded in tapping into the Churchill-Roosevelt exchanges through a Continental connection to the main cable.) The monitoring of Japanese communications was also facilitated because Tokyo routed its cable traffic into Britain's extensive global network of transoceanic cable system. The Typex cipher machines used for secret high-level British government and military communications also offered a high degree of security for Foreign Office cables. In contrast, the State Department ciphers were not secure, as Churchill well knew because they had been penetrated by the GC&CS code-breaking teams at Bletchley Park. The assumption was therefore made that they were also vulnerable to the German cryptanalysts, although the captured wartime records are still being withheld by the British and Americans.

20. American Embassy Angora (Ankara), 8 September 1940, 331, circulated 13 September 1940 as BJ 09543, HW 1/64, and American Legation Dublin to Mr. Hull, Washington, 64, decrypted and circulated 23 November 1941, as BJ 98061, HW 1/251, PRO.

21. FO 371/26565, PRO.

22. Requests to GCHQ, via the Foreign Office, have not yet produced any specificity because of the limited manpower resources that are currently being devoted to the declassification procedure.

23. Letter, prime minister to president, 25 February 1942, Kimball, *Churchill & Roosevelt*, 371.

24. Ibid.

25. On 29 May 1942 Bletchley Park intercepted a Luftwaffe Enigma Signal to *Fliegherfuehrer Afrika* that relayed a lengthy report received on 16 May detailing how the RAF was "making no use of the technical courses established by the Americans," resulting in "a dreadful waste of equipment and material" involving U.S.-supplied *Kittyhawk* aircraft. The German intercept identified the origin of the information as "from a *particularly reliable* source [emphasis added]." CX/mss/1027/T17, Italy and North Africa, HW 1/641, PRO.

"What action?" Churchill had penned on the report, picking up the clue that the Germans might have read an American military cable from the telltale reference to a "particularly reliable source," which was intelligence jargon for information provided by a spy or signals intelligence. The leak was tracked down to a cable General Henry H. Arnold, chief of the U.S. Army Air Force, had sent to General Maxwell of the American Mission in Cairo on 16 April 1942 in the U.S. military attaché cipher, which had been worded with almost precisely the same words. The inclusion of the original of this cable points to the continuing facility of the Bletchely Park code breakers with the American military ciphers despite the assurance given the president by Churchill four months earlier. The 9 June report by the assistant chief of the air staff for intelligence also noted that on information apparently received from the Americans at Cairo "Dope given in German report suggests information obtained Washington as Signal AMSEG 540 not decoded here until 17th. Breaking of American code another possibility." Quoted in full, Duty Office Hut 3 (Bletchley Park), by ACASI, on 8 June 1941, AI 3A(1), in teletext message of 6 June 1942, HW 1/641, PRO.

On 12 June "C" advised the assistant chief of air staff that "as a result of my communications with the American Cryptoanalytic Bureau there has arisen an element of doubt as to whether the Germans were reading an American cypher and there is a possibility that a traitor is providing the Germans with contents of certain American messages." He concluded that until the investigation was completed "I feel sure you will agree that it was best for me not to explain this alternative form of leakage to the prime minister at the moment." C/9744 to CAS, 12 June 1944, HW 1/642, stamped HISTORICAL SOURCE DOCUMENT. Two days later Menzies changed his mind and advised the prime minister about the possibility that the leak was the result of the work of a traitor. C/9761 to prime minister, 14 June 1941, HW 1/646, PRO.

On 16 June "C" was able to report what he had evidently known all along from Bletchley Park cryptanalysts, but which he could report to Churchill only after receiving confirmation from Washington, "that the American military cipher is compromised and I have asked that this should be changed to a cypher providing the highest security, but without furnishing any reason for the change-over." Menzies added that in his opinion "the Germans have succeeded in photographing the American cipher book," suggesting that it was impossible to "rule out the possibility of a traitor in the U.S.A. where the book is printed." C/9779 to prime minister, 16 June 1942, HW1/652, PRO. On 19 June he reported that "the U.S. Authorities have now changed their cypher" and that "no further leaks should occur from 25th July 1942." Menzies added that "if leakage continues, then there must be a traitor with access to the American telegrams in Cairo, transmitting by Secret Wireless from Egypt, but available evidence does not support this likelihood." C/9871 to prime minister, HW 1/676, PRO.

26. Final item of a "Note" of arrangements, dated 5 August 1941, in Prem3/485/6, PRO, reads as follows:

3. As regards papers to be sent [presumably by air courier to Newfoundland or the securest British cipher], the following would be responsible for the selection:

Boniface [ULTRA]	"C"
B.J.	~~Foreign Office~~ [Hand written] Major Morton
Agents Reports	Major Morton
Foreign Office Telegrams	Foreign Office to make suggestions
Service Telegrams	Office of the Minister of Defence

27. The typed up copy, bearing the BJ serial 98563 was circulated 12 hours later, the next day. The "Advance Diplomatic BJ/88" teleprinter sheet of the same intercept, time stamped 1652/4/12/41, was annotated "Prime Minister" and sent under C/8246 of 4 December, which advised after the report contents "Typed copy of this message will leave B[Letchley] P[Ark] 07.30/5th December for Foreign Office, Admiralty, War Office and Air Ministry." HW 1/298. "Advance BJ/89" arrived the following morning, giving the prime minister a three-hour head start on a typed-up copy of a similar notice. Advance Diplomatic BJ/89 teleprinter sheet of 1150/5/12/41 the "Typed copy of this message will leave B.P., 5th December, 1315 for FO, Admiralty, War Office and Air Ministry." HW 1/298, PRO.

28. The 41 Bletchley Park Purple ULTRAs are printed, verbatim, complete with the BJ serials and circulation lists as Exhibit 8 PHH 35:686.

29. The subtle differences in translation of the three extant versions of the "Winds" code setup indicate that they were intercepted and decrypted independently by the code breaking teams in Melbourne, Washington, and Bletchley Park.

The Australian version of the instruction paragraph for action to be taken on hearing the "East Wind Rain" broadcast reads: "The signal will be given in the middle and at the end as a weather broadcast. When this is heard please destroy all code papers etc. This is as yet to be a completely secret arrangement." Circular Foreign Ministry Tokyo, 19 November 1941, in CRS A5954, Australian National Archives, Canberra.

The Bletchley Park version reads: "The appropriate phase will be broadcast twice in a resolute voice and you should act accordingly [group corrupt: destroy by fire] code documents etc. The above is to be treated as strictly confidential." Circular from Foreign Ministry Tokyo, 19 November 1941, BJ 098127, Clausen Exhibit 8, PHH 35:686.

The American version reads: "This signal will be given in the middle and at the end as a weather forecast and each sentence will be repeated twice. When this is heard please destroy all code papers, etc. This is as yet to be a completely secret arrangement." Circular from Tokyo Foreign Ministry, 19 November 1941 SRDJ 017025, RG 457, NAW.

30. Exhibit 8 PHH 35: 686 et seq.: "The following documents comprise intercepts obtained from British sources. They consist of 41 documents extending over the period 21 November 1941 to 22 November 1941." Also reproduced in Clausen and Lee, *Final Judgement*, 354.

31. PHH 3:1444.

32. H. Montgomery Hyde, *Room 3603* (New York: Farrar Straus, 1962), 293. Confirmation was also received by the author from Sir William Stephenson in a telegram, 28 February 1982.

33. Hyde, who worked with Stephenson at BSC, based his account on an "office" history written in 1943, and it is therefore more reliable a source than William Stevenson's, *A Man Called Intrepid: The Secret War* (New York: Harcourt Brace Jovanovich, 1976). An authoritative and penetrating analysis on Stephenson's true role is given by Dr. Timothy Naftali in "Intrepid's Last Deception: Documenting the Career of Sir William Stephenson," *Journal of Intelligence and National Security*, July 1993.

34. Former naval person to President of the United States, 26 November 1941, Kimball, *Churchill & Roosevelt*, 277–8. Original in FO 371/27913, PRO.

35. Covering letters, 25 November 1941, in Prem 3 469, PRO and Churchill (WSC) file FDRL.

36. Halifax Confidential Diary, 26 November 1941 entry referring to the previous evening.

37. The declassified Foreign Office records contain only the copy of Churchill's cable expressing mild concern about Chiang Kai-shek, which was copied to the British embassy in Washington as a matter of courtesy to Lord Halifax. So if there was a second message that night to Roosevelt, as the circumstantial evidence now suggests, it could only have reached the White House via the secure MI6 channel through Stephenson's BSC headquarters in New York.

38. PHH 3:1444.

39. The "Winds" decrypt bears the BJ number 098127, which would indicate that it would have been in the second batch delivered to Downing Street on 25 November under Menzies's cover sheet C/8161 *none of whose contents have been released*. C/8160 was the cover from BJ serials 098107, 098148, 098149, 098151, 098152. The presumption can be made that BJ 098127 was sent under cover C/8161, which is missing. C/8162 contains a repeat of BJ 098151, an intercepted report from the Japanese ambassador in Turkey. C/8162, C/8163, C8164, are all wanting, and C/8165 contained only German ULTRA reports.

40. Wilkinson was a businessman, acting as a sugar broker, who described himself as the "representative in the Pacific for the Secret Intelligence Service of the British government reporting direct to the British Foreign Office." Wilkinson was the branch manager in Manila for Theo H. Davies and Co., Ltd, one of the five largest trading concerns in Hawaii. His wife was the granddaughter of the British firm's founder. The manager of the company's steamship department was Harry Dawson, the local MI6 agent and Britain's vice-consul in Hawaii, who reported to Wilkinson in Manila. According to the testimony of the Honolulu FBI chief, Robert L. Shivers, to whom Wilkinson had introduced himself in July 1941, he and Dawson identified themselves as British intelligence agents, and they later supplied reports from London to Colonel Bicknell, General Short's

intelligence officer at Fort Shafter, and Captain Mayfield, the intelligence officer of the 14th Naval District. PHH 3:194-5; 4:4336–80; 35:31–44, 84–87, 109–18 39, 278–80.

41. PHH 35:133.

42. General Willoughby's affidavit, quoted in Clausen and Lee, *Final Judgement*, 146.

43. Menzies was an ex officio member in his capacity as head of the Secret Intelligence Service. JIC(41) 449, "Possible Japanese Action–Report of the Joint Intelligence Sub-committee, Final version," 28 November 1941, Cab 81/105, PRO.

44. Undated note by prime minister directing that his intelligence aide, Major Morton, be responsible for selecting the "Agents' Report" for him to see at the Atlantic summit. PREM 3/485/6, PRO.

45. Prem 3/252 5, closed for 75 years, as noted in the index in the PRO. Since the preceding open file contains Japanese intelligence reports up to 22 November 1941 (including a reference to a Purple intercept BJ 099776 of 19 November) and then continues from 1 March 1942, it would appear that the withheld documentation is precisely congruent with the critical dates.

46. Author's correspondence with the minister of state for defense, 7 December 1979, and with Cabinet Records Office, 29 September 1983.

47. For a full account of the Sorge ring, see Gordon Prange et al, *Target Tokyo: The Story of the Sorge Spy Ring* (New York: McGraw Hill, 1984), and Charles A. Willough by *A Shanghai Conspiracy: The Sorge Spy Ring* (New York: Dutton, 1966).

48. Prange, *Target Tokyo*.

49. In 1936 an agent run by Walter Krivitsky, the Soviet NKVD *rezident* in the Netherlands, had succeeded in penetrating the Japanese embassy and obtaining copies of the code books. After his defection to the United State, Krivitsky claimed that "from then on all correspondence between General Oshima [the Soviet ambassador in Berlin] and Tokyo flowed through our hands." Walter Krivitsky, *I was Stalin's Agent* (London: Hamish Hamilton, 1939), 32–6. But the Purple machine, which came into use in 1939, would have rendered the code books useless by 1941 unless the Soviets managed another penetration of the Japanese embassy in Moscow.

50. "Facts on Intelligence from the Archives of the Security Organs of the Soviet Union," *Pravda*, 9 May 1989. Confirmation provided to author in interview with Oleg Tsarev, Moscow, 1994.

51. Rastvorov was interviewed and cited as the source for this by Christopher Andrew and Oleg Gordievsky in *Inside the KGB: The Inside Story* (Hodder & Stoughton, London 1990) op. cit. 219. He did not, apparently, make clear whether this involved tapping the Purple cipher.

52. PHH 11:5178–9. See also "Signal Intelligence Disclosures in the Pearl Harbor Investigation," p.33 SRH 154, RG 457, NAW.

53. PHH 39:279.

54. Ibid. and Clausen and Lee, *Final Judgement*, 115.

55. PHH 35:204.

56. Robert Haslach, *Nishi no Kaze Hare*. Cites letter of 11 March 1965 of Captain J.W. Henning, chief cryptanalyst of Kamer 14.

57. Letter, General ter Poorten, 23 July 1960 Royal Netherlands Army Archives.

58. Report of Captain J. W. Henning dated 18 July 1960 Military Historical Archive, the Hague, Netherlands.

59. Ibid.

60. Rusbridger and Nave, *Betrayal at Pearl Harbor*, p.138.

61. The scale of Japanese treachery would have been magnified for the prime minister by indications he simultaneously received that a Japanese submarine had been involved in the sinking of a warship of the British empire. The official report of the Australian Naval Board's secret investigation into disappearance of the cruiser HMAS *Sydney* after the action with the German armed merchant cruiser *Kormoran* on 17 November is still a classified secret. The 23 November entry in the Admiralty War Diary records only "it is feared that before sinking an enemy raider, she was herself torpedoed."

The *Sydney*, which had recently returned to patrol home waters after sinking an Italian cruiser in the Mediterranean, was lost in suspicious circumstances off the coast of Western Australia after engaging the German merchant raider *Kormoran* on 19 November. How the battle-hardened crew of the *Sydney*, whose eight 6-inch and eight 4-inch guns completely outclassed the armed merchantman that mounted only six 5.9-inch guns, was sunk in such an unequal encounter remains one of the great sea mysteries of World War II. Why not a single one of the 645 Australian crew survived when 318 of the 390 German crewmen were able to make it safely to shore by lifeboat has never been satisfactorily explained. The discovery a month later of one of the *Sydney*'s life rafts, riddled with bullet holes whose low trajectory angle indicated they could have been fired from a machine gun on a U-boat's conning tower, appeared to confirm suspicions that the cruiser was torpedoed by a Japanese submarine, since there were no German U-boats in Australian waters. Reports of an aircraft spotted prowling along the coast of western Australia near the port of Caernavon the night before the action also indicated that a floatplane-carrying I-Class that was cooperating with the *Kormoran*'s prowling the convoy routes where the giant liners *Queen Elizabeth* and *Queen Mary* had sailed ten days earlier, packed with thousands of Australian troops for the Middle East.

The findings of the Australian Naval Board's preliminary inquiry of 24 November into the sinking of the *Sydney* are still classified. While they had no final proof, there was a strong circumstantial presumption that a Japanese submarine operating with the *Kormoran* had torpedoed the cruiser and had then surfaced to massacre all the Australian survivors. This suspicion would have reached Churchill, via the Admiralty, the next day, providing him with an indication of an appalling act of treachery by Japan. The theory of possible Japanese involvement in the sinking of the *Sydney* was first argued in detail by Michael Montgomery in *Who Sank the Sydney* (Sydney: Cassel, 1981), but it has been disputed by other naval writers, including Commodore Bruce Loxton, to whom I am most grateful for his critique and comments. Until the wreck of the *Sydney* is located and it is possible to determine precisely how she was sunk, her loss remains one of the enigmas of World War II.

62. Tokyo—All Fleets, SRN 115385, 20 November 1941, RG 457, NAW. These were uncovered in 1984 among the SRN series in RG 457 of the Japanese naval intercepts in the National Archives, by the late Captain Roger Pineau while researching for Admiral Layton during the writing of *"And I Was There."* The postwar U.S. Navy analysis of the pre–Pearl Harbor naval traffic that was released

to the National Archives as SRH 406, and which is the focus of Chapter 13, was not declassified until seven years later.

63. The claim is part of the theory advanced by Rusbridger & Nave in *Betrayal at Pearl Harbor*, 128. The U.S. Navy record of pre–Pearl Harbor Japanese naval intercepts does not include a sailing signal, but if such an order was transmitted from Combined Fleet headquarters ordering the Striking Force put to sea on or about 25 November, it was not picked up by the U.S. Navy. No such message has been discovered among the 2,413 JN-25 intercepts made at the time but not fully decrypted until 1945.

All of Japan's wartime transmission records had been destroyed before Japan's surrender in 1945, but according to the interrogation report of Captain Mitsuo Fuchida, who led the air attack on Pearl Harbor, this message was transmitted on 25 November. He recalled it as stating "the task force will move out of Hittokapu Wan on 26 November and proceed without being detected to the eventual rendezvous point," which he said was latitude 40 degrees north longitude 170 degrees west. It continued, "set for 3 December where refuelling and supply will be carried out as quickly as possible." PHH 13:414–18. The only extant set of orders for Combined Fleet Operation Order No. 1, which directed the opening attack of the war, contains a directive that parallels Fuchida's recollection: "The Task Force will move out of Hittokapu Wan on the morning of 26 November and advance to the standing-by position on the afternoon of 4 December and speedily complete refuelling." The geographic coordinates would have been super enciphered within the JN-25B crypto system, so if this sailing message had been intercepted and decrypted by the British in 1941, it would not have revealed that the refueling point was in the mid-Pacific. Box 36, PHLO, RG 80, NAW.

64. The claim is advanced by the late James Rusbridger and the late Captain Eric Nave in *Betrayal at Pearl Harbor* that not only were the British reading the General Purpose Japanese Fleet Code signals on a current basis before the attack on Pearl Harbor, but the U.S. Navy had also penetrated the system to the point of readability. But their account was written *before* the declassification in 1991 of the 1946 *Pre–Pearl Harbor Japanese Naval Dispatches*. Unless there was a monstrous cover-up and deception, this report proves that the U.S. Navy was unable to obtain any meaningful penetration of the JN-25B cryptosystem in the fall of 1941.

Louis W. Tordella, former deputy director of the NSA, and Edwin C. Fishel, of the NSA Cryptologic School, convincingly refute the Rusbridger/Nave claim in their joint article with Donald M. Gish "A Cryptologic Analysis" *International Journal of Intelligence and Counterintelligence* 6 no. 5 (Fall 1953). Contending that the U.S. Navy was *not* able to make any significant current penetration of JN-25B, they point out that the authors failed to take account of the additional complexity of the new "B" codebook that had been introduced in December 1940 and the lack of manpower available to OP-20-G in 1941 to make the necessary number of recoveries from both the additive tables and the dictionary book to render the cipher readable. The details are provided in the same journal article, which draws on still-classified records, by Gish, a former NSA senior historian who is the author of the point-by-point critique of Nave/Rusbridger. But lack of direct access to the FECB records leaves the case short of finality when it comes to refuting the assertion made by Nave and others that the British were making no meaningful sense of their intercepts of the pre–Pearl Harbor JN 25-B traffic.

65. F. H. Hinsley et al, *British Intelligence in the Second World War*, (HMSO, London 1979 3 vols.) 1, 53n.

66. Ibid.

67. Original Nave manuscript is in the author's possession. The publication of the Layton memoir, *"And I Was There,"* in 1985 prompted Nave to defy Britain's Official Secrets Act to tell his own story, and he had written a partially complete typewritten manuscript. He and his chosen collaborator, James Rusbridger, then invited the author to act as an adviser and assist them in finding a British and American publisher for a revised and more complete work. When the original British publisher bowed out after the government issued a "D" Notice to prevent Nave from publishing his memoir, the author of this book ceased to have any responsibility for either the manuscript or the conclusions of the work that finally appeared in 1990 under the title *Betrayal at Pearl Harbor*.

68. Paymaster Commander Raymond Mortimer, interviews and correspondence with author, 1985–1991.

69. Ibid.

70. Ibid.

71. In 1941 the FECB cryptanalysis and translation team consisted of Paymaster Captain Shaw and lieutenant commanders Burnett, Parham, Merry, Foreman, and Curnock, who were assisted by three civilian clerks. Information supplied by Commander Mortimer in correspondence with the author, 1983.

72. Telephone Interview by author 10 November 1991 with Dr. Andrew Gordon, a historian who, at 50th Anniversary Conference at Hofstra University, New York, in December 1991, delivered a paper in which he discussed to his conversation with Burnett.

73. Mrs. Malcolm Burnett, interview, in *The Hunt for the Pearl Harbor Files*, broadcast, op. cit.

74. Letter, Commander Mortimer to author, 13 January 1982.

75. Commander Mortimer, interview in *The Hunt for the Pearl Harbor Files*, TV documentary, op. cit.

76. Mortimer's 1982 letter to the author does not state that Churchill (who was no longer prime minister when the war ended) had personally ordered the destruction, as Rusbridger and Nave claimed in *Betrayal at Pearl Harbor*, 173.

77. Naval Intelligence Division, Vol. 42, "Far East and Pacific," III, Adm. 223/297 PRO. It is also significant that the Ministry of Defense had no record of a Commander Mortimer at FECB!

78. Naval Intelligence Division, Vol. 42, "Far East and Pacific," III, Special. "Japanese Cyphers," notes by Lt. Cmdr. Barham, RN dated 18 July 1942, Adm. 223/297 PRO.

79. N.I.D., Vol. 42, "H.M.S. Anderson and Special Intelligence in the Far East," unsigned, undated report, Adm. 223/291.

80. N.I.D., Vol. 42, "Collaboration of British and U.S. Radio Intelligence," unsigned and undated memorandum, Adm. 223/297 PRO.

81. Duane L. Whitlock *"And So Was I,"* (*A Gratuitous Supplement to "And I Was There"* by Rear Admiral Edwin T. Layton et al) in *"The Cryptologue,"* the journal of the U.S. Naval Cryptologic Veterans' Association, Eugene, Oregon, 1986, p. 6. Unpublished manuscript in NSA's Center for Cryptologic History, cited by Gish in "A Cryptologic Analysis" *International Journal of Intelligence and Counterintelligence*.

82. Gish, *A Cryptologic Analysis*, 377.

83. "Once the postwar decrypting, screening, selection and translation of significant text from the Pre-Pearl Harbor period was complete, there would be little reason to keep earlier incomplete and fragmentary worksheets even if they had survived to that point," commented former NSA historian Donald Gish. As of this writing, an extensive batch of microfilmed material that appears to contain some of the "missing" 1941 JN-25 worksheets had been recovered from the U.S. Navy storage facility at Crane, Indiana. The poor condition of the microfilm has made it impossible for the NSA to examine and release this material to the National Archives until proper steps are taken to preserve the crumbing nitrate stock on which it was filmed. It then has to be screened for censoring according to the NSA criteria to protect cryptologic sources and methods before it can be made available to researchers.

84. Hinsley et al, *British Intelligence*, vol. 1 p. 53n.

85. Rusbridger and Nave, *Betrayal at Pearl Harbor*, 177.

86. Louis W. Tordella and Edwin C. Fishel, their introductory commentary, *International Journal of Intelligence and Counterintelligence* 6, op. cit.

87. Costello, *The Pacific War*, 658.

88. Copy of a message for the prime minister, "received over the telephone 6.15pm on 6.12.41," PREM3/158/6, PRO.

89. Ibid.

90. Telephone Message for Mr. Martin from Captain Brockman, A.M. 7.12.41, relayed from First Sea Lord, who received it from Admiral Little in Washington, PREM3/158/6, PRO.

91. Draft Cable and note by John Martin Prem 3/158/1 PRO.

92. CinC Singapore to Admiralty, 7 December 1941. Received 1315, Prem3/158/6, PRO.

93. Ibid.

94. John Ferris, "From Broadway House to Bletchley Park: The Diary of Captain Malcolm Kennedy, 1934–1946," *Intelligence and National Security* 4 no. 3 (July 1989): 439–40.

95. During the first week of December 1941 Bletchley Park Purple was not being decrypted on the same day as far as can be established. The transmission of the first thirteen parts of Tokyo's response to the U.S. government was not complete until around midnight London time, on Saturday, 6 December. The final part would have been intercepted at five A.M. on 7 December and the delivery deadline message around eight A.M. Those Purple decrypts delivered to Downing Street on 7 December under C/8628 and C/8273, namely BJs 098633, 098650 and 098651 are listed as "wanting" in the PRO index. This is puzzling because Clausen was provided with copies of them in 1945 by Bletchley Park. They are a Tokyo-Berlin cable of 30 December and two Rome-Tokyo cables sent on 3 and 5 December. So although the serials on "C's" cover sheets indicates that there were five other deliveries of SIGINT that have been withheld by GCHQ, it is highly unlikely that any of them contained decrypts of the fourteen-part message and the delivery deadline, which would not have been available—even if they were given priority handling—until the late afternoon.

96. The BJ/91 designation on this intercept indicates that it was relayed to the prime minister the day before the typed copy of BJ 098694 was circulated in Whitehall on 8 December 1941. HW 1/307, PRO.

97. "Most Immediate" from Foreign Office to Bangkok, Dispatched 1:40 P.M., 7 December 1941, PREM 3/158/6, PRO.

98. Martin Gilbert, *Churchill: A Life* (New York: Henry Holt, 1991), 711–12.

99. W. Averell Harriman and Elie Abel, *Special Envoy to Churchill and Stalin,* 1941–1946 (London: ——— 1976), 111.

100. Ibid.

101. Churchill, *World War II*, 2:538.

102. Halifax Diary, 7 December 1941 entry in the nonconfidential version, Borthwick Institute, Garrowby, Yorks.

EPILOGUE

1. Cited by Hugh Trevor-Roper (Lord Decre) valedictory lecture as Regius Professor of Modern History, Oxford University, 20 May 1980.

2. Vice Admiral David C. Richardson U.S. Navy (Ret.), the former Commander of the United States Sixth Fleet and operational intelligence specialist, made this dictum the principal basis for rejecting the conclusion by Clausen and Lee in *Pearl Harbor: Final Judgement* that the Hawaiian commanders were principally to blame. Navy Cryptologic Veterans' Association journal, *The Cryptologue*, Summer issue, 1993.

3. Stimson Diary entry, 25 November 1941.

4. Richardson op. cit.

5. Ibid.

6. François Marie Arouet de Voltaire, *Candide*, 1759, Chapter 17.

APPENDIX I

1. Letter, Safford to Kramer, 22 December 1943, PHH 8:3698–3704.

2. The denial of any knowledge about the "Winds" setup "until I read about it in the newspapers" is repeated verbatim in the interviews of the Navy radiomen in PHLO, RG 80, NAW.

3. Letter, Safford.

4. PHH 93935–6.

5. Ibid.

6. Ibid.

7. Letter from Mrs. Eunice Willson Rice to Captain Roger Pineau, 23 June 1985. Although she had been away visiting her sister in Maine during the weeks before the Japanese attack, Mrs. Willson Rice noticed that one message was missing from the numerical sequence, which Kramer told her was the one indicating that war was imminent and which he had turned over to the chief of naval operations. She said that when he asked for it back, he received a noncommittal answer.

8. Admiral Weeks, interview with author, April 1984.

9. PHH 9:4009.

10. Copy of Briggs's 1960 entry in the 2 December 1941 personnel duty log, provided by Navy Operational Archives. "Interview with Mr. Ralph T. Briggs by the Historian of the Naval Security Group Command," 13 January 1977, SRH 051, RG 41, NAW.

11. PHH 9:3934.

12. PHH 4:1969.

13. "Information from George W. Linn, Captain USNR (Ret)," 23/10/80, SRH, 081 RG 459, NAW.

14. Linn also added to the Enigma by claiming in his 1980 deposition that he had been on duty on the afternoon of 7 December, during the attack on Pearl Harbor, when Kramer came in and asked "if we could encrypt a message in the Purple system for transmission." Kramer never explained the reason for this request and no such message was ever given to Linn for encryption or sent. But as he pointed out, had the attempt been made, the Japanese would have quickly discovered the ruse and it would have exposed that the Americans were reading the their cipher systems. Just what was behind Kramer's remark remains and unsolvable mystery. It is possible to speculate that some officer senior to Kramer might have made the inquiry with a view to including a false message in the file that was never intended to be transmitted to the Japanese but which might have been intended to confuse and coverup any subsequent investigation into Washington's failure to properly analyze and disseminate MAGIC.

15. PHH.

16. Thorpe letter in Kimmel Papers.

17. PHH 33:757.

18. Letter, General ter Poorten, Royal Netherlands Army Archives.

19. Ibid.

20. Letter, Henning, 11 May 1965, Royal Netherlands Army Archives.

21. Ibid.

22. Cedric Brown, interview with Rusbridger, 9 May 1985. cited in *Betrayal at Pearl Harbor* p. 276n.

APPENDIX II

1. John T. Flynn, *The Truth About Pearl Harbor* (privately printed New York 1944) 3, 13, and 28.

2. Charles A. Beard, *President Roosevelt and the Coming of the War, 1941* (New Haven: Yale University, 1948). Beard, who died the same year that he published his controversial but closely argued study, had studied at Oxford, Cornell, and Columbia before becoming one of the founders of The New School for Social Research. Branded as a radical during his earlier career, Beard became an outspoken critic of the Roosevelt administration and was, as a consequence, much criticized by the liberals in his later career.

3. Harry E. Barnes, ed., *Perpetual War for Perpetual Peace* (Idaho: Caxton, 1953).

4. Harry E. Barnes, *Pearl Harbor after a Quarter of a Century* (New York: Arno Press, 1972), 20 and 83.

5. Genda letter, *New York Times*, op. cit.

6. Grogan's Journal, Matson Navigation Company Collection. His account was first related in Ships in Gray: *The Story of the Matson Line in World War II*, as cited by John Toland, *Infamy: Pearl Harbor and its Aftermath* (New York, Doubleday 1982) 279–281.

7. Grogan's Journal.

8. Toland, *Infamy*, 281.

9. Ibid.

10. "Interview with Robert D. Ogg by Commander Irwin G. Newman USNR, Historian of Naval Security Group Command," SRH 555, RG 457, NAW.

11. Ibid.

12. Ranneft Diary, Netherlands Defense Ministry Archives. The page was reproduced in the illustration between pp. 240–241 in the original hardcover edition of *Infamy*—significantly it does not appear in the paperback editions.

13. Toland interviewed Ranneft before he died and became convinced that he had uncovered startling new evidence that the U.S. Navy was tracking the progress of the Striking Force, although he had been advised by the Dutch defense archivists who supplied him with the copy of the diary, which had been available in the Netherlands for a number of years, that it was "compiled and edited at some considerable time after the events recorded." When confronted with the correct translation by Robert D. Haslach, a cultural attaché at the Netherlands embassy, during a public lecture at the National Archives in 1982, Toland fainted.

14. Toland, *Infamy*, 319.

15. Dusko Popov, *Spy Counter-Spy* (New York: Grossett & Dunlap, 1974).

16. Letter, Hoover to President, 3 September 1941, quoted in research note in John F. Bratzel and Leslie B. Robert, Jr., "Pearl Harbor, Microdots and J. Edgar Hoover," *The American Historical Review* 87 no. 5 (December 1982). Memorandum from office of Naval Intelligence, 31 October 1941, in FBI 65-36994-75, Dusko M. Popov, confidential informant, espionage G.F.O.I.A.

17. Kilso O. Haan Report, 16 November and 15 December 1941, "Sino-Korean Peoples' League," 711.94.2594, RG 59, NAW.

SELECTED
BIBLIOGRAPHY

BOOKS

Agawa, Hiroyuki. *The Reluctant Admiral: Yamamoto and the Imperial Navy*. New York: Harper & Row, 1979.

Allen, Louis. *Singapore, 1941–1942*. Newark, Del.: University of Delaware Press, 1979.

Andrew, Christopher, and Oleg Gordievesky, *KGB: The Inside Story*. London: Hodder & Stoughton, 1991.

Army Times, eds. *Attack on Pearl Harbor*. Washington, D.C.: 1941.

Arnold, Henry H. *Global Mission*. New York: Harper, 1949.

Baker, Leonard. *Roosevelt and Pearl Harbor*. New York: Macmillan, 1970.

Baldwin, Hanson W. *Battles Lost and Won: Great Campaigns of World War II*. New York: 1966.

Bamford, James. *The Puzzle Palace*. Boston: Houghton Mifflin, 1982.

Barker, Arthur J. *Pearl Harbor*. New York: Ballantine Books, 1969.

Barkley, Alben W. *That Reminds Me*. Garden City, N.Y.: Doubleday, 1954.

Barnes, Harry E., ed. *Perpetual War for Perpetual Peace*. Caldwell, Ida.: The Caxton Printers Ltd., 1953.

———. *Pearl Harbor After a Quarter of a Century*. New York: Arno Press, 1972.

Bartlett, Bruce R. *Cover-up*. New Rochelle, N.Y.: Arlington House, 1978.

Beach, E. L. *The U.S. Navy: Two Hundred Years*. Annapolis: U.S. Naval Institute Press, 1987.

Beard, Charles A. *American Foreign Policy in the Making, 1932–1940*. New Haven, Conn.: Yale University Press, 1948.

———. *President Roosevelt and the Coming of the War*. New Haven, Conn.: Yale University Press, 1941.

Beck, John J. *MacArthur and Wainwright*. Albuquerque, N.M.: University of New Mexico, 1974.

Belote, James H., and William M. Belote. *Titans of the Seas: The Development and*

Operations of Japanese and American Carrier Task Forces During World War II.
New York: Harper and Row, 1975.

Bergamini, David. *Japan's Imperial Conspiracy.* New York: William Morrow, 1971.

Berle, Beatrice, and Travis Jacobs, eds. *Navigating the Rapids: From the Papers of Adolf A. Berle.* New York: Harcourt Brace, 1973.

Blum, John M. *From the Morgenthau Diaries: Years of War, 1941–1945.* Boston: Houghton Mifflin, 1959–67.

———. *Roosevelt and Morgenthau.* Boston: Houghton Mifflin, 1970.

———. *The Price of Vision: The Diary of Henry A. Wallace, 1942–1946.* Boston: Houghton Mifflin, 1973.

Borg, Dorothy. *The United States and the Far Eastern Crisis of 1933–1938.* Cambridge, Mass.: Harvard University Press, 1964.

Borg, Dorothy, and Shumpei Okamoto, eds. *Pearl Harbor as History: Japanese-American Relations, 1931–1941.* New York: Columbia University Press, 1973.

Boyle, John H. *China and Japan at War 1937–1945.* Stanford, Calif.: Stanford University Press, 1972.

Braisted, William R. *The United States Navy in the Pacific, 1897–1909.* Vol. I. Austin, Tex.: University of Texas Press, 1958.

———. *The United States Navy in the Pacific, 1909–1922.* Vol. II. Austin, Tex.: University of Texas Press, 1971.

Brereton, Lewis H. *The Brereton Diaries: The War in the Air in the Pacific, Middle East and Europe, 3 October 1941–8 May 1945.* New York: Morrow, 1946.

Brownlow, Donald G. *The Accused: The Ordeal of Real Admiral Husband Edward Kimmel, U.S.N.* New York: Vantage, 1968.

Burns, James MacGregor. *Roosevelt, the Soldier of Freedom.* New York: Harcourt Brace, 1970.

Burtness, Paul S., and Warren U. Ober, eds. *The Puzzle of Pearl Harbor.* Evanston, Ill.: Row, Peterson, 1962.

Butler, J. R. M. *Grand Strategy, Vol. II: September 1939–June 1941.* London: HM Stationery Office, 1957.

Butow, Robert J. C. *The John Doe Associates: Backdoor Diplomacy for Peace, 1941.* Stanford, Calif.: Stanford University Press, 1974.

———. *Tojo and the Coming of the War.* Princeton, N.J.: Princeton University Press, 1961.

———. *Japan's Decision to Surrender.* Stanford, Calif.: Stanford University Press, 1954.

Calvocoressi, Peter, and Guy Wint. *Total War.* New York: Pantheon Books, 1972.

Carver, Michael, ed. *The War Lords: The Military Commanders of the Twentieth Century.* Boston: Little, Brown, 1976.

Chennault, Claire L., and Robert Hotz, *Way of a Fighter: The Memoirs of Claire Lee Chennault.* New York: Putnams, 1949.

Chihaya, Masataka. *Teikoku Rengo Kantai (Imperial Combined Fleet).* Tokyo: Kodansha, 1969.

———. *Nihon kaigun senryaku hassō (Strategic Concepts of the Japanese Navy).* Tokyo: Purejidento sha, 1985.

Churchill, Winston L.S. *The Second World War.* Vols. I–VI. Boston: Houghton Mifflin, 1948–53.

Clark, Blake. *Remember Pearl Harbor!* New York: Modern Age Books, 1942.

Clark, Ronald W. *The Man Who Broke Purple: The Life of the World's Greatest Cryptologist, Colonel William F. Friedman.* Boston: Little, Brown, 1977.

Clausen, Henry C., and Bruce Lee. *Pearl Harbor: Final Judgement.* New York: Crown Publishers, 1992.

Coffey, Thomas M. *Imperial Tragedy: Japan in World War II, the First Days and the Last.* New York: World Publishers. 1970.

Cole, Wayne S. *Charles A. Lindbergh and the Battle Against American Intervention in World War II.* New York: Harcourt Brace, 1974.

Collier, Basil. *The War in the Far East, 1941–1945.* New York: Morrow, 1969.

Collier, Richard. *The Road to Pearl Harbor—1941.* New York: Atheneum, 1981.

Corson, William R. *The Armies of Ignorance: The Rise of the American Intelligence Empire.* New York: Dial Press, 1977.

Costello, John. *The Pacific War.* New York: Rawson & Wade, 1981.

——. *Ten Days to Destiny.* New York: William Morrow, 1991.

Craigie, Sir Robert Leslie. *Behind the Japanese Mask.* London: Hutchinson, 1945.

Craven, Wesley Frank, and James Lea Cate, eds. *The Army Air Forces in World War II,* Vol. I. Chicago: University of Chicago Press, 1948.

Current, Richard N. *Secretary Stimson: A Study in Statecraft.* New Brunswick, N.J.: Rutgers University Press, 1954.

Dallek, Robert. *Franklin D. Roosevelt and American Foreign Policy, 1932–1945.* New York: Oxford University Press, 1979.

David, Jules. *America and the World of Our Time: U.S. Diplomacy in the Twentieth Century.* New York: Random House, 1960.

Davis, Kenneth Sydney. *Experience of War: The United States in World War II.* Garden City, N.Y.: Doubleday, 1965.

Deacon, Richard (aka Donald McCormack). *Kempeitai: A History of the Japanese Secret Police.* New York: Berkeley Edition, 1985.

Drea, Edward J. *MacArthur's Ultra: Codebreaking and the War against Japan, 1942–1945.* San Francisco: Presidio, 1991.

Drury, Allen. *A Senate Journal, 1943–1945.* New York: McGraw-Hill, 1961.

Dull, Paul S. *A Battle History of the Imperial Japanese Navy (1941–1945).* Annapolis, Md.: U.S. Naval Institute Press, 1978.

Dyer, VADM. George C. *On the Treadmill to Pearl Harbor: The Memoirs of Admiral James O. Richardson, U.S.N. (Retired).* Washington, D.C.: Naval History Division, Department of the Navy, 1973.

——. *The Amphibians Came to Conquer: The Story of Admiral Richmond Kelly Turner.* Washington, D.C.: Naval History Division, Department of the Navy, 1971.

Farago, Ladislas. *The Broken Seal: Operation Magic and the Pearl Harbor Disaster.* New York: Random House, 1967.

Feis, Herbert, *The Road to Pearl Harbor.* Princeton, N.J.: Princeton University Press, 1950.

Flynn, John T. *The Truth About Pearl Harbor.* New York: privately printed pamphlet, 1944.

Furer, RADM. Julius Augustus. *Administration of the Navy Department in World War II.* Washington, D.C.: Naval History Division, Department of the Navy, 1959.

Gannon, Michael. *Operation Drumbeat.* New York: Harper & Row, 1990.

Goldston, Robert C. *Pearl Harbor: 7 December 1941.* New York: Watts, 1972.

Grenfell, Russell. *Main Fleet to Singapore.* London: Faber and Faber, 1951.

Grew, Joseph C. *Ten Years in Japan.* New York: Simon & Schuster, 1944.

————. *Turbulent Era: A Diplomatic Record of Forty Years, 1904–1945, Part II.* Edited by Walter Johnson. Boston: Houghton Mifflin, 1952.

Halsey, Fleet Adm. William F., U.S.N., and Lt. Cmdr. Joseph Bryan III, U.S.N.R. *Admiral Halsey's Story.* New York: McGraw-Hill, 1947.

Hara, Captain Tameichi, with Fred Saito and Roger Pineau. *Japanese Destroyer Captain.* New York: Ballantine Books, 1961.

Harada, Kumao. *Saionji Ko to Seiyoku.* Tokyo: Iwanami Shoten, 1950–56.

Harriman, W. Averell, and Elie Abel. *Special Envoy to Churchill and Stalin, 1941–1946.* London: 1976.

Haslach, Robert D. *Nishi no Kaze Hare (West Wind Clear).* Netherlands: Unieboek, 1985.

Hattori, Takushiro. *Dai-toa senso zenshi (A Complete History of the Greater East Asia War).* Tokyo: Hara Shobo, 1953.

Hearings before the Joint Committee on the Investigation of the Pearl Harbor Attack Congress of the United States, 79th Cong., Washington, D.C.: U.S. Government Printing Office, 1946.

Hershey, John. *Men on Bataan.* New York: Knopf, 1943.

Hinsley, Francis A., et al. *British Intelligence in the Second World War.* 3 Vols. Cambridge, Eng.: Cambridge University Press, 1979–83.

Hoehling, A.A. *The Week Before Pearl Harbor.* New York: W. W. Norton, 1963.

Holmes, Wilfred J. *Double-Edged Secrets.* Annapolis, Md.: U.S. Naval Institute Press, 1979.

Howarth, Stephen. *The Fighting Ships of the Rising Sun.* New York: Atheneum, 1983.

Huie, William B. *The Fight for Air Power.* New York: L. B. Fisher, 1942.

Hull, Cordell. *The Memoirs of Cordell Hull.* New York: Macmillian, 1948.

Hunt, Frazier. *The Untold Story of Douglas MacArthur.* New York: Scribners, 1954.

Ickes, Harold L. *The Secret Diary of Harold L. Ickes.* Vol. 3, *The Lowering Clouds, 1939–1941.* New York: Simon & Schuster, 1954.

Ike, Nobutake, ed. *Japan's Decision for War: Records of the 1941 Policy Conferences.* Stanford, Calif.: Stanford University Press, 1967.

Ind, Allison. *Bataan, the Judgement Seat: The Saga of the Philippine Command of the United States Army Air Force, May 1941 to May 1942.* New York: Macmillian, 1944.

Interrogations of Japanese Officials, Naval Analysis Division, United States Strategic Bombing Survey (Pacific). Vol. 1. Washington, D.C.: U.S. Government Printing Office, 1946.

James, D. Clayton. *The Years of MacArthur, 1880–1964.* 3 vols. Boston: Houghton Mifflin, 1970.

Kahn, David. *The Codebreakers.* New York: Macmillan, 1967.

————. *Seizing Enigma.* Boston: Houghton Mifflin, 1991.

Karig, Walter, and Wellborn Kelly. *Battle Report: Pearl Harbor to Coral Sea.* New York: Farrar and Rhinehart, 1944.

Kendric, Alexander. *Prime Time: The Life of Edward R. Murrow.* Boston: Little, Brown, 1969.

Kimball, Warren F. *Churchill and Roosevelt: The Complete Correspondence.* Princeton, N.J.: Princeton University Press, 1984.

Kimmell, Husband E. *Admiral Kimmel's Story.* Chicago: Henry Regnery Co., 1955.

King, Ernest J. *U.S. Navy at War, 1941–1945* (Official Report to the Secretary of the Navy). Washington, D.C.: Government Printing Office, 1946.

King, Ernest J., and Walter Muir Whitehead. *Fleet Admiral King: A Naval Record.* New York: W. W. Norton, 1952.

Krivitsky, Walter. *I Was Stalin's Agent.* London: Hamish Hamilton, 1939.

Langer, William L., and S. Everett Gleason. *The Undeclared War: 1940–1941.* New York: Harper & Brothers, 1953.

Lash, Joseph P. *Roosevelt and Churchill 1931–1941: The Partnership That Saved the West.* New York: W. W. Norton, 1976.

Layton, RADM. Edwin T. CTP. Roger Pineau, and John E. Costello. *"And I Was There": Pearl Harbor and Midway—Breaking the Secrets.* New York: William Morrow, 1985.

Leasor, James. *Singapore: The Battle That Changed the World.* Garden City, N.Y.: Doubleday, 1968.

Lee, Clark. *They Call It Pacific.* New York: Henry Holt, 1952.

Levite, Ariel. *Intelligence and Strategic Surprise.* New York: Columbia University Press, 1987.

Lewin, Ronald. *The American Magic.* New York: Farrar Straus Giroux, 1982.

Lord, Walter. *Day of Infamy.* New York: Holt, Rinehart & Co., 1957.

Lundstrom, John B. *The First South Pacific Campaign: Pacific Fleet Strategy, December 1941–June 1942.* Annapolis, Md.: U.S. Naval Institute Press, 1976.

MacArthur, Douglas. *Reminiscences.* New York: McGraw-Hill, 1964.

Manchester, William. *American Caesar: Douglas MacArthur, 1880–1964.* Boston: Little, Brown, 1978.

Matloff, Maurice, and Edwin M. Snell. *Strategic Planning for Coalition Warfare: 1941–1942.* Washington D.C.: Office of the Chief of Military History, U.S. Army, 1953.

Melosi, Martin V. *The Shadow of Pearl Harbor.* College Station, Tex.: Texas A. & M. University Press, 1967.

Middleton, Drew. *Crossroads of Modern Warfare.* Garden City, N.Y.: Doubleday, 1983.

Miller, Edward S. *War Plan Orange.* Annapolis: U.S. Naval Institute Press, 1991.

Millis, Walter. *This is Pearl! The United States and Japan—1941.* New York: William Morrow, 1947.

Miyauchi, Kanya. *Niitakayama nobore 1208 (Climb Mount Niitaka 8 December).* Tokyo: Rokko Shuppan, 1975.

Montgomery, Michael. *Who Sank the Sydney?* Sydney, Australia: Cassel, 1981.

Morgenstern, George E. *Pearl Harbor: The Story of the Secret War.* New York: Devin-Adair Co., 1947.

Morison, Samuel Eliot. *The Rising Sun in the Pacific.* Boston: Little, Brown, 1948.

Morton, Louis. *United States Army in World War II: The War in the Pacific: Strategy and Command: The First Two Years.* Washington, D.C.: Department of the Army Office, Chief of Military History, 1962.

Nakamuta, Kenichi. *Jihō shikan no kaisu (Recollections of an Intelligence Officer).* Tokyo: Daiya Mendosha, 1947.

Nihon rikukaigun no seido, soshiki, jinji (The System, Organization, and Personnel of the Japanese Army and Navy). Tokyo: Tokyo daigaku shiryo kenkyuukai, 1971.

Okumiya, Masatake. *Nihon kaigun no senryaku hasso (Strategic Ideas of the Japanese Navy).* Tokyo: 1982.

Okumiya, Masatake, and Jiro Horikoshi. *Zero!* New York: E. P. Dutton, 1956.

Pantzer, Eric F. "The Debacle at Pearl Harbor." Thesis, Indiana University, 1965.

Papers Relating to the Foreign Policy of the United States—Japan, 1941. Vol. 2. Washington, D.C.: U.S. Government Printing Office, 1946.

Perkins, Frances. *The Roosevelt I Knew.* New York: Viking Press, 1946.

Pogue, Forrest C. *George C. Marshall: Education of a General.* New York: Viking Press, 1963.

———. *George C. Marshall: Ordeal and Hope, 1939–1942.* New York: Viking Press, 1966.

Popov, Dusko. *Spy Counter-Spy.* New York: Grossett & Dunlap, 1974.

Potter, Elmer B. *Nimitz.* Annapolis, Md.: U.S. Naval Institute Press, 1976.

———. *Bull Halsey.* Annapolis, Md.: U.S. Naval Institute Press, 1985.

Potter, John Deane. *Yamamoto, the Man Who Menaced America.* New York: Viking Press, 1965.

Prange, Gordon W. *Tora! Tora! Tora!* Tokyo: Reader's Digest (in Japanese), 1966.

Prange, Gordon, in collaboration with Donald M. Goldstein and Katherine V. Dillon. *At Dawn We Slept.* New York: McGraw-Hill, 1981.

———. *Target Tokyo: The Story of the Sorge Spy Ring.* New York: McGraw-Hill, 1984.

Reynolds, David. *The Creation of the Anglo-American Alliance, 1937–1941.* London: Europa, 1981.

Rosenman, Samuel, ed. *The Public Papers and Addresses of Franklin Delano Roosevelt.* 13 vols. New York: Macmillan, 1938–52.

Rusbridger, James, and Eric Nave. *Betrayal at Pearl Harbor: How Churchill Lured Roosevelt into World War II.* Touchstone: New York, 1992.

Sanson, G. B. *The Western World and Japan.* New York: Alfred A. Knopf, 1950.

Sayre, Francis B. *Glad Adventure.* New York: Macmillan, 1957.

Schlesinger, Arthur M., Jr., and Roger Bruns, eds. *Congress Investigates: A Documented History, 1792–1974.* Vol. 5. New York: Chelsea House, 1975.

Sherrod, Robert. *History of Marine Corps Aviation in World War II.* Washington, D.C.: Combat Forces Press, 1952.

Sherry, Michael S. *The Rise of American Air Power: The Creation of Armageddon.* New Haven, Conn.: Yale University Press, 1991.

Sherwood, Robert E. *Roosevelt and Hopkins.* New York: Harper & Brothers, 1948.

Slackman, Michael. *TARGET: Pearl Harbor.* Honolulu: University of Hawaii Press, 1990.

Smith, Chester L. *Midway, 4 June 1942.* London: Regency, 1962.

Sontag, Raymond Japme, and James Stuart Beddie, eds. *Nazi-Soviet Relations, 1939–1941.* Washington, D.C.: Department of State, 1948.

Spector, Ronald H. *The Eagle Against the Sun: The American War with Japan.* New York: The Free Press, 1985.

Sperber, A. M. *Eward R. Murrow: His Life and Times.* New York: Freundlich Books, 1986.

Standley, William H., and Arthur A. Ageton. *Admiral Ambassador to Russia.* Chicago: Henry Regnery Co., 1955.

Stillwell, Paul, ed. *Air Raid: Pearl Harbor!* Annapolis, Md.: U.S. Naval Institute Press, 1981.

Stimson, Henry L., and McGeorge Bundy. *On Active Service in Peace and War.* New York: Harper & Row, 1947.

Sulzberger, C. L. *A Long Row of Candles: Memoirs and Diaries, 1934–1954.* New York: Macmillan, 1969.

Tansill, Charles C. *Back Door to War.* Chicago: Henry Regnery Co., 1952.

Taylor, Theodore. *Air Raid—Pearl Harbor.* New York: Crowell, 1971.

Terasaki, Gwen. *Bridge to the Sun.* Chapel Hill, N.C.: University of North Carolina Press, 1957.

Theobald, Robert A. *The Final Secret of Pearl Harbor.* New York: Devin-Adair Co., 1954.

Throne, Christopher. *Allies of a Kind: The United States, Great Britain and the War Against Japan 1941–43.* New York: Oxford University Press, 1978.

Thorpe, Elliott R. *East Wind, Rain.* Boston: Gambit, Inc., 1969.

Togo, Shigenori. *The Cause of Japan.* New York: Simon &Schuster, 1956.

Toland, John. *The Rising Sun.* New York: Random House, 1970.

———. *Infamy.* Garden City, N.Y.: Doubleday, 1982.

Tolley, RADM. Kemp. *The Cruise of the Lanikai.* Annapolis, Md.: U.S. Naval Institute Press, 1973.

Trefousse, Hans L. *What happened at Pearl Harbor?* New York: Twayne Publishers, 1958.

———. *Pearl Harbor, the Continuing Controversy.* Malabar, Fla.: Krieger, 1982.

Tully, Grace. *F.D.R., My Boss.* New York: Charles Scribner's Sons, 1949.

Ugaki, Matome. *Sensōroku* [war record]. Tokyo: Nihon Shuppen Kyodo, 1952–53.

United States Department of State. *Papers Relating to the Foreign Relations of the United States: Japan, 1931–1941.* 2 vols. Washington, D.C.: GPO, 1943.

Utley, Jonathan G. *Going to War with Japan.* Knoxville, Tenn.: Tennessee University Press, 1985.

Van Der Rhoer, Edward. *Deadly Magic: A Personal Account of Communication Intelligence in World War II in the Pacific.* New York: Charles Scribner's Sons, 1978.

Waller, George M. *Pearl Harbor: Roosevelt and the Coming of the War.* Boston: Heath, 1965.

———. *Pearl Harbor.* Lexington, Mass.: Heath, 1976.

Wallin, Homer N. *Pearl Harbor: Why, How, Fleet Salvage, and Final Appraisal.* Washington, D.C.: Naval History Division, 1968.

Weintraub, Stanley. *Long Day's Journey into War: 7 December 1941.* New York: Dutton, 1991.

Whitcomb, Edgar D. *Escape from Corregidor.* Chicago: Henry Regenery, 1958.

Willmott, H. P. *The Barrier and the Javelin.* Annapolis, Md.: U.S. Naval Institute Press, 1983.

Willoughby, Gen. Charles A. *A Shanghai Conspiracy: The Sorge Spy Ring.* New York: Dutton, 1966.

Wilson, Rose Page. *General Marshall Remembered.* Englewood Cliffs, N.J.: Prentice-Hall, 1968.

Wohlstetter, Roberta. *Pearl Harbor—Warning and Decision.* Stanford, Calif.: Stanford University Press, 1962.

Yakolev, A. N. *The Mystery of Pearl Harbor: Facts and Theories.* Moscow: Progness Publishers, 1988.

Yardley, Herbert O. *The American Black Chamber.* New York: Ballantine Books, 1981.

Yokoi, Toshiyuki. *Nihon no kimitsu shitsu (Japan's Secret Chamber).* Tokyo: Roku-maisha, 1951.

Zacharias, Ellis M. *Secret Missions.* New York: G. P. Putnam's Sons, 1946.

SERIES

"Magic" Background of Pearl Harbor. Washington, D.C.: Department of Defense, 1977.
> Vol. I, 14 February–12 May 1941.
> Vol. II, 12 May–6 August 1941.
> Vol. II, Appendix.
> Vol. III, 5 August–17 October 1941.
> Vol. III, Appendix.
> Vol. IV, 17 August–7 December 1941.
> Vol. IV, Appendix.
> Vol. V, Index.

Reports of General MacArthur. Washington, D.C.: Government Printing Office, 1966.
> Vol. I, *The Campaigns of MacArthur in the Pacific,* prepared by his general staff.
> Vol. II, parts I and II, *Japanese Operations in the Southwest Pacific Area,* compiled from Japanese Demobilization Bureau records.

Senshi Sōsho [War History series]. Tokyo: Defense Headquarters History Office. Dates indicated.
> Vol. 10, *Hawai sakusen (Hawaii operation),* 1967.
> Vol. 39, *Daihonei kaigunbu-rengoo kantai (4) (Imperial General Headquarters–Combined Fleet), 1970.*

SELECTED JOURNAL ARTICLES

Adair, RADM, Charles, U.S.N. (Ret.), "As I Recall . . . End of Peace in the Philippines," *USNIP,* August 1985.

Bratzel, John F., and Leslie B. Robert, Jr., "Pearl Harbor, Microdots and J. Edgar Hoover, *American Historical Review* 87, no. 5 (December 1988).

Costello, John E., "Remember Pearl Harbor," *USNIP,* September 1983.

Cressman, Robert J., "That Gallant Ship: A History of USS *Yorktown* (CV-5)," *The Hook,* Spring 1981, 11–24.

D'Andrea, Thomas M., "Marines at Midway," *Marine Corps Gazette,* November 1964, 27–31.

Davenport, Walter, "Impregnable Pearl Harbor," *Colliers,* 14 June 1941.

Edmonds, Walter D., "What Happened at Clark Field" *Atlantic Monthly,* July 1951.

Forrest, Jerome, and Clarke H. Kawakami, "General MacArthur and His Vanishing War History," *The Reporter,* 14 October 1952, 20–25.

Frank, Larry J., "The United States Navy v. the *Chicago Tribune,*" *Historian,* February 1980, 284–303.

Gish, Donald M. "Cryptologic Analysis" in *International Journal of Intelligence and Counterintelligence* 6, no.: 3 (Fall 1993).

Hannah, Theodore M., "Frank B. Rowlett—A Personal Profile," *Cryptologic Spectrum,* Spring 1981, 4–22.

Harris, Dr. Ruth M., "The Purple Code," *Pacific Quarterly* LXI (February 1981).

———. "Hawaii: Sugar-Coated Fort," *Fortune,* August 1940, 30–82, passim.

Kahn, David. "The Intelligence Failure of Pearl Harbor," *Foreign Affairs,* Vol. 70, No. 5, 1991.

Layton, RADM. Edwin T., "Rendezvous in Reverse," *USNIP*, May 1953.

———, "America Deciphered Our Code," *USNIP*, June 1979, 98–100.

Meigs, LCOL. Montgomery C., USA, "This Must Mean the Philippines," *USNIP*, August 1985.

Nubser, RADM, J. F. W., "A History of Adeling I (Intelligence) Naval Staff, Batana, NEI," *Cryptogram* XLVII, no. 2 (summer 1985).

Parker, Frederick D. "Pearl Harbor Revisited: U.S. Navy Communications Intelligence, 1924–1941," *U.S. Cryptologic History*, Series IV, Vol. 6, 1994.

Petillo, Carol M., "Douglas MacArthur and Manuel Quezon: A Note on an Imperial Bond," *Pacific Historical Review* (1979): 10.

Richardson, VADM David C. Review of *Pearl Harbor: Final Judgement* in *Cryptology*, journal of Naval Cryptologic Veterans' Association, Summer 1993.

Robinson, Walton L., "*Akagi*, Famous Japanese Carrier," *USNIP*, May 1948, 578–95.

Rusbridger, James, "The Sinking of the *Nankin* and the Capture of the *Automedon*," Encounter LXIV, no. 5 (May 1985).

Tordella, Louis W., with Fischel, Edwin C., and Gish, Donald M., "A New Pearl Harbor Villain: Churchill," *International Journal of Intelligence and Counterintelligence*, Vol. 6, No. 3, Fall 1993.

Tucker, Dundas P., "Rhapsody in Purple: A New History of Pearl Harbor," *Cryptologia*, July (pp. 193–229) and October (pp. 346–67) 1982.

Unpublished Sources

Returning to the actual message files confronts the researcher with a daunting task of having to sift through thousands of randomly filed intercepts in the SRN and SRDJ records in addition to the Cincpac message files. It provides a unique access to primary sources.

Researchers are urged to resist the temptation of some recent writers to rely only upon the SRH histories. Although these provide a digest of radio intelligence materials, they are not primary sources. In the case of SRH 012, its interpretation of the comint account of Pearl Harbor and Midway was slanted to reflect the bias of the Navy Department. It provides the historian only with Washington's view by omitting the errors of misevaluation made by OP-20-G while claiming the credit for the correct analyses.

So too does the interpretation so given the Purple intercepts in the so-called *Magic Background to Pearl Harbor*. Like the selected records presented in the congressional hearings, the decrypts are incomplete and presented out of context. In the SRDJ files, we now have the ability to analyze how the intercepts were perceived as they were actually decrypted. In the sequential pattern that emerges, it is evident that the "noise" of similar messages should have reinforced as much as some historians have argued that it confused the evaluations being made in 1941. As an anonymous wartime navy analyst pointed out, the concentration pattern of the Honolulu consulate traffic that was being decrypted in Washington ought to have triggered a special alarm to the fleet.

All of the following cryptologic documents are available in Record Group 457, Records of the National Security Agency, on file in the National Archives of the United States.

Translations of Japanese Naval Messages (SRN)
SRN   129,616–133,367   5 December 1941–25 March 1942

Japanese Diplomatic Messages (SRDJ)
SRDJ   1–2,204   (1940–March 1941)
SRDJ   9,361–19,978   (April 1941–January 1942)
SRDJ   113,785–114,197   (September 1940–April 1941)

Histories (SRH)

SRH 012 Role of Radio Intelligence in the American-Japanese naval war. Four vols., August 1941–September 1942 (2,128 pages). Appendix II, Coral Sea. Appendix III, Midway.

SRH 029 A Brief History of the Signal Intelligence Service, by William F. Friedman 29 June 1942 (18 pages).

SRH 035 History of the Special Branch, MIS, war department 1942–44 (63 pages).

SRH 041 MIS Contribution to the War Effort, December 1945 (22 pages).

SRH 043 Comment on Marshall-Dewey exchange concerning Pearl Harbor, September 1944 (14 pages).

SRH 051 Interview with Mr. Ralph T. Briggs, January 1977 (17 pages).

SRH 081 Information from George W. Linn, Capt. U.S.N.R. (Ret.), October 1980 (15 pages).

SRH 106 Special Intelligence, Specific Instructions for Handling and Dissemination, 25 January 1941, G2, DA, DNI, USN.

SRH 115 U.S. Army Investigations into the Handling of Certain Communications Prior to the Attack on Pearl Harbor 1944–45 (387 pages).

SRH 125 Certain aspects of MAGIC in cryptological background of various investigations into Pearl Harbor attack, by William F. Friedman (74 pages).

SRH 128 Study of Pearl Harbor Hearings, MIS, 1947 (39 pages).

SRH 136 Radio Intelligence in World War II, Tactical Operations, Pacific Ocean Areas, December 1942 (707 pages).

SRH 149 Communications Intelligence in the United States, a brief history, by Laurence F. Safford, Captain U.S.N. (Ret.) (22 pages).

SRH 150 Birthday of Naval Security Group (6 pages).

SRH 152 History Review of OP-20-G (13 pages).

SRH 154 Signal Intelligence Disclosures in the Pearl Harbor Investigations (147 pages).

SRH 159 William F. Friedman preliminary Historical Report on the Solution of the "B" Machine (10 pages).

SRH 177 Interrogation of Japanese Concerning Possible Broadcast of the "Winds" Message, October–November 1945 (15 pages).

SRH 207 Evacuation of U.S.N. Comint Personnel from Corregidor in World War II (99 pages).

SRH 209 Decryption Intelligence Charts, OP-20-G, 20 January–May 1942 (250 pages).

SRH 210 Collection of papers relating to the "Winds Execute" Messages (80 pages).

SRH 211 Japanese Radio Communications and Radio Intelligence, Cincpac-poa Bull, May 1945 (34 pages).

SRH 255 Robert D. Ogg, history interview (82 pages).

SRH 268 Advance Intelligence Centers in U.S. Navy (Redman memos) (2 pages).

SRH 305 History of Radio Intelligence, the Undeclared War, Captain Laurence F. Safford (29 pages).

SRH 306 OP-20-G, Exploits and Commendations, World War II (82 pages).

SRH 355 Naval Security Group History to World War II, prepared by Captain J. S. Holtwick, Jr., U.S.N. (Ret.), June 1971 (464 pages).